Peg

Happy reading

Ramesh

Jon was my Board chair
at the Red Cross — a
great guy, compassionate
but a hard nosed
businessman —

BAREFOOT
to
BILLIONAIRE

BAREFOOT
to
BILLIONAIRE

*Reflections on a Life's Work and
a Promise to Cure Cancer*

JON M. HUNTSMAN, SR.

OVERLOOK DUCKWORTH

NEW YORK • LONDON

This edition first published in hardcover in the United States and the United Kingdom
in 2014 by Overlook Duckworth, Peter Mayer Publishers, Inc.

NEW YORK
141 Wooster Street
New York, NY 10012
www.overlookpress.com
For bulk and special sales, please contact sales@overlookny.com,
or write us at the above address

LONDON
30 Calvin Street
London E1 6NW
info@duckworth-publishers.co.uk
www.ducknet.co.uk

Disclaimer: The events and conversations described in this book are derived
solely from the author's recollections. The author has made every
attempt to verify all facts against existing records, but any errors
are the product of misremembrance rather than ill intent.

Cataloging-in-Publication Data is available from the Library of Congress

Book design and typeformatting by Bernard Schleifer
Manufactured in the United States of America
ISBN US: 978-1-4683-0932-4
ISBN UK: 978-0-7156-4985-5

FIRST EDITION
2 4 6 8 10 9 7 5 3

To my dear mother,
Kathleen Robison Huntsman,
who taught me,
"Sweet are the uses of adversity."

CONTENTS

INTRODUCTION
Chasing the American Dream

H AVING LIVED ON THIS PLANET FOR MORE THAN THREE-QUARTERS of a century, experiencing more than my measure of milestones, exhilaration, triumphs, and tragedy, it is time to take stock of what I have done and observed, and to share it—all of it—including incidents and details never before made public. Many episodes will surprise, some may even come as a shock, especially to those who believe they know me. Part of my life story writes itself, but there are other areas in which details are harder to relate. Just the thought of the free falls from the highest peaks to the lowest valleys and the excruciating climbs back to the top practically gives me a nosebleed.

Don't get me wrong: My life overall has been a fascinating and rewarding experience. The payoffs were as obvious as they were enormous, though the price of success may have been just as large. Save for a couple of obvious rewrites in the script, I would relive my life in a Wall Street minute, even if it meant making the same business mistakes.

But my ride isn't over.

I have divided the chapters of this memoir into two parts: "Establishing the Fortune" and "Giving It Away." It may sound materialistic, but it isn't. As the chapters that follow will show, from simple and stark beginnings, I spent the last half-century building a global industrial empire with my family's name on the door. In the process, I made a fortune, and for the last thirty years my focus has been to use that wealth to solidify charities, defeat cancer, educate kids, feed the hungry, and ensure women and children are not abused.

I made it to where I am today because of a solid faith in God and myself and with the unwavering support of my wife, Karen, and nine children. I made it because I come from good stock, a healthy ancestral mix of preachers and saloonkeepers who provided potent DNA for embracing values and accepting others who may not think the same as you do. This nation provides incredible opportunities, especially for those who are focused, tenacious, and willing to take risks. With determination and optimism, I bought into the American Dream. Let's be honest, a bit of luck and a helping hand along the way is also crucial to success.

My entrepreneurial story includes inventing the clamshell packaging for McDonald's and other fast food companies, growing a business from a single factory in California into the largest family-owned and operated business in America, creating a global petrochemical empire, becoming the first American to own a majority ownership interest in a company in the old Soviet Union, serving in the Nixon White House, and building a world-class cancer research and treatment center.

Along the way, I teetered on the precipice of bankruptcy four times. Even in the worst of times I would make a sizeable charitable commitment before the money was there or prior to a consummated business deal. My children observe that I was always one acquisition ahead of the company going under. Perhaps that is why I have lived as long as I have. Truth be told, a good portion of my health was sacrificed on the altar of success. Along the way, I was double-crossed a couple of times, saw a son kidnapped, and had a daughter die under the most tragic of circumstances. Still, I retain my wits and there remains fire in the belly at the age of seventy-seven.

I have dabbled in the writing of this memoir, off and on, for thirty years. I am glad I waited. Some of the most significant events occurred in the last fifteen years, not the least of which was the metamorphosis of my focus from building a business legacy to one of philanthropy. In that same time frame, one son became a two-term governor and went on to run for president of the United States and another leads one of the world's largest industrial conglomerates. Others have done well in varied other areas of business. At the very least, my life is an intriguing cauldron of dreams and realities; of lessons learned and fortunes found; of unspeakable sorrows, friendships, and successes; and of adversities met and conquered.

Mine has been an intuitive life laced with commitment, values, charity, faith, and love of family. And while my wealth is now all but guaranteed, my life continues to be influenced by an often abusive father, a most caring and long-suffering mother, and early household poverty.

I made a lot of money in the second half of my life and formulated a plan for the end possessor of that fortune: to distribute it to good causes. I want to give it away—all of it—before I check out. I desire to leave this world as I entered it—barefoot and broke. To many, that may seem like an odd, unrealistic, even foolish thing. Not to me. Too many wealthy people hoard their riches, believing that dying with a large bank account is a virtue. I read about one woman who died and left her dog $10 million. What's a dog going to do with that kind of money? Help other dogs? I see it another way: If I die with nothing because I have given it away, humanity is the beneficiary. My philanthropic focus today is the Huntsman Cancer Institute, to which Karen and I have contributed, along with other worthy charities, almost $1.5 billion to date. I intend to spend what it takes to help eliminate the suffering and death that all too often accompanies this scourge.

My pursuit of the American Dream has been a made-in-America entrepreneurial journey of risk, reward, and tumult. I literally bet the farm on business deals that were economically akin to drawing inside straights. My company and I have been in the eye of more than one perfect storm. I kept the faith and won far more battles than I lost. I love to read—and on one occasion I came across the Edward R. Murrow expression that states, "Difficulty is the one excuse history never accepts." That bit of advice stayed with me during those devastating storms.

The quest for the American Dream has shaped this nation's cultural behaviors for centuries. It has fueled endless visions of freedom, fame, and fortune. It suffers neither pretense nor fraud. While the Dream's variations are many, there are but two constants: allure and risk. The American Dream dangles opportunity for all but provides a guarantee to none. For each success, there are countless disappointments. For some, the Dream shimmers like a desert mirage, forever beckoning on the horizon. For others, the relatively favorable hand this nation dealt them for openers is sufficient; they are content to let someone else chase the rainbows.

In time, the American Dream embraced all who would take the risk, in spite of cultural practices and artificial restrictions that for a time excluded certain groups. For women and people of color, the wait for basic political rights, equal career opportunities, and a level social playing field was more than two hundred years. We are still tuning the process, but in America there are opportunities for all to climb the ladder of success.

Whether due to mathematical chance or cosmic destiny, I was born in America at the right time. For a twentieth-century industrialist, there was no better time to be turned loose than the 1960s through the end of the century. It was a time when society was starting to rebuild. Some will warn that America is currently on the skids. Don't believe it. We may find ourselves facing storms of a nature that frustrate or flummox us, but they are only temporary. Every great ship of state worthy of the name eventually rights itself.

For me, the true measure of success is not how much wealth you acquire but how much of it you give back. To be a philanthropist on a grand scale, however, the first part of the equation requires financial wherewithal. You must make money to give it away. It has been my belief that men and women of means must be benevolent stewards of their wealth because that stewardship is temporary. Their job is to see that wealth, modest or vast, is redistributed.

I am certain the genesis of my philosophy of giving springs from my humble beginnings, and the memory of having been on the outside looking in. There is also the example of my maternal grandfather who ran a small, rural motel during the '30s and '40s. I remember that he would allow families without means to stay the night free. He had lost his stately home in a fire; his wife died at age forty-two, leaving him with seven young children to raise; and the depression had wiped out his vast sheep raising business. He was humble, sweet, kind, chewed tobacco, and could hit the spittoon at twenty yards.

Throughout my life, I have hustled to outrun the shadow of poverty. Booker T. Washington, the one-time slave turned respected educator, believed success is measured not so much by the position one reached or the wealth one accumulated but by the obstacles one overcame in the process.

Make no mistake, there is no such thing as a self-made man or woman. Good timing and the occasional helping hand, not to mention a few lucky breaks, are always involved. What wondrous good fortune to have found Karen, the ideal wife and partner, the perennial provider of love, support, and discipline to our children and, now, to an assortment of grandchildren and great-grandchildren, each of whom I love dearly. Let's face it, without a few fortuitous actions of others, I would not have survived my infancy, let alone received an Ivy League education or had the experiences I relate throughout this book. Most of our business plans succeeded because of persuasive talking, accurate instincts, and determination. But I am the first to acknowledge it was often a matter of being at the right place at the right time. Emotion always plays a key role, too. I am an emotional man, and I often tear up when pressure becomes too intense.

Many people may understandably picture me as a straightlaced, nonconfrontational Mormon business and family man. I surround myself with loyal people inside the corporation and believe a gracious approach is more effective than bullying. I am a committed member of The Church of Jesus Christ of Latter-day Saints (LDS Church) and for fifty-two years served in mostly senior leadership positions. My philosophy regarding my faith can be summed up by a statement I always make to our management and leadership teams: "To be a successful leader, one must first learn to be a dedicated follower." I gave time, energy, heart, healthy financial donations, tithing, and the use of one of my Gulfstream jets to the LDS Church. Almost all of my relatives had been inactive in the faith, so I began a new chapter. The Church has been an anchor for our family. I am as comfortable conversing with atheists as with the LDS Church president. I am fiercely independent. There has been no blinking and no regrets.

The time I spent as a special assistant and White House staff secretary to President Nixon put me at the right hand of the most powerful man in the world. I saw Nixon up close. I continue to respect him as a leader, albeit one with insecurities and who was served poorly by many of those closest to him. (Heck, I even liked Spiro Agnew, the vice president who pleaded nolo contendere and was saved from going to jail. He was a lonely person, disliked by Nixon and his inner guard. Hardly anyone would talk to him, but I found him entertaining and upbeat.)

It ought to come as no surprise to the reader, therefore, that it thrilled me beyond description to see my son Jon Jr. seek the White

House as president precisely forty years after I left it in 1972, never looking back.

What isn't obvious is that some close friends and folks outside my company whose association I enjoy often are swashbucklers of grand proportions. You will meet a couple of them later in the book.

I don't wear a wristwatch nor do I know how to text. My idea of social media is a handwritten note to children, grandchildren, friends, or associates. I can't abide someone texting during a meeting. I tend to conduct business on napkins, business cards, and scratch paper. I write or call my children, grandchildren, and great-grandchildren—whose population is hovering around ninety at this writing—on a regular basis. I'm organized and usually composed, yet there is a sign behind my desk that says "All men lead lives of quiet desperation." Henry David Thoreau is speaking to me.

Karen and I rarely go out to eat; we don't play golf or tennis. I don't belong to clubs. I seldom tip less than one hundred dollars because I love to see the surprise in the receiver's eye. (Gratuities mean everything to those in the service industry. I know. I lived off tips once.) Don't read too much into this, but I have a weapons-grade collection of Beanie Babies (whose billionaire creator, Ty Warner, I was shocked to learn, was convicted of tax evasion in January 2014), a modest assortment of classic cars, and I am a card-carrying devotee of Elvis Presley. Almost every one of our children and grandchildren has a totally incomprehensible nickname. My guilty pleasure? Reading supermarket tabloids.

I am neither fancy nor a connoisseur of fine art. (Karen, on the other hand, has a stunning collection of Native American art.) I am not into classical music, ballet, or opera—although I believe in financially supporting them and served for years as chairman of the Utah Symphony board of directors. Many think of me as being stuck in the fifties. I am full of contradictions: a chemical manufacturing magnate who dropped out of high school chemistry, and a lifelong Republican who jumped ship to form my own political organization a decade ago—the Cure Cancer Party. I contribute financially to a number of religions beyond my own.

Deep down, I'm a prankster. I was the one who started cake fights with the children at Halloween. I joined the kids in tossing snowballs at police cars from our hiding places, and then ran home the back way and quickly changed clothes to confuse any pursuers. And I confess to dressing as Santa Claus and delivering small, wrapped gifts to our good Mormon neighbors, including the bishop, inside of which were mini-bottles of liquor I had picked up free on plane flights.

I never hold grudges. My mantra is: get mad, not even. Tick me off and I will let you know about it. In a week, though, all is forgotten. It sometimes amuses my children that I come out of negotiations upset with my counterpart. Later, I would be seen with that same person, my arm around his shoulder, and being "dear friends" again. Peter takes this even further: "It doesn't matter if you are the doorman at his favorite hotel or a lifelong colleague, to my dad everyone is a 'dear friend.'"

Hypersensitivity can turn into a positive when connecting with other people and their struggles. When I become distressed, for example, I head over to the cancer hospital and hold the hand of someone going through chemo.

My emotions are embroidered on my sleeves and I am easy to read. What you see is what you get. While I occasionally lose my temper, I much prefer being gracious. I am an emotional person but my outbursts are rare and end quickly, and I spend the next three weeks apologizing for them. I also hate being alone. I love to hold hands with my daughters. I tear up easily. Heck, I would start getting emotional when dropping off the children at school. Daughter Christena still recalls that each time she opened the car door to skip off to class I would sing a classic Sam Cooke tune. I'd sing to her about how little I knew about history or biology, but that "I do know that I love you."

What can I say? Sentimentality is a side effect of compassion.

In the world of business, I have a reputation for being a tough but honest negotiator. I deal on emotions, which are irrefutable, rather than facts and figures, which are subject to interpretation. I have an instinctive feel for numbers. I attempt to make people believe in themselves. When it comes to bottom-line negotiating, I get right to the point and employ good horse sense. I want to get new things launched.

By looking at the big picture, I tend to avoid conflicts. Most people have to check off each of the boxes before moving on to the next step in the negotiations. Not me. Find out where they want to go and fill in the blanks on the fly. When I finish, I want the other person still to be my friend and feel he or she has won something in the bargain.

I get bored with minutiae and day-to-day operations. For me, the fun and excitement come in thinking up a new deal to add value to the company. I love it when someone comes to the meeting and opens with a "no." ("No" is only the beginning of the conversation.) It motivates me to deal harder and more creatively. I am planning my next appointment. If someone wants to do a deal it always gets done. People do deals with people, not with companies. It's person-to-person. Not everyone is a born dealmaker. You have it or you don't.

I have pulled off some three dozen large (and hundreds of smaller) business deals in my lifetime, sometimes using the seller's money to purchase their own company. I followed my negotiating rubrics in all but one of the deals. In that one, I foolishly allowed my ego to get in the way and it was a costly lesson, as detailed in a later chapter.

People today associate the Huntsman name with wealth, but I haven't always been rich. We had a big home in the late 1970s in Salt Lake City, but what people didn't know was that a number of the rooms in our "home on the hill" were unfurnished. When we took vacations, we would load up the used, seven-passenger station wagon and head for California. We would rent a single room at a motel and I would have three of the children come to the motel room sometime after I registered because ten humans exceeded the number allowed in one room. Usually, the vacation itinerary included a first night in Las Vegas. After tucking the children into bed in the motel "dorm" room, I would head out to a casino for a few minutes to earn enough money to allow us two rooms for the rest of the trip. It worked most of the time.

Once, in San Diego, we didn't even have a motel room. There was none to be had. I asked a policeman if we could sleep on the beach. He said it wasn't permitted but that the expansive library lawn permitted "the homeless" to sleep there, so we just bedded down on the grass. (We were doing just fine until the automated sprinklers created chaos at 4:00 a.m.) I gave the family a choice each day. They could choose to have a big breakfast or a big lunch, but not both. Dinners were at all-you-can-eat buffets.

It's been my experience that those who are perceived to have a lot of money evoke a great deal of curiosity. Everyone wants to know just how rich the rich are, how they got that way, and what they do with their money. I freely admit I make more money than I ever thought I would earn. After leaving military service, I received less than $450 a month in my first full-time civilian job. But I established a goal for myself. At the time, I thought it was an aggressive goal. I would strive to earn $1,000 per year for each year of my age. Given that quest, I should be drawing an annual salary of $77,000 as I write this. Let the record show that our income exceeded our age-specific goal—by a long shot.

In the fall of 2004, the editors at *Forbes* magazine estimated my net worth at $2.3 billion (down $300,000 million from the previous year), which placed me ninety-second on the annual 400 list. Big deal. I was on that list for more than twenty years, and then I was off it. My net worth fell because I had other uses for the money, namely my war against cancer. After the company went public in 2005, Karen and I began moving company stock and property into our charitable foundation. Eventually, all of our wealth will be placed there, and we thought *Forbes* would quickly forget about us. Our remaining Huntsman stock and other left-over assets surprisingly placed us back on the *Forbes* billionaire list in 2014. We will now give it away even faster than previously.

The news media continually ask how much the Huntsman family has given in philanthropic donations over the years. (When, I wonder, did how much become more significant than why?) I only began keeping track of donations in the last twenty years. I enjoyed the thrill of slipping a large check under the door of a charity or just making it from "Anonymous." Unfortunately, the IRS requires documentation on everything. Thus, part of the joy is gone.

No one achieves success in a vacuum. Along the way, as I have pointed out, I received coincidental breaks and perfectly timed help. It is not possible for me to directly compensate those who assisted me over the years in a manner remotely commensurate with the boost I received. Repayment must be in the creation of opportunities for others. To be sure, I also have been handed some bad breaks: nearly flunking out of college, four bouts with cancer, four dances with bankruptcy, a severely mentally challenged son, the kidnapping of a child, and the death of another child, to name but a few.

This book was to be a tell-all, and, in large part, that's what it is. A few things ought not to be tossed about in public, such as confidential counsel and events that by their nature ought to remain private. I have attempted to follow a long-standing personal mantra: certain things you don't need to tell everyone, but when you do tell something it better be accurate.

I have had close personal relationships with the last five presidents of The Church of Jesus Christ of Latter-day Saints. It was my privilege to travel extensively with all of them. When President Howard W. Hunter presided over the LDS Church, we traveled together to most continents. We were very dear friends. I also had the great pleasure of speaking at his funeral services, per his burial instructions. The relationships were particularly close with four of the five leaders, who became cherished friends and confided in me candidly and with trust. It is often difficult for a person in such a singular position as these leaders to relate closely to the individuals he works with daily in performing his role. Others, like me, can be called upon when needed (which, in certain situations, was often).

I represented a voice and opinion different from those of the president's full-time associates, most of whom would have responded carefully and safely, making sure their responses were inoffensive and complimentary. It is not in my nature to do that. Shooting straight is the name of my game no matter who is on the other end of the conversation. But I tend to do it gently and without condescension. The expression "one can buy brains but one can't buy loyalty" comes to mind when closely held confidences are involved. Such has been my good fortune over the past fifty years—not only with highly placed spiritual leaders but also with many of their counselors and members of our church's Quorum of the Twelve Apostles. The same relationships applied to many of our domestic and political leaders, including several United States presidents. They know my word is my bond, and so it has been. Honesty builds friendships. I will not betray that trust.

I could almost say I had done and seen it all. I had experienced full-time military service, full-time government service, full-time church service, and had been a full-time businessman. Quite a resume. How wrong I was. Something was missing. What I wasn't doing full time was making a difference for those not so fortunate. My name was and is on the door of many industrial complexes the world over. I have land developments, resorts, and two private equity companies bearing the Huntsman name. But the Huntsman entity I care most about sits on a mountainside overlooking the Great Salt Lake Valley. It is the fruition of our overriding mission and the true story of my life for the past quarter century. It is the Huntsman Cancer Institute. And other than our family members, the only legacy I desire to be known for is "the man who helped stop cancer." We have not halted the scourge as yet—although we are getting tantalizingly closer—so my life continues to have grave purpose.

Even as a youngster, I had the urge to shake the shadow of poverty, to better myself, to do something grand and important, to make a difference. It kept me going; it still keeps me going in spite of a body that is a walking medical textbook. There is a natural drive embedded in each of us that accompanies us from birth: an instinct to survive. That inner strength is as powerful as it is mysterious.

I know all about that because for me things began badly.

Part I

ESTABLISHING *the* FORTUNE

1. In the Beginning

M Y STORY DOESN'T BEGIN WITH AN AUSPICIOUS OPENING ACT. I was born "dead."

I arrived June 21, 1937—eight weeks early—in our tiny two-room basement house in Blackfoot, Idaho. I emerged as purple as a Concord grape. The family doctor, A.E. Miller, held me upside down and gave me the traditional slap on the backside to get the breathing started, but there was no sign of life. A few gentle shakes elicited no further reaction. After a few minutes, he laid me aside inert, at the foot of my mother's bed, concluding I was dead on delivery.

Miller turned his attention to my mother, Kathleen, lying there in the dimly lit bedroom/living room. He wasn't surprised at the outcome. In those days, premature arrivals usually meant serious trouble. My mother painfully raised her head from the pillow and asked, "How's my baby?" Miller, certain that I was not viable and aware that my one-year-old brother Blaine was systematically destroying his straw hat in the next room, gravely answered with a double-meaning response: "Mrs. Huntsman, you are fortunate to have another son."

Earlier, my father had gone on a fishing trip on the Salmon River, some one hundred miles northwest of Blackfoot. He returned home to find that his wife had been in labor most of the day. He called Dr. Miller, who came to our home and examined my mother. "This birth is still hours away," he pronounced, promising to return later.

That wasn't good enough for my father. Off he sped in his 1936 Ford coupe to the tiny town of Thomas, nine miles away, where he taught high school. He knew that Emily Walters Olsen, a seventy-year-old widow and experienced midwife, lived there. She had been schooled in childbirth and, over several decades, had delivered a majority of the babies on the nearby Shoshone-Bannock Indian reservation located a few miles away at Fort Hall. She accompanied my father back to the sparse half-house. One look at my mother told her the birth was imminent. I arrived a half hour later, several minutes before Dr. Miller returned to begin his effort to get me to breathe.

In this remote Idaho farmland, we were far removed from the events that would change the world and our own family's future. During this time frame Japan invaded China and World War II became closer to reality. The great dirigible *Hindenburg* exploded in New Jersey, killing thirty-six people shortly thereafter. But, there in rural Idaho, the focus of attention was on whether Jon Huntsman would join the living or remain breathless.

As the doctor tended to Mother, who had endured a difficult labor, Mrs. Olsen took charge of me. She ordered my father to carry me into the kitchen where we had an old-fashioned, wood-burning stove and a sink which doubled as the washbasin ever since hot water had been introduced into our home a few months earlier. She was going to try a lifesaving remedy she had used on the reservation, she told my father, and commanded him to turn on the hot- and cold-water taps at the same time. She had him hold me under the cold-water spigot, and then under the hot one, and to keep doing it until she told him to stop. In shock, my father did as commanded—back and forth, cold, hot, cold, hot—all the while rubbing and gently squeezing my tiny chest with his hand.

Still no vital signs. My father had a sinking feeling but did not give up. He and the midwife repeated the routine for several minutes more until, barely perceptible, the tiny mouth opened and closed—just once. Two of the three hearts in that room raced as they massaged my feet and legs. They saw a faint gasp for air. With forced calm, the midwife took me and gently compressed my rib cage, observing, to her amazement, that my chest was rising and falling on its own.

"He's breathing!" they cried in unison. My color changed from purple to a deep red—so red that my father thought maybe I had been scalded by the hot water. Still, I had not yet uttered a peep. Olsen rubbed me dry, wrapped me in a soft blanket, and laid me on the open door of the stove's warming oven. Her anxiety lessened as she watched me raise a fist to my mouth and suck on it hungrily. She washed out a medicine dropper and gave me my first nourishment: diluted condensed milk, one drop at a time. Immediately after my initial meal, I cried. With Mom holding me, everyone started crying. The year 1937 may have been one of tragedies and suffering otherwise—the *Hindenburg* explosion, Japan's brutal invasion of Manchuria, a US unemployment rate of more than 14 percent, and the disappearance of the aviator Amelia Earhart—but it turned out pretty good for me.

Mom had been reading Anne Morrow Lindbergh's *Listen! The Wind,* so she decided to name the new baby "Jon" after the brother of the Lindbergh baby who had been kidnapped and murdered a few years earlier. My father chose Meade for my middle name in honor of Civil War General George Gordon Meade. I was fortunate to be a second son and for Mother to select the name. I know for a certainty that my father would have selected one of the many zany family names from his life—like Alonzo or Gabriel or Jedediah.

To this day, my personal hero is the late Emily Walters Olsen. I am able to write my story because she didn't give up and because, alongside my father, she shepherded an infant through the agonizing time between womb and first breath. With those initial labored breaths, I began life sunny-side up. Olsen's fortuitous presence foreshadowed the good fortune that smiled on me throughout most of my life.

I do not recall ever meeting Mrs. Olsen to thank her for saving my life. I hope in the eternities to come that I can properly express my love to her. My wife Karen and I did meet with Dr. Miller in 1959 during our honeymoon when we stopped in Blackfoot for Karen to catch her first glimpse of my birthplace and the surrounding area. (She wasn't impressed.) Dr. Miller was retired but in good spirits and recalled with great clarity the three births during his forty years of practicing rural medicine (mostly on the reservation) that stood out beyond all others (which numbered more than a thousand). Mine was one of those three. He was convinced that there was no way possible I could have lived, particularly when there was no breathing after delivery. He called it the "life after death" delivery. I hugged him and cried as I left his modest home in Blackfoot.

Sometimes the best way to find out what makes someone tick is to study those from whom he or she descended. We Mormons are great ones for genealogy. At least one dedicated soul in any given family will spend considerable time and resources delving into the past to produce a detailed and far-reaching family tree. My ancestors were a resilient lot who, for the most part, toed a righteous line, although I must honestly report that a saloonkeeper or two, along with a few rascals, comprise leaves on some of the tree's branches. Most, however, were early LDS Church missionaries and leaders who managed to earn positive reputations in Utah's history and, perhaps, are more worthy role models. Only the last three generations of my family were inactive in the Church. Prior to that, the previous three generations were hardy pioneers and devotees of the founding prophet, Joseph Smith. One was an early LDS Church apostle, and many others were members of the early church leadership.

Most people who know me believe that my upbringing was well founded in The Church of Jesus Christ of Latter-day Saints (the Mormons). The fact of the matter is that the Mormon Church was the third religious organization to which I belonged. My parents were less than active members of the LDS Church and never discussed the church in my presence. Likewise, all of my living relatives were also inactive members of the LDS Church. My first baptism was at age eight in a nondenominational Christian church at the Naval Air Station Pensacola in 1945. Two years later, believing that it was a form of baptism, my forehead was sprinkled by a priest of the Catholic Church, which I attended for several months thereafter.

It was shortly before my twelfth birthday that the elders of the Mormon Church realized my baptism had not occurred at age eight, like other Mormon youth, and arranged for my submersion in the baptismal waters of the church of my forefathers. I knew little if anything about the LDS faith but attended regularly in spite of my family's inactivity. I absorbed none of the doctrine, nor the basic framework and history of the LDS Church, until after my college years when I was asked to be the LDS group leader during my two-year tour of duty in the Pacific as a naval gunnery officer. My conversion to the tenets of my faith occurred almost concurrently with that of several others who were converted and baptized under my instruction. (Upon my return home from almost a year in Southeast Asia and the Pacific, I was appointed to be an early morning seminary teacher for high school students in our Southern California area.)

Four of my great-great-grandfathers, as well as some of their family members, were early converts who sacrificed much for their faith. Most of them participated in building the LDS Temple in Kirtland, Ohio (1833–36) before giving up nearly everything they owned to join the westward migration, some coming with Brigham Young, others leading or accompanying separate parties, to the Kingdom of Zion, as Utah was called by Mormons. They were devoted to their faith and endured more in pursuit of the right to freely practice it than I can ever fully comprehend.

The paternal branches of my family tree are populated with austere, no-nonsense folks. Those with attributes of graciousness and generosity are mainly found on the maternal limbs. My maternal side was predominantly populated with polygamists. It was pioneer Utah, after all. The LDS Church did not ban the practice of plural marriage until 1890. Many Utahns provincially view the state's history as having a start date of July 24, 1847, when Mormon pioneers arrived in the Great Salt Lake Valley. They had trekked an incredible 1,300 miles to trade two decades of murderous persecution in the Midwest for a religious sanctuary in the West. It ranks as one of this nation's most amazing migrations.

Bone-weary and often ill from the ordeal, the Latter-day Saints stumbled into the Salt Lake Valley via Emigration Canyon—the harshest, rockiest entrance they could have chosen—and stopped about three hundred yards from where the Huntsman corporate headquarters building now stands. An advance party led by my great-great-great uncle, Orson Pratt, had reported back to leader Brigham Young that real estate on the far side of the pass was not all that desirable. Young, however, felt he had received a revelation from God that the valley would become the Kingdom of Zion for His flock. "This is the right place," he assured the Saints. Every July 24, Utah honors those hardy pioneers.

Utah's pioneer heritage is reenacted on that very spot most days of the year, at This Is the Place Heritage Park, in which the Huntsman family is represented prominently. Among the park's historic buildings, relocated from their original building sites, is the Huntsman Hotel and Saloon, an exact replica of the inn built in Fillmore, Utah that was operated by my great-great-grandfather Gabriel Huntsman and his descendants more than 140 years ago.

Naturally, several Indian tribes have taken exception to the expurgated view of Utah's development. And, truth be told, the first Europeans to set foot in Utah were two Catholic priests, Silvestre Vélez de Escalante and Francisco Atanasio Domínguez, missionaries who explored much of central Utah in 1776. They were seeking—in vain, as it turned out—a northern route to the California mission settlements. Apparently, the friars didn't see much potential and passed through. The state also was visited by mountain men, including Jim Bridger and Jedediah Smith; a number of Hudson Bay Company trappers; and explorer John C. Frémont.

The first Mormons set up camp in that summer of 1847 on territory that arguably belonged to Mexico. It wasn't until the following year that the Treaty of Guadalupe Hidalgo marked the end of the so-called Mexican War and put the region securely in US hands. Many of my ancestors came with or followed Brigham Young into Utah along what would become the Mormon Trail. It was from that same spot at the mouth of Emigration Canyon that my great-great-grandfather Parley P. Pratt, a respected apostle in the early Church of Jesus Christ of Latter-day Saints and a leader of the second wave of Mormon immigrants from Illinois (the group that actually pulled the famous handcarts), got his first look at a fledgling Great Salt Lake City.

The Mormons arrived in Utah before the American West, save for Southern California, had been settled and, with a concerted effort, made the desert bloom. They called their newfound kingdom the "State of Deseret" (the word *deseret* means "honeybee" in the Book of Mormon and signifies hard work and sense of community). The ambitious and controversial Young was a big-picture type of guy. His State of Deseret encompassed present-day Utah and Nevada, plus unsettled parts of Arizona, California, Oregon, Idaho, New Mexico, and Wyoming. He was a master planner who laid out streets and key community elements in a fashion that earns him praise from modern-day urban planners.

In 1850, US President Millard Fillmore signed the bill creating the Territory of Utah, an area considerably smaller than Young's State of Deseret. Moreover, having failed to appreciate the religious connotations of *Deseret*, Congress named the new region "Utah," after the Ute Indian tribe. Fillmore did find it appropriate, however, to appoint Young the first territorial governor. Young was so thrilled with the recognition he reciprocated by naming a central Utah county "Millard" and, in a further flourish of appreciation, named its county seat Fillmore—a town that did not exist when it received the honor—and declared it the territorial capital.

Millard County, home of nearly all of my pioneer ancestors, is rugged and sparsely populated even to this day. Fillmore remains a farming community of some two thousand residents, many of whom are related to me. Though I spent little time there as a child, I consider Fillmore my ancestral home. On my mother's side, my great-great-grandfather Parley Pratt had twelve wives, the last of whom he pursued and married in northern Arkansas, an event that proved to be his undoing. He was shot and then stabbed to death in Arkansas in May 1857. Mormon history books state that he was on a church mission at the time of the murder. He was killed by the estranged but no less enraged ex-husband of wife number twelve.

Pratt was a man of contrasts, simultaneously obedient to his church and fiercely independent. A visionary, he was the first to see there was a shorter way over the mountains and built the first road through present-day Parley's Summit, saving travelers several hundred miles. He is well known in Utah history, having explored the Utah territory for Brigham Young and served on the legislative assembly of the State of Deseret, among a long list of other secular and church roles to his credit. He was a missionary of incredible stamina, receiving members into the LDS Church in England, South America, the South Pacific Islands, and Canada.

Pratt's sixth wife, Belinda Marden Pratt, my maternal great-great-grandmother, has a story worth telling in her own right. She and her first husband, Benjamin Hilton, were Baptists when they were married in New Hampshire. She later converted to Mormonism; he followed her and, for a while, tried to embrace its practices. He was not successful and began to berate church leaders, giving Belinda a bad time for her fervent beliefs. Things got so uncomfortable that she ran away to Nauvoo, Illinois on the advice of one of the church's apostles, Lyman Wight. Benjamin divorced her in absentia and in November 1844 she became Pratt's sixth wife and followed him to Utah.

Parley P. Pratt is recognized widely as one of the most gifted missionaries and early leaders of the LDS Church. On March 2, 2003, at the invitation of then LDS Church President Gordon B. Hinckley, Karen and I joined Hinckley and his wife Marjorie and Elder and Sister Russell Ballard (a member of the Twelve Apostles) on a visit to Alma, Arkansas to pay our respects and put some flowers on Grandfather Pratt's grave. It was a marvelous trip with major speaking engagements along the way to large crowds in both Memphis and New Orleans. President Hinckley was so respectful and kind on that journey and read extensively to all of us from my grandfather's autobiography. He called Pratt one of his "early church heroes."

Following Pratt's death in 1857, Belinda Pratt was left alone in Salt Lake City, struggling to provide for her children and enduring more than ordinary hardships because her family had disowned her when she converted to the LDS faith. She eventually took her children, including daughter Isabella (my great-grandmother), to Fillmore in 1871. There, she held high-level positions in the church's women's auxiliary known as the Relief Society and clerked in the Relief Society's Cooperative Store. A determined and resourceful person, she taught school and took in boarders to provide for her family.

Meanwhile, on the other side of the country, another of my ancestors became one of the first converts into the fledgling church headed by the charismatic founder Joseph Smith. After joining the LDS faith in New York, Joseph Robison brought his wife, Lucretia, to Fillmore in a wagon train in 1854. Their son, my great-grandfather Alonzo, married Belinda's daughter, Isabella Pratt. Alonzo helped build the Utah Statehouse in Fillmore and, at different times, was the town's sheriff and mayor. Isabella held many church and civic positions, including school trustee and twice was elected Millard County recorder.

Isabella and Alonzo had twelve offspring, one of whom was Alfred, my grandfather. With Isabella's permission, Alonzo also took two other wives with whom he sired seventeen more children. Alonzo maintained three homes to keep his domestic life peaceful. Isabella was staunchly loyal to the extended family concept and reminded everyone each Thanksgiving that there were no half-brothers and half-sisters in the bunch, only full-fledged siblings. Unfortunately, Alonzo had to flee to Arizona to escape federal marshals who had been sent to arrest polygamists after the practice was outlawed in 1890.

During the early 1900s one of my grandfather's half-brother's sons became county sheriff and no one else was chased out of town for polygamy. Heck, in February 2014 my double first cousin—his father was married to my mother's sister who died at his birth and he later married my father's sister—passed away in Fillmore. He had spent most of his life excommunicated from the LDS Church and adhering to the fundamentalist LDS faith as a polygamist. He had six wives, thirty-nine children, and upwards of two hundred grandchildren. His obituary in *The Salt Lake Tribune* read as follows: "The deceased was survived by his loving wife and a *colony* of children, grands and greats!" On my paternal side, great-great-great-grandfather James Huntsman settled in Fillmore in 1852. He also was among the first members of the LDS Church, having converted in Perry, Ohio in 1831. A handsome but aggressive man of imposing stature and explosive temper, Huntsman had been one of Brigham Young's bodyguards. He also possessed a respectable amount of business acumen. James's son, Gabriel, married Eunice Holbrook, who looked after their business holdings when LDS Church leaders selected her husband to undertake a mission by handcart to Canada in search of converts. Gabriel later opened the Huntsman Hotel in Fillmore (later moved to This Is the Place Heritage Park). The hotel was quite successful, becoming one of the first hostelries in Utah with indoor plumbing.

All went well until Gabriel got it into his head to go looking for a second wife. Eunice tracked him to the nearby town of Holden where he was found in the company of a young woman. Eunice ordered him home and saw to it that he remained monogamous ever after.

Their oldest son was my great-grandfather, Gabriel "Riley" Huntsman. Like his father, Riley was a natural-born entrepreneur. He worked alongside his father at the Huntsman Hotel. They added a saloon, meat market, and mercantile store. After his father died, Riley bought the Huntsman Hotel and continued to operate it successfully. Riley married Hannah Hansen, a Danish immigrant whose family left the church after a run-in with local Mormon leaders. A strong-willed young woman, she remained loyal to her faith. By the time she was sixteen, she was teaching bookkeeping at the Millard Academy. Riley and Hannah were well suited for each other and operated several successful businesses. Riley cashed in the saloon business in 1894 in order to expand the meat market and mercantile, but found the building too far from the center of town. They moved the store, section by section, to a more desirable location. It wasn't long before they had the largest mercantile operation south of Salt Lake City.

Their first born, Alonzo, was my grandfather. Alonzo Huntsman was an impressive man, exceedingly bright and capable. He was put in charge of herding forty to fifty head of cattle at a young age, but he was afraid of coyotes and found he preferred the comforts of home and the safer world of academia to the rigors of the open range. A hard worker, Alonzo did well in school and was elected president of his senior class at what is now the University of Utah, where, in 1906, he graduated at the age of nineteen and landed a job as a teacher in Payson, Utah. He went on to become superintendent of schools in Millard County, while operating a fair-sized ranch on the side.

In 1909, tragedy cast an everlasting shadow over my grandfather's life. Alonzo's fiancée, Nellie Melville, and his sister, Edna, both in their late teens, were attending Brigham Young University in Provo. Alonzo was in Provo visiting Nellie and invited Edna to join them on an outing to see the new streamlined passenger train *The Flyer* as it came through town. For some reason, the three decided to walk on the tracks. Just as Edna stepped onto an iron rail, *The Flyer* came roaring through the Provo station without slowing. Edna was hit full force by the speeding locomotive and was carried for some distance. She died the next day. My grandfather never got over her death.

That event may explain in part how Alonzo came to have a volatile temper. His size and ornery disposition intimidated nearly everyone, including his children. Not exactly a warm individual, Grandfather Huntsman's favorite descriptive of certain individuals began with *goddamn*, followed by any combination of his favorite pejorative adjectives, such as *lazy, disgusting, ungrateful, stupid,* and *incompetent.* He referred to all of his grandsons as a Little Shit. I thought that was my name until I was about five years old.

Alonzo and Nellie Huntsman had five children in rapid succession. The first, Alonzo Blaine Huntsman, was my father. Because the home was crowded, young Blaine spent many of his formative years in the more peaceful Fillmore home of his mother's parents. With his typical tenacity, he took up the violin and eventually played first chair in the University of Utah symphony orchestra during the 1928–29 academic year.

By standards of the day, the Huntsmans were somewhat prosperous—that is, until the Great Depression. When the banks in Fillmore collapsed, Alonzo was left with precisely fifteen cents. My father was forced to drop out of school after his freshman year. He rode the range for the next few years, saving money to attend Armstrong College of Business Administration in Berkeley, California for a year. That ended when his money ran out. He worked as a ranch hand until 1934 when the Depression eliminated even those jobs.

My mother's side of the family was of a different world entirely. Life was hard for my grandfather, Alfred Robison. His wife Mattie died in 1925 at the age of forty-two, which was devastating for Alfred and the seven children Mattie left behind, one of whom was my mother, only fourteen at the time. A year after Mattie's death, the family's home burned to the ground. Alfred lost almost everything in the Depression, and a second wife would later leave him. Despite the hardships, Alfred was always warm and generous and he tried to stay true to his Mormon faith throughout his life. He chewed tobacco and didn't attend church, but a more Christlike man never existed. I believe he instilled in me kindness and generosity. He always found ways to help those who were less fortunate. He owned a motel in his later years and regularly provided free rooms or discounts to itinerants and those in need. I was thirteen when he died. He has been a role model for me.

It is important to note here that Grandmother Mattie's death at such a young age was probably due to breast cancer. There were no medical doctors in Fillmore then, but those who attended to her surmised that the cause of her death was cancer. Grandfather Alfred died of melanoma and esophageal cancer after suffering immensely. My mother eventually was to die young of breast cancer as well, which clearly indicates that both sides of my mother's family carried the cancer gene. My family's genetic predisposition to this horrific killer was a major influence on my decision to establish the Huntsman Cancer Institute and to devote so much of my life to fighting the disease that has been described as "the emperor of all maladies."

Some of my happiest memories involved my mother's two brothers, Lon and Hal Robison, hardscrabble farmers who enjoyed their liquor. I looked up to them, although not for that reason. I was allowed to stay with them whenever our family would visit Fillmore in the summers. I remember Lon and Hal taking Sonny (my brother Blaine's nickname) and me hunting, fishing, and camping. They were fathers in absentia. My uncles were a couple of characters, but they were kind and gracious. Being with them was one of my joys, and their good-natured ebullience taught me many positive lessons, such as looking at the glass half-full instead of half-empty. Without jobs or any money to speak of they were still upbeat. They shared what little they had. A number of town folk thought my interactions with them were steps down the road to perdition.

Unassuming Uncle Lon had no children and only a sixth-grade education. A lonely man after two failed marriages, he seemed to enjoy taking me under his wing. I idolized him. Once during World War II, Uncle Lon gave me his new shoes (we wore the same size) and his pocket watch. It was much later that I realized he barely eked out a living and that he had no business parting with necessities he couldn't afford to replace. Uncle Hal was the more formidable of the two, but he was no less kind and caring. In World War II, he received a battlefield commission and a bronze star, returning home from Germany a captain. The only intolerance he showed was toward bullies and hunters who shot deer without antlers. He genuinely liked people and had a reputation for being self-reliant, inquisitive, and straightforward. I would like to think it was their genes that helped me develop those qualities.

They were salt of the earth, albeit chain smokers and heavy drinkers. Often Uncle Lon would consume a six-pack of beer for breakfast. Uncle Hal's typical fare would consist of tomato soup spiked with Tabasco sauce and vodka. He would drink the concoction straight from the soup can. They were pure, decent souls and I loved them dearly.

Well into my first job, I decided to do something for Uncle Lon, who spent so much of his life giving me love and attention, not to mention a sense of direction and the self-confidence to head out on life's journey. Having little financial sense, Lon lived on about $150 a month. His pickup, nicknamed Old Gypsy, was ancient, although when he let me drive it as a kid on the back roads of Millard County, it was a marvelous machine. I thought I was driving a Rolls-Royce.

In 1966, I treated him to a new pickup as a surprise. My annual salary at the time was $10,000. From my California home, I ordered a $6,000 baby blue Chevy pickup from a Salt Lake dealership. Karen and I realized that we would spend a year in very sparse conditions to pay for the truck—but it was worth every penny. I arranged for a friend to drive it to Fillmore on Christmas Eve and park it in Uncle Lon's driveway. A note, thanking him for all he had done for me, was left on the front seat.

Considerable time elapsed before there was a response. True to his nature, honest Uncle Lon had seen the shiny new vehicle in his driveway. He knew it wasn't his, so he assumed one of the neighbors had parked it there. He didn't touch it or look inside until much later in the week when, after no one came to claim it, he finally found my note. Using a neighbor's telephone, he called me in California. Choked with emotion and barely able to speak, he managed to tell me what that meant to him.

I always gravitated to my mother's family. Lon and Hal seldom had much money or full-time jobs, living off the land and relying on what the government and I gave them in later life. They weren't unemployed; it was just a way of life. They considered themselves fully employed and lived off the land. They hunted and fished whenever they wanted, but only to eat. Licenses? They paid little mind to such bureaucratic nonsense. I considered them great American icons. They were handy and resourceful and could fix anything. I offered one of them a job as a mechanic, but he only stayed on the job for two weeks. He said it gave him claustrophobia.

As a boy, I was never truly comfortable with my father's side of the family. In fact, the Huntsmans and Robisons did not have a warm relationship. From the Huntsmans, I learned fear and trepidation. From mother's family came love and empathy. Mother was a real joker in school but a good student who excelled in literature and debate. Following her father's example, my mother began a two-year stint as an LDS missionary in the backwoods of the Deep South at age twenty, a rather uncommon experience for a Mormon female in the 1930s. Her experience with the adverse conditions on that mission would serve her well during the lean and difficult years ahead. Although my father and mother had known each other since they were children, it wasn't until after her mission that my father took a serious interest in her.

As my parents grew fond of one another, the Great Depression was casting a pall over the nation. Dad had to go to Salt Lake City to find employment. No sooner had he landed a job than he contracted mumps, a serious illness in those days. Mother, who had remained behind in Fillmore, traveled with a friend to Salt Lake City to check on him. Her devotion and concern confirmed that she was the woman for him. He asked her to marry him and she accepted. Once married, Dad was determined to complete his education. To earn enough to return to college, my parents opened the Arrowhead Bar in Fillmore. It started out as a restaurant, but after Prohibition ended in 1933, its best-selling product was beer.

My mother was a devout Mormon, forbidden to imbibe alcohol let alone to be a purveyor of it. Nevertheless, she understood these were hard times and did her best to support her husband. She quit her job as a dental assistant and pitched in with the new business. Dad was a member of the LDS Church, too, but he did not practice his faith. Honoring the preferences of church leaders took a backseat to his desperate need to earn enough money to get back into school. While many Mormons were scandalized by the sale of alcohol in the restaurant, other folks were thirsty, ensuring a brisk business in homemade pies, sandwiches, and beer. During the Pioneer Day celebration in 1934, my parents reported clearing an astounding forty-five dollars. Brave souls entering through the front door had to pass by the city marshal who had his nose pressed against the window, keeping tabs on who was buying what. My father recalled selling a lot of beer out the back door that day. "The whole county was thirstier than I ever suspected," he told later.

By the end of that summer, my father signed a promissory note for the tuition and entered Brigham Young University at Provo. He graduated in the spring of 1935 with a business degree and a Utah teaching certificate and began scouting for rare teacher openings. A school district in Salt Lake County had a position open which paid $85 a month, but when Dad learned of another opening in the tiny eastern Idaho farm community of Thatcher that offered $125 a month, he hitchhiked north to apply. He found the district's clerk and the chairman of the school board in the latter's ranch corral. They said they would award him the job, primarily because he did not smoke, but there was a major problem: he lacked the requisite credits for his Idaho teaching certificate and a specific certificate in science, one of the subjects he would be teaching. Dad told the clerk he would obtain the necessary credits by attending summer school at the University of Idaho in Moscow, located in the state's northern panhandle region, knowing full well he had no way to pay for it. Nevertheless, he told the Thatcher school officials to sign him up and he headed back to Provo to discuss the situation with his new bride.

Always supportive, Mother responded by selling her precious cache of bottled fruit to their landlady and used the money to buy two bus tickets to Moscow. They somehow scrimped through, renting a shabby apartment near the UI campus for fifteen dollars a month. Through pure tenacity, Dad earned the necessary credits for an Idaho teaching certificate but still needed the critical science certification. Without enough money for the return trip to Fillmore, my mom and dad hitchhiked as far as Provo. They stayed with relatives while Dad tackled the missing science credits, the final impediment to the Thatcher post. He enrolled in a correspondence course and a sympathetic BYU chemistry professor named John Wing left the lab window unlatched so my father could crawl through early each morning to set up his experiments. Wing would arrive to supervise his work. After a week of ten-hour days in the lab, Blaine took the exam and passed with a C grade.

In the late summer of 1935, my parents left for Thatcher, with their combined belongings stowed in a trunk and a twenty-five-dollar loan from a cousin in their pockets. Uncle Lon drove them to Idaho. Thatcher consisted only of a couple of buildings. My parents rented a room in the back of the barbershop.

It was a pioneer existence—no hot water, no indoor plumbing, no car. When Mother became pregnant with Blaine Jr., she and Dad would hitchhike thirty miles each month to see the doctor. Toward the latter half of the school year, they were able to move from the barbershop apartment to a small home and, at last, to buy a car. It was in that newly purchased Ford that my father drove my mother to Fillmore in late April to be with her family for the birth. After nineteen hours of labor, Alonzo Blaine Huntsman Jr. arrived on May 26, 1936, during a fierce electrical storm that caused a power outage in the doctor's office. The physician had neither a flashlight nor candles and relied solely on a small battery-powered examining light to facilitate Mother's delivery in the darkness.

My father was determined not to return to Thatcher. It was too small and remote, especially with a baby. There weren't any teaching jobs in

Millard County, so he accepted a position at the larger high school in Thomas, Idaho. My parents rented a tiny basement apartment in the nearby city of Blackfoot for ten dollars a month, spending another three dollars a month to rent a wood stove for cooking and heating. Things were a little better there, but it was another year of rustic existence, especially for my mother. Full indoor plumbing was a luxury yet to come. Compared to Thatcher, though, Blackfoot was a metropolis. My father was happier in Thomas, where he was welcomed as the handsome, sophisticated new teacher from BYU. One of only four teachers at the high school, he taught English and math, directed the school orchestra for another five dollars a month, and played his violin at community events for a few extra dollars.

Mother never complained about having to wash my brother's soiled diapers outdoors in the elements. Bundled against freezing temperatures, she pumped icy water into a large pail, braced herself against the wind, and rinsed and wrung out every diaper with her bare hands. My mother always set a loving example. She was a wonderful, accepting person, totally dedicated to her family. She was a Robison. I loved her more than words can describe.

My father was stern, strict, and quick of temper. Anger was his sole emotion. I seldom saw him smile, even around his grandchildren. He brooked no impertinence with regard to his authority. At times, he was verbally and physically abusive to us. A private and antisocial person, he would not permit my mother to join any organizations, attend church, or drive a car. This left her somewhat a prisoner in her own home. Yet, she acquiesced to my father's will, bearing isolation with dignity and grace. Her faith in her sons, which eventually would number three, was freely practiced and absolute. With love, generosity, and graciousness, this angel on earth, Kathleen Robison Huntsman, instilled in me a high level of self-confidence. She, more than anyone, is the reason I had the courage to dream and to follow that vision as the primary inspiration for the Huntsman Cancer Institute, which was to follow many decades later.

Yet I had a certain admiration for my father, as uncompromising and abusive as he was. His ambition exposed us to a broader world than we would have known had we remained in eastern Idaho throughout his career. He demanded a work ethic that serves me to this day. His exacting standards drove us to excel. Nor can I overlook the fact that Alonzo Blaine Huntsman saved my life—literally (at birth) and figuratively (some twenty years later when I nearly flunked out of college).

My religious education waxed and waned during much of my childhood. My mother was devout in her heart, but my father was inactive and harbored ill feelings toward the church of his ancestors. Because he sold beer in Fillmore, he and mother had to marry in a civil ceremony rather than in the LDS Temple. Dad resented having been denied this privilege for what he felt was a ridiculous reason. He was being penalized for trying against steep odds to make a living during the Depression. (Eventually, my parents did marry "for time and eternity" in the Logan, Utah LDS Temple.)

My mother deeply regretted the absence of full participation in church activities, but she stayed away out of loyalty to Dad. Later, after the war, when my father was away in the navy, however, she would take us to LDS services that had started up a considerable distance from where we lived. We were residing in "navy housing" in nearby Warrenton, Florida, whose population contained no Mormons other than us, let alone an LDS Church. Occasionally, she would send us to the nearby Catholic Church or to the nondenominational Protestant services that met each Sunday morning in the naval station auditorium. I was actually baptized the first time by a Protestant naval chaplain in 1946. It wasn't until we returned to Idaho that I was baptized into my ancestral LDS faith, when I was nearly twelve years of age.

Perhaps it was this intermittent exposure to several religions that allowed me to be comfortable in my adult years with people of other faiths. But as is often the case, my spotty background in the LDS Church put me in a position of being on the outside looking in when we lived in heavily Mormon areas. I was an observer as much as a participant; I had more opportunities than some to think hard about what I saw. My independent streak sometimes led me to question things that others took for granted.

Christmas morning 1945, I received a note under the tree from Santa Claus. I had asked Santa for a bike. The note said because of the war, the government only "made rubber" for the military, so he could not bring me a bike because he couldn't get rubber for tires. Until he could get rubber, the note concluded, no bike. When Santa finally did bring a bike two years later, it was only half a bike. I had to share it with my brother Sonny.

The first home I remember was a two-room stone structure with an outhouse. Sonny and I had plenty of backyard in which to play. During bad weather—which was much of the time in that neck of the woods—my mother sang songs, read us poems, and organized indoor games. We had no radio and precious few toys. Entertainment was limited only by our resourcefulness. Such an environment inspired creativity and self-reliance.

We were just getting the hang of making up games in the cornfield out back when my father felt it was time to move on. I was four, Sonny a year older. There was a teaching vacancy in Pocatello, twenty-five miles to the south. It was the region's largest city and the site of the two-year southern branch of the University of Idaho (later to become Idaho State University). The Pocatello teaching post was more prestigious than the position at Thomas High—and it paid more. Dad held out little hope of landing the job, but he went to Pocatello for the interview. Dad and Mom caught up with the superintendent just as he was leaving for a golf game. "Well, we won't keep you," said my father after he had introduced himself and left an application. "Have a good game." Apparently, the man did, perhaps associating his great golfing round with my father. Whatever the reason, a teaching contract arrived in the mail a few days later. Dad would be teaching math and English for $140 a month plus an extra $10 to direct the junior high band and orchestra.

We rented a cramped apartment in Pocatello, but this time the Spartan living was worth it. My parents' scrimping enabled them to build a home on a small parcel of land in an alfalfa field on the outskirts of the city. Board by board, Dad constructed our first real home. He took a second job at a gasoline station to help underwrite construction costs. Sonny and I helped by clearing away rocks, stacking lumber scraps, and doing clean-up chores. I am not sure how effective we were at that age, but it provided our first taste of work. The new house was small and cost $4,000, but we felt like royalty. The first year we lived in the basement while the upper story was being finished. When we finally inhabited the main floor, Sonny and I had a bedroom to share. No longer would we be sleeping on camp cots at the foot of my parents' bed. And, if that wasn't swanky enough, we finally purchased a radio.

The house still stands today at 510 E. Stansbury Street in Pocatello. Of course in the past seventy years it has been enlarged several times and is comfortably located in a real neighborhood. We drive by to show the children and grandchildren, as we do the old house on Fisher Street in Blackfoot where I was born. For my sixtieth birthday all the family rented a Greyhound bus to make a tour of the area. The town of Thomas did not exist, but short of that everything else was hardscrabble but surviving.

I became fast friends with the only child of the couple next door. The relationship with Jim Fogg was to last a lifetime. Fogg spent so much time in the Huntsman household that my parents often referred to him as their third son. Like most people in those days, we would gather in the evening to listen to the radio. The only broadcasts I can recall were radio episodes of *The Lone Ranger* and his trusty companion Tonto and President Franklin D. Roosevelt talking about developments in the war and the devastating effects both in the Pacific Islands and in Europe.

Jim and I started school in 1943. The following spring, my father's youngest brother, Clayton, was killed in an army flight-training exercise in Virginia. The death deeply affected Dad and he enlisted in the navy. Because he had a college degree, the navy sent him to officer training school in Pensacola, Florida. Mother, Sonny, and I moved back to Fillmore to await our next move. Late in 1944, Ensign Huntsman sent for his wife and children and we drove across the country to the Pensacola naval base. The neighboring Warrenton School had only the first four grades, all in the same room. We felt like outsiders, which we were. The only friend I had was Sonny. Yet, as I look back, those three years in Florida were the happiest time of my childhood. My big brother and I became close, like Huck Finn and Tom Sawyer. The weather was wonderful and we spent time at the beach on the Gulf with our dog, Cruiser. Left to our own devices, imagination fueled our adventures. The comings and goings of great ships and airplanes provided a glimpse of the outside world.

When the war ended, the only thing I can remember is joining people moving up and down Pensacola streets cheering at the news. Best of all, I knew we would soon be moving back to Idaho.

During the summer of 1946, we returned to Fillmore to stay with family. Sonny and I enrolled in school and soon Mother was again pregnant. Because she had access to free medical care at the naval hospital, my father signed up for an additional year in the service and back we drove to Pensacola. This time our school was a new base facility for military dependents. My father was its first director. Clayton arrived on April 5, 1947, the only one of us to be born in a hospital. He was named in honor of Dad's deceased brother. A month later, my father was discharged from the navy. He accepted an offer to be dean of boys at Pocatello High School for the unbelievable sum, at least to us, of $279 a month.

We headed back to Pocatello—Dad and I in our 1936 Ford coupe and Mom, Sonny, and the baby on the train. I don't remember hearing how the train ride went, but our journey in the car was a harrowing experience. We slept in motels without bathrooms, in people's homes, and in the car. My father and I got lost once, had a mechanical breakdown in Texas, and ran into a cyclone in Colorado. I was scared to death the entire trip. To this day, I dislike long car trips.

Back in Pocatello, there were no bays, beaches, or bayous to explore, but they were replaced by streams with the enticement of fish. We pedaled our bikes more than ten miles to get to those fishing holes. It was there that I developed a passion for fishing that has remained with me. Except for the fishing and occasional hunting trips, Pocatello was real city living. We turned to the streets, cemeteries, makeshift baseball diamonds, and empty lots for our adventures.

The New York Yankees were our heroes, with Yogi Berra, Phil Rizzuto, and Joe DiMaggio, yet when Jackie Robinson joined the Brooklyn Dodgers in 1947, it didn't mean much to our gang because Pocatello was a railroad town and all races gravitated there for employment. I think our school classes looked like the newly formed United Nations.

Sonny, Jim Fogg, and I became part of the Bremmer Park Lions, a neighborhood gang of sorts. Our domain, as we saw it, extended a half-mile in each direction. The Huntsman boys were leaders of the Lions and competition between Sonny and me was fierce. No matter how much I ached after wrestling or fighting my bigger brother, I never gave up. As a group, though, we joined forces against the Ross Park gang, most often in tackle football and sandlot baseball.

It was around this time that Sonny and I learned to put plywood in the backs of our pants. When our father came home from work, he would give each of us a hard kick in the pants "for the damn things you did today that I don't know about." It hurt, so we occasionally would pad our pants with a piece of plywood to absorb the impact. He never discovered this bit of creativity.

The Huntsman boys were not angels by any stretch of the imagination. Pranks were the Bremmer Park Lions' main order of business. Sonny masterminded them, but it seemed I always paid the price when we were caught. I remember one of the Lions buying a frightful Halloween mask with a deformed face. Sonny decided we should add a beat-up overcoat and hat, go around knocking on doors after dark, and ask for handouts. It was such a hoot we repeated the prank the next night. One of the neighbors didn't appreciate such nonsense and called the police. As soon as we saw the flashing red lights approaching, we split up and hightailed for cover. Fogg and I hid in a cornfield until things quieted down before making a break for it. Alas, we ran right into the waiting arms of Alabam Dawson, a Pocatello cop of considerable size and notoriety. He opened the door of his squad car and invited us in.

As we got older, the pranks became more aggressive. When I was fourteen and smitten by a sweet thing named Alice Johnson, we decided to attract her attention by throwing tomatoes at her house. Alice's not-so-sweet mother came out on the porch with a shotgun, threatening to shoot if we didn't clean up the mess. We did so with such civility and respect that, by the time we had finished, Alice's mom thought us a great bunch of boys and laughed off the prank. Wishing us a good night, she went inside. As the door closed, tomatoes flew anew and we scattered. This time, Mrs. Johnson called the police and we were again apprehended.

My mother always stuck up for her sons with a commitment forged in the unwavering belief that we were perfect. She could not imagine her boys doing any of the things of which we were accused. No matter what the allegation, no matter how strong the evidence, her defense of us was consistent, her faith in us absolute. On the other hand, my disciplinarian dad, like his father before him, was a firm believer that punishment should be swift and commensurate with the offense. He had an explosive temper and an unreasonable streak, both of which were manifested frequently. I learned to be cautious in dealing with him.

One day, while in the neighborhood grocery store, I attempted to steal something. When Mrs. Edwards, the proprietor, was in the back of her store and I was sure she couldn't see me, I slipped an ice cream sandwich into my pocket. When she came back up front, I mumbled something about going home and moved toward the door. "Don't you think you had better pay for that ice cream sandwich in your pocket, Jon?" she inquired matter-of-factly. I froze. *This is it*, I thought, *jail time*. Sheepishly, I handed the purloined booty to the proprietor. She didn't scold me or threaten to call the police, and I never again felt the urge to take something that wasn't mine.

If Sonny or I wanted spending money, we had to earn it. My first paying job was selling and delivering the Pocatello newspaper door-to-door at the ripe old age of nine. I bought the daily papers for three cents a copy and sold them for a nickel. My father insisted I sell all my papers before coming home. Once, while doing my best to get them all sold, I wet my pants rather than take time to find a bathroom.

Just out of the fifth grade at Whittier Elementary, Sonny and I opened what we touted as the best lawn-mowing service in town. The following year, my father thought we were ready for real work and convinced the principal at Whittier that we could maintain the school grounds for the summer. The schoolyard was a block-long expanse of grass that had to be cut twice a week. Our hand-mower was too heavy for either of us to push individually, so we each took a side of the handle and shoved. It was painfully slow going. By the time we finished one cutting, it would be time to start another. We worked an eight-hour day, but it paid seventy-five dollars a month, an astonishing sum for two young boys in 1948. The job provided us with our first real spending money. Flush for the first time in our lives, we bought a second bicycle, clothes, and some sports equipment. With that job, however, came the clear but sad message: childhood was over. No more carefree summers. From then on, we were responsible for our clothing, medical, transportation, and entertainment expenses.

Under the combined influence of my mother and father, I grew up with a strong sense of caring, responsibility, and self-worth. My brother and I were contributing members of the household. We were putting in longer hours and accomplishing more than just about anyone we knew. Looking back on it, we learned a great deal from that experience. We managed to have fun while working hard and, in 1949, my fellow students elected me sixth grade class president. While the role at that age was not one of great impact on my classmates or the school, it turned out to be the first of several opportunities to participate in student government and it was rewarding to receive the vote of confidence.

My life, however, was about to lose its innocence. Up to now, I didn't even know how poor the family was. I would soon find out. We would be moving again—this time to California. That was followed by a trek back to Idaho and then back to California. The moves were based on opportunities for my father, but they were also a fortuitous development for me. As a result, I met my future wife and received an opportunity to attend a prestigious Ivy League school with a paper baron picking up the tab—but not before nearly blowing it on both counts.

My destiny was starting to take shape, and rapidly.

2. Leaving Home

I N THE SPRING OF MY SEVENTH-GRADE YEAR, MY DAD REALIZED HIS dream of becoming a school superintendent would be limited without an advanced degree. He was accepted into Stanford University's graduate program in education and, with a year's leave of absence from the Pocatello School District, we were headed for California. It was June 1950, and the beginning of a nomadic existence for the Huntsman family.

My father somehow believed we could survive the eighteen months on his GI Bill allotment of $120 a month. He rented a unit of the married-student housing in Stanford Village, which in reality meant living in one of twenty World War II Quonset huts that had cardboard for interior walls—a few clicks downhill from our Thomas, Idaho two-room hovel with outdoor plumbing. For those unfamiliar with the Quonset hut, *Webster's* defines it as "a semi-cylindrical metal shelter having end walls, usually serving as a barracks, storage shed, or the like." Using one of these six-hundred-square-foot units as family living quarters presumably constituted the "or the like" part of the description. Most occupants were young married couples or very small families. Our family was the largest group in Stanford Village. Needless to say, we literally lived on top of one another.

It soon became obvious that $120 per month wasn't going to cut it. Of necessity, my mother made it a practice to go to the meat market near closing time when she could buy stew scraps for ten cents a pound. Mom was skilled in making do with little, and sometimes the butcher would just give her leftover meat. On the occasions I went with her and witnessed what she went through to put food on the table for us, tears of sympathy and humiliation filled my eyes.

At school, the trappings of affluence among students from nearby upscale Menlo Park and Atherton brought home to Sonny and me just how poor we were. The disparity didn't seem to matter to our peers, though, as I was elected president of my eighth-grade class. We didn't have what others did, however, so Sonny and I concluded hard work would get us what we needed.

We found after-school jobs at Cook's Seafood Restaurant in Menlo Park. Sonny was a waiter; I bussed tables and washed dishes. We earned seventy-five cents an hour plus tips and all the food we could consume. We ate next to nothing during the day but stuffed ourselves on the freebies at night. Our earnings helped pay for necessities our parents couldn't afford. When a dentist announced I had nineteen cavities—which could have cost us the equivalent of my father's monthly income—my restaurant earnings paid for a mouthful of fillings.

The year 1950 also was significant because I met Karen Haight at the Palo Alto Ward of the LDS Church. A shy girl, a year younger than me, Karen was the daughter of Ruby Olson and David B. Haight, the respected owner of a hardware store who would in a few years become mayor of Palo Alto. Later, in 1976, he was called to serve as a member of the Quorum of the Twelve Apostles, the governing board of the LDS Church. Meanwhile Ruby Olson Haight was a woman of remarkable grace, beauty, and charm, with far more outward strength and confidence than I saw in my own mother, who was diminished by a domineering, belittling husband. Ruby was an intriguing example of a different sort of womanhood. Little wonder Karen grew up self-assured and passionate about life.

I was terrified during this period of time because the Korean War began and I was all but certain that my dad would be called back to military service. Thank goodness, it wasn't to be, and by the end of the summer of 1951, my father had his master's degree and it was time to return to Idaho and the Pocatello School District. Karen thought she would never see me again.

Back in Idaho, Jim Fogg was delighted to see his best friend return. During my freshman year at Pocatello High, I decided to run for class president. I had to stay home the day of the election because I was ill. Fogg somehow engineered my victory as a compromise choice when the frontrunners found themselves in a stalemate. Serving as class president in 1951–52 prompted me to think about leadership and to develop a social philosophy for the first time. It also dawned on me that being class president was bigger than winning a popularity contest. It carried the opportunity—and the responsibility—to make a difference.

Sonny and I went to work at the Whitman Hotel in Pocatello on rotating shifts as combination bellboy/elevator operators. One of us worked from 3:30 p.m. to 11:30 p.m., the other from 11:30 p.m. to 7:30 a.m. We received twenty-five cents an hour plus tips on the swing shift and thirty-five cents an hour and tips on graveyard. After several grueling weeks, we approached the manager with a request that he shorten our hours so we could finish our schoolwork—either that, or we wanted an increase in pay. He refused both options. We resigned on the spot and left the building, but not before pulling the main light switch, leaving the hotel and surrounding businesses in darkness.

I did odd jobs for a while, such as picking potatoes for six cents per fifty-pound gunny sack until I got another job assembling wagons and tricycles at the Payless Drugstore. Christmas Eve, the store manager presented me with a box of cherry chocolates and the news that I was laid off. His cold, offhand manner taught me a lesson about how not to treat employees. As it turned out, losing that job was of little consequence because after Christmas my father decided to return to Stanford once again in order to work toward a doctorate degree. The Huntsman family packed our things into a rented trailer once again, said good-bye to friends, and traipsed back to Palo Alto, the Quonset hut, and Karen Haight.

In February 1952, Sonny and I enrolled in Menlo-Atherton High where the student body almost exclusively came from wealthy and upper-middle-class families. During high school, I was even more sensitive to the contrast between their sprawling homes and our "chicken coop." I never invited friends over to visit. Neither were my two school shirts and two pairs of pants on par with the fashions of my peers, who never seemed to want for cash. I confess there were times when I told other kids my father was an associate professor at Stanford rather than admit that he was a student.

Those were hard years for the world—the Korean conflict, the hydrogen bomb, the Cold War—and, on a more provincial scale, the Huntsmans. At times, it looked as if we had only one purpose in life: to get Dad through school. I resented my father's ambition. I could not understand the frustration that he often vented in explosive displays of temper on Mom, Sonny, and me. Dad was the one who brought us to that place; he had opted to work toward his doctorate. Why couldn't he attempt to be easier to live with? My mother would try to convince us that our hardships were merely temporary, that the goal was lofty and worth the sacrifices. All I knew was that we were poor and everyone else wasn't. The sting of poverty was humiliating and made a lasting impression.

Looking back more than a half century later, I can partially write off that segment of my life as a learning experience. My father's obsession did set an example. He could have remained a rural schoolteacher, but he lifted himself up. He demonstrated how to set and attain goals, no matter how great the challenge. The experience also taught me there are mountains to climb and challenges to overcome. Show me someone who spent their teenage years in a Quonset hut and I will show you an overachiever. Having nothing gives one something to prove.

Other childhood images come to mind, mostly pleasant ones of Sonny and me, but it saddens me that my memories seldom feature our brother Clayton. Because he was ten years younger, I did not bond with him as I had with Sonny. Clayton's childhood was quite different than ours. From the age of eight, he was the lone child in the household that, by then, offered a relatively stable middle-class existence, so he never experienced the insecurity of poverty. At different times later in life, Clayton became antibusiness, antiestablishment, and antireligion. Nevertheless, he is a good, thoughtful, decent person, and I respect him for finding his own way in life.

By mid-1952, my father had received his doctorate degree and an offer from the Los Altos School District to be assistant superintendent. (Years later, he would be named superintendent of the nearby Los Altos Mountain View Union District.) For the first time, my father's annual salary exceeded $5,000. As a result, we were able to rent a small house in Palo Alto proper, a real home with a yard and an actual street address where I could invite friends without feeling ashamed.

Moving to the new residence meant transferring to Palo Alto High, our third high school in little more than a year. Sonny was a junior; I was a sophomore. Palo Alto High offered a terrific secondary education with its low student-teacher ratio, access to exciting clubs, student organizations, and traditional sports. I lettered in football and baseball as a sophomore, although my first love was basketball. I had to skip basketball my sophomore year because of a knee injury sustained in football. To make sure that didn't happen again, I turned out only for basketball the next year.

Though the family may have been doing better financially, Sonny and I were still required to work. We were hired first as stockers at the Palo Alto J. C. Penney store, and quickly promoted to sales clerks. It wasn't long before we were earning our best wage to date: $1.25 an hour, impressively higher than the 75-cents-an-hour minimum wage at the time. It didn't hurt, either, that our work performances impressed store manager Merrill Vanderpool, who happened to chair the Palo Alto Board of Education. More advantageous from my perspective, Penney's was located across the street from David Haight's hardware store.

Karen made it no secret she was pleased I had returned to California, and we took advantage of the proximity of the two stores. Between my job and school activities, the only time we could be together, aside from heavily chaperoned church functions, was when she came into Penney's to try on shoes. I made sure I was the one who waited on her, my heart skipping all the while. I deliberately brought out the wrong size footwear to prolong her stay. She favored red or navy 1950s-style flats but went along with the game and tried on whatever old-lady styles I would produce to allow us more time together.

We seldom saw each other outside of church events or at the store. I didn't know it at the time, but she wrote our names in wet cement and referred to me as her "boyfriend." I was fifteen before I got up the nerve to hold her hand at an LDS ward dance, and even then a chaperone told us to knock it off. It was another year before I again reached for her hand, and two more years before I kissed her. In the interest of full disclosure, I had been seeing another girl on and off for five years. Annie Lease was a gracious, gregarious, upbeat young woman from Pittsburgh whose father had been transferred to the West Coast by his company. She helped me learn many of the social skills that I would later find were second nature among the eastern prep school boys at Wharton. There were a couple of other girls, too, but I was shy and naïve, and still pretty young. And the decade of the fifties was a carefree age of quasi-innocence. Drugs, liquor, and sex were generally not part of the equation.

Where Karen was concerned, it was love at first sight. But it wasn't until my junior year in college that I decided she would be The One. Compared to my family's circumstances, Karen led a privileged life. I saw her as a bit out of my league. Both families took summer vacations: the Haights to Hawaii and the Huntsmans to Utah. Because of her family's elevated financial position, I was in awe of her parents and a bit insecure around them. Karen had her reasons to be nervous, too. She was attracted to me, she says, because I was cute, positive, and especially kind to my mother, but she was afraid my father would never let me marry her. She was dyslexic and struggled for grades. She worried that, as assistant superintendent, he could pull her school records and discover what she viewed as her shortcoming. It wouldn't have mattered if he had.

Karen was exuberant and beautiful, and we easily bonded. Her father became my advocate throughout the courtship. In the senior Haight's eyes, a teenager who worked after school to help out the family was someone worth knowing. Moreover, Haight was brought up in Idaho and was determined that his only daughter would marry someone from a similar background.

During the summer, I worked full time at J. C. Penney, secured a second job as a plumber's assistant, and began saving money for a car. I was a terrible plumber's trainee. The first bathroom I installed in a nearby church had to be totally replaced. When a toilet flushed, all the water taps would turn on. There was no hot water, and the drainage from the sink terminated somewhere in the church chapel. Nevertheless, by my junior year, I was the proud owner of a 1947 Plymouth that cost three hundred hard-earned dollars. It was a rather humble vehicle, which wasn't helped by my do-it-yourself paint job (it looked like it had been painted with a broom), but having a car gave me a sense of freedom previously unknown.

At the end of my junior year, I was elected as an assemblyman at California Boys State where we debated the news-oriented topics of the moment, such as the Supreme Court's decision to integrate public schools and whether Senator Joseph McCarthy should be censured for his over-the-top hunt for communists. Just prior to my senior year, I was elected to student body president after running on a platform focused on giving everyone a fair chance to be involved and to receive the attention and recognition they deserved. My election campaign received considerable help from the senior class through Sonny's efforts, while Karen recruited support from the sophomores.

Once elected, I was presented with numerous opportunities to put my promises into practice. For instance, a senior named Ron Chappel had been disfigured from plastic surgeries and had an artificial leg. He had suffered severe burns as a baby. He had no friends and usually sat alone in a corner of the cafeteria during lunch period. One day, I left the table where I had been talking with friends, walked over to his table, and sat down. We chatted and continued to do so for several days afterward. Before long, the student leadership table shifted from the center of the cafeteria to Ron's corner. We included him in social events and group pranks, making him a card-carrying member of our crowd. It turned out to be a great year for him—and for us.

Even though I lacked top grades, my school activities and work habits apparently caught the eye of our principal, Dr. Ray Ruppel. I would have flunked typing class had the teacher not also been the assistant basketball coach. (And get this: I, the future petrochemical magnate, dropped Dr. Engelkay's chemistry class after three days, believing I would never have a use for that science.) Nevertheless, the remaining grades were As and Bs and I felt good about applying for scholarships at Stanford and the state universities in California. But everything changed in the spring of 1955, when Principal Ruppel summoned me to his office—the resulting proposal would turn out to be the opportunity of my lifetime.

Harold Zellerbach, president and CEO of Crown Zellerbach Paper Corporation, then the second-largest paper company in the nation, had previously come to Palo Alto High School to ask an important question. Zellerbach, a 1917 graduate of Penn's prestigious Wharton School (known then as the Wharton School of Finance and Commerce), had asked Ruppel a few days earlier why, upon graduation, his seniors attended Yale, Princeton, Harvard, and Stanford but not the University of Pennsylvania, the oldest university in America. Next to Zellerbach was Dr. Ray Saalbach, director of admissions for the University of Pennsylvania, who noted that Palo Alto was a prestigious high school and asked if there was a reason why UPenn—particularly Wharton—was not a destination school for Palo Alto students.

Ruppel responded that their interest in PAHS was gratifying and promised a greater focus on Pennsylvania, but he was curious. "Is there some significance to your timing?"

Zellerbach explained his family was prepared to offer to a qualifying Palo Alto senior a full scholarship to the University of Pennsylvania's Wharton School, and wanted the principal to recommend a student with academic strengths and an all-around performance that set him apart from other students. (At the time, only males were permitted to attend Wharton.)

I found out later Ruppel and David Haight were fellow Rotarians and, at the organization's weekly luncheon the following day, Ruppel asked my future father-in-law if he knew of a deserving student. Indeed he did, said Haight. Apparently, Karen's father's opinion carried weight, because the next morning, when a teachers' conference had preempted normal classes, I received a phone call from Ruppel at home. Hearing from the school principal so early on a non-school day was a little disconcerting, especially when all he said was, "Could you arrange to be in my office later this morning, please?"

Oh, brother, I thought, *what have I done*? Zellerbach and Saalbach got to the principal's office before me, eager to learn who Ruppel would nominate for the scholarship. Ruppel told them he had a student in mind, one with satisfactory grades, good work ethic, and who was well liked and rounded. He is a bit different than most of the student body, Ruppel continued, in that he comes from one of the less affluent families in our area, but he has shown himself to be a leader and has demonstrated a concern for fellow students. Ruppel opened the door to his outer office where I waited and beckoned me to enter and sit down.

A nervous rush of feelings swept over me as the impressive Zellerbach spelled out the situation. I had not heard of the Wharton School and could scarcely comprehend the significance of what I was receiving. A little stunned by this out-of-the-blue offer, I said I was grateful to be considered, adding that I had been planning to pursue a degree in business, but that an out-of-state university would pose a financial problem for our family. I said I didn't know anything about Wharton and didn't know what to say. Zellerbach said we should get to know each other a little better.

Over the next three days, I was treated to concerts, athletic events, and social functions the likes of which I had never before seen. But at an enormous barbeque at Zellerbach's San Francisco home, two Wharton graduates figuratively doused me with cold water. "You're all right, Huntsman," I recall one of them saying, "but you'll never make it past your freshman year without a prep-school background." Crestfallen, I thought my future at Wharton was doomed.

Zellerbach didn't seem concerned. He offered me a no-strings-attached scholarship of $3,200 per year. Wharton's Ivy League price tag was among the highest in the nation, and though I had saved some money for school, $3,200 would not be sufficient. I thanked him for his generosity but said even with that scholarship I would not be able to swing the costs. Zellerbach would not be denied. He came up with another $1,000 a year from Pennsylvania's Northern California Alumni Scholarship Fund. This put a new spin on things. I would still have to get a job while in school, but $4,200 a year was close enough. It was an enormous scholarship package in 1955 dollars, nearly equal to my father's entire salary as assistant superintendent.

I expressed my sincere appreciation and vowed I would repay him one day with a return on his investment. "You can repay me by doing the same thing for someone else when you become successful," he replied.

Over the years, I have tried to do just that by awarding thousands of scholarships to the children of company employees and many underserved students. At last count, we had sent more than five thousand students to schools or universities around the world, all with a nod of appreciation to the Zellerbachs for sending a financially challenged boy to Wharton. (Fate can be fascinating. During Ray Saalbach's last decade, he was forced by failing health into assisted living because he had no family to look after him. For many years, I picked up the $36,000-per-year tab with gratitude and love. He died at age ninety-three in 2011, fifty-six years after our first meeting with Harold Zellerbach.)

Walking the halls during my final days at Palo Alto High, I was haunted by the warning from the two Wharton alums. Would I be able to compete with students who were so much better prepared? Whatever the future would bring, Palo Alto's Class of 1955 received diplomas in May and I was on my way to the best business education in the nation. The Penney's store manager offered me the position of department head in a last-minute attempt to persuade me to launch a career with his company. I declined. I was about to unfurl my sails.

Having sold my Plymouth for one hundred dollars, I had just enough money left over from summer jobs to buy my first-ever plane ticket and to cover my initial food and housing expenses on campus. Packed into my single suitcase was my first business suit, a $29.95 Penney's special made of silvery gray fabric that more or less glowed in the dark—perfect, I figured, for seeking one's destiny nearly three thousand miles to the east.

Within days of landing in Philadelphia, I realized those fellows at the Zellerbach's barbecue had been right: I was woefully unprepared. My classmates had been groomed in exclusive eastern academies and were accustomed to the grueling schedule and fierce competition. They were imbued with discipline, diligence, and a foundation in economics and finance. They knew what to expect; I didn't have a clue.

From the start, those of us with public school backgrounds were left in the dust. Many gave up and dropped out. Those who hung in there found themselves running at the tail end of the race. Just as degrading was the feeling of being a social misfit. Wharton, founded in 1881 as the nation's first business school, seemed to epitomize the stuffy, formal, old-world atmosphere of elite traditional institutions. For me, the term "higher learning" took on a new meaning.

Wharton was home to the upper crust. Coats and ties were mandatory and many students wore conservative dark suits to class. We were to look and act like Wall Street barons whose ranks we were supposed to be joining in four short years. In my case, I drew sideways glances and more than a few sniggers in my Penney's suit and bright red tie with a glowing yellow sun in its midsection (my father's gift, which had been hand-painted by Navajo Indians). To make matters worse, it was tied incorrectly. I stood out like a tattered suitcase on a Four Seasons luggage rack. My "howdy-do" smile and country cousin personality worked fine back in high school, but they failed to penetrate the sophisticated aloofness at Wharton.

When the students learned I was from Idaho, my nickname became Blackfoot, a pejorative reference to my rural birthplace. The nickname fit, I concluded dejectedly, and I felt like a lonely outcast.

I tried to stay positive. I had coped with adverse situations before, although not of this magnitude. I was no shrinking violet, I reminded myself. Given enough time, I will fit in. I focused on adjusting to the big-city ways, to the academic rigidity, and to the air of sophistication meeting me at every turn. In the process, I made a friend.

Peter Riley, a rugged westerner from Spokane, Washington, was another struggling product of public schools. Like me, he had to work his way through school. We both waited tables in sororities and delivered flowers throughout West Philadelphia. During my freshman year, I attended the annual senior class Hey Day ceremonies, a tradition dating back to Penn's founding in 1740. Four honor students were recognized at the event for having excelled in academics, athletics, personality, and leadership. The highest of the four awards was called "the Spoon." I could only dream of winning that award one day. Considering my academic performance at the time, the notion was a fantasy.

In the second half of my freshman year, I joined a fraternity. Sonny, a sophomore at the University of Utah, had threatened to disown me if I didn't pledge Sigma Chi. His call proved to be very fortuitous. The friendships formed in the fraternity worked wonders toward dispelling my sense of being lost and alone. With this support system came a glimmer of hope that I might get through this nightmare after all. Peter and I barely made it through our freshman year and we each hitchhiked home to summer jobs. Neither of us could afford airfare nor owned an automobile. I worked as a plumbing apprentice during days and sold Penney's shoes in the evenings.

In the fall of our freshman year, the two of us signed up for the Naval ROTC because it paid an extra fifty dollars a month. I gave basketball a final fling during my first two years at Penn, playing on the freshman team and making the varsity squad as a sophomore, albeit as a bench jockey. In the last game of the season, against Cornell, I got into the game in the final minutes and was fouled with thirty seconds remaining. Standing on the free-throw line, I knew this was my only chance to score for Pennsylvania, the only opportunity I would have to get into the official record, albeit in asterisk-size type. I calmly sank the free throw. That just may have put me in the record book, as well. As far as I know, my single-point career still stands as Penn's lowest scoring seasonal effort by any player.

On the social scene, things picked up nicely. And that was exactly the problem: my social life was doing me in academically. The way it was going, I was on track to become the most popular washout in Wharton's history. Sigma Chi provided lessons in etiquette and proper dress, including how to knot a tie. The rough edges were being made smooth and the loneliness faded. I was meeting girls from nearby Vassar, Smith, and Bryn Mawr. I had become a man about campus. Never had I imagined such enjoyment while receiving an education. The movie *Animal House* somehow comes to mind when I think back on my sophomore year. As it turned out, one of the best decisions of my life was to join Sigma Chi Fraternity. Since graduation I have been an active alumnus and faithful financial supporter, helping many young men who are Sigma Chi's get through school. The Fraternity's values have assisted me through many of the challenges I faced after completing college.

Letting the good times roll, however, was playing havoc with grades, which weren't that good to begin with. I nearly failed my political science and foreign commerce classes. In order to remain in school, I would have to retake and pass those two final exams on my return in the fall. I realized I was on the verge of losing my scholarship, my career, and my future wife. Discouraged, I hitched a ride to California for the summer. My father was waiting and was not pleased with my academic performance. "It is plain," he bellowed, "that you will never measure up at Wharton. You'd better get yourself into the School of Education and become a teacher. What was good enough for my father and for me is damn well good enough for you."

I was humiliated, to say the least, and angry—partly at my father and partly at myself. I didn't want to be a teacher. I wanted to be an entrepreneur. I had always seen business in my future, but now I was blowing a golden opportunity. I resented my father's insults and lack of faith in me. Yet, he was right. His kick in the rear turned out to be the catalyst for change and prompted an academic epiphany: Success in high school had been too easy, a walk in the park on a much different playing field. Only total commitment was going to get me through Wharton with any hope of success. Otherwise, I would be condemning myself to a life like the one I was trying to leave.

This particular thought reminded me of the vow I took while enduring the humiliating life in Stanford Village: whatever the cost to get out,

I would pay it. I forced myself to right the ship. Screwing around was a thing of the past. I spent the summer on a construction crew during the day, sold shoes at night, and in between studied for the exams I would have to retake.

The fall semester was as different from the previous one as Blackfoot is from Philadelphia. I aced the makeup exams. My professors, former Ambassador Robert Strausz-Hupe and Dr. W. T. Kelley, wanted to know what had happened during the summer. I devoured my first-semester courses in marketing, industry, naval science, economics, and history, and my grades reflected the effort. I made myself focus on cutting through trivia and concentrating on the heart of the matter. Only three things were important to me now: Karen, my faith, and a career in business.

Karen had let it be known she wasn't so sure about me anymore. She had heard rumors of my lifestyle and was not amused. The fact that I had dated other girls bothered her more than the partying. She felt she could get me in line if she were nearby, but we were too far apart—in more ways than one. At the time, she was a popular student at the University of Utah, involved with sorority activities, group dates, and nice guys. "I always knew I would marry a Mormon," she said later, "but I found there were other fish in the LDS sea." A future together was no longer a sure thing.

Karen's father never lost his faith in me, counseling her that I needed patience, support, and time to find myself. She later acknowledged it was partially her father's optimism that led her to allow me another chance to rekindle the relationship. Whenever Karen wrote to her father that she was interested in a new guy, he would fly to Salt Lake City from California to meet him. When he got back home, he would phone her to say he didn't particularly like the person. "I like Jon," David kept repeating.

I idolized David Haight. He was like a second father to me, possessing traits found on the Robison side of my family. He was nonjudgmental, even-tempered, and kind. From the time I was thirteen, he had taken me under his wing. I am sure he always had in mind that I would someday be family. While he was not 100 percent sure of me in the beginning, he kept telling Karen that he liked my confidence and optimism. "Jon will get knocked down a peg or two on occasion," he would say, "but he is strong and knows where he is going." My future father-in-law also had a sense of humor. He loved to joke years after Karen and I married that his son-in-law was "still on probation. I am waiting for Jon to come through and amount to something."

I hitchhiked to the University of Utah during my junior year to see Karen. I made it clear to her that she was looking at a new man and that we were meant for each other. I only hoped she believed me. Hitchhiking may be a dangerous way to travel today, but back then it was a common practice, especially for those in the military. It was almost unpatriotic to drive by a member of the armed forces without giving him a lift. I thumbed my way across the country eight times while at the University of Pennsylvania, always in my navy ROTC uniform. On one occasion, three cars stopped at the same time. It was an exciting way to travel, going straight through from Pennsylvania to California without sleep. All kinds picked me up—the intoxicated, the sleepy, or those desperate to talk. They seemed to enjoy having a young midshipman as a passenger. Often, I helped drive.

The downside of thumbing it was that you could not always be assured of a direct route. Once I was headed home to Palo Alto and found myself in Phoenix. The next driver to pick me up was going to Los Angeles. He let me drive, which was good because he was drinking and passed out halfway there. When I got to LA, the man was in the backseat, still sawing logs. *What the heck*, I thought, and steered the car north to Palo Alto, some 380 miles up the coast. He woke up just as I drove to the front of my home. He got back behind the wheel, assured me I just had a couple of hundred more miles to go, and drove off. I don't know how long it took for him to realize he was nearly 400 miles north of his original destination.

As most who know me will tell you, I am never more focused than when facing a crisis. Throughout my junior year, I mainly ignored the party scene. I hit the books hard and, for the first time, made the faith of my ancestors an integral part of my life. Mormons were a rarity at Ivy League schools. Most people in that neck of the woods thought we were screwballs. Each Sunday, though, a few of us would convene in the ceremonial room in the basement of the fraternity house. I led the services, often after pushing aside empty beer cans strewn about from the previous night's festivities.

At the end of my junior year, I had a 3.5 GPA and was elected to the junior honor society and president of my fraternity. On top of that, Blackfoot, the guy with the Navajo tie and the cowboy smile, was nominated in the spring to run as senior-class president, the university's equivalent of student body president. My opponent was John Huggins, the starched-shirt scion of a prominent Philadelphia family. The contrast in backgrounds was striking, but there was another difference. Students from all walks of life seemed comfortable with me. I tried to be nice to everyone, irrespective of religion, demographic status, or background. Those factors didn't—and still don't—matter to me. Huggins was a fine man, a close friend, and he would have been a strong leader. Yet, to my astonishment, I won by a landslide.

Besides my newfound study habits, a sure sign of my maturation was getting serious about the future and focusing on Karen as my intended. During spring break, I hitchhiked back to Salt Lake City once again to see her. I only had forty-eight hours before I had to return, so we stayed up late at night and took long walks. I made the most of my limited time with Karen and assured her I was interested in no one but her. That next summer, between my junior and senior years, Karen and I spent as much time together as we could. I spent eight weeks at sea as part of my Naval ROTC training, but we managed a day trip to Yosemite National Park, which ranks as one of the most memorable of my life. We left at 4:00 a.m. in her father's car, armed with his Diners Club credit card.

Just prior to leaving, I gave her my Sigma Chi pin. Actually, the pin belonged to a fraternity brother, Hugh Kirkpatrick. I had already given my own pin to the African-American cook and custodian of the Sigma Chi house, who wore it faithfully. (Blacks, in those days, were precluded from joining Sigma Chi, so I made him an honorary member.) For the current purpose, Kirkpatrick's pin worked just as well. With that pin, Karen and I became "engaged to be engaged."

As a senior, things continued smoothly except on the financial front, which continued to be a struggle. I needed $600 for an engagement ring, which I planned to present to Karen over the Christmas break. One of my fraternity brothers, Clark Smith, of the family who owned Kimberly-

Clark, received an allowance that exceeded his annual tuition, fees, and overhead by $10,000. (Peter Riley and I used to update our meager wardrobes by rummaging through Clark's discards.) Clark loved to play poker. I played the game well and since Clark had a reputation for being the worst player in the fraternity, I decided to finance Karen's engagement ring by cleaning his clock at the poker table. I went to Clark's apartment and engaged him in a low-stakes (by his standards) game that lasted most of the night. I took home $120—peanuts to Clark but 20 percent of Karen's ring for me.

I "reinvested" those earnings to obtain the balance. Some friends invited me to the Garden State Park Racetrack in New Jersey. I didn't have a clue about the ponies—I had never been to a horse race—but decided it was worth the risk and bet my $120 on a mare. She won and paid an additional $180. I was halfway home.

The following Monday I went to the jeweler in whose window resided the flawless emerald ring I coveted for Karen. I explained my financial dilemma and, bless him, he had an idea. Noting that I was senior class president at the University of Pennsylvania, the jeweler proposed that I represent his store on campus. If I sold just two diamond rings at full price, Karen's ring would be mine at a 50 percent discount. Eventually we shook on it. I sold one ring to Peter Riley, who had fallen in love with a Philadelphia girl and planned to ask her hand in marriage that same Christmas. The second went to John Mangum, captain of the tennis team, who was marrying a lovely coed from California. True to his word, the jeweler handed over Karen's ring and I had it wrapped for personal delivery. No piece of jewelry would ever be more important or, considering my income, more expensive.

Getting home for Christmas required nearly as much ingenuity as buying the ring. During the past year, I had upgraded my hitchhiking technique. I would get free transportation by donning my midshipman uniform and hanging around the Anacostia Naval Air Station in Washington, DC until I could catch a military plane headed west. How far and how directly west that plane flew was another matter. I would just keep hitching rides on westbound planes, hoping to land somewhere close to my destination. If no planes were flying, I would resort to extending my thumb on the highway.

Usually, this was a piece of cake, but by Christmas the military had changed the rules. NROTC students were now required to have written orders to fly on military aircraft. Those orders were not easy to obtain, even after my promotion to the rank of battalion commander over our entire NROTC unit. It was imperative I get home with Karen's ring, so I took matters into my own hands and fabricated travel orders on official navy stationary. It wasn't foolproof, not by any means, but I rationalized that military orders are seldom scrutinized. That proved true at Anacostia and I was given a seat on a military plane to Chicago.

My luck didn't hold at the Naval Air Station Great Lakes, where an alert marine major read my orders, studied the signature, and looked at me sideways. "This document doesn't look official," he said.

"No," I admitted, "it doesn't look official, does it? But getting home is important to me. I hope you won't mind these orders not being as official as they should be. You see, I'm getting engaged as soon as I get home." The major smiled, looked the other way, and I boarded the plane to Los Alamitos, California. From there, I hitchhiked to Palo Alto to present the ring to Karen, which she sweetly accepted.

Our future together was assured. As part of the engagement formalities, an LDS Church official pronounced a special blessing on us, invoking in me a feeling of peace beyond any I had experienced. We set the wedding date for June 20, 1959, in the Los Angeles LDS Temple, a week or so before I would report to the USS *Calvert* (APA-32) on active duty.

Our otherwise blissful Christmas was marred by the sad news that Peter Riley, who had purchased the first ring from me, was killed in a car accident in Ohio as he hitched his way home to get engaged. I was crushed. The loss of this dear friend had an impact on me for years to come. My second son, Peter Riley Huntsman, was named in his memory.

Returning after the holidays, the remainder of my senior year was filled with studies, student activities, and, to my surprise, a number of honors—the Alumni Award of Merit to the top graduate of the university, election to the Sphinx Senior Honor Society, and induction into Kite and Key, the oldest university service organization in the nation. For a second year in a row, I was elected president of the university chapter of Sigma Chi and, at graduation, was selected as president of the alumni class of 1959. To top it off, I was presented with the Zellerbach Foundation Fellowship for the most outstanding senior student in the US.

The best was reserved for last. Three years earlier, I had fantasized about the Spoon award, the highest of the University of Pennsylvania's four annual honors. The university chaplain, Reverend Edward Harris, had counted the votes several days before the ceremony and secretly tipped off Karen that I had won. Her father arranged to fly her to Philadelphia to surprise me at the awards ceremony. The Cane, Spade, and Bowl awards were announced first. My heart fell as they made ready to announce the grand prize, the Spoon. The name Jon Meade Huntsman rang over the PA system. I could not believe my ears. As Blackfoot came on stage, there was not a single dry eye in the house.

A few days after graduation, I was in New York City interviewing for a job that I hoped to start once my navy obligation was over. A friend tracked me down to inform me that I had won the International Balfour Award, given annually to the most outstanding member of the Sigma Chi fraternity throughout the US and Canada. The presentation would take place June 18, 1959, in Kansas City, two days and 1,500 miles away from our California wedding. I shared the Balfour platform with the late Senator Barry Goldwater of Arizona. In my first formal speech, I spoke of the commitment and fortitude of my pioneer ancestors, of how they believed in something, of how they instilled in me the determination to accomplish good for mankind. I said the award was more theirs than mine.

I owe a great deal to the Wharton School. It has become something of a standard in our family. My brother Blaine later received his doctorate there. Three of my sons and two sons-in-law continued the tradition. I have served as chairman of Wharton's Board of Overseers. Wharton broadened my world, provided a clearer sense of my potential and of life's possibilities, and opened unimaginable doors. In 1996, I was honored to give the graduation address and to receive an honorary doctorate from my alma mater, the University of Pennsylvania.

Each new adventure in life leads us to ponder whether we are in over our heads. I have come to realize it is simply a matter of persevering until the challenges are overcome. In the summer of 1959, I was about to test out this thesis for a second time as I charged into an environment light years away from Blackfoot. The world beckoned. It looked neither cold nor cruel. To me, a business career was enticing, even though I had not a clue what it would be.

3. Taking Flight

O N THE DAY BEFORE OUR WEDDING IN CALIFORNIA, I WAS STILL IN Kansas City. Just hours before I had received the Sigma Chi's International Balfour Award. I caught a red-eye flight to Los Angeles and I arrived at that city's LDS Temple so early on that bright June morning that I helped the gardener with his dawn chores while I awaited Karen and her family.

Thinking back over the nine-year relationship, mostly spent apart, I thought about something my mother had told me: a person never really knows another until they have lived together. As I tried to imagine what sharing my life with Karen would be like, the memory of one of our first dates came to me.

Karen was fifteen and I a year older. My goal had been to take her to the drive-in for a burger and float, a standard dating activity in the 1950s. I had neither a car nor driver's license, but I did have a learner's permit and a friend, Charlie Van Wagoner, who let me borrow his car. It was no ordinary set of wheels. I am talking about a 1941 Ford convertible. My best girl and a convertible—how good could it get? I lowered the top and, with a jaunty air, collected Karen from her home. The only things missing were the white sport coat and the pink carnation.

Being on display was not as exhilarating for Karen. Feeling conspicuous as she sat close to me in the convertible at the drive-in, Karen announced that she felt a little queasy. No doubt her anxiety was compounded when the football team, honking and yelling, pulled up to either side of us. "Hey, Hunts, how'd you rate such a cute chick?" they called out in that obnoxious tone unique to teenagers without dates of their own. Karen slumped lower in her seat, but I smiled proudly and waved them off.

Maybe it was the razzing from the football team, or perhaps she was coming down with something, but suddenly Karen started to cry. My first emotion was sympathy, which instantly turned to horror when, without warning, she vomited on the dashboard, the seat, and the floorboard of Charlie's car. She was mortified. I got us out of there fast and drove back to her house. She ran inside, hardly looking back.

I was concerned for Karen, but I had a bigger problem. The car's interior was a disaster. No way could I return it to Charlie in that condition. With the top still down, I drove to my house, grabbed the garden hose, and filled up the car to the windows. Then I opened the doors and let the water pour out. After the seats were dried, the car looked as good as new. I returned it to Charlie, none the worse for wear. Charlie never knew what I went through to get his car back to normal.

There I was, on the temple steps chuckling over the incident, when Karen approached, flanked by her parents. She was especially radiant and gave me a disarming smile. Birds were trilling in the cool morning air. A wave of warmth and peace washed over me. (Her smile was probably one of relief that I showed up on time, or at all, for that matter. She told me later her father kept reassuring her on the way to the temple that "he'll be there.") Karen and I entered the temple and received our wedding instructions in preparation for the sacred ceremony.

The next day, June 20, 1959, we were joined in marriage for "time and eternity."

Ruby Haight loaned us her car for the honeymoon. We went as far as Gilroy, California, "Garlic Capital of the World," where, after a sumptuous dinner of hamburgers and milkshakes at the Dairy Queen, we registered at a local motel called the King's Rest, hardly a five-star operation at the rate of ten dollars per night. As blissfully happy as we were, it seemed like the Ritz.

Following a stop at Yosemite, we set a course for Fillmore, Utah, so that I could show off my new bride to relatives. We slept outside in our sleeping bags. From central Utah, we drove to Pocatello, Idaho, land of my childhood memories, so Karen could meet Jim Fogg, who was himself engaged to be married and working as a civil engineer at his father's roofing business. Then it was on to my birthplace of Blackfoot, Idaho. But our honeymoon was necessarily brief because I was due in San Diego to begin a two-year navy stint to fulfill my NROTC obligation.

• • •

We gathered our few belongings, left Palo Alto behind, and headed for Coronado Island. I reported for duty on the attack transport USS *Calvert* on July 20. With the rank of ensign, I was one of thirty-five officers on board and was assigned to a bunkroom with five men of similar rank. Initially, we didn't sail far out to sea, allowing me to spend many weekends at home.

Before long, Karen announced she was pregnant. I was away enough of the time that Karen returned to Palo Alto to stay with her parents. As luck would have it, the *Calvert* was ordered north and was in dry dock for repairs for two months at Hunters Point near San Francisco, a half-hour's drive from the Haight home. But after sixty days, the *Calvert* took me back to San Diego and Karen remained with her parents.

In March 1960, to be with Karen for her birthday, I hitched a ride to San Francisco on a twin-engine Beechcraft. It was important for me to be with her—our first child's arrival being only weeks away. As the plane approached the Alameda Naval Air Station, the tower radioed that the aircraft's landing gear wasn't down. The lowering mechanism had malfunctioned. My heart sank. We flew over San Francisco Bay to dump fuel while the ground crew foamed the runway. Terrified, I held my breath and prayed for deliverance. The pilot began a second approach. Moments before we hit the foam, he tried one last time to get the landing gear to drop. Miraculously, the wheels lowered.

Karen experienced the first signs of labor the day after her birthday and on March 26, 1960, Jon Meade Huntsman Jr. was placed in my arms. Over a harrowing twenty-four hours, I had gone from nervous wreck to happy father. Gazing down into that serene little face, Karen and I hardly imagined what an extraordinary future this child would have.

Within a few weeks, Karen, Jon Jr., and I returned to San Diego to an apartment I had rented, only to find ourselves on the first shoal of our marriage. Karen took one look at the sooty walls and dubious "amenities" of our humble abode and declared it the dirtiest, grimiest place she had ever seen. She threw down her suitcase and started to cry. The apartment looked okay to me, but what did I know? I had just spent three years in a fraternity house where the décor could hardly be described as gracious living. Karen's negative assessment notwithstanding, the apartment still beat some of the homes I had lived in as a youngster. But I located a suitable substitute without argument.

Another faux pas was unwittingly committed a short time later. I came home from the naval base one evening and inquired casually, "What did you do today, Sweetheart?"

"What did I do?" cried Karen, "What did I do? I'm here with a three-month-old baby and you ask what did I do?" In fifty-plus years of marriage, I never again asked *that* question.

That summer, the USS *Calvert* sailed for Japan and Southeast Asia on an eight-month tour of duty, separating Karen and me for the longest time in our lives. We kept in touch through the mail, which a few months into my tour brought the sad news that Karen miscarried. It was the first of two miscarriages. Despite my letters attempting to console her, those times were especially hard for Karen.

In December, my promotion to lieutenant (junior grade) bestowed upon me the dual roles of gunnery and public information officer. My PIO duties involved being dispatched ashore several days before the *Calvert* anchored in a port to organize public relations opportunities for the captain and crew. We were part of President Eisenhower's post-WWII, people-to-people program under which we conducted friendship programs in many foreign ports. And we needed to shore up the nation's image. During my tour of duty, an American U-2 spy plane was shot down over Russia, nearly one thousand US military advisers were in South Vietnam, and the civil rights movement in the South was highlighting that the "Land of the Free" mantle didn't cover everyone. But I also had a new commander-in-chief, who had also served in the navy. John F. Kennedy was a relatively young, energetic president who prompted all of us to ask what we could do for the country, rather than the other way around.

There was sufficient free time on those advance assignments to allow me to study military law. This led to my being assigned to defend sailors facing a court martial on various infractions. Many were still teenagers who had committed foolish and fairly minor acts. Even so, their actions put them at risk of harsh, outdated, and, at least to me, unjust penalties.

Representing them seemed a worthy cause and it was easy to find loop-holes in the Uniform Code of Military Justice.

There were few active Mormons aboard the *Calvert*. Catholics had a full-time chaplain and Protestants had a part-time chaplain, but the handful of Latter-day Saints on board only had me. The LDS Church had called me to serve as the LDS navy group leader over eight ships in the squadron. In that capacity, and since I held the highest rank among LDS on the *Calvert*, I found myself presiding over services, although only two people showed up for the first gathering. It marked the first time in my life that I looked closely at the Bible or sought to learn more about my faith since I was raised in an inactive LDS family.

I did not serve a traditional Mormon mission. My mother served a mission in the Deep South and her father also was a missionary, as was his father. My "mission" took place in the navy and it truly made a dif-ference in my personal life. As the LDS group leader, my role was similar in some ways to that of a Mormon bishop. I baptized three crew mem-bers into the faith. LDS meeting attendance aboard the *Calvert* increased to the point where we traded meeting places with the Protestants.

The immorality of some of the crew often troubled me. Many mar-ried personnel were blatantly unfaithful to their wives. I didn't like being assigned to shore patrol because of the things I would witness. It was a patrol officer's job to round up the crew from a port's bars and brothels when it was time to get under way. It wasn't my place to preach to them or to be openly judgmental. Nor did it seem right simply to look the other way. Instead I found not-so-subtle ways of suggesting more respectable behavior. My roommate on the *Calvert* was an officer named Hans. Fol-lowing free time in ports of call, Hans often returned to the ship and re-galed me with tales of his bawdy antics. "That's great, Hans, but listen to this exciting thing that happened in the twentieth chapter of Matthew," I would playfully counter. Hans would listen to my stories from scripture and I would let him expound on his adventures. I don't think he ever got the message, but we maintained a compatible relation-ship and respected each other's differences. We remained friends after leaving the navy.

It was in April 1961, near the end of my tour of duty, that I nearly destroyed the fleet. Some seventy-two ships from six countries were participating in a Southeast Asia Treaty Organization (SEATO) exercise off the coast of Borneo. Because of the event's importance, an admiral was stationed temporarily aboard the *Calvert*. His presence made our vessel the flagship of the flotilla. One evening, at 3:12 a.m., the order came to change course to 330 degrees on the compass. As the officer of the deck, I passed along the direction change to the helmsman, and the fleet was to follow the flagship's lead. The helmsman misunderstood my order and I missed his mumbled confirmation. "Course three hundred, aye," he confirmed. As we came about to 300 degrees, some of the vessels in the fleet correctly used 330 degrees. Chaos ensued as paths began to merge. In the ensuing execution of uncoordinated emergency maneuvers, some ships reversed engines, others continued on, still others turned hard to starboard or to port. The flotilla's formation was in disarray.

The bedlam ended when the admiral and the *Calvert*'s captain, both in pajamas, rushed to the bridge to restore order—and to have a pointed discussion with me. For the rest of my watch, I was a model seaman. I redeemed myself several weeks later when another ship lost its steering and was headed straight for the *Calvert*. I ran to the bridge, literally knocked down the helmsman, and spun the wheel. The collision was avoided by about forty yards.

My honorable discharge took place at Naval Station Treasure Island near San Francisco on July 17, 1961. I was deeply moved to see Karen and fifteen-month-old Jonnie waiting at the gates. My absence for seventeen of the last twenty-four months had been rough on both of us. The future was a clean slate. I set out to make a living and launch a career.

I owed the Zellerbach family. Their family and foundation had underwritten most of my Wharton education. Harold Zellerbach had taken a chance on me and I wanted to show my appreciation by working for the company when my military service was completed. So confident was I this would happen that my Wharton undergraduate thesis was titled, "Vertical Integration of the Paper and Pulp Industry." A riveting read it was not, but it was evidence of the extent to which the paper company figured into my career planning.

I fully expected to work for Zellerbach in my first sortie into the workforce. I landed an interview with Harold Zellerbach's son, Bill, who oversaw distribution operations, and informed him of my desire to repay the family's kindness by bringing value to the company. He arranged for me to spend a few days at headquarters and to meet key people. I appreciated all that I observed and felt I could make a contribution. Therefore, I was caught off guard when the attractive offer they presented was immediately followed by a contrary recommendation from Bill.

Bill told me that the Zellerbachs had been watching my progress for the last six years. Their sense was that I was a natural-born entrepreneur. Rather than working for them, the family thought I should learn a business from the ground floor to prepare me for starting my own.

At first, I felt rejected. However I soon came to realize it was sound, thoughtful counsel. An offer was extended to me for a position at IBM's marketing division with a tempting salary, but I decided to accept a lower paying job, at $450 a month, with the eccentric but brilliant recluse Dudley Swim, something of a legend in business circles.

The distinguished-looking Swim was a bit like Howard Hughes. He owned a six-hundred-acre ranch in Carmel, California overlooking the Pacific Ocean. From his incongruously Spartan office amid such glorious surroundings, Swim controlled large blocks of stock in more than four hundred US and Central American companies. From what I had gathered, he also owned most of Guatemala. He was on the boards of many public companies and solidly connected in Republican circles. I first shook hands with Swim at a chance meeting while still in the navy. He later wrote to say I was the kind of person who could play on his team "anytime, anywhere." It was impossible to resist this once-in-a-lifetime opportunity to learn from the silver-haired Swim. There was clearly no future in the job, but a voice inside me said: "Take it. Go for the experience and what you can learn." I took him up on his offer and he seemed glad to have me, but I started my employment a little fearful of this mercurial man.

My workspace was even more austere than his—an army surplus desk propped up by bricks. My main responsibility was to get him ready for board meetings at which he would arrive armed with artillery derived from my findings. He would utilize these facts and figures to skewer the company's executives who he usually depicted as blithering idiots. "There is nothing lower in life," he would often say to me, "than to work for a large, bureaucratic company and to be a pawn to its board of directors." He used every opportunity to prove the point by being the most demeaning director any of those pawns ever attempted to appease.

Swim was a shrewd businessman—a lonely, contentious man hacking through the corporate jungle with his mean-spirited strong-arm tactics. I did not enjoy working for him and decided the most important lessons I would glean from the experience would come from his examples of what *not* to do in dealing with people. Swim's unsavory brand of leadership was not inspiring, and I began to search quietly for a new opportunity. An unpleasant run-in with Swim after only three months erased any reservations I had about moving on. "Unless a person earns straight As in college, as I did at Stanford," he bellowed out one day, "he has no chance to make it in business."

"I don't believe that's true," I responded with a measure of temerity. Swim held stubbornly to his argument and went so far as to demand to see my transcript. Still sensitive about my freshman and sophomore grades, I declined. That made him even more insistent. The badgering continued until I drew a line in the sand. I told him if my college grades meant more to him than my loyalty and performance, then it was time I terminated my employment. True to his style, Swim didn't blink. We found ourselves at the end of the line. I cleaned out my desk and felt nothing but relief as I drove my Volkswagen Beetle, my first new car (which put me back $1,568), past the three security gates that guarded Swim's mountain bunker. I never looked back. A dozen years later, the lessons I learned from Swim's eccentric ways probably kept me from facing a congressional Watergate committee investigation, as I will relate in the pages to come.

It was mid-October 1961. Karen and I packed Jon Jr. and most of what we owned into our VW bug, happily heading out for the next experience, whatever it would be. Unsure of where we were headed, we pulled over at the outskirts of Gilroy at the crossroads of US 101 and State 52. Which way should we go? We had two options: north, to familiar Palo Alto and a job with Karen's father and her brothers in the family's expanding hardware business; or south, to sprawling Los Angeles and a job with Karen's uncle Dean Olson and a chance to start at the bottom of his egg business. The latter carried the potential of working my way up the ladder at Olson Brothers, Inc., at the time the nation's largest independent egg producers and distributors. Karen and I weighed the alternatives and made a decision: south it would be.

Olson Brothers (Dean and his brother Glenn) turned out to be the right career choice—with the wrong boss. My experience there would be invaluable, but it would come at a steep emotional price. Twelve years later, I would be suing my uncle-in-law for libel. At the moment, though, I was happy to start a career selling eggs.

My starting position at Olson was no suit-and-tie job. The dress code on the egg ranch called for rubber boots and coveralls. Before long, I could balance four eggs in one hand as I checked their quality. I reached the point where I refused to eat eggs for breakfast.

Assembly-line techniques were easy to master and I soon became fully engaged. Before long, management asked me to conduct an efficiency study of the operation. My report must have been received well because I was promoted to truck driver. For six months, I sold eggs to supermarkets and larger restaurants throughout the LA area. Jon Jr. grew up in the back of my Volkswagen or egg delivery trucks, accompanying me on my runs when his mother would permit. I delved deeper into the workings of Olson Brothers' operations, looking for ways to improve efficiency. I got to know assembly-line workers, truck drivers, and foremen. Mixing with them was easy. They saw I understood the work; my hands and overalls were as dirty as theirs were.

In 1962, I was elevated to the role of chief financial officer (CFO) and assistant secretary of Olson Brothers, Inc., which included the duty of preparing for its board meetings and overseeing most of its financial group. Although there was always something to do, restlessness constantly plagued me. My Wharton classmates were advancing in the rarified environment of finance and commercial banking. They wore suits, starched collars, and expensive silk ties to classy, urban offices. Occasionally, a few would send condescending notes, such as: "What is it you're into again? Fish or eggs?" It bothered me. My factory work was uninspiring; I sensed I was falling behind my peers.

To ensure I made professional progress, I enrolled in an MBA program at University of Southern California. Attending night classes twice a week, I finished the course work in two years but receiving the degree proved more of a challenge. When it came time for my comprehensive exams, Dean Olson sent me to Pennsylvania to establish a poultry farm partnership with grocery chain Food Fair. The next year, I again prepared for the exam but something else came up. (I wouldn't receive my MBA degree until 1971.)

By 1968, Karen and I were the parents of five offspring: Jon Jr., Peter Riley, Christena Karen, Kathleen Ann (named for my mother), and David Haight. To keep us afloat, I had begun moonlighting several years earlier in what was my first entrepreneurial venture. Karl Engemann, a trusted and loyal friend, who also shared responsibilities with me at our LDS ward (church), worked for Capitol Records. We formed a record company in 1963 called Continental Productions Company (later changed to Continental Dynamics). The plan was to make records that would appeal to Mormon audiences. We managed to produce two albums over the next year, but we were a long way from making the big time. The main problem was that neither of us had time to manage the venture. We lost track of inventory and receivables. It was more of a challenge than we had expected. Then a Christmastime visit to a tire store propelled us in the right direction.

The local Goodyear and Firestone outlets had a successful holiday promotion in which a Christmas-themed album was offered for a dollar. The album was a collection of some artist's previously recorded yuletide songs. I thought if people made a special trip to a tire store to purchase a Christmas record, wouldn't they be even more likely to buy one at a supermarket where they routinely shop? I approached the grocery giant Safeway. Nearly everybody shopped at Safeway and Lorenzo Hoopes, a trusted friend, was senior vice president of the chain. He had been in charge of Safeway's egg purchasing unit at one time and I had met him through Olson Brothers. (His son, David, later became my deputy at the White House.) Hoopes warmed to the idea and agreed to launch our promotion the following Christmas. There was one catch: Danny Kaye was the Safeway chairman's favorite singer, and Hoopes said his songs must be on the initial album. *Perfect*, I thought darkly, *how do we make that happen?*

I stalked Danny Kaye for days. I trailed him to the CBS studio where he was making a TV special and to a Los Angeles Dodgers game. He showed not the slightest interest in talking to me. Ever. When Hoopes learned of my predicament, he reluctantly settled for Nat King Cole. The artist had died the year before so nostalgic interest would be high. We successfully combined sixteen of Cole's yuletide songs. Several were previously unreleased; eight featured the orchestral backup of Fred Waring and his Pennsylvanians. It had possibilities.

By Thanksgiving, Capitol Records had produced and delivered 250,000 records at 50 cents a platter. We sold them to Safeway for 75 cents apiece for nationwide distribution. The stores, in turn, charged customers a dollar. After only 10 days, every album had been snapped up. Safeway was thrilled at the popularity of this venture. Hoopes called for more records, but there weren't any more. We were sold out, and there was not enough time before Christmas for a second stamping. We couldn't meet the demand. Even so, Continental Productions enjoyed its first profitable year.

Engemann was coming under increasing pressure from Capitol Records whose managers, perhaps justifiably, were concerned about his conflict of interest. He ended up selling his interest to me for $5,000, leaving me to run the company on the side while working 10-hour days for Olson Brothers. Not surprisingly, Safeway was eager to repeat the promotion the following year. In a moment of madness, I asked Hoopes to name the star he would like to feature next time around, assuring him that I would get whomever he wanted. "Bing Crosby," said Hoopes without a second's hesitation.

"Crosby it is," I said bravely but with private remorse. I had put myself in a pickle again. That year, I sought out the crooner with the same dogged stalking used on Danny Kaye. I haunted every place Crosby lived, worked, or visited, but I could not get near him. Eventually, Bing's brother Larry said he would see me. He listened to a sales pitch that would have made my former boss at Penney's, Mr. Vanderpool, proud. Larry was intrigued but hesitant. "With the exception of 'White Christmas,'" he said, "Bing hasn't sold a Christmas record in years."

"This album will bring him back," I argued. "I have an order for seven hundred thousand records." (There would be no shortfall this year.)

I said they would go for a dollar apiece in Safeway stores across the country and assured him that every other major grocery chain in the US would join Safeway in the promotion because it was so successful last year. "At that price," I closed, "every American family can afford to have Bing sing to them this Christmas."

Larry Crosby succumbed, signed the rather toothless contract I had drawn up, and supplied me with the family Christmas card photo of Bing, Kathryn, and their children to use on the album cover. This time Decca Records cut the album.

Yet just as visions of dollar signs danced in my head, Bing Crosby's tough-talking business manager/attorney called, ordering me to immediately cease and desist. "You are not to release that album," he yelled into his phone. Incredulous at his outburst, I responded that I had a signed contract from Larry Crosby empowering me to do just that.

"Larry Crosby is not Bing's agent," he fired back. "He can't sign anything on Bing's behalf. No one can do that but me." Images of bankruptcy notices immediately replaced the dollar signs that, only moments before, had swirled in my head. I had borrowed $100,000 to cover production costs, and all of it was spent. I had no choice but to get this done. What I resorted to set the precedent for the tactic I would employ many times in my career: sell like crazy to someone who had no desire to buy. I asked the agent for an audience.

I rushed to his office and with all the charm and persuasiveness I could muster, asked him to understand that we were talking about my entire business, that I was putting out a wonderful, wholesome product and was proud of it. "You will be proud of it and Mr. Crosby will be proud of it, too," I bantered, noting that a charming Crosby family photo will be on the cover. I flashed the photograph Larry Crosby had given me and he almost fainted. Undaunted, I continued to press my case.

"I have come here in good faith and have a valid and enforceable contract. I have borrowed an enormous sum of money to produce the album. My family and I will be ruined if you shut this down." He gritted his teeth and uttered assorted expletives. I held my breath and prepared for the worst. After several seconds, he relented. "All right, you can do it this one time. I don't know how you got Larry to sign this thing, but this will never happen again."

Nearly three-quarters of a million records went on their merry way to Safeway stores that sold out long before Christmas. Safeway gradually expanded the deal by allowing other grocery stores in non-competing markets to join. More than a million albums were sold in the ensuing years. Glen Campbell, Perry Como, Julie Andrews—all were among the stars whose pictures graced my album covers.

I was making big money—big for me anyway. The part-time moonlighting was netting $100,000 a year. My day job at Olson Brothers grossed $12,000 annually, and I was working ten- and twelve-hour days. So why didn't I go full time into record sales? Because I knew it was a shaky venture. Safeway could have pulled the plug at any time. It was like blowing up a balloon knowing it eventually would pop. The part-time enterprise brought us millionaire status within a few years, but much of its success was attributable to Lorenzo Hoopes, and running it alone just wasn't the same. I would end up selling my interest in the early 1970s. But it was just the beginning of hawking products on TV, which had been untested up to that point. Still today, I chuckle every time I see a late night infomercial that ends with "If you act now . . ."

By 1968, our family was doing well enough for us to install a swimming pool in our backyard. Karen was expertly managing the home front, caring for six children under ten years of age with energy and grace. She tolerated my absences, sometimes days at a time, but expected me to be a participating husband and father when I was home. I devoted each Saturday to the family and Sundays were spent at church. I had been called to the bishopric of my LDS ward back in 1992 (an assignment that would last for seven years). A Mormon bishop is the rough equivalent of a minister or priest, but the calling is for a set number of years. He has two assistants, called counselors. There are no professional Mormon clergy; all are volunteers. I was to serve as our bishop's counselor. Our Los Angeles years were perhaps the happiest of our child-rearing years.

In the four years I worked for Olson Brothers, I successfully fulfilled Uncle Dean's mandate to learn the egg business from the nest up, and he appointed me vice president of operations. The company had doubled in size during my time there and had plants throughout the West. I was given a free hand, which meant a lot to me. By this time, though, I had handled enough eggs that I didn't care if I never saw another.

The desire to own my own business was beckoning seductively. Dean and his brother, Glenn, each had children of their own waiting in the wings to play major roles in the company and who, I assumed, would eventually own Olson Brothers. There were no more rungs on the ladder for me to climb.

I hinted to Dean and Glenn they ought to consider grooming someone to take my place. I told them I had gained invaluable experience at Olson Brothers and that my five years with them had been wonderful, but my dream was to build something of my own. Dean seemed dismayed, saying I had become indispensable to the business, implying that one day the company's presidency would be mine. I wasn't sure being head of a family-owned egg company was what I envisioned at the end of my rainbow, but I agreed to stay another year. My longing for a greater challenge grew more intense with each passing day. It was the challenge of coming up with a better egg carton that temporarily suppressed the inner turmoil.

With all the social and political upheaval of the 1960s—anti-Vietnam protests; the Cuban Missile Crisis; the rise of a radical left; civil rights marches and murders; three presidents, one of whom was assassinated—the crying need for better egg packaging probably didn't register with the average American. It was, however, at the top of my agenda on Thanksgiving Day 1967 as Olson drove me to our Pico Rivera plant near Whittier, California.

The operation was a joint venture between Olson Brothers and Dow Chemical Company named Dolco, a homogenization of the parent company names. Dolco was pioneering a revolutionary plastics polymer called polystyrene. Up to that time, egg cartons were made of light cardboard known as paperboard or a similar type of mesh paper called chipboard produced from recycled boxes and discarded newspapers. Neither offered much protection, and eggs inside easily broke. By contrast, polystyrene was lightweight, flexible, leak-proof, and inexpensive. Dolco's experiments so far, however, had been a costly disaster. After eighteen months of trial and error, all Dolco had to show for its efforts was a simple, flat tray like the ones found in grocery store meat departments. Not a single usable egg carton had been created.

As I surveyed the plant, its interior looked more like a scrap yard. We waded through a sea of discarded foam sheeting that had emerged unusable from the carton-making machine. Dow's technical wizards—a few engineers and an executive "expert" hired from Shell Chemical— were getting no closer to solutions. The monetary losses were staggering, and Olson Brothers was at wits end.

"Jon," Olson said, "someone's got to take over this plant or the financial losses will take down our business. It's got to be you or me, and I'm almost sixty. I can keep track of egg production a lot easier than I can learn a new technology. That leaves you." In fact, Olson already had discussed with Dow executives the matter of my taking the helm. Dolco was structured such that Olson Brothers supplied management and marketing while Dow, which had dabbled at making polystyrene meat and fruit trays since the early sixties, provided the technicians. Dow was willing to give me a try even though I was not an engineer. My mandate was short and sweet: turn Dolco around and do it fast.

It was a tall order, but I jumped at the opportunity. It wasn't the same thing as starting my own company, of course, but the offer had three things going for it: it was an intriguing challenge, I would have carte blanche authority, and I would be president of a company at age thirty. That might reduce the number of condescending notes from fellow Wharton alums. Plus, I would have Dow Chemical Company executives as my primary mentors. I could learn an entire new industry from the titan itself. I couldn't pass up the opportunity.

When I returned to the Dolco plant as its president, not knowing a vacuum former from a polystyrene sheet extruder, I was looking at a one-hundred-thousand-square-foot facility littered with igloo-shaped piles of polystyrene foam and a business several million dollars in the red. Before me was a twenty-four-carat challenge.

Tray products didn't require much engineering. They were flat and square with no labels, no coloring. An egg carton was a different matter. It needed sides, a lid, and depressions to keep the eggs from touching each other. It required some kind of lock and had to be strong enough to withstand printing. The worst problem was that the sheets of polystyrene foam Dolco had been making were too flimsy to maintain their shapes.

Once again, I donned coveralls and a hard hat and spent more than eighty hours a week crawling under the machines trying to figure out how they worked and why they weren't producing what we needed. Our thermoformers had been custom made exclusively for Dolco by Portland Company Machines in Maine. They were supposed to stamp out two usable egg cartons or four meat trays at a time. They didn't do that. Obviously, changes had to be made to both machinery and personnel, including many of the Dow executives and engineers. The technicians I inherited couldn't wait to tell me why we would never make polystyrene do what we wanted it to do.

Knowing less about the technical process than they did, initially, I couldn't counter with cogent arguments. What I did know was that there was no time to waste rehashing it. The bottom line was that we *were* going to make it work, and it was imperative that we get some people in there who had open minds and a little optimism. I didn't care if my new team knew anything about polystyrene. I wanted young newcomers without hang-ups or preconceptions, people who knew nothing about the process and who would have to use their ingenuity to come up with a design. There was no place for useless paradigms or cop-outs, such as "it can't be done." To this day, that's my least favorite phrase. Shortly thereafter, I fired ten Dow people, mostly engineers, and brought in my own team.

As fate would have it, Jim Fogg, my fellow dreamer from the Bremmer Park Lions, showed up in Los Angeles about this time looking for work. He hoped to employ his civil engineering degree in some way other than roofing houses. An interview with Mobil Oil had brought him to my neck of the woods. While he mulled it over, a little bewildered by the big-city commotion and knowing next to no one in Southern California, Fogg called me a week after I had taken over Dolco's reins.

"Fogg, you're in LA!" I was delighted to hear his voice. "Stay right where you are. I'm coming to get you." I picked him up and drove him to my house. Over dinner, I told him that going to work for Mobil was a bad idea and that I had a much better job for him. He spent that night with us and the next morning we drove to the Pico Rivera plant, whose floors were still buried in drifts of shiny white polystyrene scrap. I laid out the challenge and explained the potential, closing my pitch by saying there was an operations manager position open with his name on it.

"Sounds great to me, Jon," said Fogg, and we shook hands. "I'll make my apologies to Mobil." Neither of us knew anything about the technology we would be developing or the mostly undiscovered process of forming products from polystyrene pellets, but that mattered little to either of us. Four days later, he put his Pocatello home and roofing business on the market. Before he could even spell *polystyrene*, he was off to California to become an expert in it. My core team numbered five, including Lynn Mathie, our marketing manager, and Dean Mackintosh, our hotshot accountant from BYU. The managers worked on the floor in a hands-on approach to developing a plan of attack. Both Mathie and Mackintosh were recruited by Ray Goodson, a Stanford MBA graduate and the first executive to join my new young team in the capacity of executive vice president. Goodson was an excellent manager and assisted with sales and overall operational needs.

The process for manufacturing polystyrene foam was at once simple and complex. (Whenever you see "expandable polystyrene" or "EPS" on these pages, think Styrofoam, the trademarked name for a similar product turned out by Dow.) Simplicity or complexity wasn't the issue. We simply couldn't get the machinery to work.

The challenge was threefold: the sheet's thickness had to be even, strong, and flexible; the product's shape had to be uniform—no breaks or thin spots; and we had to figure out how to print on the product without the ink running or the foam getting flattened in the printing process. Eventually, through trial and error, by never uttering the word *impossible*, and by listening to Bob Webb, a millwright and mechanical wizard, we got there.

Our first egg carton was paper-thin and wouldn't close, but it was the genuine article. That breakthrough was followed by months of fine-tuning. Webb reengineered every machine in the plant. I kept the pressure on, refusing to allow Dow's costly and time-consuming R & D mentality to derail us. We were not researchers; we were businessmen. We had to get the foam out of the extruder and the cartons formed, printed, and off to market fast. Karen ran R & D from her kitchen, by putting our new products through her dishwasher. If they passed the rinse test—whamo!—they were ready for market. Our R & D budget was zero.

Olson Brothers and Dow Chemical had been impatient from the beginning. In the months we spent tinkering with the machines, they occasionally dropped by to meddle. Dow kept attempting to install its personnel. I finally had to issue an ultimatum: "If you want to send me someone, send me someone who wants to work. Don't send me people you think I need. You don't know what I need."

Worse, Olson couldn't stop being my boss even though I was the venture's president. At 6' 4" and 250 pounds, the former all-conference University of Utah football player was an intimidating guy. He would drive to the Pico Rivera operation and start yelling about the way something or other was being handled. I would fire back: "Dean, this isn't helpful. You have no idea how to make egg cartons. I'll appreciate your visiting less often. We'll get it done."

After our first major breakthrough, we went on to perfect a decent plastic egg carton. Finding the market for it was another set of headaches. The most significant competitors were Keyes Fibre, which made meat trays, egg cartons, and apple dividers from wood pulp; Diamond International; and Mobil Chemical Company, which had begun experimenting with polystyrene about the same time as Dolco. Pulp manufacturers had enjoyed a corner on packaging sales for decades and it was against this competition that the battle for market share would be waged. We had a new product made of a new material, but the big boys would not allow a market conversion to be won easily.

We possessed an arrow or two in our quiver that helped level the playing field, namely my grocery chain relationships formed through the Olson Brothers egg business and the Christmas album promotions. We started selling our space-age products to those guys. They were happy to get cartons and trays that were colorful, lightweight, inexpensive, and superior. Dolco turned a profit within the first year. Within two years, we had captured enough of the market to keep three plants busy twenty-four hours a day, producing four hundred million egg cartons and two hundred million meat trays annually.

How we were able to make Dolco work was clear: We used chemistry, vision, and optimism. Another key factor was that our core managers enjoyed common bonds: all of us were young, ambitious, and Mormon. We had a common purpose and a common work ethic that sustained us through long, hard days. We trusted and were comfortable with one another. We tried to inspire the same chemistry in each of the 180 employees. The heady feelings did not last forever, though.

In the process of making Dolco work, I had worked myself to a frazzle. We had three plants, located in California, Georgia, and Washington. I was racing back and forth among them, overseeing every aspect of the business. One night in late 1968, I worked nearly until dawn at the Wenatchee, Washington plant, caught two hours sleep, and was back at the plant by the time the morning shift arrived. After that, I drove to Seattle to catch a flight to Salt Lake City where I was to meet my parents. Our destination was Fillmore and the fall deer hunt. (In some parts of Utah, the opening day of the deer hunt is more sacred than Christmas. It is rumored that Utah's deer hunters make up the fourth largest army in the world.) During the flight, sharp pains ran through my arms and chest. By the time we landed, I was in trouble. My parents met me at the airport, took me straight to the hospital, and I checked into intensive care.

At the age of thirty-one, I was having what the doctors termed a "mild" heart attack. As I slowly recovered, my mother, who had remained with me at the hospital, began to feel pains in her own body of a different kind. The breast cancer she had survived four years earlier had returned. An optimistic prognosis had followed her mastectomy and chemotherapy treatments, but the disease would not be denied. While my convalescence in Salt Lake continued, Dad took my mother home to Palo Alto where she could be seen by physicians at Stanford. That her condition was terminal quickly became obvious.

These events represented a double crisis. In my case, it was clear that some lifestyle changes had to be made. For mother's sake, and for mine, I cut back on my Dolco hours and spent weekends with her in Palo Alto. The thought that she might leave this world without knowing how deeply she was loved and appreciated was unacceptable. Her last months were fraught with pain, eased only by the shots of morphine I was taught to give her. As her condition worsened, she became emaciated and, at times, incoherent, but she never complained. Her pain required increasingly larger doses of morphine. Administering the shots was almost as painful for me as for her. I watched as she steadily wasted away.

My father couldn't handle it. He had depended on his wife for everything. Now, with his spouse helpless and in need of his support, he lacked the inner resolve to stay at her side until the end. Unable to face the reality of her slow, awful death, he withdrew and began drinking more than he had in years. Mother's brother, Paul Robison, a man of constancy and great generosity, came to be at her side throughout her final weeks. I would spell Paul on weekends and made sixteen trips from Los Angeles to be with her before she slipped into her final coma.

On April 8, 1969, she began to shake uncontrollably. Uncle Paul and I rushed to her side. I picked up my mother's frail form and cradled her in my arms. There was an unmistakable moment when I could feel the change as her spirit left. Although heartbroken, I felt at peace that she died in my arms with the knowledge she was loved. My prayer that her suffering not be prolonged was answered. Her passing was a blessing. From then on, she would rest in peace.

My brothers and I conducted two funerals for Mother, one in Palo Alto and the other in Fillmore. I drove my station wagon from California to Utah with her casket in the back. After the Fillmore service, she was buried alongside other family members in the cemetery there. I wondered if her later years had been easier than the first two decades of my life, when times had been hard in so many respects. I decided they probably had been easier after pondering a different question: whether my father was introspective enough to look back and recognize that he hadn't been a kind husband. He seemed to have mellowed over time. Perhaps his hunger for attention was appeased by his Stanford doctorate and his self-respect bolstered by his school superintendent status in a nice part of Los Altos, with a Mercedes to drive, and the recipient of community respect. After achieving those milestones, Dad seemed less angry, less intimidating, and less of a drinker.

Having come into his own professionally, there were fewer reasons for my father to take out his frustrations on my mother. She had always tolerated his behavior. She wasn't strong in a way that would have enabled her to lay down an ultimatum of her own. She did seem more at peace in her final years. Mother never had many amenities. She never owned a clothes dryer, not even when Dad had two luxury cars in the driveway. I don't recall her ever asking for anything for herself, but there was nothing she would not do to make life better for her family.

My brothers, Blaine (by which he was known as an adult) and Clayton, a navy ensign at the time, joined Dad and me for the funeral and burial services, coming together as a family for the first time in many years. Blaine and I, the Pocatello pranksters who could do no wrong in mother's eyes, said our good-byes. To this day, when visiting Fillmore, her grave is the first and last place I stop.

As I left the cemetery after her burial, I made two vows: I would lead my family differently than my father had led his and, if I ever attained the financial wherewithal, I would someday find a cure for cancer. I would move heaven and earth to eliminate the suffering that goes with it. That vow to conquer cancer constituted a sacred commitment. I didn't know how and I didn't know where and I didn't know when. But I did know it would happen.

What also was becoming increasingly apparent was that I needed new challenges, to see other things and to work for myself, running my own business where I could engage my entrepreneurial ideas. By early 1970, the new Nixon Administration had made its second attempt to get me to Washington, D.C. Serving government was something I thought I should do—but not as a career. Thus, when an administration recruiter offered me a position helping to direct the nation's social welfare programs for the Department of Health, Education and Welfare, I accepted. I had exceeded my goals at Olson Brothers, including creating the egg carton, and it appeared that Dean's successor would be one of his children. Nevertheless, I knew my leaving would not sit well with Uncle Dean, who by this time considered me part of the "family" at the business. He would take it personally. What I failed to fathom was how persistently ugly and detrimental his reaction to my departure would become.

What happened next was beyond anything I had ever imagined.

4. Good Morning, Mr. President

THE VOICE OF FRED MALEK, SPECIAL ASSISTANT TO PRESIDENT NIXON in charge of White House personnel recruitment, who had lured me to my administrative post the previous year, was tense. His message was as ominous as it was succinct: "Haldeman will be calling you. He is seeking candidates for White House staff secretary. I recommended you. Officially, there are fourteen candidates, but you're the front-runner. He will be calling you within ten minutes. Don't leave your desk. Don't panic. And don't miss his call."

Haldeman, of course, was White House Chief of Staff H.R. "Bob" Haldeman, Nixon's loyal majordomo and arguably the second most powerful person in Washington. He would become infamously involved in the Watergate cover-up scandal within two years. Haldeman controlled every aspect of the president's schedule, staff and contact with others and ruled with an iron hand.

Malek didn't offer particulars in that February 2, 1971 call other than to say the job encompassed granting White House perks and attending to administrative details. As it turned out, as Bob Haldeman's right hand, I would also have under my purview being the president's gatekeeper for all correspondence and memos in and out of his office and his written link to cabinet and executive department heads.

I sat frozen in my chair, not knowing what to think. Had I known what the job would demand of me, I might have gone out for a Coke and missed the call.

Just moments before, I had been busy in my spacious office in the Department of Health, Education, and Welfare (HEW), comfortably wearing the title of associate administrator of Social and Rehabilitation Services (SRS). It didn't take me long after taking the job in 1970 to come to the sobering realization that I was overseeing some of the most needed—and most abused—programs in the federal government. I oversaw six major federal-state programs in the Welfare section of the department:

Assistance Payments (better known as the country's welfare program), the Administration on Aging, Community Services (overseeing low-income issues), Medical Services Administration (Medicaid), the Office of Juvenile Delinquency and Youth Affairs, and Rehabilitation Services (for the mentally challenged and physically handicapped). We badly needed new strategies to address the problems of a bureaucracy that had grown rigid and resistant to change.

There were certainly success stories at HEW. One of my areas of responsibility encompassed the program to assist Cuban refugees as they landed in Florida, who were hitting the beach at an average of 150 per day (two flights per day from Havana). Within sixty days of arriving, we had more than 80 percent of them on their feet and off public assistance. I became close to the refugee leaders, who confided in me about the Bay of Pigs fiasco, a US-sponsored invasion of Cuba nearly ten years earlier in which air support was pulled at the eleventh hour by President Kennedy. (That information proved fortuitous three years later.)

I was also involved deeply in working to shore up the welfare programs. For me, compassion is a nonpartisan issue, inseparable from the concepts of philanthropy I have espoused throughout my life. Welfare benefits were a legitimate government service, programs created by Congress for the specific purpose of meeting an acknowledged need. My job, as I saw it, was not to undermine these programs, even if my fellow conservatives viewed them as liberal mechanisms for spending more taxpayer dollars. It was to assure the programs operated as efficiently as possible within the intent and the spirit of the laws that created them, and that benefits were paid in a manner that neither demeaned nor diminished the people receiving them.

Singing this song as consistently as we did brought a measure of success. Within six months, our efficiency measures saved $100 million without eliminating or scaling down programs. In that half year, something else happened, as well. I realized that I had fallen in love with ordinary working people, not just machinery.

My jump to the federal government in 1970 was the right thing and the right time. I had done what I had been asked to do at Olson Brothers, and I had made my first million, primarily from the Christmas recording business. It was time for the next adventure.

Roland Rich Woolley was a legendary Southern California trial lawyer with whom I became friends after moving to Los Angeles. One day, he called me out of the blue to suggest I consider a job in the Nixon administration. It wasn't just talk. He had the political connections to turn food for thought into a gourmet meal.

Soon after the November 1968 election, Woolley received a letter from Richard Nixon, as did thousands of prominent Republicans, seeking recommendations of up-and-comers to fill posts in the new administration. Woolley submitted my name to Nixon and to Robert Finch, a former lieutenant governor of California who had been appointed secretary of the then-called Department of Health, Education, and Welfare (HEW). Both were close friends with Woolley.

By early spring 1969, I received a telephone call from Malek, then Finch's deputy undersecretary, who said he was looking for young talent to revamp and improve HEW, considered by most Republicans even then to be an out-of-control, bureaucratic monster. He flew to Los Angeles to interview me. We got on well. In fact, that interview was the start of a lifelong friendship. He offered me the position of regional HEW administrator for the Western United States based in San Francisco. I surprised him by declining after realizing I wasn't quite ready to leave the businesses I was juggling. The timing just wasn't good. But I asked him not to forget about me. He didn't, and a year later, Fred called again, asking me to consider the job of deputy commissioner of Education at HEW.

I flew to Washington to interview for the job. One of the sessions was with HEW Assistant Secretary L. Patrick Gray, who later would be appointed to succeed the controversial FBI director J. Edgar Hoover. Gray's out-of-the-box question was a doozy. Referring to the LDS Church's barrier against black people holding the priesthood (which the church later removed), he opened by asking what I would say to an angry black person who, after being denied a welfare check, walked up to me and claimed the reason was because I was a Mormon and therefore a bigot?

My response was immediate: "I would put my arm around that person's shoulder and say, 'We are all children of a loving Heavenly Father.

Neither color nor religion has anything to do with the way I conduct department affairs.'" It seemed to satisfy him.

Elliot Richardson had replaced Finch as HEW secretary three days before my interview (and would end up heading the Justice Department in the darkest days of the Watergate investigations). Following a meeting with him, Richardson told Malek that instead of placing me at Education he would rather see me working to revamp the Welfare leg of the HEW tripod. The offer they extended to me was for the position of associate administrator of the office of SRS in charge of field operations. My role, in essence, was chief operating officer of the entire spectrum of US social programs. I accepted without hesitation and flew back to California to put my affairs in order.

Dean Olson was not pleased when I told him I was resigning to take the HEW job. He felt betrayed, even though I had been dropping hints that I would be seeking a new challenge for more than a year. He got angry—and when Dean got angry, he got mean. He would attempt to torpedo me for the next decade, but first, he tried an inside move.

Our board of directors included Ezra Taft Benson, a powerful personality in the LDS Church. He was a member of the ruling Quorum of the Twelve Apostles and was in line to assume the role of president of the church, which he did fifteen years later. Benson had also served as secretary of agriculture under President Eisenhower (who called Benson "the most ungrateful person it has ever been his misfortune to know"). We had worked together closely during the past decade as fellow board members. Olson asked Benson to pressure me into turning down the government position and staying with the company.

Benson was an outspoken supporter of the John Birch Society, a national right-wing organization whose members saw a communist under every bed. Instead of giving me a pep talk for remaining with Olson Brothers, Benson's approach was to warn me about the federal government. "The Department of Health, Education, and Welfare is the most socialistic arm of the federal government," he declared. "It will be even more so now that such liberals as Nixon and Richardson are running it."

Benson saw Washington, DC as the epicenter of leftist philosophy in America and warned that I would be sucked into that liberal quagmire.

I would become corrupt and adopt socialism as my core philosophy. I politely reminded him that he had served under Eisenhower and seemed to have avoided the liberal pitfalls. "That," he said, "was because I have a strong belief in America and its Constitution."

"So do I," I countered, adding that I could represent my position well. But it was unsettling for me. Instead of challenging Benson further, I sought the advice of another trusted source, Eldon Tanner, one of two counselors to the president of the LDS Church and, thus, a member of the First Presidency. My father-in-law, David Haight, accompanied me to that meeting. He had recently been called to serve as an assistant to the Quorum of Twelve and later would become a sitting member of that governing body. He knew Tanner well. Tanner urged me to accept the Washington job. Put aside Benson's forebodings, he counseled, underscoring that the appointment was a great opportunity to serve my country.

Reinforced, I respectfully reported my decision to Elder Benson: "I feel I could not, in good conscience, look my children and grandchildren in the eye and tell them their father or grandfather, when requested by the president of the United States to take a key position in government, had rejected it. No, sir, I will not do that."

Two years later, following my return from Washington, Benson would call to congratulate me. He referred to my White House stint as "an appointment from heaven." His opinion had turned 180 degrees. He underscored what a great friend he was to President Nixon and that he had received several "personally signed" letters from him while he was in office. I inwardly chuckled, having personally run that boilerplate correspondence through the automatic signature machine before mailing them. (The president disliked signing personal letters. Thus, our automatic signature machine, referred to as "autopen," could mimic seven slightly different "Richard Nixon" signatures and two RN-encircled signatures for more intimate and personal letters.)

Karen and I packed our six children in the car and drove across the United States. At 9:00 a.m. on September 21, 1970, I entered the Social Services Building at HEW and found my new office on the top floor. It was the largest office I had ever seen. A stadium-like room, it contained thirty-two chairs. I began to comprehend the breadth of my responsibility.

HEW had a $15 billion budget, roughly the same as that of the Pentagon at the time, much of it mine to manage.

Six months later, I had what looked like another job offer.

Ten minutes to the second after Fred Malek's call, the phone rang. A woman's voice said Bob Haldeman wished to speak to me. Before I could thank her, Haldeman was on the line. He skipped any semblance of pleasantries: "We are considering you for an appointment to staff secretary. Don't get excited. You may not be what we're looking for." He said the White House was aware of my work at HEW implementing the president's efficiency programs. "I'll see you here at the White House in fifteen minutes." Click.

It would take me at least fifteen minutes in Washington traffic to reach 1600 Pennsylvania Avenue. I felt surprisingly calm, although I recognized a Haldeman summons could portend a major change in my world. As fast as one can drive in DC traffic, I hustled to the White House gate and prepared to show my identification. The first thing that came out of my wallet was an American Express card. I showed it to the executive protection officer as I fumbled for something more official. He waved me through. I had not been to the White House before but found a gardener who directed me to the West Wing waiting room.

After my rush to get there, I was allowed to cool my heels for an hour and a half, lest there be any misconception on my part that Haldeman was excited about the possibility of my joining the team. Finally, Haldeman's deputy, Alexander Butterfield, escorted me inside Haldeman's office. Instead of a desk, the room was anchored by an imposing circular table made of rich, dark wood so finely polished the finish seemed three feet deep. Off to one side was a comfortable seating area with a blazing fireplace, the only warmth to be found that day.

Haldeman, a good-looking man in his forties with a signature crew cut and an air of aloofness, sat at the table. Though he was impeccably dressed in a white button-down shirt, conservative tie, and dark suit—the uniform in the Nixon White House—it struck me as incongruous that he was slouched in his chair, jacket unbuttoned, with his feet up and ankles crossed on that elegant table. Rumor had it that Haldeman could be both charming and ruthless, each to intense degrees. Prior to attaching himself to Nixon, he had been an executive with the J. Walter Thompson advertising agency in Los Angeles where he perfected his talents for schmoozing when it served his interests and for intimidation when that would better serve. He displayed a bit of each at the interview.

The chief of staff covered every aspect of my background, including my Mormon faith. He listened quietly to my responses. At one point, he implied I might be overqualified for the position, but I responded that no one could be too well qualified to serve the president of the United States. Haldeman told me he was a Christian Scientist who neither smoked nor drank alcohol and he appreciated that I, as a Mormon, didn't either. He indicated clearly that he frowned on such behavior by his staff. (Pat Nixon would later confide how she could never relax with a martini on the campaign trail without Haldeman eyeing her with disdain.)

Our meeting went well and, initially, Haldeman and I seemed to view each other with tentative respect. More interviews were arranged in the West Wing, one of which was with Vice President Spiro Agnew, who engaged in polite banter. I suddenly realized I was wearing my Spiro Agnew wristwatch, given to me as a gag gift by some Democrats on my HEW staff. My crew thought it funny, but I doubted the vice president would be amused if he had spotted it. I spent the rest of the interview with my right hand covering my left wrist.

In the early afternoon, Butterfield invited me to join him for a late lunch in his office. I continued to be in awe of the atmosphere, but the longer I sat with him the more at ease I became and the more apparent it seemed the staff secretary's position was mine. Butterfield knew most everything that went on behind the White House scenes. He had been a UCLA classmate of Haldeman's, an air force colonel who flew with the Thunderbirds aerobatic flying team and who resigned his commission to serve President Nixon. A pleasant, positive man, we hit it off. He was adept at collecting information, which I discovered as he prodded me to share what Haldeman had said in the interview. I had just started to relate the highlights when Butterfield's office door flew open and in blew Haldeman.

"Are you a full tithe-payer in the Mormon Church?" he asked, referring to the practice many religions urge in which ten percent of one's income is given to the church.

"I am," I responded.

"Good. We have no room here for people who don't live up to their commitments." With that, he left the room. That was the sum of the notification I received that I would be the new staff secretary and special assistant to the president of the United States—regardless of whether I wanted the job. I had some reservations, unfinished work at HEW primary among them. Moreover, I had doubts about fitting in at the White House. Notwithstanding those concerns, I wanted the job. Who wouldn't?

With H. R. Haldeman, however, the decision was never mine. It was his. On February 7, I began gearing up to go to work for the president. Our seventh child, James, was born the same day. Haldeman had demanded I transfer to the White House immediately. I asked for two weeks to finish up at HEW and to meet with my business associates in California. Haldeman permitted me one week—the first of many omens that I was no longer in control of my life.

I reported to the White House at 7:45 a.m. on February 14, 1971, to begin my new duties. I had the benefit of one day of succession training with my predecessor, John Brown. The job's pressures, he told me, had made him physically ill. That was not reassuring. I met Kenneth Cole, who had the distinction of being the first staff secretary under Nixon. He was also the man who Haldeman later reassigned to support John Ehrlichman which, some said, was to make sure the president's domestic advisor didn't get out of line. Cole rendered this advice: Be independent if you want to survive. Take a stand and refuse to be run over by Haldeman and his yes men. "That will take all the powers of resistance you can muster," he said in closing.

No one told me it also would require all the forces of the ethics and values instilled in me since childhood to survive with my moral compass intact.

There is no way to exaggerate the scope of the role I had undertaken. It was apparent from my first day I had landed in the epicenter of White House activity. My desk was the clearinghouse for information going in and out of the president's office, every official document distributed among the cabinet, the White House staff, and the president's daily "Eyes

Only" CIA briefing called the Red Book. Every piece of it had to be condensed, summarized, and approved by me. I had authority to classify documents and to determine who could read them. Haldeman insisted that Nixon's name not appear on any memos so, while I was there, a goodly portion of the 1,800 memos passing across my desk from President Nixon went to their recipients under my name.

My role extended to oversight of White House finances and certain personnel, office assignments, and keeping the West Wing's operations within its budget. The staff secretary also was one of only a handful of people who had direct access to the president.

Each day began with the news summary from Mort Allen, a member of a speech-writing team that included Patrick Buchanan, William Safire, and Ray Price. In the wee hours of each morning, Allen would assemble and condense relevant news stories from the daily papers and have them to me by 7:00 a.m. I would have that briefing ready for the president's eyes by the time he entered the Oval Office, usually around 8:15 a.m. Allen's news summaries always made life interesting. No matter what he read, Nixon always scribbled notes and instructions in the margins. One page of scribbles in Allen's news summary could mean half a day's work for me.

Nixon hated negative press. It set him off to read a story that quoted "anonymous White House sources." He would write in the margin, "Find out who said this and why." I would try to discover which reckless soul had dared talk to the press without authorization, but my efforts were fruitless.

Technically, the organizational chart showed me as Butterfield's deputy with a dotted line to Haldeman. But make no mistake: Haldeman called the shots. The three of us had control over White House administrative matters and anything or anybody having to do with the president's schedule. Butterfield was secretary to the members of the cabinet, which left me to serve as assistant secretary to all the heads of the sprawling executive branch of government.

Working in the White House was heady stuff, but it came at great personal price. After my fifteen-hour workday, I would make my way home, exhausted, and try to catch a few hours of sleep. Even that time was not my own. My personal and family life went out the window. Our kitchen had a red phone and a direct line from the White House. I was always at Haldeman's beck and call. I seldom got to church because I worked most Sundays, unless the president was at Camp David or out of town. Even holidays were treated as regular workdays.

Karen had been trained for this lifestyle by the example of her father, who was a caring but often absent husband and parent. She took it all in stride, as part of normal life. She was supportive and steady through those years, always a guiding hand to our children. I would sometimes bring the older children to the office on Saturdays. They would draw pictures, play games, and run around on the South Lawn of the White House. Initially, when they were outdoors, I would check on them periodically until a Secret Service agent told me not to bother. White House security had the children under constant surveillance and assured me they were safe. Despite the demanding schedule, most of the older children have fond memories of Washington, recalling how I helped coach them or took them on outings, ensuring that each one was a memorable experience.

As in most administrations, the proximity of the advisors' offices to the Oval Office indicated their levels of power. An office in the East Wing meant a person was several rungs removed from the top of the ladder. Although, since First Lady Pat Nixon didn't like the limelight, she and her staff were quartered in the East Wing, along with military attaches and others. Most East Wing staffers did not have security clearance for the West Wing, which was quite restricted. That way Nixon could stroll about the corridors, if so inclined, without being accosted by someone he didn't want to see.

Daniel Patrick Moynihan, a Harvard professor who at the time ran Nixon's National Domestic Council, made an interesting point on this matter. When asked why he opted for a tiny office in the West Wing in lieu of a suite in the Old Executive Office Building next door, Moynihan remarked: "A West Wing office, my boy, means I can pee standing next to Haldeman in the same bathroom."

As staff secretary, my office was in the West Wing, on the ground floor, or "the basement." It was a three-room suite, elegantly furnished but only about a third the size of my office at HEW. On either side of my office were the Office of National Security and the locked-and-guarded Situation Room, where the president and his top staff would confer during wartime or national emergencies. Twenty-five feet away and up one flight of stairs were the offices of Kissinger, Butterfield, and Haldeman. Between Haldeman and the Oval Office resided Nixon's personal secretary, Rose Mary Woods; Appointments Secretary Dwight Chapin; and Press Secretary Ron Ziegler. Also upstairs were George Shultz, Nixon's chief economic advisor, and John Ehrlichman, head of the Domestic Council.

With the exception of Kissinger and Woods, all were subject to Haldeman's personal orders. Haldeman shielded Nixon from his own staff as much as he did from the public. Even White House Counsel John Dean, later a high-profile figure in the Watergate hearings, spent several months in the White House before meeting the president. (Dean's office was in the Executive Office Building adjacent to the White House.)

Since I had access to the president, I often found myself a go-between for cabinet members. Housing and Urban Development Secretary George Romney, father of Mitt Romney, came to my office one day complaining he had not been able to visit with the president on HUD matters for three months. "Can you line me up with him?" asked the former Michigan governor. The best I could do was to arrange a meeting with Ehrlichman, the domestic affairs point man. Romney could never get Nixon's attention on matters of serious concern and felt slighted. Nixon was an internationalist. Domestic issues did not command his interest unless they were brought up by Treasury Secretary John Connally or his former law partner, Attorney General John Mitchell.

Thanks to Haldeman's vigilance and the hell-to-pay consequences whenever he saw anything he didn't like, the West Wing was constantly tense. But its denizens also basked in an atmosphere of power and privilege. Most were fascinated with the idea of the perks to which such privilege entitled them—perks which were mine, as the staff secretary, to bestow. Office assignments, staff increases, use of limos and tennis courts, and other status symbols were jealously sought and guarded as evidence of superiority. In the first few months on the job, I always checked with Haldeman and Butterfield before approving perks and privileges. Before long, though, Haldeman trusted me to grant them at my discretion. After that, I was lobbied endlessly.

Outside the White House, few knew my position existed, let alone who filled it. Inside the porticoed mansion, I performed as a backstage logistics specialist, a camouflaged force who, like the Wizard of Oz, wielded pulleys and cables from a concealed spot behind the curtain. In such a role, I came across a good deal of low-level insider information and more than a few dirty secrets. President Nixon's favorite wine, for example, was expensive. It was served to him alone at every formal dinner, a towel carefully obscuring the label, while his guests' glasses were filled with the nectar of a less pricey grape.

Then there was the matter of the presidential "throne." One of my first orders from Haldeman was to swap out the high toilet that the lengthy and bulky Lyndon Johnson had installed in the Oval Office's private bathroom. Nixon complained LBJ's toilet was too tall for him, and that his legs dangled when he sat on it. He also complained about LBJ's shower, which aides referred to as a car wash. By the power vested in me, I issued the crucial executive order for White House Government Services Administration (GSA) czar Charlie Rotchford to replace the toilet with a lower one and to make the president's shower less like Niagara Falls.

The secrets of White House salaries were also within my purview. I knew how much everyone was making. Even bearing in mind that this was the early seventies, White House salaries were surprisingly modest. Haldeman, Ehrlichman, Kissinger, and presidential counselor Donald Rumsfeld were at the top with an annual wage of $42,500. Rumsfeld's assistant, Dick Cheney, earned $28,317. Press Secretary Ron Ziegler received $37,500, and he had a diligent and hardworking research assistant, Diane Sawyer, who was paid only $12,615, a figure that pales against her current television network anchor contract. Butterfield earned $35,000, as did John Dean, Utah's own Tom Korologos (who went on to become a high-powered lobbyist and then US ambassador to Belgium), and William Safire, all special assistants to the president. Speechwriter Pat Buchanan was paid $34,000; Alexander Haig, deputy to Kissinger, made only $22,500. My pay was about $2,000 less than Rose Mary Woods, who handled the president's personal correspondence and whose controversial eighteen-and-a-half-minute erasure of presidential tapes would make her a household name. At $30,000, my salary was some $6,000 less than what I was making at HEW.

One of the friendships I forged was with Manolo Sanchez, Nixon's devoted valet, who may have been the only apolitical person in the building. I often would arrive at work early to make contact with Sanchez before starting my day. He would let me know what sort of mood his boss was in, whether he had had a before-breakfast conversation with Haldeman of which I should be aware, and whether it was "safe" to take piles of paper into the Oval Office.

Richard Nixon may have been president, but it was H. R. Haldeman's White House, from the people he hired to his zero-defects management code. Presidential assistants were bright, clean-cut young males whose obedience was robotic, or else. Haldeman's team became known as the WASPs, all being white, Anglo-Saxon Protestants. (As a member of the LDS faith, I was the lone exception.) Haldeman demanded of every member of the team the same fanatical fidelity to Nixon that he maintained. He was committed to protecting the president from the pressures and stresses of office. Unfortunately, he did so by hermetically sealing Richard Nixon inside the Oval Office.

Often without fully understanding the inherent powers of the president of the United States, Haldeman's top priority was to carry out his interpretation of the president's will. "We are here to serve the president, not the people," he would tell me. "The president is sacred and above reproach." Haldeman felt any task Nixon ordered, or which, in Haldeman's opinion, the president should have ordered, must be carried out to the letter. He expected flawless and specific performance and he usually got what he wanted.

For his part, Nixon had great confidence in Haldeman and acquiesced to his suggestions to remain above the fray. Aside from Haldeman, the president's next most trusted staff member was Butterfield, who enjoyed more informal contact with Nixon than perhaps anyone else. Butterfield earned his trust in every way I could detect. He was perfect for his position. It was gratifying that the president's confidence seemed to extend to me, as well. Naturally, Nixon reserved for Haldeman and his advisors the discussions on affairs of state or those of personal concern to him. He confined his brief conversations with me to topics of an administrative or general nature. On those occasions, I enjoyed our interactions and was pleased when he signaled his trust in me in small but noticeable ways. When I presented each day's voluminous stack of documents and letters requiring his signature, he would sign without reading them, asking only, "Jon, do these all meet with your approval?"

"Yes, Mr. President."

"Has Haldeman reviewed any of them?"

"Yes, sir, he has."

And that would be the end of it.

Haldeman was perturbed by anything that occurred without his specific approval. J. Willard "Bill" Marriott, the hotel magnate and whose son Bill Jr. was my best friend and neighbor, was a friend of Nixon's and one of the few outsiders whose visits the president liked to receive. That irritated Haldeman to no end. Each year at Christmastime, Marriott would show up in the West Wing to hand out home-baked fruitcakes to White House personnel. Following their 1971 fruitcake delivery, Haldeman snapped at me: "Huntsman, you've got to figure a way to keep the Marriotts out of here."

"Bob, they are my dear friends," I answered. "More importantly," I hastened to add, "they are the president's friends. If you want them to stay out, you tell them not to come." Haldeman didn't do that, of course. Rather than speaking up to the influential, he preferred to find ways to circumvent or undercut them. But he also made cracks about what he thought was the inordinate number of Mormon visitors to the White House. There weren't that many, but four probably seemed excessive to him. I began to sense that Haldeman, who, in our first meeting, had expressed respect for Mormons and their values, had developed a bug in his bonnet where Latter-day Saints were concerned.

Or maybe it was just a "bug" in my office. Ever vigilant, Haldeman had noted that a dozen or so Mormons had "infiltrated the ranks." There was no agenda on my part for bringing Mormons on board. As secretaries and aides were needed at various levels of staff, I recruited people from all possible sources because capable people who could pass White House Security were indeed difficult to locate. I did on occasion invite a resume from a member of my church whom I knew to be qualified. One of those was my deputy, David Hoopes, who became a valued member of the White House staff and stayed on after I left, serving Nixon and Gerald Ford. Hoopes proved to be devoted to Nixon and earned his respect.

Let the record show that I recruited capable talent of any stripe. It was a source of particular pride, both at the time and later on, to be part of the hiring process of a brilliant Harvard Law graduate, Elizabeth

Hanford—who was certainly not a Mormon. After the interview, I recommended her for the position of deputy to Virginia Knauer, the first White House director of consumer affairs. Hanford later became a member of the Federal Trade Commission, a special assistant to President Ronald Reagan, and later secretary of the departments of Transportation and Labor. Her name changed when she married Senator Bob Dole, the Kansas Republican who, in 1996, challenged Bill Clinton for the presidency. Elizabeth Hanford Dole served as CEO of the American Red Cross from 1991–99. In 2002, Elizabeth became a US senator from North Carolina. She has long been a special friend and confidant.

Yet for whatever reason, Haldeman was bothered by the number of Mormons on the payroll—so much so that one day he made an issue of it. "Jon, don't you think we have enough of the Mormon Mafia now?" he snarled. Mormons weren't even close to being the largest slice of the demographic pie chart, but Haldeman decided to take a stand. Not only did he put a stop to the hiring of LDS personnel, but I saw that he started using his authority to make problems whenever possible for the two Mormon cabinet members, Treasury Secretary David Kennedy and HUD Secretary Romney.

No one in the White House other than Haldeman seemed preoccupied with my religion, although at least once the subject came up to humorous effect. Most practicing members of the LDS faith wear what are called "sacred garments" their entire adult lives. These garments possess a deep symbolism, not unlike vestments and accoutrements worn by people of other religious beliefs. Garments are bestowed upon temple-worthy adults with their initial temple endowments, usually preliminary to a mission or marriage. They are meant to remind Mormons of the sacredness of their bodies and their temple covenants. Garments are white and look like truncated long johns, but of lighter material. The tops are styled something like a tee shirt; the bottoms are similar to shorts and are hemmed just above the knees. Today, garments are two-piece in deference to modern fashion, but when I started wearing them, they were a single piece of clothing. Practicing Mormons wear garments except when participating in sporting events, bathing, or when work requires a specific form of dress. Some Mormons feel uncomfortable discussing these garments, which may be why non-Mormons are curious about them.

The presidential "gym," which Chief of Staff Haldeman had authorized me to set up when I first started my job, was located in a small room in the Old Executive Office Building basement (now the Eisenhower Building). It was really just a weight room with a few exercise machines, a couple of showers, and a steam bath. The president never used it. A select few in the West Wing did. Since I had authorized its construction, I was one of twenty-one senior staff with access.

Late one day, I was in the steam room after a quick workout when John Ehrlichman and Henry Kissinger came in and sat down on a bench directly in front of the locker containing my clothes. I didn't want to dress in front of them because I was concerned about what they would think of my "full coverage" temple garments, so I remained in the steam bath. The two became heavily engaged in conversation and didn't budge. They didn't move for what seemed like an eternity. I was becoming overheated.

Feeling faint, well done, and red as a lobster, I burst out of the suffocating steam, took a breath of air, and said "excuse me" as casually as possible while squeezing between Kissinger and my locker. I reached in and tucked the legs of my one-piece garment into my suit pants, hoping to slip into both in a seamless move. It didn't work. My foot caught on the underwear and pushed it out the bottom of the pant leg. There, at the feet of National Security Advisor Kissinger, was a sacred garment. The conversation between Kissinger and Ehrlichman stopped. I separated my clothing and started over, this time donning one piece at a time. "Vaat is daat?" asked Kissinger in his signature basso profundo accent.

"Umm, this is special underclothing worn by people in my church," I said, quickly pulling them up over my shoulders and reaching for my pants. It wasn't enough for Henry and John. I had to elaborate, which I did as briefly as possible, but their incredulous faces didn't change. I threw on my shirt, tie, and coat and left them to wonder.

Throughout my time in the Nixon administration, Haldeman protected the president to such an extent that he effectively presided over the executive branch of government. He did so with President Nixon's acquiescence but with little deference to the lessons of history. He had no previous experience with or knowledge of the workings of national government.

He just made it up as he went along and took the ringmaster's role to stunning levels of brilliance, vengeance, and unethical behavior.

I didn't think much of his approach to his job. It may have been Haldeman's ruthlessness on the campaign trail that helped get his hero elected to the most powerful office on the planet, but with Haldeman's appointment as chief of staff came the ultimate test of his coarse management style. And it failed. The degrading manner in which Haldeman ran roughshod over staff might have been forgiven in the context of an intense presidential campaign, but, as time eventually proved, his continued, no-holds-barred code of conduct was intolerable in any other scenario and was especially inappropriate in the White House. I quickly would discover the depths to which the Nixon White House had descended.

For the most part, my dustups with Haldeman were nothing more than blips on the radar screen. Take, for example, the "H incident." There were fresh legal pads at the president's side twenty-four hours a day on which he could scrawl notions and directives intended for his team. I received these jottings twice a day and would convert them to memo form, dispatching each to the appropriate recipient. Each entry began with a single letter designating the team member for whom it was intended, *K* for Henry Kissinger, *Z* for Ron Ziegler, and so forth. I assumed the one-letter designations were universal staff shorthand. One day, while still new on the job, I sent a memo from me to Treasury Secretary John Connally, signing off with the letter *H*. It boomeranged back to my desk, never having reached Connally. Haldeman had intercepted it and scrawled across the top of the page in heavy, red letters: "If you think *H* stands for Huntsman, you are crazier than I thought." Signed, *H*. Thereafter, I settled for *J*.

Another unpleasant encounter occurred when my mentor, Roland Rich Woolley, visited me at the White House hoping he also would be able to say hello to the president with whom he had been on friendly terms in California. As luck would have it, Nixon was returning to the White House by helicopter that afternoon. I escorted Woolley to the South Lawn to await his friend's arrival. The helicopter landed and Nixon approached us. I stepped forward: "Mr. President, say hello to your old friend, Roland Woolley." The president looked exhausted, but he brightened when he saw Woolley, greeting him warmly. The two chatted about old times for three or four minutes before Nixon excused himself and continued to his quarters. No sooner did we turn back toward my office than I spotted Haldeman with a glare icy enough to freeze a lava flow. "Huntsman," he hissed, "don't you ever detain the president again without prior approval."

Over time, I developed a thicker skin for Haldeman's bullying, if for no other reason than I had to in order to get work done. My loyalty was to R. M. Nixon, not H. R. Haldeman, whose surliness was his trademark. My tolerance for boorishness had a limit, however, and he overstepped that line in early June.

Nixon was in Key Biscayne for the weekend and Haldeman was with him. As our routine dictated, I would send a daily mail pouch by air force courier for Nixon and senior staff. This particular day's packet contained material for a speech Nixon was planning to give to the Veterans of Foreign Wars convention in Miami Beach later in the week. I had just gathered materials from speechwriters Pat Buchanan and Ray Price when Dwight Chapin called from Key Biscayne to say the speech had been canceled. On the strength of that information, it seemed reasonable not to include the speech material in the pouch. When the packet arrived later that day, sans speech, Haldeman went ballistic. He phoned me and, as usual, didn't bother with any semblance of a salutation.

"You son of a bitch, Huntsman," he raged in my ear. "Why didn't you carry out my orders? You had no authority to pull that speech material."

"I'm sorry, Bob, but Chapin told me the speech was canceled. The president wouldn't need the material, so I didn't send it." Haldeman was never interested in explanations, reasonable or otherwise. I had seen plenty of his flare-ups, but I was shocked at the vehemence of this particular tirade. I became angry at being the target of this over-the-top abuse. As abruptly as he had started his barrage, he ceased fire and hung up, only to call back a few minutes later to carry on with renewed vigor. I had had enough.

I told him that I had been the target of enough of his insults and degradation and that, as much as I would hate to leave the White House, I had no desire to work for him under current circumstances. "If my performance isn't good enough, you can take this job and shove it." This time, I was the one to slam down the phone.

Angrier than I ever remembered being, I gathered the speech materials, called a White House limousine, and ordered the driver to get me to Washington National Airport on the double. Flashing my White House ID at anyone who attempted to stop me, I climbed aboard a commercial Eastern Airlines jetliner about to take off for Miami and opened the door to the cockpit. (Obviously, this was long before strict FAA security regulations.) Handing the sealed envelope to the astonished pilot, I said in an official tone: "This material is for the president of the United States. It is not to be out of your sight until you place it in the hands of Colonel Jack Brennan," explaining that the latter was the president's military aide who would be meeting the plane at Miami International Airport. "Do you understand?"

"Yes, sir," replied the pilot, almost snapping to attention. "I will see to it."

By eight o'clock that evening, materials for the speech that was "never delivered" were on the president's bedside table with a copy to Haldeman. I didn't know whether I still had a job and didn't much care. Nothing was said about it when Haldeman returned from Key Biscayne later that week. Four days later, Larry Higby, one of Haldeman's assistants, walked into my office to say, "Bob said to tell you that he appreciates the way you got the speech to the president. He wants you to start attending the ten a.m. staff meetings." I already was a regular participant in the daily 2:00 p.m. scheduling meetings, but the 10:00 a.m. "superstaff" meeting was a gathering quite different. Rather than losing my job for returning fire, my presence was being requested unexpectedly in the White House's most exclusive inner circle.

It soon became clear the super-staff huddle, with all its lofty connotations, was not something one anticipates with eagerness. I arrived at Haldeman's office for my initial meeting a few minutes ahead of time. Seated around the table were Special Assistant Fred Malek, White House Counsel John Dean, Appointments Secretary Dwight Chapin, Speechwriter Ray Price, Special Counsel Chuck Colson, Press Secretary Ron Ziegler, and Haldeman's deputies, Butterfield and Higby. Haldeman didn't believe in small talk, so no one spoke as we waited for the meeting to begin. Haldeman sat with his back to the group, looking through the French doors that led to his private garden. At ten o'clock sharp, he whirled in his chair and pointed a finger at the person on his right.

"Begin."

"Pass," came the response.

Haldeman continued counterclockwise around the table, pointing his finger like a pistol at each man, who either gave the "pass" response or introduced a matter for discussion. The tension increased as Haldeman shifted his aim from one target to the next. What made it worse was that the chief of staff ridiculed nearly everything presented or chewed out its author. Chapin and Higby, the youngest members of his staff, received the worst abuse. Why Haldeman found it necessary to be so venomous toward those two, I never understood.

Only Colson, having become a Nixon favorite in recent months, was unfazed by Haldeman's threatening manner. In fact, he seemed oblivious to it. Colson reportedly had been quoted as saying he would walk over his own grandmother to get Nixon reelected. No one, including Haldeman, doubted his loyalty. Nixon's confidence in Colson led to a higher level of prominence—and accompanying self-importance. With his star rising, Colson used super-staff gatherings to widen his circle of control, always pushing for more staffers, more office space, and more power. Colson's staff increases almost invariably came at the expense of White House Communication Director Herb Klein's dwindling team. Haldeman found Colson obnoxious. And he, better than anyone, ought to have known an obnoxious person when he confronted one.

John Dean, usually slumped in his chair, seldom said a word. Like Jeb Magruder, Dean aspired to become a Haldeman insider and would have done anything to wear that badge. His only job was to investigate new staff members for conflicts of interest and, therefore, he did not have a lot to contribute to the agenda. I worked closely with Dean because of my role overseeing certain personnel. He didn't impress me as overly bright. He was so intimidated by Haldeman and so eager to please that he rarely offered an independent opinion.

Super-staff meetings lasted anywhere from three minutes to half an hour. Taking notes was not allowed. Haldeman availed himself of every opportunity to keep participants on edge. He liked to use one person's folly as a warning to others. Rufus Youngblood, head of the president's Secret Service detail, was a frequent target of this technique. For example, late that fall, Nixon attended an Eisenhower Theater gala where an elderly woman got near enough to corner the president. In the staff meeting following that incident, Haldeman employed exceptionally eloquent expletives in discussing what he felt was Youngblood's security lapse, declaring, "Somebody ought to demolish that man."

Haldeman was thrown into a tizzy on another occasion when the Secret Service roped off the entrance to Nixon's box at the Kennedy Center, inadvertently blocking access to the women's restroom. Not to be deterred at intermission, women simply climbed over the velvet ropes, crowded outside the door of the president's concert box, and waited their turn to use the facilities. When Nixon opened the door to leave, he found himself in line for the ladies' room.

And imagine, if you will, Haldeman's reaction when he learned that his aide, Bruce Kehrli, had sent an important individual a personal letter—a letter which still had attached, for the recipient to see, Haldeman's notes on whether it should be sent. Haldeman's zero-defect mentality did not suffer human error well.

It was during my first month at the White House, in February 1971, that Nixon made the fateful decision to install a voice-activated taping system in the Oval Office and in the president's quarters in the Old Executive Office Building. Only four people knew about it—Haldeman, Butterfield, Higby, and the president.

My duties kept me so busy that I did not sense the darkness enveloping the West Wing, but by late spring the deterioration of morale was unmistakable. The warm weather brought an increase in anti-Vietnam war marches. On May 1, in remembrance of the Kent State shootings, a quarter of a million antiwar demonstrators converged on the nation's capital to vent outrage over Vietnam. I made my way to work through streets that were either full of rubbish or had been blocked. More than seven thousand arrests were made on May 3, a day that saw the White House surrounded by protesters and cut off from the rest of the city. The air was filled with smoke and tear gas. Chanting from the demonstrators could be heard inside the White House. The protests continued for a week. Nixon took it personally.

On June 12, 1971, I watched from an office window as a beaming Richard Nixon gave his daughter Tricia's hand in marriage to Edward

Cox in a Rose Garden wedding ceremony. The next morning, the radiant bride and her father were pictured on the front page of *The New York Times*. Next to that photo was a much different story under the headline "Vietnam Archive: Pentagon Study Traces Three Decades of Growing US Involvement." The article detailed findings from a secret Pentagon-commissioned study of America's role in the Vietnam conflict which had been released to the media by Daniel Ellsberg, a military analyst for the prestigious think tank the RAND Corporation. In the course of his research for the forty-seven-volume digest, called the *Pentagon Papers*, Ellsberg had changed from hawk to dove. Believing the public's understanding of the Asian conflict's evolution might bring it to an end sooner, Ellsberg leaked portions of the study—but only those sections, he maintained, that did not compromise national security.

All hell broke loose in the West Wing that morning. An apoplectic Kissinger pounded his fists on the president's desk, demanding that something be done about the leak. For months, Nixon and his advisers fretted over minor leaks that resulted in negative press. Now something colossal had happened, something into which reporters could sink their teeth. Nixon's inner circle viewed the leak as a heinous, frontal attack that could not be allowed to go unanswered. Several reporters, such as columnist Jack Anderson, were put under FBI surveillance.

I didn't know it at the time, but the Anderson residence, his workplace, and his comings and goings were being closely observed, day and night. The constant surveillance extended to his visitors, as well. Among the stealthy characters soon spotted transferring material to Anderson would be White House staffer Jon M. Huntsman.

On one of the rare Sundays I managed to get to church, I had an extra responsibility. I had been asked to fill in for the out-of-town Anderson as a Sunday school teacher in my Chevy Chase, Maryland LDS ward (church). Anderson, who grew up in Utah, also was a member of that ward. He had left his teaching aids for me in the church office after I had agreed to fill in. Following the lesson, I drove to the Anderson home a few miles from mine to return the materials, totally unaware of the FBI agents on stakeout in the dark sedan across the street. The FBI was assisting in the search for leakers of what the Nixon White House called classified documents. A few days later, a pair of surly FBI agents visited me at the White

House. They told me I had been observed delivering a packet to Anderson. What sort of documents had I given him, the agents wanted to know? My simple explanation assured them the incident was a nonstarter. God only knows how word of the Huntsman-Anderson connection was received in the White House, but I never heard anything more about it.

Plugging the leaks became top priority for Haldeman and Kissinger. Nixon wanted a plan of action. I was not privy to their discussions—some of which took place in San Clemente—but I was aware the president had prohibited anyone other than Press Secretary Ron Ziegler from talking to the news media. Nixon also summoned his cabinet to alert them that Ellsberg's "leak of all leaks" was an issue of "highest national priority." In that meeting, each cabinet member was assigned responsibility for monitoring staff—even to the extent of bugging offices and homes, if necessary. Nixon warned his agency heads to keep their people under control. The bureaucracy and the press were out to get him, he noted, and heads would roll if any more information was leaked.

He dubbed Haldeman his Lord High Executioner to deal with leakers and anyone who got out of line. Nixon's parting comment to them was, "Don't come whining to me when he tells you to do something. He'll be doing it because I asked him to, and you are to carry it out." Having issued his edict—no one but the president said a word at that meeting—Nixon stormed out of the room. A witch hunt was under way, with Haldeman in charge.

FBI Director J. Edgar Hoover, who, unknown to all, was in his final months of life, had ceased providing surveillance data on potential leaks, having become uneasy about how the information was being used. Haldeman came up with a backup plan: an intelligence squad under his personal control. The aptly named Plumbers leak-capping team was formed with Ehrlichman's deputy, Egil "Bud" Krogh, and David Young as its leaders. John Dean was assigned to coordinate intelligence for the reelection campaign, and he was happy for the opportunity to prove his worth. Jeb Magruder was reassigned to the Committee for the Re-Election of the President (CREEP, as it came to be nicknamed). Its mission was to discredit Nixon's opposition in the 1972 election and the mechanism for doing so would be the Plumbers, coordinated by Colson.

To handle the expanded responsibilities, Dean recruited Gordon

Liddy, a gun-toting former FBI agent with a tendency to spot enemies everywhere he looked. Colson brought in Howard Hunt from the Mullen Group, a public relations agency that the CIA had used as an occasional business front. It was run by Bob Bennett, who later became a US senator from Utah. The Plumbers unit was open for business. The group had seedy goals in mind. Its undertakings ended up toppling the Nixon presidency.

To secure his control over their operations, Colson hoped to add the Plumbers as members of his staff—which meant that he would have to win my support. I did not know what Hunt's and Liddy's assignments were, but when Colson asked me to lobby to add the group's positions to the White House staff, I flatly refused. The proposed job descriptions were vague and Colson's staff already was one of the largest. Colson brought both men to my office, hoping I would agree to make them White House consultants, but I refused. My responsibility was to hold the line on expenses. I told Colson adding new positions would further exceed his already hefty budget and would have required restructuring our White House budget by reducing other personnel allotments. "It just won't work," I warned him. I also alerted Haldeman that White House regulations would not permit additional personnel on Colson's staff and that creating new jobs could invite trouble with Congress.

Haldeman didn't care. Nixon wanted Colson to have the necessary people, so, without my knowledge, Haldeman brought Liddy and Hunt aboard, not as staff members but as one-hundred-dollar-a-day consultants. The Plumbers quietly were assigned Room 16 of the basement of the Old Executive Office Building. Colson now had his "gestapo." The Old Executive Office Building's basement contained a number of hidden offices and quiet corners that made it easy to remain out of sight. Behind the double doors of Room 16, the Plumbers enjoyed a clandestine base and quietly operated under the supervision of Dean and Magruder.

The Plumbers never did plug any information leaks, but the group managed to create an efficient "black bag" operation that infiltrated political camps, planted misinformation, and gathered or manufactured dirt on Nixon's opponents. Nixon told Krogh the first priority of his unit was to find out all it could on Daniel Ellsberg as a matter of national security. Any dirt Colson could feed to the press on Ellsberg was fine. Apparently, leaks were okay if the "good guys" were doing it. The Plumbers had been turned loose and, though he may not have realized it, Haldeman's tight control began to slip.

One afternoon, shortly after I had resigned my White House position but still held the position of consultant, Dave Young took me downstairs in the Old EOB to Room 16. Above its secured door, a new blue sign read: The Plumbers. I was curious why he decided to make me aware of the secret operations' headquarters. In a conspiratorial tone, he said the Plumbers were going to "get" Jack Anderson, who had continued to cause the Nixon administration considerable heartburn in newspapers across the nation that carried his column. It was not clear to me what *get* meant in Young's context. (It was later revealed that Colson had suggested putting a poisonous substance on the steering wheel of Anderson's car.) What was clear was that Nixon believed the news media had more power than the presidency to shape public opinion. "The media always have the last word," he would say. He was prepared and determined to do whatever was necessary to silence offenders.

Ironically, the Nixon administration almost went another route on the *Pentagon Papers*. Richard Allen, an international-affairs scholar from whom Nixon often sought counsel, recommended doing nothing about the disclosure. He told Haldeman the leaked information showed how the United States became mired in Vietnam through the actions of previous Democratic administrations and actually placed the Nixon administration in a comparatively favorable light. Haldeman took that to the president and called Allen back the next day to relate that Nixon liked the idea and was going to take his suggestion a step further. Nixon intended to trump Ellsberg by declassifying the entire Pentagon study. That, Allen said, would give Nixon a legacy of leveling with the American people. Unfortunately, paranoia and vindictiveness won out and the plan that made good sense never came to fruition.

The White House atmosphere, already ethically challenged, became toxic no less than six months after I got there. I was being pulled on all sides: my duty to the president, Haldeman eyeing me for his inner circle, and muckraker Jack Anderson seeking to groom me as a source inside the administration. Upon my two-year anniversary in government service, I began to look toward an exit.

5. Deep Throat

I T WOULD BE WRONG TO LEAVE THE IMPRESSION THAT INTRIGUE AND QUES-
tionable ethics alone characterized the Nixon White House. Policy
and diplomatic breakthroughs occurred left and right, and the president enjoyed great popularity as his reelection neared. Nixon's crowning
achievement would give his ratings yet another boost. After months of
secret negotiations, in the summer of 1972 Kissinger announced the electrifying news that an historic presidential visit to China was scheduled
for October. From time to time, when eleven-year-old Jon Jr. was with
me, he would observe Kissinger as he departed the White House. On one
such occasion, he carried Kissinger's briefcase to the waiting limousine,
asking him where he was going.

"Don't tell anyone," Kissinger answered, "but I'm going to China."
Jon was impressed. Who knows—that conversation may have prompted
Jon to focus on the Far East as he matured, and to learn as much as he
could about China and its neighbors. Years later, when Jon was appointed US ambassador to China by President Barack Obama, after being
elected twice as governor of Utah, Jon Jr. and Kissinger had lunch together at the Metropolitan Club in Washington, DC. Upon entering the
dining room, Kissinger picked up the young ambassador's briefcase and,
with eyebrows raised, as if to ask, "Shall I carry this for you?" as he ges-
tured in the direction of the reserved table. After forty years and a role
reversal, Kissinger was offering to return the favor.

Yet even as the president's popularity rose, a select coterie of power-
hungry insiders scurried about in an ethical void, desperate to climb the
White House ladder. I had arrived at the White House in time to witness
the beginning of the end.

From my perspective, there were several positive aspects of being staff
secretary. I was fascinated with the disparity between the private Richard

Nixon and his public persona. Outside the White House, he was seen as cold and aloof. My closer view inspired a different kind of affection for the man. I saw only the cordial Nixon, who graciously charmed his visitors; the appreciative Nixon, who treated staff with kindness; the relaxed and tanned Nixon, who liked to talk golf; the personable Nixon who remembered names (even without my help); and the gentle Nixon, who was always kind to staff families.

Nixon was especially good to my children. One day, I invited Karen and the children to the White House to watch the president's helicopter take off. The president was running late, so the children became restless and I decided to herd them back across the South Lawn to my office. As we walked among the colonnades separating the West Wing from the White House, out came Nixon. He shook hands and briefly chatted with each member of our sizable family, including three-year-old David, who asked, "Are you really the president?"

"Yes, David, I am the president," he said quietly, almost as if he were reminding himself. "I am Richard Nixon." When young Christena further inquired if he was also Santa Claus, the president, initially taken aback by the question, assured her there was a Santa Claus but that he wasn't St. Nick.

President Nixon earned my further admiration for initiating his War on Cancer, which emphasized the importance of the devastating disease. On December 23, 1971, I gratefully attended the president's press conference at the White House and stood by as he signed the National Cancer Act allocating $1.5 billion in federal funds for cancer research. I still have the signing pen given to me at that event in commemoration of the occasion, and it will always represent an historic occasion that was of deep, personal significance to me. My mother had passed away only three years earlier after a painful battle with breast cancer. Nixon's act reinforced my emerging dream of creating a major research and medical treatment center to eradicate the disease.

Yet the tenor of machinations within the White House was growing darker. Haldeman began to confer more power on Larry Higby and Bruce Kehrli. Although still in their twenties, the pair took to bullying cabinet members and White House staff and interfering with their communications to the president. They tampered with cabinet correspondence, sidelining or altering memoranda addressed to the president. Research documents with cover memos from cabinet members disappeared en route and reemerged behind cover memos signed or initialed by Kehrli or Higby. Sometimes they would alter only the dates and names and claim full credit for the content. Other times, they completely altered the tone or essence of the sender's communication, further isolating Nixon from reality.

In mid-August, the initial version of the three-hundred-name "Enemies List" came to light—an invention of Dean and Colson. The latter skillfully played on Nixon's paranoia of the press and political opponents. Kissinger persuaded Attorney General John Mitchell to authorize a wiretap of National Security Council members, as well as some reporters. Preoccupation with leaks and enemies overshadowed all else. I didn't know everything transpiring on King's Row and in the Plumbers' office in Room 16 in the Old EOB, but I knew enough to note in my diary there was "a calamity in the making."

One evening after church, I confided my thoughts about resigning to Jack Anderson. Through our church relationship, I considered Anderson a friend and I believed he thought the same of me. "Can we talk off the record?" I asked. I had spent almost eighteen months in the Nixon administration, and the last year of that in the West Wing. I described the tense atmosphere at the office, the stress of the job, and the sense that something wasn't right in the White House. I related my run-ins with Haldeman, the Higby-Kehrli shenanigans, and my concern for how the White House was being managed. "Things are not as they should be in the White House and I think it's time for me to leave," I said, as much to myself as to him.

"There are two ways you can look at the situation," Anderson responded. "One is to get out before the house falls in. The other is that maybe you are the very person they need to have around to keep it from falling in. Maybe they need somebody who can talk back, somebody with integrity who will stand up to Haldeman. Besides," he added with a wink, "if things really do start to fall apart, I will need a good source in the West Wing."

Anderson knew the depth of my loyalty to Nixon. He was critical of the president but never in my presence. But as soon as he learned I was a member of the super-staff group and that I had concerns about

Haldeman, he tried to get me to discuss what transpired in those meetings. I realized he was a journalist first and a friend second. While I never said a word to Anderson that was negative regarding Nixon, I was determined not to compound the error of taking him into my confidence. I said nothing further and regretted having turned to this man for advice in the first place.

Anderson later described me as one of the only people working for Haldeman who was "not for sale." He confirmed later in an interview that I didn't tell him anything about the White House he hadn't already known. "Jon was a loyalist to Nixon," he would say, "but he and Haldeman were destined for a fallout."

The ill wind blowing through the corridors of the White House created a heightened sense of urgency to return to the private sector. A dinner cruise on the Potomac River was the catalyst. With the president out of the country, White House Chief of Staff Haldeman invited members of the super-staff and their spouses to join him and his wife, Jo, aboard the presidential yacht, *Sequoia*, for a relaxed evening. Karen and I had never socialized with coworkers, and my lifestyle was not predisposed to high-dollar entertainment. To assure our attendance, Alex Butterfield and his wife picked us up and drove us to the Potomac. Already aboard were the Dwight Chapins, the Ron Zieglers, and the Chuck Colsons. John Dean came alone, having recently divorced. And an elegant affair it was.

The weather was perfect, the yacht breathtaking. We were afforded only the finest cuisine, all served on presidential china. Haldeman was so charming and gracious that I wondered for a moment whether we were on the right boat. He spread compliments like confetti—totally out of character. When he got around to Karen and me, he made a good-natured jab about the size of our family. Haldeman playfully asked the group, "What are we going to do about Jon, who works all day and doesn't play? What do we have to do to get Huntsman out of his office to socialize with the rest of us?" It was presented as a joke, yet it seemed more than that. Why would it matter to him whether I became chummier with colleagues or why make a point of singling me out?

Something about his tone sparked, with icy clarity, the realization that he was trying to snare me into the "inner circle"—and had been for some time. That was why I had been invited to join the super-staff after crossing him. That was why I was let in on some of their secrets. He had been trying to get me to become one of the boys. That way, perhaps, I could not claim ignorance that the administration was operating in two realms, a public one and a clandestine one. Other than attending the super-staff meetings, I hadn't taken the bait. This soiree on the yacht was his next gambit.

Haldeman continued playing the perfect host, but I noticed others were watching my reaction. They apparently didn't trust me, because I continued to walk the straight and narrow path. From that moment, the humor seemed forced and the smiles pasted onto faces. It was a disheartening development. It wasn't that I inherently disliked any of these people—not even Haldeman, surprisingly. As often happens in a workplace, something akin to a familial relationship evolves. I knew things in the White House were not as they should be but, after all, were we not all working toward the same goal of helping the president of the United States carry out his agenda? Otherwise, there wasn't the slightest similarity between anyone on that boat and Karen and me—or with any of the people in my life whom I truly admired. I suddenly wished she and I had stayed home with the kids.

Within a matter of months, most of the party guests aboard the *Sequoia* that night would be disgraced. Many ended up serving time in prison. I didn't know at the time that Chuck Colson, sipping fine wine directly across from us at the table, would in two weeks authorize the Plumbers unit to break into the California office of whistle blower Daniel Ellsberg's psychiatrist to obtain detrimental information in Ellsberg's medical file. All I knew is that I had no intention of ingratiating myself to Haldeman by becoming a confidant. In my early college days, I had adapted my life to accommodate those around me. That had been a mistake. The closer I got to Haldeman the more often I heard Ken Cole's voice advising me to stay independent. In return for my appointment to the super-staff, Haldeman expected me to be as loyal to him as he was to the president. But I had drawn the line at carrying out any order that my moral compass told me didn't point true north.

One example of Haldeman asking me to do something unethical that would "help the president" remains vivid. Congressional Democrats were questioning one of Nixon's nominees to head an agency. During a committee hearing, they grilled her about a rumor that she had employed undocumented workers in her business. Haldeman asked me to use my connections to check out a factory owned by a Democratic member of that committee which was located not far from my own business in California. Haldeman suspected a number of the senator's factory workers were undocumented. To find out the truth, he wanted me to enlist some of the Latino workers in my Fullerton business. If illegal workers were discovered, Haldeman planned to make sure there would be enough news media coverage to embarrass the congressman who was leading the opposition to the nomination. Either way, my following Haldeman's orders would amount to an act of industrial espionage.

Everyone in the West Wing was under enormous pressure to follow Haldeman's orders unquestioningly. It was that thoughtless momentum which led me automatically to pick up the phone and call the head of our Fullerton plant. Yet just a few moments into the conversation, I stopped. "Wait a minute, Jim," I said. "Let's not do this. Forget I called."

This act of disloyalty was tantamount to saying good-bye to the White House, because it was yet another indication I wasn't going to go along to get along. In the end, though, this sound judgment and independence saved me from a connection with King's Row and the morass of Watergate. From this time forward, Haldeman saw me as a potential problem. My failure to come into the fold meant my next move would be out the White House door. That wasn't long in coming.

About a month after the sea-going social on the *Sequoia*, Fred Malek came to my office. He exchanged pleasantries before coming to the point: my name had been suggested for an "important appointment." My White House service and ability with people, he said, qualified me to be director of ACTION, the acronym for the agency administratively responsible for the Peace Corps, Vista, and five other domestic volunteer organizations.

It was common knowledge in the West Wing I had crossed Haldeman once too often. "So this is how Haldeman will get rid of me," I said to Malek. "I've almost been expecting you." Fred did his best to assure me I had earned this promotion and it had nothing to do with Haldeman. He painted what was intended to be a tantalizing picture of glamorous travel, a salary increase, and an opportunity to inspire young people. It was nonsense. All I wanted was to serve out my White House commitment and keep my promise to my partners to return to our embryonic business within two years of entering government.

My choice was an easy one. I informed Malek and Butterfield I would soon be returning to the private sector. Malek did his best to keep me on the Nixon team, offering in November the role of assistant secretary of the Interior with responsibility for the Bureau of Land Management and the Bureau of Indian Affairs. Again, I declined. My one-year commitment to the White House had an end date of February 1972. Observing how ungrateful I was after his generous offers, Haldeman got nastier by the day. His deputies, Higby and Kehrli, became more brazen than ever. Not only were the two doctoring cabinet memos intended for Nixon's eyes, they now were pulling the same tricks with my own correspondence to the president. They regularly removed my cover notes and replaced them with their own or they altered or distorted the ones on which my signature was retained.

The final straw came one Saturday in December 1971. Having caught up with my work and having been briefed by my deputy, David Hoopes, on how to handle the next day's agenda in my absence, I flew to Ohio where a new Huntsman manufacturing plant was breaking ground. I had arranged for the day's documents to be taken to Haldeman's home for his inspection prior to the courier delivering them to the president. Just as the groundbreaking ceremony was about to commence, a phone call came from Higby informing me that Haldeman was demanding my immediate return to Washington. I told Higby to tell Haldeman the president's papers were in order and that if he needed anything further, Hoopes was more than capable of obliging. Higby was undeterred and insisted I return at once, so I immediately boarded a plane to Washington. I personally delivered the papers to Haldeman's house by 1:00 p.m. only to have him rifle through them quickly and dismiss me. Needless to say, I was seething. My departure from the White House couldn't come soon enough.

The news media often lumped Haldeman, Ehrlichman, and Kissinger together with references to the "German Guard" surrounding the president, but the latter two did not operate in sync with Haldeman and should not have been counted among his storm troopers. Kissinger, a genius at foreign affairs, was difficult for Haldeman to manage but was a source of intellectual strength for Nixon. In the breakthrough with China, it was Kissinger's negotiating skill and uncanny understanding of the Chinese psyche that created the diplomatic coup for which Nixon received the credit.

Ehrlichman, too, was worlds apart from Haldeman. Before the Senate Watergate Committee hearings, he was portrayed as every inch the defiant Nixon henchman—a far cry from the man I knew. Honorable, personable, and straightforward, Ehrlichman had an impressive grasp of domestic issues. In a December 1971 memo-to-self, I predicted the story would be written one day that it was only Haldeman and his toadies who created the totalitarian legend about the Oval Office and who isolated Nixon to his detriment. I was already getting the impression by this time that Nixon was not fully aware of what went on outside the Oval Office in which Haldeman kept him safely sealed. Haldeman showed only his congenial side to the president and his visitors. Nixon probably didn't know just how abusive Haldeman could be with staff and how woefully ill-suited he was for managing.

Throughout my experience at the White House, I kept my distance from the activities that would land the others in court. The nearest I came to being trapped in an unethical situation was in December 1971. It involved the eccentric Dudley Swim, my first employer after getting out of college. When Haldeman learned that Swim intended to visit the president, and knowing I had worked for Swim in California, the chief of staff assigned me to solicit a $100,000 campaign contribution for the Committee for the Re-Election of the President. My orders were explicit: accept only cash. Swim was a strong Nixon supporter and had been a past contributor. He would be offered the ambassadorship to Australia during this visit and it would be my job to let Swim know that a cash donation would be expected in return. After being offered the appointment, Swim turned it down but said he would be happy to contribute to Nixon's re-election.

"But why does it have to be in cash, Jon?" he questioned. He said he would make a donation, but preferred to send a check after he returned to California. Upon Swim's departure, Haldeman asked if I had landed the hundred grand. I told him Swim had not left cash but that he would make the donation once he returned home. Haldeman demanded I get on an airplane to California and personally pick up the money. In January, I told Swim I was coming to Carmel and asked whether he could have the donation ready. He told me he wasn't feeling well but that he would have it for me when I arrived. He still was puzzled as to why it had to be cash. That made two of us. What I didn't know at the time was that CREEP was laundering donations through Mexican bank accounts to finance illegal campaign operations.

The day before I was to pick up Swim's six-figure contribution, Swim's wife, Kay, called me to say he had died of a heart attack. The donation died with him. Dudley Swim had been a challenge to work for, but his passing saved me from becoming a bagman in an illegal contribution scheme. And for that, I remain forever grateful.

Alex Butterfield, who I personally liked, probably knew more than anybody about what was going on behind the scenes in the White House. Butterfield always struck me as about as suave as James Bond. He seemed well suited to his role as chief White House liaison to the FBI and CIA. For the longest time, I suspected he might be the Deep Throat source on whom *Washington Post* reporters Bob Woodward and Carl Bernstein relied for some of their stunning revelations about the Nixon administration. Butterfield had a comprehensive knowledge about what transpired in the Oval Office. He knew everything Haldeman knew, and he even knew of things Haldeman did not know, such as exactly what was on those Nixon tapes because the recording system was in the closet of his office, immediately adjacent to the Oval Office.

Other than the president, the system was known only to Butterfield, Higby, and Haldeman. I was as stunned as the millions of viewers who heard Butterfield first describe it during the televised Watergate hearings. (Since then, it was revealed President Kennedy clandestinely taped cabinet meetings and President Johnson secretly recorded telephone conversations. Nixon, however, was the first to engage in full-time recording of everything uttered in the Oval Office.)

When it was finally revealed in June 2005 that Deep Throat was Assistant FBI Director Mark Felt, it made perfect sense. I knew Felt from his many visits to the West Wing, yet the connection to Woodward never

crossed my mind. As the number two person in the FBI, Felt was the
bureau's liaison to the Nixon administration. I knew from chats with
Felt that he was ambitious and maneuvering to be J. Edgar Hoover's
replacement upon his retirement. Three months after I left the White
House, Hoover died. The president selected my old boss at HEW, L.
Patrick Gray III, to be the acting head of the FBI. I thought Gray was a
great choice, but many senior FBI executives, including Felt, did not.

Woodward and Bernstein have since suggested that Felt, whose iden-
tity was kept secret until he revealed his informant's role in a 2005 *Vanity
Fair* magazine article, was not their only White House source. What they
received from Felt more or less confirmed or supplemented what they
had learned from other sources—some of whom were senior Republican
senators and White House staffers alarmed about the goings-on in the
White House. However, the two *Post* reporters made a big deal in the years
after Watergate about the value of Deep Throat, whose information, it
subsequently turned out, was not always on point.

Felt's motivation for leaking the information, some of which he obtained from his field agents involved in investigating Watergate and some
from his own sources inside the White House, was to disgrace Gray, as
has been extensively documented in author Max Holland's book *Leak:
Why Mark Felt Became Deep Throat*. Holland details how veteran FBI
brass, including Felt, considered Gray an outsider who was not up to the
job. Felt and a couple of others were jockeying for the position. The
Nixon administration sought the identities of *The Washington Post*'s
sources and by the fall of 1972 Felt was under suspicion. (William Ruck-
elshaus, named FBI director after Gray, suspected Felt was leaking to the
press as well, and forced Felt's resignation in 1973. He died in 2008.)

There was no question that Felt was the two reporters' Deep Throat.
But who was feeding Felt the White House dirty laundry? I may have
been a concerned staffer but I was no Deep Throat. While there, I was
one of three persons who had access to the type of information Felt was
given, who, in turn, passed it along to Woodward, about the infighting
inside the administration. But the proof that it was not me is the time
frame. Felt didn't start his dance with Woodward until a few months
after I had resigned.

H. R. Haldeman was the second suspect with access to high-level information. His perverted sense of loyalty, however, would never permit him to double-cross his boss.

My money is on the third possibility, Alexander Butterfield, who knew everything Haldeman did. He was a straight shooter, troubled by what was going on, and he also happened to be in charge of the taping. Butterfield was the White House contact person for the FBI. On a number of occasions during my work, I would notice the white-haired Felt sitting outside Butterfield's office awaiting an audience. (Later, Ehrlichman became Felt's official White House contact.) Butterfield was adept at information gathering and seemed to enjoy telling others what he knew. And, with direct and unfettered access to both Haldeman and Nixon, he knew a lot.

As my resignation date approached, Haldeman selected Bruce Kehrli to be my replacement and asked me to work with him to effect a smooth transition. There was no love lost between Kehrli and me, so I was not pleased either with the choice or with the request to prepare him. My final official meeting with Haldeman came in late January. We parted on professional terms and with guarded mutual respect. I was given the status of unpaid consultant, the duties of which were left vague.

Each of us remained loyal to the president. Each of us was governed by his ideals and commitments. The similarities ended there. We were miles apart in personality and only one of us embraced the concept that the end justified the means. He did surprise me as I left the office when he said: "Don't ever try and run a business the way I have run the White House." It was a curious thing for him to say. I always had thought he viewed his management style as above reproach. Either way, he did not have to worry about my imitating him.

Bob Haldeman and his troubles became the subject of countless stories in the ensuing years. It was sad, in a way, to see him sentenced to prison for his role in the Watergate affair and other crimes although, once his complicity was revealed, the conviction came as no surprise. I did not see him again until 1990 when both of us were invited to a dinner honoring Russian General Secretary Mikhail Gorbachev attended by some forty invited guests. It struck me as odd when Haldeman told me that evening in Minneapolis that he was upset that I had neither visited nor written him while he was in prison.

My letter of resignation was submitted to President Nixon on January 12, effective February 5, 1972. It read, in part: "This past year in the White House and the preceding six months with the Department of Health, Education, and Welfare have been one of the most satisfying, as well as the most challenging, periods of my life. What will always stand out among my memories of this time is my personal observation of a truly gifted president. I am especially grateful that Karen and our children have had the opportunity to know you and to experience something of the White House. I know their lives have been enriched and strengthened by their association with this administration."

The following afternoon, Richard M. Nixon met with the Huntsman family in the Oval Office and posed for a group portrait. My parting gift to him was a leather-bound copy of the Book of Mormon signed by the First Presidency of the Church of Jesus Christ of Latter-day Saints. Nixon read a few passages aloud. (His reading was recorded on the taping system, which later, I'm told, puzzled Watergate investigators.) In his formal acceptance of my resignation that he penned on February 2, he wrote: "Yours has not been an easy job, being faced each day with a seemingly endless number of new and demanding responsibilities. Yet, you have handled every one with a competence and cheerfulness that properly won for you the respect, admiration and gratitude of all of us here."

Three days later, I left the White House with my reputation intact. Seventeen months later, Richard Nixon left the White House in disgrace.

Watching Nixon's fall was painful. When Vice President Spiro Agnew resigned in the wake of revelations of kickbacks he accepted while governor of Maryland, it came as no surprise. But Karen and I were distraught over Nixon's traumatic departure on August 7, 1974. He had been a friend and we had believed in him. I am loyal to the people I believe in, and I had believed in him. When those I admire are found to be dishonest, it's heartbreaking.

Richard Nixon had a dual personality. On the one hand, he was a good husband and father who believed in basic family values. Nixon had bold ideas and a courageous sense of destiny. Respected more abroad than at home, his foreign policy remains his legacy. Even in the areas of domestic affairs, there were lesser-known moments of brilliance. To this day, for example, most Native Americans point to Nixon as the president most in tune with their plight. He was a painfully antisocial and lonely man; he had a hard time making friends, yet he loved to be around children—perhaps because he didn't have to prove anything to them. This was the Nixon for whom I had empathy and admiration.

Then there was the other Nixon—the Nixon I did not respect. This was a man driven by ambition, who believed that the president could do no wrong. This Nixon surrounded himself with amoral loyalists and kept at arm's length all but an ill-chosen few. He was secretive, spiteful, and angry. He hated the news media and governed from the depths of his alternating moods of suspicion and hostility. Worse, as president, he betrayed the American people and the democracy he was elected to defend.

I choose to believe that the kind man was the real Richard Nixon. History, unfortunately, does not permit individual perspectives to be the final portrait of those who make it. The gleam of Nixon's legacy must forever be viewed through its tarnish. I will remember him affectionately. Richard Milhous Nixon was a complex man, but he was kind to me and to my children. Let's leave it at that.

The day I walked away from the West Wing for the final time, late in the afternoon of February 5, 1972, it struck me that the only connection that would remain was the unpaid consulting agreement and I had only a vague idea what it entailed. Haldeman had put the document in front of me and commanded me to sign. Not giving it a second thought, I did so and put the White House behind me. My time there had been exhilarating and eye-opening. Best of all, it was over.

The Watergate scandal was the primary news topic throughout 1972. I watched with horror and fascination as the drama unfolded. Having been close to most of the players, I was deeply troubled. I began receiving calls from the White House asking that I deliver a series of speeches around the nation on behalf of the president. The consultant agreement I had signed must have obliged me to comply, but I was reluctant to promote the Nixon administration while these revelations were still unfolding. I kept the White House at bay with legitimate excuses of business pressures. However, within months of leaving, I did do the White House one favor.

My consultant's status did allow me to come and go in the White House even though I no longer was part of the administration. They agreed that I should keep my White House pass—a perk not extended to everyone. It was a nice gesture on Haldeman's part, considering the battles he and I had. I soon received a call from John Ehrlichman, informing me that Bill Marriott Jr., to whom I became close in college days, had been asked to babysit President Nixon's brother Donald during the 1972 Republican Convention in Miami. Ehrlichman didn't want Don to do anything that might grab news media attention while his brother accepted the nomination for a second term and he asked Bill to help out. I joined in to assist.

Bill and I and our wives arranged to take Don and his wife to dinner in Miami during the president's speech. Marriott happened to know a Mafiosa leader who was connected to the largest Italian restaurant in South Florida, and that's where we were to have dinner. The mob shut down the restaurant for this six-person event and picked us up in three stretch limos. We would be out of circulation for the evening. Two-dozen waiters served us a feast that lasted four to five hours—well past the concluding sentence of Nixon's acceptance speech. Our task was completed. Even Haldeman was impressed.

Then in July 1973, as Karen and I were in the process of relocating our eight children to Salt Lake City from Washington, DC by car, I was astonished to receive an early evening telephone call in our motel room. The caller was Scott Armstrong, assistant to Sam Dash, majority counsel for the Senate Watergate Committee, and he was calling to inform me that my name was on a long list of White House staffers who had been subpoenaed to testify before the Select Watergate Committee.

The day before the call, Alex Butterfield had dropped a bombshell. He had been randomly asked by one of the investigators, in a classified interrogation the previous day, whether he knew of any system for recording conversations in the White House. Butterfield answered truthfully. The astounded counsel then asked him who else knew about it. "H. R. Haldeman, his assistant Larry Higby, me, and the president himself," answered Butterfield.

Butterfield's under-oath response to the same question in front of TV cameras the next day unfairly earned him the disdain of White House colleagues. It immediately put him in the same traitorous league with John Dean, who had talked of a "cancer" in the Nixon administration. When I heard Butterfield's testimony, I was flabbergasted. That cupboard behind the TV console in Alex's office, a desk that I occupied for weeks at a time when covering during his absences, apparently hid a sophisticated voice recording system. All of my conversations with the president had been captured without my knowledge. Why would Butterfield, who knew his conversation was being recorded, have commented derisively on Pat and Dick Nixon's sex life as he went about arranging sofa cushions in that room? What about all the off-color jokes he used to tell me in the Oval Office? All had been recorded for posterity.

Butterfield's sworn testimony notwithstanding, Armstrong believed others also knew about the recording equipment and that I had to be one of them. "You must have known," he said in that evening's call. "You had to know when it was installed and for what purposes." He said he needed me to testify before the Watergate Committee as soon as possible.

I assured him I knew absolutely nothing about the taping system until Butterfield's public testimony. "You are on a fishing expedition and I resent your pointing a finger at me when you have already been told by the person who knows the most about it that I was not one of the few aware of it." Karen and the children sat spellbound as they listened to me argue with Armstrong. They knew something ominous was occurring, but only Jon Jr., Peter, and Christena were old enough to comprehend the implications of the conversation. Their dad was getting bundled with his old White House colleagues who were in serious trouble.

"Well," said Armstrong, "even if you didn't know about the taping system, you were the staff secretary at the time of the break-in of Ellsberg's psychiatrist's office in California." He said his staff believed information about that came to the president through my desk. "You must have information concerning the president's involvement in that incident. We want you here to testify tomorrow."

My voice rose as I enunciated for Armstrong's benefit: "The president of the United States never received an iota of information from me concerning any illegal activity. That is something I would clearly remember. You are fishing again, Mr. Armstrong, and I happen to be tied up at the moment." I was furious and had no intention of returning to

Washington and leaving my family to make their way to Salt Lake on their own.

Armstrong backed down a bit by saying he could give me a couple of days leeway for an appearance, but that they would need me in Washington by the following Monday at the latest. A car would pick me up at the airport.

"Fine," I responded, lowering my voice, "but first let me mention a couple of things that, as former staff secretary and assistant to the president, I intend to include in any testimony I might be called to give." Our church always encouraged members to maintain a personal journal, and I had maintained a detailed daily diary during my White House time, notwithstanding the fifteen- to sixteen-hour days. I knew I would have plenty of solid material to which I could refer in preparing to testify.

On the telephone, I began to rattle off from memory, in my most solemn testimonial voice, several bits of information a self-respecting Democrat would not want to hear. My audit of accounts conducted when I became White House staff secretary showed Lyndon Johnson's daughters had ordered at taxpayer expense $50,000 worth of gold-embossed letterhead stationery after LBJ had left the White House. Then there was the matter of the two-dozen TV sets, ostensibly in the custody of the White House Communications Office, which could not be found by the incoming Nixon staff. Subsequent checking revealed LBJ had all twenty-four sets carted off to his Texas ranch to give to visiting VIPs as personal gifts. "And let's not forget," I added in summation, "the four-point-five million, FAA-approved control tower and landing strip built on the LBJ ranch shortly after he announced he would not be seeking reelection." These were not matters of current national consequence, I told Armstrong, but since taxpayer money was involved, they certainly raise questions of integrity that may be of public interest. Should his committee want something else of national interest, I continued, I enjoyed a close relationship with Cuban refugees while I was at HEW and even later at the White House. Their leaders gave me a fascinating account of how, on the night before the invasion at the Bay of Pigs, Bobby Kennedy talked Jack Kennedy into withdrawing military support and dooming the expatriate force. "It behooves your committee to investigate the character and actions of other recent presidents, including Kennedy," I concluded.

There was a long silence, as if Armstrong was finishing detailed notes. Karen and the children sat wide-eyed and breathless. Finally, Armstrong said that these points should be given an airing. If I would assemble notes on the matters he would try to schedule me sometime during the following week. He would be in touch. I never again heard from him or the committee.

I saw Nixon again in September 1975, a little more than a year after he resigned. His aide, Colonel Jack Brennan, had followed Nixon into exile and still served as his attaché at Casa Pacifica in San Clemente. Brennan called me out of the blue one day to inquire if our family would like to visit the former president. He said Nixon had only a few visitors in the previous year and that he would enjoy seeing our family again. I was touched and said we would come.

There was another reason for our invitation, of course. Frank Gannon, an aide from the president's last years in the White House, was helping him write his presidential memoirs. Much of Nixon's papers and White House documents at the time were still in the hands of Watergate investigators or the Justice Department and Gannon asked whether I had files or documents that might help Nixon write his book. I readily agreed and loaded three boxes of relevant materials, plus our nine children, Karen, and a carload of family luggage into an eleven-passenger van and off to San Clemente we drove. We spent a day with Richard and Pat Nixon. It was a delightful experience.

Unfortunately, the next time I saw Richard Nixon was eighteen years later at Pat's funeral. A heavy smoker but one who never allowed herself to be seen in public with a cigarette, the former First Lady died of lung cancer on June 22, 1993. She was a woman of remarkable strength whom the White House staff loved and respected. A number of former staff members gathered for the funeral of the president's lifelong companion, a loyal, poised, and gracious lady who stood by him throughout the unprecedented heights and humiliating depths of his public life.

Karen and three generations of Huntsmans—Jon Jr., and grandson Peter Jr. and I—attended the funeral held at the Nixon Library in Yorba Linda, California. Following the services, Nixon invited former White

House staff members into the library. Kissinger, Buchanan, Haldeman, and Higby came. Butterfield, Dean, and Ehrlichman had not been invited. They had been ostracized for their respective roles in the Watergate investigations. Despite the solemn occasion, the former president was happy to see us, complimenting each of us by name and thanking us for our service. As for H. R. Haldeman, time had softened the sharp edges. He had become a thoughtful and interesting man. For the first time, I enjoyed his company.

Despite his questionable tactics, the White House operated efficiently during his oversight. I learned a number of lessons from him, in both the what-to-do and what-not-to-do categories. Five months after Pat's funeral, Harry Robbins Haldeman died. The Christian Scientist who didn't believe in doctors passed away less than a month after it was discovered he had stomach cancer.

Richard Nixon, the thirty-seventh and perhaps most misunderstood president of the United States, died April 22, 1994, precisely eight months after his only real companion in life passed on. I was out of the country when the funeral was held, but Jon Jr. represented the family. Like many in history, Richard M. Nixon is better appreciated in death than he was in life.

As for my life, I would be returning to my private-sector roots. No more egg cartons or working for someone else. I needed to make money, to build a business, to be my own boss. Fortunately, it was the right time to be thinking and betting big. It was a period that allowed my entrepreneurial style and deal-making talent to bloom. It took me a couple of years to discover the right business fit, and I nearly went bankrupt doing it. But, as the next chapter relates, I ended up striking it rich with the Big Mac.

LEFT: *Parley P. Pratt, my great-great-grandfather and early Mormon apostle.*

BELOW: *Huntsman Hotel and Saloon (1872), relocated from original site in Fillmore, Utah to "This is the Place Heritage Park" in Salt Lake City.* ABOVE, RIGHT: *Complimentary spending tokens, Huntsman Hotel and Saloon, including the family favorite, "Good for One Drink or Cigar."*

LEFT: *My big brother Blaine Jr. ("Sonny") and me in 1938.*

BELOW: *First family photo: My parents Blaine and Kathleen, my brothers Blaine Jr. and Clayton, and me in 1948. (Note: My brother is barefoot. I call this our "Grapes of Wrath" photo.)*

LEFT: *First string varsity hustler, Palo Alto High School vs. San Jose High School, 1954.*

RIGHT: *Palo Alto High School Student Body President Jon M. Huntsman, 1955.*

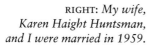

LEFT: *University of Pennsylvania's top four graduates of the Class of '59 planting ivy: Jon M. Huntsman, Spoon Award; Robert McCafferty, Bowl Award; Carl Shine, Cane Award; and George Katterman, Spade Award.*

RIGHT: *My wife, Karen Haight Huntsman, and I were married in 1959.*

LEFT: *With then-Secretary of Defense Thomas S. Gates, 1959, prior to my commissioning as Ensign, United States Navy.*

BELOW: *I served aboard USS* Calvert *from 1959-1961.*

LEFT: *In Navy Whites, 1960.*

ABOVE, RIGHT: *After two plus years of active duty, I was honorably discharged from the US Navy in 1961. I received my Lieutenant bars in 1964, after three additional years in active reserve, with brother and fellow officer, Blaine Jr.*

LEFT: *Holding three-month-old son Jon Huntsman Jr. in Coronado, California, 1960.*

ABOVE: *In Oval Office with President Nixon and former employer Dudley Swim, who would be offered the position of US Ambassador to Australia, 1971.*

BELOW: *In my office in the West Wing of the White House, 1971-72.*

ABOVE: *Conferring with Richard Nixon in the White House, 1972.*

BELOW: *President Nixon in the Oval Office with my family and Alexander Butterfield (right), Staff Assistant Stephen Bull (center), reading a passage from the Book of Mormon gifted by me as I left the White House in 1972.*

6. Contention, Creations and Clamshells

I WAS FREE OF THE WHITE HOUSE, SORT OF, AND EAGER TO GET MY company going. Prior to my heading to Washington, DC, my brother Blaine and I, along with Ray Goodson (who had worked with me at Dolco) formed a business plan for a new enterprise called Huntsman Container Corp. We were fortunate to establish a relationship with Hambrecht & Quist, a small start-up investment firm in San Francisco that agreed to invest $1 million in the venture. Blaine and I added $300,000 in capital out of my profits in album sales. There was no returning to Dolco—it had become clear as soon as I had left to work for the White House that I had burned my bridges with Dean Olson.

When I went to his office to bid farewell and to express my appreciation for the opportunities afforded me at Olson Brothers and Dolco, as well as to wrap up departure details and final compensation, Dean had become belligerent. "You can walk out that door," he said, "but you'll go through it empty-handed. You may think you're entitled to commissions and accrued vacation, but I don't agree. That is not going to happen." He launched into a tirade and implied my performance at Dolco, into which I had poured my heart and soul for three years, had been lacking. He stormed at me that *I* owed *him* money for his investment losses and, adding insult to injury, made an accusation I couldn't believe: my decision to work for the government was based solely on mercenary instincts.

I stared at him in bewilderment. Was it possible he was referring to the federal salary I would be earning, which was about $6,000 a year higher than what Dolco had been paying me? (People in Washington later teased me that I was probably the only corporate CEO in America to receive a pay raise by going into government service.)

In retrospect, Olson no doubt thought he was justified in feeling betrayed with my leaving the "family business." Although he had children of his own, he apparently saw me as the heir apparent; he had taught me all he knew. After that rancorous parting, Olson remained bitter and his vindictiveness would haunt me for years. His opening volley came while I still was in the White House. In the fall of 1971, White House Counsel John Dean brought me several anonymous, malevolent missives to see if I knew what they were about. I told him they could only have come from one source, my wife's uncle and former employer who was irate because my new container business would be competing against his.

John Dean seemed satisfied with that explanation and said no more about it, but I was furious that Olson would send anonymous letters of that kind to the White House in an attempt to make trouble for me. I fired off a letter demanding an end to the character assassination. After yet another anonymous letter arrived, I sought counsel from Los Angeles attorney Roland Woolley, the man who had initially recommended me to the Nixon administration. He advised me to file a countersuit, which I eventually did, but not before an additional egregious issue cropped up.

As soon as Dow Chemical and Olson Brothers saw Huntsman Container pulling ahead of Dolco in the race for new markets, they brought a series of legal actions to impede us. Even after the court dismissed their 1971 lawsuit, they continued to pursue us with one trumped-up claim after another. Clearly it was time to take Woolley's advice.

Blaine and I filed a countersuit against Dow Chemical and its senior vice president for antitrust violations through harassment and restraint of trade. It was based in part on information of which I had become aware during my Dolco days. Dow had rebated excessive amounts of money to certain accounts based on sales volume. This seemed unfair and illegal, as I complained to Dow's legal beagles at the time. Our countersuit was a bold strike against the chemical giant, and we hoped it would be sufficiently distasteful to Dow that it would pressure Olson Brothers to ease up.

Dow hadn't anticipated the counterclaim, which the company executives realized would not play well with a jury. No one is sympathetic to big boys beating up on small, start-up competitors, and no company ever welcomes allegations of antitrust. Apparently eager to smooth over the situation and move on, Dow's brass flew us to its headquarters in Midland, Michigan. Praising our entrepreneurship and complimenting us to the skies, Dow assured us there would be no future action on its part if we dropped our counterclaim. We agreed, shook hands, and, at least as far as Dow was concerned, the matter was dropped. Dow became a corporate friend and we have remained partners in many ventures throughout the world, supplying each other with raw materials and products. The Olsons would prove to be another matter entirely.

My government service had kept me from interacting closely with my partners in Huntsman Container Corporation or with my New York recording company, now operating as Continental Dynamics and headquartered on Park Avenue. When I joined the Nixon administration, I left Doug Poulson and Larry Crane in charge of Continental Dynamics and its joint venture with *Family Circle* magazine, a subsidiary of *The New York Times*. I had come to the realization that, while lucrative, the record distribution business no longer held any appeal for me. Preferring to focus squarely on Huntsman Container, I sold my interest in the record business to Crane, who immediately sold it to CBS.

Blaine was Huntsman Container's chief financial officer. Jim Fogg and Bob Webb, experts in the design and operation of polystyrene packaging plants, were in charge of operations. Without much input from me, they had taken the Fullerton, California plant through its trial-and-error phase and were doing the same at the new Troy, Ohio site. Ray Goodson was head of sales and having a devil of a time luring away the accounts of established suppliers in a competitive arena. The operation needed a shot in the arm, and that would only happen with a full-time CEO.

Instead of moving back to California after my time in the Nixon White House, Karen and I kept our home in Chevy Chase, Maryland, and I opened a small office there and another in New York City. Karen expected to see more of me now that I was out of the White House, but that wasn't to be. It was necessary that I spend as much time as possible at our Fullerton, California and Troy, Ohio plastic products manufacturing plants, implementing the management policies and techniques I had developed during my short nights while still at the White House. That entailed a lot of time in airplanes and any time not spent at our sites was devoted to making sales calls. Huntsman Container needed sales volume to offset heavy start-up costs. We were able to meet that need through two major contracts.

The first, Pacific Growers Cooperative (Nulaid Farmers), signed a multiyear contract for 50 million egg cartons a year from the Fullerton operation at 1.8 cents each, well below the 2.6-cent break-even cost. But we brought in other accounts at full value to turn a modest profit. Pacific Growers elected me to their board of directors, practically guaranteeing future business.

The second lifesaver was Kroger's supermarket chain in Cincinnati, which ordered 55 million egg cartons from the Troy, Ohio plant for 2.6 cents a carton. Those two contracts saved our bacon. By the end of 1973, Huntsman Container was turning a profit after sustaining $1.6 million in annual losses. Our forward momentum increased as we developed more products that would revolutionize the fast-food industry.

At this juncture, I moved Huntsman's headquarters to Salt Lake City. Karen's father, David Haight, was by then a general authority of the LDS Church, and he and Ruby had moved to Utah so he could fulfill his calling as an assistant to the Quorum of the Twelve Apostles. (A few years later, he was called to serve as a member of that twelve-person body.) By July 1973, we had built our Salt Lake City home, and Karen and I packed up our eight children and drove westward, making something of a vacation out of the trek.

After Blaine and I settled our disputes with Dow Chemical, Dean Olson and his son, Peter, who remained 50 percent owners of Dolco, and who had also moved to Salt Lake City, became more vitriolic than ever. Fifty percent owner Dow Chemical honored agreements with Huntsman Container and we were actually purchasing some of our raw materials from them.

Yet additional anonymous letters blasting my character continued to arrive at the White House, even after I had left. This time, acting White House counsel Fred Fielding, who had taken over for the departed John Dean, brought them to my attention. I told Fielding who I suspected was sending them and why. He suggested I tell Olson I was no longer on the staff and that the White House wasn't interested in unsigned letters about former staffers.

The Olsons turned next to the news media, which was alert to any story dealing with a Nixon White House staffer given the atmosphere of suspicion created by the Watergate revelations.

Peter Olson reached out to Thomas O'Toole, a one-time writer for *The Washington Post*, and informed him that they were in possession of some vital information involving a former White House senior staff member—Jon Huntsman. After spending two days interviewing the Olsons, O'Toole's article gave ink to the innuendos and half-truths they fed him. For example, it alleged I had taken Julius Goldman, owner of Egg City (an enormous poultry farm and an Olson Brothers competitor), on a personal tour of the White House and introduced him to influential people in the Department of Agriculture. According to the story, the department then offered Goldman's firm the highest indemnity ever paid for chickens slaughtered after Newcastle disease devastated the poultry industry. The story further claimed that, as owner of a related business, I stood to benefit from Goldman's recovery in the form of egg-carton sales. Basically, O'Toole implied I had used my White House position to influence the Agriculture Department in return for a Huntsman Container egg-carton contract with Goldman.

As a matter of fact, I was no longer on the White House staff when I met Goldman and didn't even have White House security clearance at the time. Moreover, Goldman met no one of consequence during the brief White House tour that I did arrange for him through staff I had worked with when I served there. His visit to the Department of Agriculture, however, was altogether independent of me. The Olsons knew this, but during the Watergate era everyone who served with Nixon was tainted by association, so O'Toole forged ahead on that premise. Never mind that government records show that Goldman's indemnity payments were lower than those paid to other chicken ranchers, that I had never done business with Goldman, and that he never bought Huntsman egg cartons. (Goldman eventually did sell his farm to Kroger and the food chain later used Huntsman Container as its egg carton supplier.) Dean Olson, and now *The Post*, had it wrong.

Before his front-page story was published, O'Toole called and read it to me over the phone, asking whether I cared to comment. The story made me physically ill. Of course, I had comments. "All of this is untrue or misrepresented, and I'm pretty sure I know the source of your misinformation." I told O'Toole I would like to meet with him to go over errors contained in the story. We made an appointment for the following

Monday. *The Post* published the story on August 23, 1973, a day before we were to meet. The headline read: "How to Succeed in Business as a White House Assistant." My photo ran alongside the story some two-and-a-half years after I had completed my White House assignment.

There are no superlatives to describe how angry I was. I called O'Toole again and got him to admit he hadn't checked out Olson's allegations with the Agriculture Department because his call to them was put on hold. Still, he did not apologize and stuck to his position that some of the information from Olson had to be true because, as he assumed, every other former Nixon staffer was guilty of something and I probably was no exception. "Well, I am the exception," I fumed, and demanded a retraction. Three days later, the *Post* ran a half-hearted disclaimer admitting to errors in the article.

The ink was barely dry on *The Post* article when the *Chicago Tribune* followed with a story of its own. A few days later, *The Salt Lake Tribune* reprinted the *Chicago Tribune* story, which alleged I had used my White House influence with the Small Business Administration to get special treatment for Donald J. Long, another competitor of Olson Brothers. Long and I had once worked together at Olson Brothers, but we'd had no contact since then. Long subsequently left Olson, too, and apparently went to Washington to seek an SBA loan to start his own egg business. I never met with Long nor with SBA officials and had no idea what the *Tribune* was talking about, but the Olsons clearly were attempting to kill two birds with one stone by going after Long and me for having had the temerity to "abandon" them and open competing businesses. Dean Olson was a spiteful man, to say the least, and it would eventually lead to his company's demise.

I contacted my good friend, Congressman Ed Koch of New York, who was on the SBA subcommittee in the US House of Representatives (and later mayor of New York City). He looked into the matter and reported back that Peter Olson had been the source of the information and that there had been no favors given to Long. Koch said he sympathized with me and that I was being accorded the same media treatment as other Nixon associates: "guilty until proven innocent."

A few weeks later *The New York Times* called. Based on the *Washington Post* and *Chicago Tribune* stories, *The Times* was getting ready to run a story on the same subject. Once again, I made the case that Olson's "facts" were distortions planted by a person trying to sink my business. The reporter was unimpressed and read me the story for reaction. Essentially, it was a replica of the other two. Those stories have been retracted or proven wrong, I countered. None of what he wrote had been verified, I said, noting that the reporter had not bothered to interview me concerning any of it. I asked if he thought that was fair. The reporter didn't waiver. He said it was the news media's responsibility to inform the public as best it could about the abuses of power that occurred in the Nixon White House.

"None of this is true," I shouted into the receiver. I struggled to remain calm and lowered the volume. I tried another approach, informing the reporter that my record business in New York City enjoys a fifty-fifty partnership with *Family Circle*, which happens to be a *Times* subsidiary. I said I had spoken to its chairman, Fred Thompson, who was a friend and a member of *The Times*' board of directors. I added that I told Thompson that *The Times* was about to print absolute lies and statements that are unverifiable. The reporter said he would check out the facts but that it was too late to pull the story. It was too far along in the process to stop.

Fifteen minutes later, the reporter was back on the line with me, announcing the paper would not be printing the story, saying he had spoken with Thompson who said the rumor was started by an unhappy business competitor. Apparently, the presses had not started after all.

This nerve-wracking nonsense had to stop. I sued Dean Olson for slander in a California court. His lawyers approached me at one point in the proceedings and asked what it would take to settle. All I truly wanted was to get Dean to admit publicly his accusations were lies.

I received a monetary settlement and a letter of apology from Olson. Each side agreed to drop its lawsuits against the other. At the time, I thought the mudslinging was over. As I would learn in the years to come, I was wrong.

With Watergate and the Olson fiasco ostensibly behind me, I focused on business and not a second too soon. Our management team was heading for a major crisis. From an industry standpoint, the first three quarters of 1973 should have been ideal for rejuvenating a business. President Nixon, in an attempt to distract the focus from Watergate, abolished wage and price controls and devalued the dollar by 10 percent, leading industrial nations to chart a 6 percent growth rate. Unfortunately for Huntsman Container, the period also brought with it a Category 5 catastrophe. Conflict in the Middle East and an OPEC-inflicted embargo, partially in retaliation for the West's alliance with Israel during the Yom Kippur War, strangled oil supplies and produced a full-fledged energy crisis. The traditionally strong international hand that Nixon could have played to mitigate this crisis was hampered by an administration being sucked ever deeper into Watergate quicksand.

In March 1974, the oil embargo eased but the price per barrel nearly quadrupled to around forty dollars a barrel. (While it fell off highs, it would approach eighty dollars a barrel in less than a decade and more than triple the 1974 figure in another decade.) Auto manufacturing, tourism, and petrochemicals were hardest hit. Churning out plastic products by the millions relied on a ready supply of petrochemicals that we could neither obtain nor afford. The Fullerton plant had been buying polystyrene raw materials from Diamond Plastics in Long Beach on an as-needed basis at nine-and-a-half cents a pound on ninety-day terms. Almost overnight, Diamond raised its price to sixty cents a pound, cash on delivery. Worse, Diamond and the larger suppliers were locked into existing contracts and had nothing to spare at any price since they, too, teetered on bankruptcy. This was devastating for Huntsman Container. No polystyrene, no cartons. The company lost about half its net worth the first year of operation, sustained a similar loss in the second year, and eked out a small profit the third. But shortages and cost overruns were killing us. Huntsman Container was on the brink of disaster.

My partners were seriously talking about shutting down. It had been an uphill battle from the beginning and some felt we had struggled long enough. Each of our homes had been mortgaged as collateral, the company had borrowed past its limit, and it appeared we might not make the next payroll. Our two plants were operating at half capacity. Even Blaine, who considered his younger brother America's best salesman, started to question my management skills. As its CFO, he said the company was insolvent. Its net worth had fallen to negative $1 million from the original investment of $1.3 million.

Two of the four directors wanted to declare bankruptcy. Yet I was determined that my name would never be associated with bankruptcy. Nor would I go back to the wellhead, venture capitalists Hambrecht & Quist, which had underwritten the start-up. I had a plan that I was sure would get us out of our predicament. "Trust me," I implored the directors in an emotional speech. "The ship may be leaking badly, but it will still float." The directors agreed to ride out the storm.

As a bandage measure, I contacted a past associate from the recording business, Morris Levy. After I outlined the situation and the company's potential if we survived, he offered to lend me enough money, interest free, to meet the payroll. (Levy was later indicted for Mafia dealings, which surprised me. At the time, though, his money was good and I was grateful.) Levy's infusion bought us time, but we still had to deal with the chemical shortage and high raw materials prices.

For the longer term, my plan was theoretically simple: Rather than going down as a result of the petrochemical shortage, we would capitalize on it. Since we were unable to buy polystyrene crystals, we would barter for what we needed. It was ingenious, if I say so myself, and proved that necessity is indeed the mother of invention.

Once we got started, the process took on a life of its own. It worked this way: Chemical Company A would ask for a product which we would find for them through Company B, which, in turn, needed something else which we found available at Company C, which had needs of its own. We would contact whoever could fill Company C requirements, and so on. We fashioned a chain of trades that secured for each company the materials it needed, sometimes reaching three or four products out and often at black-market prices. Financing for some of the deals was based on purchase orders. We essentially became petrochemical brokers.

At the time, no one was doing this sort of thing. Petrochemical users were accustomed to picking up the phone and ordering what they needed, the same way they would order a pizza. They hadn't a clue what to do in this new environment of scarcity. We became the answer. It still tickles me that one of our customers, ARCO, a major oil company, came to us for styrene monomer, which we discovered one of their own subsidiaries stocked in abundance. We bought a barge full of styrene monomer from the subsidiary and sold it to parent ARCO at a $600,000 profit.

It was about this time that Terry Parker, a trained CPA, joined Huntsman and became involved in these trades. He took over for Blaine, who had been absolutely brilliant at these trades, particularly in arranging letters of credit from banks. Blaine was my closest friend and the smartest man I knew. (He was one of only three students who received a PhD in 1967 from the Wharton School.) But Blaine became exasperated with some of the shortcomings and high-wire antics of our initial ventures. I was dreaming audaciously and betting on the future. I made deals looking at the bigger picture, filling in the blanks on the fly. Blaine was more cautious, analytical, and detail oriented. He didn't have a high tolerance for risk. He returned to the more ordered and predictable world of academia and was appointed dean of the business school at the University of Utah.

We formed two auxiliary companies, Midwoods Petrol Development and Huntsman Chemical & Oil, through which we handled our bartering transactions. Granted, the system was difficult to track, but it worked wonderfully and we saw positive results right away. In the first year of bartering, our company netted $5 million in profit and obtained all the polystyrene it could use. We were making more money brokering raw materials than from manufacturing and selling plastic containers. Our survival plan had turned into a lucrative enterprise. Everyone had predicted this strategy wouldn't work. I was confident it would and others in the petrochemical industry picked up on my optimism.

Each of us has untapped reserves on which to call in times of trouble, but sometimes it takes hitting the lowest of lows, economically speaking, to be jolted into locating these reserves and learning how to draw from them. The experience taught me three lessons: First, don't finance business deals with personal assets. Second, the petrochemical business is cyclical. Supply will exceed demand one year, but a year or two later the reverse will be true. Feast-or-famine cycles train one to know when to hold and when to fold. Finally, the thrills and spills of the business world far exceed the dubious rewards of bureaucratic service. Times were tough, but those are precisely the times when one's entrepreneurial tenacity is put to the test.

Bartering chemicals whetted my appetite to tackle the larger petro-chemical industry and there soon came a breakthrough that propelled Huntsman Container into the big leagues. My small, three-person packaging development team created a new product—a clamshell container that, if accepted in the marketplace, would alter the concept of fast-food packaging. In point of fact, it ended up forever altering food packaging throughout the world.

In 1974, McDonald's Corporation was the fast-food industry's leader. Founded in California in 1940 by the McDonald brothers and later purchased by Ray Kroc, it had been in business for some thirty-four years. I knew that if I could sell such a clamshell container to McDonald's for the Big Mac sandwich, Huntsman's future would be spectacular.

I attempted to reach out to McDonald's executives to show them what we had. For weeks, I contacted anyone I could think of who might help me get an audience but I was blocked at every turn. I traveled cross-country from Fullerton to McDonald's Oak Brook, Illinois headquarters. For three days, I tried in vain to meet with someone in marketing or distribution with decision-making authority. So I decided to get the attention of McDonald's by other means.

Tony Burns, an old friend who later became chairman and CEO of Ryder Systems (and later an outstanding director of Huntsman Corporation), knew the senior buyer of Burger King and helped me arrange a meeting. Burger King's executives, it turned out, were receptive to new-product pitches. They welcomed the news that the newly minted Huntsman clamshell container would keep food fresher, hotter (or colder), and more sanitary, which would enhance the product and boost sales. Burger King, while excited to have a leg up on McDonald's, was hesitant to utilize the container with its best-selling burger without a market test of some sort. The company was in the process of phasing out the ham-and-cheese sandwich, but they reconsidered after our meeting and opted to discover whether better packaging would renew customer interest. As soon as that sandwich got placed in our clamshell it became a hit. The successful trial gave Burger King the confidence to use our packaging for its top-selling, have-it-your-way burger.

Two months after Burger King introduced the clamshell into the marketplace, two dark-suited men walked into our office at the Fullerton plant looking for me. The receptionist asked for their names. "When Mr. Huntsman agrees to see us, we will give him our names," they told her. She came into my office and told me there were gentlemen out front who either had to be from the FBI or the CIA. "One has his briefcase strapped to his wrist," she whispered excitedly, taking considerable delight in the intrigue. *Wonderful,* I thought, *another wave of Watergate investigators.* I told the receptionist to show them in.

The shadowy pair entered and closed the office door. They introduced themselves as McDonald's vice presidents and one of them unlocked his briefcase and brought out a Burger King clamshell container, and asked why I didn't come to McDonald's first with this new container. I informed them, with some inner relish, that McDonald's was my first choice, and that I had tried for weeks to show it to company executives. "But I couldn't get anybody to talk to me. What can Huntsman Container do for you?"

Before long, Huntsman Container was working with McDonald's to design a container specifically for the Big Mac that featured a new and improved locking device. McDonald's bought hundreds of millions. So did its competitors.

Our relationship with McDonald's, for the most part, was positive. It did have its moments, particularly when a few of its hard-nosed middle managers threatened to withdraw its business if we didn't turn over the legal and technical rights to the clamshell and stop selling to competitors. My colleague Ron Rasband and I were summoned by McDonald's senior brass to a meeting in its corporate headquarters where we were presented with this unreasonable ultimatum.

I listened quietly to their demands, then picked up the phone. I remarked that perhaps we ought to speak to the US Attorney General Richard Kleindienst about this and dialed the White House phone number from memory, asking to be put through to Kleindienst. One of the McDonald's guys took the phone from me, gently placed it on the cradle, and assured me I had misunderstood them. Some scrambled from the room while those who remained said all they meant to do was to increase McDonald's orders with Huntsman Container Corporation. I knew what they meant and refused to be bullied. From that day until I sold the business, the relationship was smooth.

Huntsman Container had no manufacturing operations in Utah—as true in the mid-'70s as it is today with our worldwide enterprise—but I never regretted the decision to make Salt Lake City my base of operations. In fact, operating out of Utah sometimes has the effect of disarming competitors. They assume we are hicks from the sticks and often let down their guard. Too late, they realize the miscalculation.

To my disappointment, though, there was also a downside to basing in Salt Lake City, one I had not anticipated. Some of our middle children were subjected to subtle taunting at school, by students as well as a few teachers, about their "big house" on the hill and the rumored Watergate connections of the man who had built it. We really were not that wealthy in the beginning, so the three oldest children grew up in fairly middle-class surroundings. And the others usually rolled with the teasing. I told them to be gracious to everyone and that those who have more must give more. We would help people no matter what was said.

The lowest blow personally originated once again with my old nemesis, Dean Olson. Dean had formally retracted his accusations with the settlement of my lawsuit, but he continued to impose his venomous influence to anyone who would listen. This became apparent when I received a calling to serve on the high council of Salt Lake City's University Stake of the LDS Church. This was not my own home area stake but was composed entirely of students attending the University of Utah. (A stake is the administrative entity of approximately six–twelve wards, or congregations, in the church's structure.)

The day before I was to be installed, I was called into the office of my home area stake president who told me Peter Olson, Dean's son who lived in Salt Lake City, had visited him and had leveled serious allegations regarding my business dealings and White House relationships. Olson had been most persuasive and probably provided the stake president with copies of the *Chicago Tribune* article. As a result, the stake president advised me, my high council installation would be postponed until matters could be sorted out. I urged him to talk to my father-in-law, David Haight, who was an assistant to the Quorum of Twelve. I told him Elder Haight could give him the real story from beginning to end because he, too, had served on Olson Brothers, Inc.'s board for several years and that Dean Olson was his brother-in-law. Haight knew all the facts and was a straight shooter.

Fortunately the stake president eventually did get the full story. Several weeks later he apologized, and I was appointed to the high council on schedule. But that meeting with him had been most disheartening and, with my church appointment up in the air, I left his office feeling at least temporarily estranged from the church, an institution that had been my anchor throughout my adult life. I have revered LDS leaders always, usually finding them to be kind, understanding, and fair. But the stake president's attitude during our interview had none of those attributes and the speed with which he turned against me left me shaken and resentful.

After all the Watergate fallout and Olson's personal attacks, I had withstood all I could take and needed time to sort things out. An opportunity to do that presented itself in California while attending a Pacific Growers Association board meeting. Between sessions, I slipped away and listened to the surf and the seagulls and contemplated the genesis of the endless ill will between Olson and me. His longstanding grudge cast an ominous cloud over the family. There had to be a way to defuse his animosity.

I thought back through our history, recalling how emotional Dean was when I, his protégé, left the company to start, of all things, a rival business. What had I expected he would do? After each Olson lawsuit tossed out by a judge and after each false attempt at reconciliation, the relationship steadily had worsened.

The level of pettiness on the part of the Olsons seemed to know no limit. The wealthy establishment in Salt Lake City—then and now—belonged to the exclusive Alta Club, an historic good ol' boys tree house. I am not a private club person—and never have been. I would never have desired to be a member of the Alta Club, but without my knowledge, my name had been submitted for membership. Soon after, the Olsons fed someone on the membership committee tainted stories and I found myself blackballed.

I was hurt, but the incident made me wiser and stronger. Several years later, when the Alta Club sought me out for membership, I declined and continued to do so to this day. (When Jon Jr. became governor, he had occasion to give speeches in the stately club. He always prefaced his remarks with a good-natured, "I am committing a grave family sin by being here.")

Clearly the feud between Dean and I had to end. David Haight suggested a conflict-resolution committee consisting of a prominent member of the Quorum of the Twelve and another from the Quorum of Seventy (the governing level just below the Twelve) and himself. Olson and I agreed to appear before the committee. Facing one another in the same room would be difficult.

While preparing for our confrontation, I learned Dean and his brother were having serious legal problems. In 1974, Olson Brothers was charged by a grand jury in Utah for price fixing and conspiracy, similar to a 1942 California price-fixing charge against the company. The latest incident, however, forced Ezra Benson and other directors to resign from the board of the Olson business. It was clear that Karen's uncle, now much older and in desperate straits, deserved whatever kindness and magnanimity I could muster.

We aired our differences in front of the committee and it became apparent that the dispute boiled down to money. We ended up agreeing on a settlement figure that reflected what each felt the other was owed. We shook hands and agreed never to speak ill of each other again. It was finally over.

In the end, it was like all business conflicts. The adversaries more or less collapsed from exhaustion. Revenge saps so much of one's resources, energy, and focus. I had always tried to be positive, upbeat, and even respectful of Dean. He was finishing his life's work (except for a Justice Department indictment he would have to work through and a number of civil lawsuits involving significant legal payments to some of his competitors) and I was just beginning mine. It was time for us to go forward with positive energy. And we ultimately were successful in doing that.

In fact, in the late-1980s, out of the blue, Olson called. "You know, Jon," he said genially, "you were the only executive I ever had in the business who was worth a shit." Good old Dean, genteel to the core. He asked if I would consider running the egg business as part of our plastics operations. Here was Dean Olson, my longtime nemesis, reaching out to me in friendship. It prompted me to say what should have been said to my first industrial mentor years ago. "I didn't start out as a seasoned executive," I answered softly, "but I was trained by a great businessman, and that was you." I told him that our chemical business had moved on and that I could not honestly see a good fit for the egg business. Offering my highest regards, I wished him well. It pleased me that we had had our first civil chat in fifteen years. It also turned out to be our last. He died not long after that, in 1993. His son, Peter, ran the company until he died of a heart attack in 1998. Today, Olson Brothers, Inc. is all but gone.

As the 1970s drew to a close, my company was growing and changing. After exploring Japanese and European ventures and opportunities for further expansion, I learned Keyes Fibre Company of New Jersey was looking to partner with an aggressive and independent plastic packaging company. Years earlier, Keyes had discovered how to mold wood pulp into disposable plates. The demand for molded fiber products had gone international and, to meet modern-day market needs, Keyes also wanted to produce plastic products.

Keyes was a small company without much imagination. Its managers were stodgy, Ivy League types in love with the status quo. Keyes approached us about merging, creating both a compatible expansion opportunity and a means of meeting our need for an infusion of capital. It would allow me to play a role in Keyes' management while retaining independent status as a subsidiary. The merger was consummated in March 1976. I became a Keyes director and its executive vice president, while remaining president and CEO of Huntsman Container. I had authority to expand and grow and we injected some juice into Keyes' operations. The company signed a lease for a new one-hundred-thousand-square-foot Huntsman plant in Memphis. The $3.5 million facility would join the Fullerton, California and Troy, Ohio sites.

In the midst of this frenzy of building new businesses, our family took a motor home trip to California with two other families. Each family had nine children—so it was no small entourage. The long drive began in Salt Lake and terminated at Disneyland in Anaheim. While crossing the hot Nevada desert, the news on the car radio announced that my singing idol, Elvis Presley, had died. I shall never forget that date: August 17, 1977. The caravan pulled over to the side of the road to conduct our own Elvis memorial service.

Not long afterward, we added facilities in England and Australia, my first international acquisitions, although these were under the Keyes-Huntsman banner. Sales boomed. Two more plants were built, one in Spain and the other in Italy. But on November 30, 1978, Keyes Fibre was acquired by Arcata Corporation and renamed Molded Container Group. Up to this point, Arcata had been one of the largest commercial printers in America and dealt heavily in redwood products. One of the first moves by Arcata was to disband the Huntsman marketing-management team and to begin selling fiber and plastic products under a single sales organization. It was like abandoning a child. Throughout the 1970s, Huntsman Container technicians had come up with more than eighty new varieties of polystyrene packaging. It had been a thriving enterprise. Products ranging from plastic plates to carryout food containers were created at the Fullerton plant by a small team of loyalists. We had revolutionized food packaging. Our sales of the Big Mac container took off like wildfire around the world.

Operating under the Arcata banner, the Keyes-Huntsman business was no longer under my control nor in need of my services. After I fulfilled the four-year obligation to which I had committed in accordance with the 1976 merger, I resigned in 1980. By 1981, Arcata had divested the Keyes-Huntsman subsidiary to a Netherlands company. During the prior year, Arcata bought back its stock from shareholders and went private in order to resell the stock. I was paid in cash for my share of Keyes-Huntsman at a premium price, more than $10 million on my 1970 personal investment of $300,000, not to mention some forest acreage of redwood trees in California which, unknowingly, would come in handy in a future negotiation.

The 1970s had spawned my love affair with the chemical industry and a creative financial means to dive into it. My future was spelled: p-l-a-s-t-i-c-s, and pronounced petrochemicals. The whole adventure taught me a great lesson: next time, do it alone. Over the years, I have entered into all sorts of joint ventures, and not one of them succeeded when the family was not managing and operating it. For me, joint ventures have never been a way to make money. They have been stepping stones in paving the way forward.

Alas, at this point my plans for the next venture were delayed yet again by another move to Washington, DC, this time to accept a multi-year, uncompensated commitment overseeing missionaries in a four-state area, including the nation's capital. My church assignment demanded three full, uninterrupted years of my life when I was in my early forties, the father of nine, and about to start a new business. No other faith that I am aware of requires this sort of mid-career dedication and commitment. We could have produced a number of excuses for why the timing was not right, but I was honored, as was Karen, to be requested for the assignment. I had promised myself when we were married that family and faith would always come first. And they have, and it has strengthened the moral principles that constitute my philosophy.

Moral values play a crucial role in our personal lives and are equally important in business. Sadly, they are often missing ingredients in that sphere, as the headlines in our nation's newspapers underscore nearly every day. Because I so often found in my dealings with some people that morals and ethics are the first to go out the window when they become inconvenient, I decided a few years back to write a little primer reminding people of some of the basic rules we are taught from childhood but either forget or choose to disregard as adults.

Being an active Mormon is extraordinarily demanding of one's time, behavior, and resources in a way that non-Mormons simply cannot fathom. Many people, even some born into the faith, won't make that commitment, which may account for the number of less-than-active Mormons—perhaps as many as 65 percent of those born or converted into the faith. Most of these people are well-meaning, decent individuals who follow the teachings of Christ in their everyday lives but find they cannot devote their energies to doing all that is required of active members. Most remain proud of the LDS heritage. Thus, in 1980, when Karen and I were called to head a mission in Washington, DC, it meant dropping everything and reporting for duty. We responded to our mission call in the belief that it was the right thing to do as a family. I further believed that when our mission was fulfilled, I would leave Washington better prepared to pursue my dreams for a successful business.

Three marvelous years ensued where Karen and I (together with all our children) devoted our energies, efforts, money, and patience to overseeing over 600 full-time Mormon missionaries. They were tough but rewarding years. We grew in stature, spirituality, and love for one another. The missionaries were our family and we left all we had to devote 100 percent of our time to this incredible endeavor.

It was an interesting time to be in Washington, DC. Ronald Reagan was elected president and ended the standoff with Iran revolutionaries over embassy personnel they had taken hostage more than a year earlier, but was wounded by a would-be assassin's bullet fifteen months after taking office. Sandra Day O'Connor became the first female Supreme Court justice, but the Equal Rights Amendment failed to be ratified. And the US invaded the Caribbean island of Grenada in what turned out to be little more than an overblown military training exercise.

What followed that mission was an acquisition from Shell Oil Co. that defined me as a creative, straight-shooting national player on the petrochemical field. The big boys took notice of this one. From that point on, I was on their radar. Thinking three deals down the line, I juggled the moves among three of the oil giants. Shell was determined not to do this deal. It was the most complex, excruciating transaction of my nearly five decades of buying companies. It was a winner-take-all transaction. If I failed, the company would be broke and the Huntsmans would not have a home.

It began on a napkin in a Metroliner club car toward the end of my Washington mission. It ended with me lying on the floor of Shell's Houston headquarters building with two cracked vertebrae, still negotiating. On paper and in most people's minds, the odds were heavily stacked against me. It wasn't possible. I saw it otherwise and bet the farm. It was a signature Huntsman deal.

7. Riverboat Gambler

O N THE CRISP MONDAY MORNING THAT WAS NOVEMBER 25, 1985, walking down the streets of downtown Houston toward One Shell Plaza, I found myself on the brink of great changes. My company was on life support; my career, reputation, and family home were on the line. I was about to meet with Shell executives at the giant's headquarters in a last-ditch effort to salvage a deal essential to resuscitating my company, and achieving my American Dream. The fact that Shell's CEO was even seeing me was itself a miracle. The last time we had talked, he said coming to Houston would be a waste of time. Yet, I was determined this most desperate hour would be my finest.

It is neither a plot spoiler nor a surprise to relate here that the Huntsman business did not die. What may amaze you is how we stayed alive. For me, the feat epitomized both who I am—how I operate and why I ended up where I did—and my favorite kind of deal, one designed on a napkin to include fluidity and flexibility in the spirit of never say die. While this signature deal may not have been my most lucrative or headline grabbing, it was certainly the most complicated. But that final walk to One Shell Plaza began a long way from Houston and several years before.

Let history mark 1983 as the genesis of the Huntsman chemical industrial empire.

I was near the halfway point in my life. I had made more than a million dollars a couple of times over—first by moonlighting in a Christmas record album business and then by developing plastic containers to keep Big Macs and other fast food warm, fresh and safe. Under the banner of Huntsman Container Corporation I had established a tradition of either plowing corporate gains into expanding my businesses or buying new ones. By then, Karen and I had begun a wonderful family and I had been named a mission president in Washington, DC for the LDS Church. On several levels, my life at this point might have been described by many as "as good as it gets." From my perspective, that wasn't the case.

For one thing, Huntsman Container had seen better days. I was running out of money—not a good thing for an entrepreneur. My early dabbling in the petrochemical industry had spawned a desire to venture further into it. Notwithstanding the fact that I had a couple of relatively small operations in place, I was still a minor player. What I needed was a bold, creative, jaw-dropping deal that would get me on the radar. The tricky part was that the deal would have to be done with someone else's money. I certainly did not have the personal or corporate wherewithal to pull off much of anything, let alone a major purchase or a global presence.

The petrochemical industry is dominated by some of the world's largest corporations operating in a low-margin, capital-intensive environment characterized by roller-coaster cycles that carry the players from dizzying heights to nerve-testing troughs and back up again. The price of admission can be prohibitive, especially since the best time to buy a petrochemical business is when economic conditions are at their worst. Buying even a small petrochemical manufacturing plant would require a hundred million dollars, best-case scenario. I had been told I would never make it in the industry as an individual, but my philosophy has always been to look for the right opportunity and to worry about raising the money later. I paid close attention to Dr. Kline, one of my professors at the Wharton School, who opened every finance class with a timeless business motto, "Buy low, sell high."

In the early 1980s, petrochemicals were in a funk. The nation was nearing the end of the worst recession since the 1930s. Unemployment hovered in the 10 percent range. Interest rates broke into double digits for only the second time in history. Big oil companies were cutting back on petrochemical investments, canceling capital projects, and closing operations. With profits low and supply languishing in warehouses, the industry was demoralized. It was the perfect time for a fledgling company like mine to take flight. The best point of entry is when everyone else is heading for the door.

The timing otherwise wasn't so hot. While planning this big-bang approach to building a petrochemical empire, I found myself in charge of two hundred or so nineteen-to-twenty-one-year-old LDS missionaries in Washington, DC. For two years of their lives, I was their father, confessor, bishop, teacher, bodyguard, and best friend. No job on earth can match the exhausting, exasperating, and wonderfully rewarding challenge of being an LDS mission president. Karen and the children were remarkably supportive. It was a family effort and I am happy to have done it. It is, however, a life experience I need enjoy only once.

On the personal financial level, my future was anything but assured. With the money from the sale of Huntsman Container in the late 1970s, prompted by environmental liabilities that were looming over clamshell containers, my longtime, trusted associate Ray Goodson and I had started a property management company and small petrochemical business known as Huntsman-Goodson Corporation. Our assets consisted of a condominium project, a shopping center, and miscellaneous real estate. I also owned a half interest in a small polystyrene plant in Troy, Ohio. I had to leave all this in Goodson's hands while I detoured to Washington, DC for the mission presidency.

While depressed times bring about the best bargains for those looking to buy, they have the opposite effect on those who own properties. High interest rates had devastated the real estate market, our properties were generating no income, and debt equaled marketable assets. To put it bluntly, Huntsman-Goodson was in shambles. This was another reason I had no choice but to put together the next business and rebuild my financial base by working out the most creative deal of my life—above board and fair but based on an idea so audacious, it was almost comical.

LDS Church officials knew I would be working during the last months of my three-year commitment to establish Huntsman Chemical, and they tacitly approved as long as it did not interfere with my mission responsibilities. Therefore, most of the planning had to be done late at night. Some days, I worked around the clock, squeezing between midnight and 8:00 a.m. whatever work I could do for the business from my little office in a back bedroom of the mission home. Any absences from the mission home could only be for a few hours at a time, and business-related travel required tight scheduling to ensure I did not neglect the missionaries. I knew the rules and honored them. Our Washington, DC mission led all others in North America in convert baptisms. Morale with our missionaries was high. Our constant leadership of these great young men and women had kept them energized and positive. Karen and I loved every missionary, each dedicated and diligent, each unique and special to us.

My past business partners had gone in different directions, making it crucial to form a new team for my proposed company. Its first member was Ron Rasband, a top salesman and trusted lieutenant from my first solo foray into the packaging industry. Solid and dependable, Rasband had joined Huntsman Container before it was purchased by Keyes Fibre Company. Originally, I had hired him during his junior year at the University of Utah. I found him to be a quick study and loyal, almost to an extreme. Later, when I recruited him for Huntsman Chemical, Rasband was living in a beautiful home in Ridgefield, Connecticut, poised for a promising career. I was asking him to make a leap of faith and become second-in-command of a company that existed only on paper. To my amazement and everlasting gratitude, he agreed to become the first employee.

Initially, Rasband split his time between helping launch the new company and sorting out my foundering property management affairs. Things were so bad on the latter front that I ended up selling my interests in the real estate projects for a single dollar. Then, in what proved to be a most fortuitous move, I actually paid almost $800,000 to my partner Ray Goodson and then conveyed to him my 50 percent interest in our Troy, Ohio styrene monomer manufacturing plant. (In other words, I paid him to assume ownership of my half.) Shortly thereafter, it experienced a terrible explosion—but by then I had no ownership liability.

Terry Parker was the second to come aboard. He had helped me in a chemical bartering operation in the mid-1970s, my initial dabbling into the industry taken on a whim. He possessed an exceptional grasp of all things financial. Jack Calton, who worked with me earlier, signed up as well. Another founding member of the Huntsman Chemical planning team was Brent Stevenson, a talented young lawyer who had advised me for several years while in private practice. These guys operated from our downtown Salt Lake City offices. It didn't seem to bother them that I underwrote their salaries from personal funds. I had the best lieutenants possible, especially since I was not yet at liberty to perform the necessary legwork to create the business. Now, time was of the essence. The budding Huntsman Chemical Corporation was about to bloom, with Shell

Oil, an eager seller and new best friend, as its partner—although Shell was not aware of that at the time.

Our first major acquisition would be a sizable North American petrochemical plant. That I had no money with which to purchase it made things even more interesting. In late 1982, we considered buying two small polystyrene plants, one in Massachusetts and the other in Kentucky. I bid on the Massachusetts plant, which was in bankruptcy proceedings. I knew it was an iffy proposition when the first thing the annoyed bankruptcy judge asked me was, "Who the hell are you?" Obviously, we lost out on that plant, as well as the Kentucky plant. It was just as well. Had we acquired those two properties, we never would have gone after the plant we did buy in Belpre, Ohio, which was ten times larger.

Entrepreneurs are strange, self-torturing creatures at times, but we thrive on the challenges. Turndowns and defeats are the tests of our mettle; setbacks only defy us to set the bar higher. My plan to buy our first site with neither purse nor portfolio was unlikely but thrilling. My new team spent much of its time holding its collective breath and fastening their seatbelts for the white-knuckle ride for which they had been assembled.

In an Amtrak Metroliner cafe car on an August 12, 1982, trip from Washington to Philadelphia, I outlined my plan to Ron Rasband on a napkin. (Rasband still has it.) The two of us were on our way to Philadelphia to meet with executives in the chemical division of Atlantic-Richfield Company (ARCO), which recently had constructed a plant in Texas to make propylene oxide, a basic building block for plastics. For each pound of propylene oxide generated, two pounds of styrene monomer were produced as a byproduct. This left ARCO with excess supply of the stuff. They were desperate to find a market for it.

I had become acquainted with ARCO's styrene monomer manufacturing operations from my days brokering chemicals. That was also how I came to meet the folks running Shell Chemical's polystyrene plant at Belpre on the Ohio River and to learn this site was a prime user of monomer and was not operating at full capacity. We had negotiated a good price from ARCO for its excess monomer and paid Shell to convert it into polystyrene—an arrangement known as "toll conversion." We made a few pennies on each pound. It wasn't much, but it got us started and created valuable relationships within ARCO and Shell.

As unlikely as it sounds, my plan was to buy Shell's Belpre operation using ARCO's money. Rasband and Parker thought it was the wildest pipe dream ever and predicted long odds of succeeding. But I knew a couple of things they did not: First, ARCO's chemical division had been in a downward slide for years. Second, major manufacturers of styrene monomer were badly in need of sales outlets. We were among Shell's largest customers, accounting for about one-third of Belpre's manufacturing capacity. I figured Shell eventually would decide to unload its polystyrene plant. Whether Shell would sell it to me was only a matter of timing.

As I anticipated, it wasn't long before Shell executives called a meeting to discuss our existing business relationship. We had to meet in Washington because I wasn't free to travel to their offices in Houston. Rasband set up a dinner at the Marriott Hotel near Dulles International Airport. Midway through our meal, I spontaneously said to the Shell executives: "Since we are going to become your biggest customer, why not just sell us the Belpre plant?"

It happened so abruptly that Ron nearly fell out of his chair. The Shell folks looked at me as if I had lost my marbles. Shell didn't know much about me, though they may have started to sense that I was somebody of consequence when hotel magnate Bill Marriott Sr., who I had gotten to know several decades earlier, stopped by our table to warmly shake my hand and say hello. All Shell's executives knew for certain was that Shell had been converting styrene monomer for us for less than a month and had invested $67 million in the well-engineered Belpre plant. They replied that Belpre wasn't for sale. However, my audacious question sowed a seed. In about a week, Henry Sullivan, a brilliant chemical engineer who oversaw Shell's polymers and plastics business, called Rasband and asked if I was serious.

It turns out my hunch had been right. Shell's leadership had been considering selling the plant. In fact, it had talked with chemical giant BASF about a purchase. The Belpre plant had a 300 million pound annual capacity but was only producing about 240 million pounds. Making only about $1 million per year (EBITDA), the plant was performing below Shell's expectations. The business was growing too slowly and Shell's people had guessed polypropylene was going to replace polystyrene in the industry. Fortunately for me, they guessed wrong.

I expected my finance guys, Terry Parker and Jack Calton, to be skeptical about my offer to buy the plant. Always safe and conservative, they typically err on the side of caution, finding a host of reasons why a deal couldn't be done. That, of course, was why I needed them—to open a discussion of the opposing point of view. One detail over which they fretted was my net worth. At the time, it was about $2 million, much of which was tied up in my home in Salt Lake and the condos I owned in New York and Arizona. They knew I had ten mouths to feed (eleven, if I wanted to eat), and had been without a paycheck since accepting my mission call almost three years earlier. (Church assignments, such as my full-time LDS mission service, are undertaken without compensation. It is volunteer service.)

In short, I had no money and Parker thought I was nuts. I, on the other hand, believed that if you are creative enough, you can do anything. It just takes ingenuity and a strong stomach. In all the complex deals I have cut, I always visualized a way to do them. To be sure, improvisation was required, but when push came to shove it didn't seem like such a stretch. Once I had engaged Shell to talk about selling the plant, I considered it a done deal.

Shortly after the dinner at Dulles, I slipped away from Washington for a day and flew to Houston to meet with Peter De Leeuw, a sharp young manager in Shell's plastics business. (He went on to become CEO of Sterling Chemicals, Inc.) De Leeuw didn't think anything would come of my offer, but he was curious enough to receive me. His opinion seemed to change when I offered $17 million for the plant. The spontaneity of my offer took him by surprise, but De Leeuw said it wasn't high enough and countered with $27 million plus an additional $20 million or so for inventory and receivables. Karen was back in Washington, taking care of the two-hundred-plus missionaries, so my one-day absence had to be productive. Securing the deal that day was imperative. I gazed at him across that cavernous gap, pondered its depth and breadth, and said, "Let's eat lunch."

"Seventeen million is not a deal," De Leeuw said when we got into it again. "Maybe twenty-seven million isn't, either. If we were to split the difference at twenty-two million, I think I could sell it to management, but that is the very bottom."

"Okay," I said, eyeing him calmly as I pondered the instantaneous $40 million undertaking (including inventories and receivables).

Stunned, De Leeuw stared at me. When he found his words, he said he would draw up a draft agreement. I sat right there and waited while he did that, and then we read through the document at the coffee table in his office. It looked like he had covered everything—price, number of employees, wages and benefits, environmental liability, the lease on the land, and general statements about how Shell would provide power, fire protection, and storage at cost. We went through it paragraph by paragraph. I made minor changes, pulled out my pen, and signed it. De Leeuw's expression grew even more incredulous.

"To this day, I've never had a deal happen like that—not by a long shot," he told someone later. "No lawyers, no financial advisors, just Jon by himself." He suggested my lawyers look at the agreement, but I said I trusted him. Besides, other than Brent Stevenson back in the office, Huntsman Chemical didn't have any lawyers. I assured De Leeuw that if either of us found a mistake we would work together to resolve it.

De Leeuw, of course, required final approval from Jim Street, Shell Chemical's president and CEO, who definitely would want Shell's attorneys involved. De Leeuw could not bind Shell by signing on the spot as I had done. But my immediate signature underscored I was serious and showed him that Huntsman's decisions were not to be made by committee. The agreement included the standard language and after De Leeuw's colleague Henry Sullivan went through it, he said that if I promised to take good care of the Shell employees who would transfer to me with the purchase, he would see that the deal went through. He told me the plant worked like a small community—employees knew and looked out for each other. No one would be happy if I planned to let anyone go. I assured him I would retain the workforce, salary structure, and benefits.

Shell's attorneys worked their way through the details which delayed the closing for a while, but that only worked to my advantage. With each passing month, Shell became more invested in seeing the deal go through. We developed a rapport, which was crucial since the sale was only the first phase of my plan. In its final form, the deal would be unlike any Shell had ever experienced. Signing the draft agreement was just the first step in making De Leeuw feel obligated. I knew he wanted to sell, but I had to get him to commit to selling it to me, notwithstanding the fact that I had no money with which to buy it, something he did not know at the time. Earning his trust was pivotal, as it is in any deal.

Through the next six months, we dealt with one roadblock after another, the last of which wasn't removed until ten minutes before closing. We signed the draft agreement in November 1982 but didn't achieve an actual binding contract until January. We didn't close until March 1983. (All this time, I was still serving as mission president, keeping up with the weekly duties such as interviewing missionaries and speaking before large congregations. My release from the three-year assignment remained four months away.)

What I had to do now was come up with $40 million. As I said, I had zero liquidity. To most people involved, the Shell deal was a long shot if for no other reason than my negotiating time was limited and because bankers generally don't have the stomach for the kind of financing I had dreamed up. They are especially wary if they can't see how you plan to repay. It would be a hard sell, I acknowledged to Rasband and Parker, but by showing how we would cut costs and increase production I was confident we would raise the money. Persistence and character would win out. Besides, bankers always like a confident, seasoned businessman, so I set about convincing them that's who they were dealing with.

One thing working in my favor was that I had established an unblemished line of credit over the years, beginning with my early days when I would borrow a thousand or so dollars from this or that bank and repay it several months later. I didn't do anything with the money; I just borrowed it and then immediately repaid it to demonstrate I was a good credit risk and to establish a history of early repayment in anticipation of the day when I would need a couple of million dollars. The hard fact, however, was that I would not get $40 million from the banks for this deal no matter how trustworthy I was. It had to be obtained in a more creative way.

That is where ARCO Chemical came into my plan. I went to Jack Kleiderlein, an executive overseeing ARCO Chemical's styrene monomer business and my primary ARCO contact, and agreed to buy 150 million pounds of styrene monomer annually for 10 years, 3 times the amount the Texas plant sold to its previous top customer, Goodyear. I let him know that I wanted to buy the Belpre plant from Shell and market the polystyrene through the newly formed Huntsman Chemical Corporation. Kleiderlein found that attractive—until I dropped the bombshell.

I looked him squarely in the eye and asked: "Jack, can ARCO lend us ten million to help buy the Shell plant?" Kleiderlein's jaw dropped and his eyes widened, a reaction I had fully expected. He looked ashen when I added the proviso that it wouldn't be a loan in the traditional sense. "What I'm talking about, Jack, is more of a continuous, revolving float."

In short, we were asking ARCO for $10 million in styrene monomer with 90 days to make our payment in exchange for the 10-year contract of which we could opt out after 4 years so long as we repaid the loan. This would allow Huntsman to order styrene the first day we owned the plant and have 90 days from the last day of the month to pay for it. By the time each due date arrived, we would have ordered an additional $10 million of styrene. Basically, we were going to continuously roll over a $10 million loan, interest free. At the closing of the Belpre sale, ARCO would transfer $10 million in styrene to Shell, which then would sell it on the open market. The proceeds would be applied to the plant's purchase. In effect, ARCO would be lending us $10 million toward the facility's purchase price.

To my mind, it was ingenious financial engineering, particularly since I had no alternatives. It was a complicated maneuver but good for everybody. As in any deal, one must paint a clear picture of how the other side benefits. The other party isn't interested in what you will receive from the deal. He must be made to see himself as a winner. Otherwise, the deal falls apart. To me, this was just simple math, a thoughtful game plan. To the others, it looked like risk, chaos, and confusion.

Good chemistry between the players also is crucial. We had to have someone we could trust inside ARCO, someone who would understand the loan was good for ARCO and be confident that we would repay it. He must be able to see the benefits for ARCO's side of the bargain. Jack Kleiderlein was that person. He became our advocate. Jim Madden, a creative, energetic ARCO salesman who later joined Huntsman, also worked with us.

Following his initial reaction, Kleiderlein began to warm to the notion of helping make the Belpre deal happen. ARCO stood to win a big customer, and there were other reasons just as persuasive. ARCO's Texas City plant produced propylene oxide, a high-margin product, and there weren't many of these plants in the petrochemical business. The byproduct of each pound of that product was two pounds of styrene monomer. ARCO had been running the plant intermittently, and repeated shut downs and start-ups are expensive. Kleiderlein's boss, ARCO president and CEO Hal Sorgenti, had been asking whether Kleiderlein could sell all the styrene if they were to run the plant full time. Our ten-year contract would allow the facility to operate at near capacity. ARCO didn't have the $10 million to lend, but it certainly possessed the equivalent in styrene.

The more Kleiderlein and Sorgenti thought about it, the more the deal became a win-win. I knew Sorgenti was a tough but fair leader and had a reputation as a hard sell, but we liked each other. And Kleiderlein and I always got along well. We had a running joke: whenever our business talks broke down, I would start talking religion. That tactic always brought him back to the table. Even given both men's inclination to proceed, sealing the deal became an uphill battle once ARCO's legal team got involved. Attorneys love to kill deals and this was no exception. The lawyers fought it from the start, calling the plan outrageous. "Huntsman has no means of repaying the loan," they warned. "No collateral, no money. Unheard of!"

At one point after signing the draft sale agreement with Shell, I asked Shell's Pete De Leeuw to join me for a meeting with ARCO in Philadelphia in hopes of speeding up the process. But after spending a good part of the day listening to ARCO's lawyers rake the deal over the coals, De Leeuw advised me to walk away. "Pete, I can work it out," I told him, noting that all the executives on the business side wanted this to work. The business types will prevail over the lawyers, I predicted, and they did. Against all odds, ARCO agreed to the $10 million, interest-free "floating" loan. The attorneys went crazy.

Yet even after all this wheeling and dealing, I was still $20 million shy. Prying money from the banks proved more difficult than getting it from ARCO. Bankers simply were not interested. Then I remembered Mark Buchman, a college friend from the Wharton School, who had just left Manufacturers Hanover Trust Bank in New York City to become executive VP of corporate banking at Union Bank in Los Angeles. He was my last chance, but I was optimistic because Buchman was a rare bird: a risk-taking banker. Buchman went to bat for Huntsman Chemical and I appeared with him before his loan committee to make our case. Union Bank's lending policy was traditionally focused on Southern California businesses seeking "small loans" of $500,000 to $2 million. I wanted 10 times that amount for an Ohio business.

Buchman did a brilliant job and deserves full credit for convincing the loan committee to trust me, but meeting the committee's collateral and guarantee requirements presented a special challenge. Most banks make loans backed by tangible assets, such as buildings and land. The Belpre assets consisted of pipes, tanks, and extruders standing on leased land in the middle of a huge Shell facility that produced Kraton polymers and a wide range of other products. Our small landlocked operation would have little or no value in a foreclosure. If we didn't plan to manufacture polystyrene, the assets would be all but worthless. Of course, Shell had a first claim to all assets, so Union Bank's valuation was greatly diminished. Miraculously, Union Bank tentatively approved $18 million on condition that $6 million of the loan would encumber the plant's remaining assets and that collateral for the $12 million would include everything I owned—my home and condos in New York and Arizona. (I even offered Karen and the kids, but the loan committee had no way of appraising such assets.) I also threw in what we called those "redwood-taking claims" I mentioned earlier.

After I sold my 25-percent share in Huntsman Container to Keyes Fibre for $8 million in stock, Keyes, in turn, sold it to Arcata Corporation, which owned some redwood forestlands in Northern California that had been confiscated by the federal government to enlarge Redwood National Park. The value of that land was in litigation. While it was litigated, the Redwood land was placed in trust for Keyes' former stockholders, which included me. The government had paid for the Redwood land through the process of eminent domain, but if the court ruled the price hadn't been sufficient, former Keyes stockholders would stand to gain about $1.35 million each, I estimated. Regardless of the court's decision, the combined

value of my home, real estate holdings, and my potential "windfall" from
the Redwood lawsuit was assessed at well below the $12 million in col-
lateral the bank wanted. At the last minute, the Union Bank loan committee got cold feet and the tentative approval evaporated. Union Bank
would not lend the $12 million unless it was guaranteed by Shell.

By that point, Shell badly wanted to sell me its polystyrene operation.
Selling a piece of a company is as much an emotional decision as a business one. I had worked desperately to get their executives on my side,
and De Leeuw and Sullivan emotionally were ready to pull the trigger.
Even so, Shell's response to Union Bank's demand was less than enthusiastic. Shell wouldn't guarantee the loan, but De Leeuw asked to see my
financial statement to see whether I had anything left to bundle with my
collateral.

Parker thought that request was a bit invasive, but we itemized my
assets. The list wasn't long. It included the four older condos in Park City
and my partial interest in the Grubstake Restaurant there. It bears mentioning that, in 1983, Park City wasn't the trendy resort town that it is
today, so this property at the time may have been more of a liability than
an asset. But the bottom line was that Shell liked to pick its partners and
had decided that its partner would be me. Shell finally agreed to accept
those holdings as collateral for its loan guarantee. The reasoning was
that, if Huntsman defaulted, Shell could always reclaim the plant and retain the $10 million rollover deal from ARCO and would end up owning
a marketable restaurant in Park City.

De Leeuw later said that the decision came down to this: "What was
the alternative? If we were going to make this deal, we had to work with
Jon. We didn't have any other buyers and we were going to get a decent
price from Huntsman." To my way of thinking, it boiled down to a matter of mutual respect. We were all honorable people, and each side was
committed to keeping its word.

Reassured by Shell's guarantee, Union Bank lent me the $18 million
and opened an $11 million line of credit as working capital. But another
wrinkle swiftly emerged—a technical issue that threatened the entire deal.
ARCO's plant produced propylene-oxide styrene monomer, a type of
styrene not approved for use in the Belpre plant. Shell would have to sell
this styrene on the spot market. Since it could not be sold the same day

it was produced, Shell did not want to assume the risk that the price might fall before it could unload the product. Huntsman Chemical had to give Shell a $10 million note. Shell would credit Huntsman its actual sale proceeds and we would have to make up any shortfall.

Finally, having worked through that issue, we thought we were home free. Wrong. On the day before the deal was to close, an overzealous Shell lawyer popped the question: How would Shell know it was getting title to the styrene? That forced us to go to ARCO for a letter stating the styrene purchased in our ninety-day agreement belonged to Shell and that Huntsman Chemical had no claims on it. We spent that entire night before closing faxing letters back and forth to ARCO. Shell's people were getting increasingly nervous. It was a case of "go or no-go" as far as they were concerned and to say there was tension in the air was an understatement.

We worked far into the night. For sustenance in the wee hours, I went to the popcorn machine in the employee cafeteria several times as we ironed out the final wrinkles. I was on edge because I had to be back in Washington, DC for a 9:00 a.m. missionary zone conference. Remember, I was only supposed to be working on any of this during nighttime hours. Nobody in Washington except Karen even knew I was gone. Time was running out.

Truth be told, every business deal I have ever undertaken has had last-minute complications. Most deals have been accomplished with little or no cash and were tightly wired. This first deal merely set the precedent for many others to come.

After our nightmare on the eve of closing, and with only ten minutes to spare before we were to close the deal with Shell, we received ARCO's final acceptance letter. It had taken six months, but we did it.

Forbes magazine described the $40 million deal as "one of the most creative on record." Only $500,000 of that $40 million came from my pocket, and that was used primarily for outside expertise, salaries, and other expenses. In return, my company gained an immediate revenue stream of about $100 million a year. Seasoned entrepreneurs know that as long as hard dollars are not involved in a transaction there is exceptional flexibility. The Huntsman forte is finding substitutes for real cash.

Stitching together and closing this deal put me well on my way to building an empire and proved to be one of the most excruciating, exciting, and exhausting experiences of my life. To this day, people still are amazed I persuaded ARCO to lend me $10 million and Shell to guarantee a $12 million bank loan. Yet, all of us—ARCO, Shell Chemical, Union Bank, and Huntsman Chemical—came out winners. When the Belpre sale was announced, *Modern Plastics* magazine likened me to a "riverboat gambler." De Leeuw saw the article and immediately knew what to bring to our formal dinner celebrating the closing: a bronze statue of a riverboat gambler (which is still prominently displayed in our Salt Lake City headquarters). The inscription read: "From your friends at Shell." This deal was small potatoes compared to others that followed, but I savored the moment for the triumph it was.

Following the backslapping and congratulations all around, it was time to turn my attention to the Belpre employees who would make or break the operation. Employees understandably were apprehensive, but I was determined to make them feel good about their new owner. Rasband and I stressed they were starting afresh, working on the ground floor of a family business—this would be a collaboration between my family and theirs.

We assigned new titles and responsibilities and laid out our goals, emphasizing that each person's effort would make a difference in the company. That concept was foreign in a company of Shell's size but we assured them that, as Huntsman employees, each had the opportunity to show his or her creativity and to contribute to our success. We let them know we would be running the plant in a more entrepreneurial manner, with faster decision-making and more customer focus, at a lower cost. The employees listened, they performed, and not a single worker bailed out or was laid off. At the end of the first year of operation, each employee received a new TV set in appreciation for his or her part in the transition.

Belpre was the start of our petrochemical empire. As it turned out, Belpre was not highly profitable but, as our only asset, it became the foundation of our portfolio. Most importantly, that deal gave us a reputation as a risk-taker, though I saw the acquisition as an act of entrepreneurial creativity. We reveled in the achievement of buying the Belpre plant with someone else's money. We were proud to have finessed the acquisition of a $100 million facility, through a succession of ingenious, hard-won events. But even as the confetti settled, we still had no liquidity and precious little equity. Our financial rubber band was stretched to the limit. What we had just achieved was but Part I of the plan for salvation. Huntsman Chemical would not be out of the woods until Part II was accomplished.

July 1, 1983 marked the culmination of my service as mission president and a return to Salt Lake City where I could become a full-time leader of the business. For me, the mission experience presented a precious opportunity to renew a connection with Karen and the children and a time to mature personally. Most of our children weathered the challenges and made the transition back to life in Salt Lake City well. Daughter Kathleen, however, in her mid-teens, encountered difficulties adjusting to the relocation at an impressionable phase of her development when she was vulnerable to the emotional aspects of change. It pains me to realize that those problems marked the beginning of a downward spiral that eventually would take her life. Karen and I worked with Kathleen as patiently as we could and hoped that, with love and the passage of time, her anxiety would be calmed. We did all for her that we knew how to do.

Once back in Salt Lake City, phase two of our plan began with an assertive campaign to raise capital. We sold a 10 percent interest in Huntsman Container to Dyno Industries of Oslo, Norway for $5 million, in exchange for which Huntsman Chemical acquired a 30 percent share in a small plant in Singapore that produced expandable polystyrene. Just like that, we were international. The $5 million helped, but it didn't solve our financial problems.

Next we approached our friends at Shell about buying 15 percent of Huntsman. Shell already was guaranteeing $12 million of the loan to buy the Belpre plant and here I came, asking them to buy back a piece of Belpre, at a proportionately higher price than Shell had sold it to me. I proposed the idea as an investment in Huntsman Chemical, confident that Shell had an incentive to work with us. Someone without a stake in our future would never have considered buying an interest in an undercapitalized, fledgling company. I knew the investor had to be an insider and there were only two: Shell and ARCO, and the latter already had loaned us money. It helped that Shell was a supplier, but the key to getting Shell's cooperation was to raise the ante with something it did not have—a long-term raw materials contract.

Once again, Henry Sullivan proved an invaluable advocate inside Shell's hierarchy. Sullivan, who oversaw Shell's polymers and plastics business plus its investments in other companies, had grown up in the 1960s. As Shell's youngest vice president, Sullivan wore his hair long and reminded me of a flower child. He was also fair and versatile and, as I had always done in my career, Sullivan maintained his independence within Shell. Without Sullivan, I never could have maintained the relationship I enjoyed with Shell. (He proved so valuable that Huntsman Chemical Corporation eventually elected him vice chairman of our board.) Thanks primarily to his support, Shell bought a 15 percent share for $7.5 million—another helpful cash injection but not enough for the long haul.

Between 1983 and 1986, we had added small polystyrene plants in England, Georgia, and Canada. Huntsman Chemical was growing, but our profits were still slim. We needed a much firmer capital footing.

My strategy for the mid-1980s centered on two premises. These held that Huntsman could operate more flexibly than bigger companies and that we had to remain an active player in what was then a buyer's market. Whenever a door opened, we walked through.

The next door that opened led to the purchase of a small polystyrene plant in Carrington, England owned, once again, by Shell. It was a minor part of a massive chemicals complex outside of Manchester. Carrington annually produced eighty million pounds of crystal polystyrene, the simplest to produce of the three main polystyrenes. With a mere forty employees, it was barely a third the size of Belpre. When I learned Shell was planning to shutter the plant, I flew to England to meet with John Collins, chief executive of Shell Chemical UK, a subsidiary of Royal Dutch Shell. After inspecting the run-down facility I concluded that, if it offered a means of getting cheaper styrene monomer, the plant could be profitable. Buying the Carrington facility would bring us a second manufacturing plant and give us a foothold in the European marketplace.

Collins let it be known that Shell would sell the plant for next to nothing if the employees could retain their jobs. We reassured him on that point and were able to close the deal in July 1984 at a price of $2.25 million, basically the cost of the inventory and receivables. I also struck a deal to buy styrene monomer from Shell at a discount. The plant itself was pure junk—dirty, rusty, and barely operating, but, as I told a British newspaper, "We can make rust work." The quote made the paper's "Top 10 Quotations" list at year's end.

The acquisition's timing couldn't have been better. We landed monomer at a discount and the polystyrene market in England improved within a year, allowing us to make money immediately. Shell ended up retaining several of its employees after the sale, which allowed us to operate at full capacity with a more manageable payroll. Our new employees jumped to the task at hand. They had gone from working for one of the world's largest corporations to being employed by a small company with a name that few recognized. They soon developed a sense of ownership, however. They also knew that if they failed, I would fail; if I failed, they would be unemployed. Over the years, we expanded the Carrington plant dramatically, transforming it from a dilapidated disaster into a modern manufacturing model, much to Collins's amazement.

I went on to buy an expandable polystyrene plant in Rome, Georgia and a compounding plant in Farmingdale, New York from Georgia Pacific. As long as the market was depressed, our no-money-down buying spree continued. Next, I struck a deal to buy half interest in Polycom, Inc., owner of small compounding plants in Conneaut, Ohio and Donora, Pennsylvania, south of Pittsburgh. Polycom was headed by Ralph Andy. Shell was one of Polycom's customers and Andy and I met while working on the Belpre purchase. He is one of the finest people it has been my pleasure to know. My first inclination was to buy his company outright, but I had a better idea. I proposed selling our new Farmingdale plant to him. Polycom's sales were about $17 million a year versus $50 million for Farmingdale. "It was a case of the fish eating the whale," Andy later would say, but we shook hands on what turned out to be a great deal.

Polycom paid $3.5 million for the equipment, customer list, and other assets of the Farmingdale plant. Huntsman paid $4 million for a half interest in Polycom. No money changed hands at the closing in June

1985 because neither of us had any. I borrowed the $500,000 that made up the difference. Polycom-Huntsman was a different example of making rust work. Andy made brilliant use of the Farmingdale operation and ran a first-class business. He was an ethical, professional partner, and we each benefited from our respective contributions. After what amounted to a $1 million net investment in Polycom-Huntsman, the business was sold in 1999 for $135 million.

In those days, everything we touched absolutely had to work. We had no financial reserves on which to fall back. Though these deals were small compared to what was to come, each was a crucial component of my plan to gather rosebuds while they were cheap and then stand back and watch them bloom when the upturn inevitably came.

Huntsman was still dangerously undercapitalized. The cash from Shell and Dyno helped considerably. Maintaining a positive cash flow was a continuous juggling act. We did okay our first year, but in 1985 polystyrene prices fell to 33.1 cents a pound from 38.9 cents the year before. The 15 percent decrease was greater than our profit margin. For Belpre, it meant $17 million in lost revenue. Prices fell again toward the end of the year, causing Huntsman Chemical to hemorrhage red ink. With our mishmash of assets, depressed polystyrene prices, and our lack of capital, we had to do something quickly. The down cycle had lasted long enough that an upswing had to be near, but nobody knew precisely when that would be. Meanwhile, Huntsman Chemical was in peril.

Though it may have seemed counterintuitive, it was time to launch the larger piece of Part II of my growth strategy. If it worked, it would double the size of the company.

Huntsman Chemical's deal of the decade had actually begun to take shape a year earlier. During a visit to American Hoechst's headquarters in Bridgewater, New Jersey, I inquired about the availability of a small business it owned in Sandusky, Ohio that made polystyrene cups. It turned out Hoechst also wanted to sell a Manchester, New Hampshire plant that made a high-performance plastic called engineered resin. Hoechst executives didn't take me seriously, probably because it must have seemed like we were too small to buy these bits and pieces. Those sites weren't promising enough for us to justify pressing the issue, but the discussions did get my foot in the door and established a relationship with president and CEO Dieter zur Loye, a straightforward guy who gave me a clear impression that American Hoechst was not enamored with either the polystyrene or styrene monomer business produced at its plants in Illinois, Virginia, and Texas. I told zur Loye he should sell them to me.

It took more than one conversation, but I finally got zur Loye to agree to present my idea to his parent company, Hoechst AG, in Germany. Zur Loye would have preferred to wait for the economy to improve, but his German bosses had been pressing him to rid the company of those plants. Hoechst already had sold the company's European polystyrene operations and was delaying future acquisitions for the American subsidiary until zur Loye divested the Bayport, Texas monomer operation and the polystyrene plants at Chesapeake, Virginia and Peru, Illinois. The combined annual polystyrene production at Peru and Chesapeake was about five hundred million pounds. The Peru facility also manufactured about eighty million pounds of expandable polystyrene a year. Expandable polystyrene enjoyed good profit margins and the Chesapeake site consisted of a new plant with modern technology. It would be a prize.

Initially, my goal had been to produce additional grades of polystyrene in order to enter other markets. It didn't take long to realize that in order to maximize revenues from its polystyrene business, Huntsman needed to make its own raw material—styrene monomer. Doing so would allow us to better weather the market's storms. To build a monomer plant from scratch would have required several hundred million dollars. In our financial condition, that was out of the question. But if we had American Hoechst's latest state-of-the-art styrene monomer Bayport plant, we could produce a billion pounds of styrene monomer each year. Bayport was the newest, most efficient, and largest single-reactor operation in the world. It would be a jewel in the crown.

Because zur Loye's German executives were eager to dump these sites, they agreed to talk. I had to make this deal work. Failure to close on those money-generating plants would mean Huntsman Chemical was dead. If we could close, we would become the largest polystyrene producer in the US. On this side of the Atlantic, zur Loye and American Hoechst's CFO, Harry Benz, were my initial contacts, but I wanted to make some inroads with the brass in Germany. My chance to do that came with a Utah Symphony engagement in Frankfurt. At the time, I was chairman of the Utah Symphony's board of directors, so I arranged to cosponsor the evening with Hoechst AG, whose top officers attended the performance. Hoechst chairman Jörgan Dormann and I jointly intro-duced the orchestra to a full house. The event proved to be a fortuitous icebreaker and solidified our partnership.

Huntsman Chemical's financial position was approaching disaster. We were on the verge of bankruptcy and here I was, consummating the largest acquisition in our history. Somehow, I had to negotiate terms by which all payments of the related debt and the up-front cash component would be postponed to some future date. The Lord had helped me before, and I needed Him again, big time. He must have been watching over me because, by July 1985, after two days of intense negotiations, I held in my hand a letter of intent from Hoechst to sell its two polystyrene plants to Huntsman Chemical for $50 million and its styrene monomer facility for $55 million.

Hoechst knew our financial resources were severely limited, so for this and other reasons Hoechst agreed to be paid in installments. For the poly-styrene plants, the first $15 million was due on October 1, 1988, an addi-tional $15 million a year after that, and the final $20 million was to be paid by October 1, 1990—all without interest, bless Hoechst's heart. For the Bayport monomer plant, Hoechst gave us until October 1, 1990, to pay them $55 million. Huntsman would pay $30 million per year to operate the facility until the debt was retired. Huntsman Chemical would provide the required raw materials, primarily benzene, ethylene, and natural gas.

Once the agreement was announced in July, I knew Huntsman Chem-ical was saved. As with earlier deals, my first concern was getting the commitment, and raising the money was secondary. Hoechst was a mo-tivated seller, but it was not in dire need of cash. Its forbearance was a godsend. No matter how the cards fell, this was a no-lose contract for Huntsman. Once again, necessity had been the mother of invention. The news that Huntsman Chemical was to become one of the largest poly-styrene producers in the United States was met with mixed reaction from competitors. One styrene producer was quoted in *Chemical Marketing Reporter* as worrying I would be a disruptive influence in a market that already lacked discipline. Another opined that Huntsman could provide a needed leadership role that actually would help other makers of the material. My hope was to do a little of both—shake up the market and provide leadership—but I had to earn my wings. Huntsman still was not perceived as a serious player when it took over Hoechst's plants. We had been in the business fewer than five years and the feeling in some quarters was we wouldn't make it to six.

That was apparently the feeling of the people at Muehlstein, one of Hoechst's chemical distributors. European petrochemical companies like Hoechst often employed distribution agents to hawk their products rather than selling direct to customers, as we did. Muehlstein was Hoechst's largest chemical distributor and, within weeks of closing our deal, we were invited to dinner with ten of its executives at New York's 21 Club. After an elegant meal, the company's brass fired up cigars. As the smoke swirled in our faces, the chairman announced Muehlstein would be moving most of its Hoechst accounts to Dow Chemical, stating that if we proved ourselves and were still around in six months it might throw us a few bones. Had that actually happened, it would have diverted about $60 million in business from the newly enlarged Huntsman Chemical Corp., bankrupting us before we got out of the starting gate.

When the condescending chairman was through pontificating, I rose from my chair, peered through the clouds of cigar smoke, and told him to do something to himself that is anatomically impossible. "We will see who wins this war," I fumed. Rasband and I turned on our heels and marched out. I don't normally use that kind of language, but I have found that summing up one's feelings in a few well-chosen words can be highly effective on select occasions.

As soon as Ron and I left those cocky executives at their smoke-enshrouded table in the 21 Club, we returned to our hotel to set up a war room. We promised each other we would not lose one account. This really would be an all-out war, and we were fired up for it. Here was a case, like so many times before and since, when the New York boys significantly underestimated the country kids from Utah. Throughout the subsequent weeks, we made the rounds to customers, camping on their doorsteps until they agreed to see us. We made each the proverbial offer-they-couldn't-refuse: if they would buy polystyrene directly from us after the closing, instead of going through the distributors, we would cut the price they had been paying Hoechst (via Muehlstein) by five cents a pound, in essence a 20 percent loyalty discount.

Dow couldn't match that price because it had investors to satisfy, and we knew it. In the end, Huntsman Chemical did not lose a single account. We fixed Muehlstein's wagon and eventually sent it into bankruptcy. In the process, we gained the industry's respect and established a reputation to be taken seriously in the future. We also proved to a skeptical chemical industry we were a tough, no-nonsense operation.

Still, closing the Hoechst deal wasn't over yet. We had hung onto Hoechst's clients, but we still had to make things official. That process ended up a white-knuckle ride that came close to falling apart at least four times before we finally closed in March 1986. Throughout the negotiations and preparations for closing, polystyrene prices continued to tumble and our financial condition became bleaker and bleaker. Before I knew it, I was back at One Shell Plaza, once again working to get Shell on board. It would prove to be one of the most difficult, and potentially disastrous, efforts yet.

When I unfolded the Hoechst deal before Shell's Peter De Leeuw in Houston, he was not pleased. "Jon," he said, "you have got to be kidding."

He knew I was in violation of Union Bank's loan covenants and he strongly recommended I focus my attention on the plants we already owned. But the Hoechst plants were such good a deal and so crucial to Huntsman's future, I argued, I couldn't afford not to purchase them. They would triple our size. Besides, I concluded, one cannot lose what one does not have. Buying large businesses exposes a company to higher risks, but whether it was a $10 million or a $100 million acquisition, the risk of becoming a victim of an industry downturn is the same. Since the market was already at rock bottom, better to position the company for the coming upturn. For me, the glass is full until it's totally empty.

Because there was so much riding on this complex transaction, I engaged Wertheim & Co., a Wall Street investment bank, to guide us around the obstacles. Its fees scared the daylights out of me, but we got more than our money's worth. Wertheim assigned Jack Cuneo, Dan Klipper, and Ted Cook to the project. They had no idea what they were getting into. Cuneo later described his experience as being lashed to the mast for seven months. Because we had no money, they recommended recapitalizing Huntsman and bringing in Chase Manhattan Bank to do it. The challenge was to come up with a transition structure that would entice Chase to grant the loan. How we managed to do that in the midst of a vicious market downturn is what separates this deal from the rest.

The book value of Hoechst's eight-year-old styrene monomer plant at Bayport was $75 million. I paid only $55 million and Hoechst didn't want to post a loss, which was one reason it was willing to wait until 1990 to collect. By then, depreciation would reduce the facility's book value to $55 million. The delay worked for Huntsman, too, but when American Hoechst's tax experts saw the agreement the deal nearly disintegrated. They said if Hoechst had a contract to sell, it would have no choice but to book the sale and post a loss. My attorney, Brent Stevenson, offered an ingenious solution. He suggested Hoechst give us an option to buy the plant at the end of 1990. That way, American Hoechst would not have to book the sale until it actually happened and Huntsman would not have to record a $55 million debt on its books.

We were a small company without much experience. Wertheim's people said I needed to persuade a big-time player to get behind us to enhance our credibility. Shell came to mind. Hoechst's styrene plant was linked by pipeline to a Shell plant, and Shell had excess ethylene, one of the materials for styrene monomer. My initial idea was to buy ethylene and benzene from Shell. Hoechst would convert the ethylene into styrene for a fixed fee, giving us styrene at close to cost. But stodgy Chase Manhattan wouldn't touch that scenario, no matter what our cost of styrene would be. Chase simply did not feel Huntsman was strong enough to survive an extended downturn in styrene prices. Historically, styrene had been a lousy business. Prices swung wildly, which was why Hoechst wanted to get out of it in the first place. But Hoechst also wanted assurance we were going to be around five years down the road when the bill came due. The last thing it wanted was to take back the plants should we default. The financing would have to be strategically structured to eliminate downside exposure to styrene price volatility.

I proposed that Shell supply the ethylene and benzene for the Bayport plant. Hoechst, which would be operating the plant for us under our agreement, would convert those raw materials into styrene and Shell would pay Huntsman 4.25 cents a pound for it. At a billion pounds a year, that would give us $12.5 million more than the $30 million I was paying Hoechst to operate the plant. That $12.5 million would be used to repay Chase Manhattan.

There was just one hitch: Shell hadn't made much money from styrene in recent years and its people were starting to wring their hands over the proposed arrangement. I was asking Shell to expand its presence in a market in which it wasn't making money. Shell was understandably nervous, but I argued there was money to be made on ethylene and benzene.

On July 25, 1985, we managed to obtain a verbal commitment from Shell to buy the styrene at 1.5 cents a pound below the low-contract price. We agreed to that in principle, but the devil is always in the details—and the machinations of the corporate lawyers. Therefore, nothing was cast in concrete at that point. Closing was a moving target, what with simultaneous negotiations with Hoechst, Chase Manhattan, and Shell; purchasing plants; recapitalizing the company; and crafting a supply agreement. Each piece of this puzzle had to fall into place at precisely the same time. Everything had to be done before anything could be done. Just when we thought we could pull the trigger, we would wake up to further deterioration in the polystyrene market and a new rut in the road.

Chase Manhattan wasn't too worried by the tentative agreement with Shell, but it added new loan requirements that, in turn, forced us to go back to Hoechst and renegotiate. The bright side was that Hoechst kept coming up with increasingly better arrangements for us. For example, when Chase said Huntsman could make no payments to Hoechst for the plants until the bank had received its money, Hoechst obligingly delayed all repayment until 1990. The bank then announced a new condition for its approval, a $40 million price tag on the two polystyrene plants—$10 million lower than agreed. Hoechst balked at that one, but we managed to compromise at $45 million. Had Hoechst walked away, it would have had to shutter its plants to staunch its losses. Therefore, it was motivated to hang in there, but there was a limit to its patience. Zur Loye said later his company came close to pulling out because of the delays. The only thing keeping the discussions going was that zur Loye continued to trust me. (I've found in business that trust and loyalty mean everything. Plus, a little personal warmth never hurts either.)

To keep Union Bank from calling in its loan and forcing Huntsman into bankruptcy, Wertheim's Ted Cook flew to Los Angeles twice to dissuade the bank from its intentions. More than once, I had to reassure Mark Buchman, who by now was an executive vice president of Union Bank, that his old Wharton colleague would not let him down.

In some ways, having no money worked to our advantage, but it meant every deal was always on the verge of collapse. At one point, Parker warned me that if we didn't find more money fast, Huntsman Chemical would be bankrupt in ninety days. I flatly told him the b-word was not in my vocabulary and that I would never declare bankruptcy. I had rejected bankruptcy before and worked through the problems, and I would do so again, and again, and again if necessary. There was a crisis every week, but I saw them as tests of my resilience. It was imperative to stay positive and display nothing but confidence— to my people; to Hoechst, Shell, and the banks; and to the guy in the bathroom mirror who looked increasingly haggard each morning. To our partners, I had to be the businessman to believe in, no matter how challenging the obstacles or how preposterous the project. Everyone loves a positive, determined CEO. The Academy should have given me an Oscar.

But the situation was a precarious house of cards. Huntsman Chemical required the three Hoechst plants in order to stay afloat since all of our previous purchases of plants were losing money. Acquisition of those lifesaving facilities hinged on Shell's participation. Without a toll-conversion agreement with Shell, Chase Manhattan would not lend us the money to buy the Hoechst plants. Shell had serious reservations about proceeding and, so far, it had given us only a verbal agreement. On November 1, Davis Richardson, president of Shell Chemical, telephoned me to hotly express his concerns about our credit situation.

"Shell knew full well we had no credit, and has known it from the start of negotiations," I reminded him.

"The transaction," shouted Richardson, "must be put on hold until I meet with the CEO of our parent company, Shell Oil."

It was the end of the line for us if Shell bailed. Three days later, Richardson called back with worse news—all aspects of the proposed transaction were under review while Shell attempted to work out a solution to the credit problem. Things were beginning to look grim.

Monday, November 11 brought what I feared would be the coup de grace. Richardson informed me that despite dozens of trips we took to Houston and months of working out the details, the deal was off. Shell had no interest in going any further.

I was upset but remained calm. I have always regarded *no* as the beginning of the conversation, in which I would have to talk faster and more persuasively.

"There is no way you can turn this down after approving it (in principle) on July twenty-fifth," I said crisply. "Our teams have worked five months to resolve the details, and your representative told Chase Manhattan this deal is properly structured. Moreover, Shell has said its option for an additional fifteen percent of Huntsman Chemical stock would be exercised for seven-point-five million."

"Jon, the debate is over," Richardson flatly replied. "The matter is settled."

I knew that I had to keep him on the phone. If he hung up, the door was closed. I restated my conviction that the deal was structured to the benefit of Shell and Huntsman. I reiterated the ethical considerations of our verbal agreement and reminded him what it would do to Huntsman Chemical if Shell reneged. I closed by asserting I would be coming to Houston to discuss the matter in person.

Richardson insisted there had been no binding agreement and that Shell didn't want to be in the styrene business. He hit close to home when he intimated that Huntsman couldn't even guarantee its own survival. To my frustration, our transaction with Great Lakes continued to drag on and, while its $54 million cash injection was maddeningly close, it was still not within our grasp. "If Huntsman fails," Richardson continued, "Shell could be stuck with $22 million in styrene with no buyer for it. I can't let that happen." He ended the conversation by saying, "I will see you in Houston next week if you want to come, but you'll just be wasting your time."

The deal could not be allowed to fail. I had nine children at home and I had accepted the LDS Church's call to serve as a stake president and preside over the Salt Lake Monument Park Stake with responsibility for some five thousand church members. I felt blessed by the calling and loved the people, but the challenge of that heavy load, the stress of the deal, and the pressures on our business were taking their toll. On top of all that, I had broken two vertebrae in Hawaii a few months earlier and had actually conducted our negotiations to this point while lying flat on the floor.

When Brent Stevenson and I arrived in Houston on Monday, November 18, neither of us was at our best. My back was killing me, Stevenson's son was critically ill, and Houston was experiencing a record-breaking cold snap. We were miserable, but we spent all of Tuesday arguing with Shell. My back pain was so excruciating that I again resorted to lying prone on the floor during our meeting with Richardson and other Shell executives. It probably didn't hurt our side that I looked half dead. We left Houston later in the week, armed with a ray of hope. We hadn't come to an agreement other than to convene again on November 25.

But on November 22, the day after Thanksgiving, the roller-coaster ride plunged me to the depths of my emotional reserves. Richardson called me at home and once again declared the deal was off and the decision was final. Karen burst into tears, but I assured her there was no way in the world Shell could do this. Richardson will just have to reverse himself, I told her. I clenched my teeth and vowed that I would not let Shell do this to me.

That's the way life is, sometimes. People say no, banks say no, large oil companies say no. They all mean it when they are saying it. That doesn't preclude the possibility they might change their minds after further persuasion. Shell and Huntsman Chemical did have an agreement—an oral agreement, to be sure, but no less binding if Shell's word was its bond. I had no choice but to hold Richardson to it.

I called him at his home the following day and curtly informed him that I would not allow Shell to destroy us after leading us on for months.

We were a small family business, after all, and I hinted that Huntsman Chemical might well sue Shell Chemical for putting us out of business and perhaps for causing us to lose our family home. I laid it on thick assuring him that he, personally, would be a defendant. To big corporate moguls, being named personally in a lawsuit is the kiss of death. (Earlier in my career, I had to do the same thing to a Dow senior vice president in a matter involving illegal kickbacks, and he capitulated immediately.) Richardson finally said he would bring Shell Oil Company's top executives together to discuss the issue with me on Monday. On Sunday, I flew to Houston and the next morning, I was walking down Houston's streets to face my fate in Richardson's office.

Strain was evident on every face in the room. Among those at the morning meeting was Jim Street, president of Shell Chemical Company, who I knew to be a straight shooter. As I shared my feelings on the strength of a verbal contract, of the importance of keeping one's word, and of the ethical price Shell might pay for obliterating my company, I realized I was weeping. Months of stress had taken their toll. I struggled to regain control.

Street listened carefully and then quietly suggested we adjourn for the moment and meet with Shell Oil's CEO Frank Richardson, Davis Richardson (no relation), and other senior Shell executives later in the day.

I walked back to my hotel a little less briskly than when I left it that morning. After a brief rest I resolved to keep my emotions in check and returned to One Shell Plaza to meet CEO Frank Richardson. He was in a difficult position. He had not been party to the most recent discussions but would be the referee in the dispute over the oral agreement. I summarized for him, in minute detail, what had transpired throughout the past six months. I did not disparage Davis Richardson to Frank because I highly respected Davis and suspected he was acting on advice from overcautious lawyers and number crunchers. I was sure they saw Huntsman Chemical on the verge of going down the drain and had strongly advised Shell's executives to pull the plug. Nevertheless, I clearly stated my case. We had an agreement and I expected Shell to honor it.

It was a matter of pure brinkmanship. Shell and I were staring down each other's loaded barrels. The threat of a lawsuit infuriated Frank Richardson. I didn't look forward to the prospect either, but he knew I would do it if it would save my company. He also knew that juries tend to side with the small businesses claiming to have been injured by a big company. I would file the suit in Utah and have the hometown advantage. It might be even worse for Shell if it were filed in Texas where, only months before, the Texas Supreme Court upheld a contested handshake agreement between Pennzoil and Texaco for billions of dollars.

We knew Shell had an internal memo acknowledging the oral agreement that we could obtain in legal discovery. We had done our homework and it gave us confidence as we negotiated the dispute. If I went under, Shell stood to lose $12 million of a guaranteed loan to Union Bank and a $7.5 million investment in Huntsman Chemical. Moreover, we owed Shell $8 to $10 million for raw materials which it would never see if we backed out.

In the end, Shell blinked. They agreed to go forth with the deal. That's all we wanted.

Like dominoes, everything would now fall into place. The final provisions gave Shell downside protection on styrene prices—$7.5 million over five years—under a complex formula based on production. Shell limited its credit exposure to $10 million, about half the value of the styrene inventory it normally would keep for us. We dropped our fee to Shell to convert ethylene and benzene into styrene. Almost to the end, Chase Manhattan continued to add demands. The bank would not let Shell off the hook for its $12 million loan guarantee to Union Bank and required Shell to guarantee $30 million of the Chase loan. Chase had a sweet deal before it was over, but I had $60 million. Wertheim's bill was $1.5 million. I sent a check for $1.8 million, insisting bonuses of $100,000 each go to Cuneo, Klipper, and Cook.

Enter Great Lakes Chemical Company, a major supplier of bromine products to Huntsman. In 1986, after lengthy negotiations, Great Lakes agreed to purchase 40 percent of Huntsman Chemical for $54 million. It took me a while to reach an agreement with Chairman and CEO Emerson Kampen, but eventually we sealed the deal with a handshake. It was disconcerting, then, that I didn't hear from Kampen or his people for what seemed like a long time after the oral agreement. About four months later, Great Lakes' lawyers called to enlist our participation in drafting the documents and we became embroiled in the deal phase, the period in which we have to satisfy the lawyers and which never ceases to frustrate me.

Corporate attorneys probably have cost the chemical industry more in lost time and asset value than any other segment of the business world. They overanalyze every phrase and generally view it as their role in life to hold up the process. Maybe it's their way of making sure the parties are serious about closing, or perhaps the idea is to drag out the hours to justify higher fees. By the time this fairly simple purchase agreement was put to paper, between handshake and final documentation, nearly seven months had elapsed. Within that time frame, the price of raw materials decreased substantially and Huntsman's margins reached all-time highs. Profits tripled during that period, and we still weren't ready to close.

Out of the blue, Kampen telephoned one day with a proposal that provided a refreshing insight into his character. He said his bankers informed him that 40 percent of Huntsman Chemical was worth $250 million as he spoke. "We shook hands on a fifty-four-million-dollar price over six months ago," he continued. "I can't commit Great Lakes to making up the full estimated value, but how about splitting the difference?" His offer represented an extra $100 million to our coffers. Because of that phone call, I always have thought of Emerson Kampen as one of the most principled people I have ever known. My answer, however, was no. It would not be right to use the appreciated value or to expect Great Lakes to split the difference. "We agreed to a price of fifty-four million and that is the price I expect you to pay," I said in a tone meant to close the discussion.

"But that's not fair to you," he countered.

"You negotiate for your company, Emerson," I said, "and I'll negotiate for mine."

My adherence to our original agreement made a lasting impression on Kampen, the degree to which I did not fully realize until his death years later. I was never personally close to Emerson, but his family members followed his instructions for funeral arrangements and invited two selected speakers: Indiana Governor Evan Bayh and me.

I could have taken advantage of the situation and allowed Great Lakes to pay the extra $100 million for its stake in Huntsman. But a basic tenet of my value system is that my word is my bond. Kampen and I eventually closed on precisely the deal to which we had originally agreed. The entire chemical industry, as well as many banks, took note. The Huntsman brand became linked with integrity. This one gesture with Great Lakes saved me hundreds of millions of dollars in acquisitions, divestitures, and deals later on. People want to see fairness and honor in one's business practices and the value of trust is immeasurable.

Within weeks of our taking possession of the Hoechst plants, the polystyrene market swung upward. In the first months after the purchase, Parker went over the plants' books five times, trying to figure out what was amiss with the accounting system. He could not believe the numbers he kept getting. *It can't be this good*, he thought. We were seeing profits we had never seen in our lives, and it only got better. The average contract price for polystyrene jumped from 32.9 cents in 1986 to 48.8 cents a pound in 1987 and 58.3 cents in 1988. Suffice it to say, the deal worked out well for all parties. We had hit a big-time home run, and just in time.

Hoechst never looked back. After selling its polystyrene and monomer plants, it acquired Celanese Corporation the following year. Shell found a long-term customer for its ethylene and benzene. David Willetts and Chase Manhattan became big names in the chemical industry. Great Lakes' public stock leaped skyward, mostly because of the Huntsman investment. We now became a major player in the industry. By 1989, we had become the nation's largest producer of polystyrene. After teetering on bankruptcy's edge in 1985, I had been named one of *Forbes* magazine's wealthiest people in America by 1988. It came about through old-line business savvy, a dash of ingenuity, guts and a great team effort.

I hasten to note that it was entirely possible the market could have gone the other way. You've heard the saying "no risk, no reward." Well, we risked everything and reaped a big reward. Consider the saying: "Some people build bridges. The rest of the people drive over them." I would add that Huntsman seems to build bridges during hurricanes. The return on the investments was in the hundreds of millions of dollars because we bought the plants for no money down. Some luck was involved, but a person has to make his or her own breaks.

Profit margins during the late 1980s and early 1990s were at record highs. We were able to purchase fifteen to twenty more plants and facilities around the world. We were off to the races—and big time. Philanthropy became a central theme with the heavy profits we were reeling in. So many great causes, but cancer was my gravest concern. We had to stop this dreaded disease at all costs.

I was keenly aware after my travels around the world for the past twenty years that charitable funds and contributions basically do not exist in Europe and most of the countries of the world. The United States is almost single in their citizen zest to build great centers of hope and inspiration through personal donations. "The state will take care of us" was always the answer that one would receive when seeking charitable donations outside of the United States. I believe it is a mindset for those living abroad. It has become a bit more commonplace today, but even the wealthiest of citizens rely on the state for charitable and noble causes that wealthy citizens of the United States make happen from their heart and personal emotions.

It was time to shift into overdrive. The idea of a major cancer research center and clinical facility became an even deeper and more determined goal. I made some mistakes along the way and on occasion got diverted. But I needed more deals and a lot more money if a world-class cancer center was ever going to happen.

8. Expanding Horizons

B Y THE LATE 1980S, OUR GROWTH STRATEGY WAS PAYING OFF HANDsomely. We had purchased troubled operations precisely at the most fortuitous time in the petrochemical industry's turbulent cycles. From their depressed levels, Huntsman Chemical's profit levels had ascended to heights never before experienced. For an entire decade, the industry had witnessed no new plant construction, no additional production, and no new supply. As a result, we were in the catbird seat as the 1980s waned. Our industry's peers were starting to take us seriously. While bargains were not plentiful after the upswing, Huntsman Chemical continued to grow, particularly in global markets. The sky was the limit.

In little more than a decade, Huntsman would become the largest privately held petrochemical company in the world and the fifth largest over all. And, if that wasn't enough, we also pulled off an historic business coup in the Soviet Union in the process.

Sometime prior to the completion of the Hoechst-Shell venture in 1986, we approached General Electric about a supply contract. GE was the largest American buyer of the type of plastic Huntsman produced. GE, unfortunately, was unreceptive and continued to purchase mostly from American Hoechst and Chevron. Finally, in January 1986, at our third annual customer seminar at Park City, Utah, GE's representative was impressed enough to make Huntsman a supplier. I approached Glen Hiner, the dynamic president of GE's plastics division, with a proposal for a joint venture to develop an unfinished GE-owned polystyrene facility in Selkirk, New York, which had been mothballed in the mid-'80s because of the sluggish economy. The financial benefit to us would be substantial, but the real prize was the prestige of being allied with General Electric. Six months later, the deal was sealed and the plant began production in February 1988. It did not go unnoticed that one of the largest corporations in America had chosen Huntsman Chemical over the big boys.

My relationship with GE Plastics led to additional joint ventures under the name of GE-Huntsman with plants at Bergen op Zoom in the Netherlands and at Bay St. Louis in Mississippi. General Electric boss Jack Welch got his start on the plastics side, having run the Pittsfield, Massachusetts plant in his early years. Jeff Immelt, GE's current CEO and chairman, also came from the plastics division. At the time of our fifty-fifty venture, Immelt was a relatively young mid-manager who sat on the GE-Huntsman board. Eventually, Huntsman sold both operations back to General Electric. Hiner and I remained close throughout our lives; later he became CEO of Owens Corning. Jon Jr. was invited to serve on his corporate board of directors. Immelt and I became trusted friends.

Another worthwhile overseas transaction occurred in the mid-1980s when Shell's Peter De Leeuw, who was always looking out for ways to assist Huntsman, called to say that one of Shell's partners was interested in building a polystyrene facility in Taiwan and that Shell hoped to license Huntsman technology for fire-retardant polystyrene to be used in manufacturing TV consoles for the Asian market. We struck a deal with Grand Pacific Petrochemical Corporation's Jeffery Koo, president of Chinatrust Investment and a principal in Grand Pacific, and in April 1988 Huntsman Pacific Chemical opened a plant in Gaoshan, Taiwan. At the ribbon-cutting ceremony, Koo and I jointly announced we would double the size of the plant immediately.

Koo was also kind enough to try to help me relieve the upper back pain that had plagued me for most of the decade. While I was in Taiwan, he arranged an appointment with an acupuncture specialist who, it turned out, was blind. Koo accompanied me to the small backroom office located in the middle of the teeming vegetable market district of Taipei. With the help of Jon Jr.'s fluent Chinese, the sightless doctor located the correct spot on my back and drove in the needles. Surprisingly, it didn't hurt. Nor did it work. At a reception that evening, Koo informed me that nine more acupuncture sessions had been arranged. With as much gravity as I could muster, I expressed deep regret that we had to leave the country the next morning.

The following day, then-Senator Jake Garn of Utah and I were to meet with Singapore's prime minister, Lee Kuan Yew. This wasn't a business trip. Elder Russell Ballard of the LDS Church had asked if I would give a pep talk to the handful of Mormon missionaries serving in the island state. He also hoped we could influence the prime minister into relaxing Singapore's stringent missionary quota which, at the time, excluded English-speaking missionaries.

We spent most of our allotted thirty minutes with him trying to find an opening to introduce the missionary issue. It was looking hopeless. As Lee started to wrap up, he changed the subject from diplomatic niceties to a concern for Singapore's small-family tradition, which at the time averaged 1.4 children per couple. He said a birth rate of 2.4 per family was required to support the nation's economy. Garn and I responded that we had sixteen children between us. Lee asked how he might steer Singapore couples in that direction. At last, our opening.

Permit more LDS missionary visas, we suggested, adding that these young men and women would teach the value of larger families, something for which Mormons are known. Lee suggested the LDS Church apply for additional visas. It did so, and they were granted.

Prime Minister Lee was a marvelous friend to Jon Jr. when he became the United States ambassador to Singapore (1991–92). From Singapore, we flew to Bangkok to discuss a forthcoming joint technology venture at Rayong, Thailand, and then on to meetings with an Indian company for a similar arrangement in Mumbai.

Back on American soil, Huntsman Chemical acquired Shell Oil's Woodbury, New Jersey polypropylene plant. We had been seeking this option for two years, trying to persuade Shell that its $60 million asking price was too steep for an outdated facility. Eventually, we agreed on $48 million after Shell threw in three hundred acres of prime industrial sites. While the Woodbury plant was indeed dated, Shell's maintenance had been impeccable and the quality of its polypropylene was legendary. To build a new plant with the latest technology would have cost us at that time between $200 million and $300 million. To buy it for a fraction of that was the best of all outcomes. Shell agreed to carry $8 million in paper, the banks financed about $36 million, and my children and I put up the remaining $4 million. (It represented the children's first financial investment in the family business.) Shortly afterward, Huntsman Chemical bought the facility from the family, generating sale proceeds of about

$30 million that we reinvested in several new packaging operations, including Goodyear Tire & Rubber in 1992.

Perhaps out of paternal interest, I continued to track the fortunes of my first corporate child, Huntsman Container, which we had sold to Keyes Fibre in the late 1970s only to watch it be swallowed whole by Arcata. In 1989, Huntsman Chemical bought back the Keyes' container manufacturing plants in England, France, and Spain for $10 million. The buyback was not solely for nostalgic reasons. We knew the plastic container business better than just about anybody, and Keyes' customers all knew us. We rolled the plants into a subsidiary called Huntsman Container Corporation International, got the operations on track, and ran it for nine years before selling it for $35 million to a subsidiary of the Finnish company Huhtamäki.

It was around this time that for the first time, I seriously debated taking Huntsman Chemical public. I didn't want to answer to stockholders or to an outside board and I definitely appreciated the independence of operating as a private company, but the time was right to at least consider an initial public offering (IPO). The nation had come out of the recession by 1984, but the petrochemical industry, typically the slowest of all industries to recover after an economic slump, didn't rebound until 1986. When the industry did come back, however, it was with gusto. Earnings in 1988 and 1989 were the highest in the industry's history. In 1988 alone, Huntsman made $400 million in profit and carried zero debt. Had Huntsman been publicly owned in such heady times, its shares would have traded robustly.

That said, petrochemicals are susceptible to downturns. We knew the industry would eventually tank again (as it did in 1991 and again in 2001). Volatility is in the nature of the beast, and an entrepreneur must read the tea leaves correctly or be prepared to lose everything. For those reasons, 1988 would have been a good time to go public if we were of the mind to do so. In the fall, I called a meeting in the boardroom of our Salt Lake headquarters to discuss the matter. I gathered the children along with their spouses and our senior staff, including lawyers and finance executives, and invited Russell Palmer, dean of the Wharton School, to join us as a consultant. We had done extensive research on IPOs and, as a possible alternative, we also had a billion dollar offer on the table from Quantum Chemical.

The discussion went back and forth for five hours. The crux of the matter for me was philanthropy. Essentially, the company had been a one-man band since its inception, giving me the freedom to direct its revenues as I saw fit. If Huntsman Chemical went public, shareholders would screech if profits went to anything but dividends. It all came down to what was most important to the Huntsman family: having more money on the bottom line or for charitable giving. The children were deferential, saying they would go with whatever I chose to do. Karen, however, was against selling or going public. I left the meeting to do a bit of soul searching. Philanthropy won the day and the family concurred with my decision.

The next time the subject of selling arose was eight years later when we received a $4.5 billion stock offer from the Hanson Group of the UK. In 1996, selling would have netted the family nearly $3 billion, which would have allowed us to establish a sizable foundation. Again, we decided the timing wasn't right. That decision turned out for the best. Hanson didn't perform well and a year later sold its business entities and its stock plummeted. We would revisit the issue a third and final time nine years later.

While the chemical industry boomed and business performed well, I found myself looking for a new challenge. In the late 1980s, I became serious about pursuing a longtime interest: newspapers. They intrigue me, even to this day when many people write them off as old-style media. I also wanted to invest some of our out-of-state earnings in a Utah enterprise. The *Deseret News*, owned and operated by the LDS Church, became a flashing beacon. Started by Brigham Young in 1850, the *Deseret News* was the first daily newspaper in the western United States. It was the smaller of Salt Lake City's two daily papers with less than half the circulation of *The Salt Lake Tribune*. In 1952, the afternoon *Deseret News* was financially strapped and sought out a cooperative business arrangement with the morning *Tribune* under a joint operating agreement (JOA). Such a federally sanctioned arrangement allows competing newspapers to skirt antimonopoly laws by sharing advertising revenue, production facilities, and distribution networks in the interest of maintaining independent editorial voices.

When I looked into buying the *News*, it had a circulation of about

55,000, which hadn't changed much over the years. (Today, it puts most of its resources into a digital edition.) Its growth problem was ownership. Church-owned newspapers historically have not enjoyed wide circulation—not even in a state like Utah where two out of three residents, at least nominally, are Mormon. If the LDS Church were inclined to divest itself of the publication, why not sell it to a Mormon of good standing who would continue to steer the paper in a direction compatible with the previous owner's interests? The move would create an independent news outlet more palatable to general readership. That also was the thinking of J. W. (Jack) Gallivan, then-publisher of the *Tribune*, who encouraged me to seek a sale agreement from the LDS Church. Under the joint operating agreement, the *Tribune* received 58 percent of the profits; so any growth by the *Deseret News* would have benefited the *Tribune*. While the church's First Presidency politely gave my proposal a hearing, it was not inclined to relinquish control of its newspaper and the matter was dropped.

My experience in the Nixon White House was not bad enough to immunize me from having a keen interest in politics. In the late 1970s, I served as the finance chairman for the Utah Republican Party and personally extinguished a $42,000 party debt. I successfully ran for national committeeman in 1976 and in 1979 was elected chairman of the Western States Republican Conference. There was talk at the time of my running for governor of Utah, but it didn't go anywhere. Nine years later, however, I decided to seek Utah's highest office and filed candidacy papers.

My political campaign ended up being the shortest in the state's history. Its brief duration notwithstanding, the experience was enough to forever quench any thirst for public office. While I never officially announced in that 1988 gubernatorial flirtation, in the four weeks between an indication of my intention to announce and pulling out I raised more than $300,000 in campaign donations (all of which I returned). The experience underscored for me how contentious the relationship between press and politicians can be.

At that time, the Republican incumbent, Norm Bangerter, and the lone Democrat, Salt Lake City Mayor Ted Wilson, were dwelling on the issues of education and taxation. These were important, to be sure, but Utah was in the grip of a recession and I felt strongly that the next governor's focus ought to be on economic development and job creation. I decided to become the candidate who would introduce those issues. GOP party bosses were less than thrilled that I was challenging the incumbent in a primary. That didn't bother me, particularly, but something else did.

The Salt Lake City NBC television affiliate decided to produce a three-part series on my candidacy and my life. During the interview for that series, any interest I might have had in politics evaporated when the reporter's questions turned to the Nixon presidency, my White House position sixteen years earlier, and the notion of a potential link to Watergate escapades. The reporter also asked questions regarding Dean Olson's scurrilous accusations, apparently having failed to note that they had been retracted.

Midway through the interview, I became disgusted and told the reporter as much. Furious that the guilt-by-association theories still lingered, I got up, threw down my microphone, pulled the plug on the camera lights, and left the room. The interview ended up being broadcast anyway, including footage of my unceremonious exit. It surprised me that the incident didn't have much of an effect on public opinion. A poll taken a week later showed my support had actually grown since the previous survey.

The TV station admitted it received anonymous material prior to the on-camera interview, and Peter Olson subsequently admitted to sending it. But that did not stop the station from taking backstage credit for my leaving the race.

My decision to withdraw was made a few days after I received phone calls from Shell Oil and Exxon, my two largest US raw material suppliers, and from other businesses crucial to Huntsman Corporation ventures. Having learned of my potential candidacy, they made it clear that if I chose to run for governor instead of keeping my eye on the business, they would pull away. They were our largest suppliers of raw materials—and I couldn't let them or my employees down. It was either politics or business. That made for an easy choice.

On April 12, with the assistance of Senator Jake Garn, Bangerter's campaign chairman (who would join Huntsman Corporation as vice chairman a few years later), I contacted the governor and asked him if he would meet with me quietly—just the two of us. An empty parking lot behind the state capitol building was chosen as the site, which has more of a cloak-and-dagger connotation than was the case. I informed Bangerter I was withdrawing from the race, requesting only that he not harbor ill will against my supporters and that I be allowed to help somehow with Utah's economic development. He agreed.

A week later, I was named Utah's first economic development ambassador. In my new quasi-official role, I urged local governments to come up with utility and industrial bonds and tax incentives to attract new businesses to their cities and counties. Over the next four months, I hit the road selling Utah. I visited nineteen major domestic firms and five foreign corporations. I also worked closely with Utah entrepreneurs to create a financial organization that would provide limited venture capital and expansion funds for existing Utah firms and new enterprises interested in moving into the state.

Bangerter and I ended up political colleagues, although he never fully forgave me for threatening him with a primary. (Evidence of that surfaced in Jon Jr.'s 2004 gubernatorial race.) Karen and I contributed $33,000 toward Bangerter's reelection in a come-from-behind victory with 40 percent of the vote. Wilson received 38 percent and Cook got most of the remaining votes. That was my last dance with politics. Henceforth, first and foremost, I would focus on business and philanthropy.

I am a lifelong Republican, the first of five inductees into the Utah GOP Hall of Fame. Former Vice President Dick Cheney has been a friend since our days in the Nixon White House. We have fly-fished together on the Snake River in Idaho. At the dedication of Huntsman Hall at the University of Pennsylvania's Wharton School in 2002, Cheney graciously told the audience, "(Jon) has to rank among the most successful and public-minded citizens any place in our nation. In every setting, public, private, and personal, I have found him to be one of the people I most admire—a man of discernment, character, and humanity. In his creative gifts, in his business success, in his great philanthropy, in his human qualities, Jon Huntsman stands in a class of his own."

Humbling words from a man a heartbeat away from the presidency, but my concern for the less fortunate occasionally turns me into a closet

Democrat. In areas of economic policy, military, and moral values, count me a card-carrying conservative. On other social issues, though, I find myself on the side of compassion, probably as a result of my youth and growing up as a have-not. I empathize with traditional Democratic philosophy on many of these issues involving the relief of human suffering and tend to be one of those bleeding heart, left-of-center softies when it comes to people in need.

Between 2000 and 2008, the Huntsman family contributed a half million dollars to candidates in federal and state elections. (This did not include Jon Jr.'s race for the governorship or the presidential nomination, but my contributions to those were minimal. Jon wanted to do it on his own.) Of the half million, about 60 percent went to Republicans and 40 percent went to Democrats. Since zeroing in on cancer, I have supported both Democrats and Republicans who include fighting this insidious disease on their agendas. This has bothered some Republicans, but I gave up worrying about partisan politics years ago. I want to keep those in Congress who will help conquer cancer.

That isn't to say I don't have political standards. I admired some of President Bill Clinton's economic policies, but I declined an opportunity to get too close. Jim Harmon, a former Wall Street business acquaintance and Clinton's appointee to the presidency of the Export-Import Bank, called in 1998 to inquire if we would host the Clintons for eight days at our Deer Valley lodge. He wanted me to invite top leaders of the LDS Church, senators from Utah and surrounding states, and other dignitaries to meet with the president in a social setting. I have always had great respect for the White House and I thought Clinton had debased it by some of his practices, including selling overnight stays in the Lincoln bedroom as though it were a Motel 6, tending toward casual attire in the Oval Office, and exhibiting the moral standards of an alley cat. After giving it serious thought, I told Harmon it would be disingenuous of me to host a social event for someone I could not endorse in good conscience.

I must admit, though, that the economic policies and monetary affairs during the Clinton administration were the best of the latter half of the twentieth century. I since have grown to admire Bill and Hillary Clinton.

While my own days as a politician were few, I had opportunities to become familiar with a number of the country's most prominent political figures, including several US presidents. Gerald Ford was among those with whom I occasionally interacted while in the White House. He was appointed vice president by Nixon when Spiro Agnew resigned and became president when Nixon left August 8, 1974. I found Ford to be consistently gracious and considerate.

I knew President Jimmy Carter, but only slightly. I was among a number of western business leaders called to Denver for his summit on how to deal with high inflation and interest rates. I couldn't get a read on him but, when former British Prime Minister Margaret Thatcher stayed at our Deer Valley home in 1996, she referred to him as the "weakest leader" she had ever met from any Western nation and said he was "ill equipped" to be president. On the other hand, I always have thought he got a bum rap when he acknowledged in a famous interview that on occasion he "lusted" in his heart. He received a raft of criticism from the righteous types. Give me a break. I think about that, too. What man doesn't on occasion? That's why I have nine kids.

Speaking of the late Mrs. Thatcher, I had a fairly good relationship with Maggie until I inadvertently hurt her feelings. I thought of her as one tough cookie until I discovered that she was as thin-skinned as the rest of us. The former prime minister had agreed to dedicate our new headquarters building while she was visiting in Utah in connection with our state's centennial celebration. Lady and Sir Denis Thatcher touched down late in the evening, accompanied by their security team. I escorted them to our spacious Deer Valley home and its one-hundred-plus acres of secure surroundings about forty miles from the airport, where they would stay through the week. I showed them to the master bedroom suite and left the Thatchers and their security people to themselves until I returned for them the following morning.

I arrived at about 9:00 a.m. to find Sir Denis roaming the long, winding driveway of our mountain home. He looked ghastly and asked for a spot of gin. I apologized, saying that I had no alcohol in my home, and asked him if anything was wrong. He confided that I had put him in the same bedroom with Margaret with whom he had not shared a bed in more than two decades. "It was dreadful," he moaned. I immediately dispatched a member of my own security staff to the liquor store in nearby Park City to purchase a case of English gin (which was consumed within the week).

Several years later, a reporter for the London *Observer* came to Utah to interview me on business matters. He noticed the plaque in our lobby acknowledging Thatcher's involvement in the building dedication and inquired about it. I told him of the public event and then "confidentially" told him about Sir Denis's ordeal, adding indelicately, "I suppose if I had to sleep with Maggie, I'd be looking for gin in the morning, too." The reporter's gales of laughter should have been a clue that my comment was not going to end up off the record. My remarks were published in *The Observer* and I felt terrible, realizing the Thatchers would read them. I should have reached out to her but didn't know quite how to approach it. I was sorry to have offended her. That was never my intent. But we remained friends through much of the Thatchers' lives.

My first meeting with Ronald Reagan was when he was governor of California. Roland Rich Woolley, with whom Reagan was close, took me to meet the governor in 1970. Without realizing I was about to leave for Washington to join the Department of Health, Education, and Welfare, Reagan visited with me about an appointment to the State Board of Regents for the California university system. My second trip to Washington in 1980, as an LDS mission president, coincided with the start of the Reagan administration. That three-year church commitment superseded several opportunities Reagan's team offered me to serve in senior positions in his new administration. However, any time I wanted access to the White House during the Reagan years, it was a done deal. There were several Nixon holdovers on Reagan's staff, making each visit somewhat of a homecoming. Reagan was a great president. I was honored to have worked on his initial campaign and am friends with many on his senior staff.

George Bush the First worked closely with me when I was White House staff secretary, initially when he held the position of Republican National Committee chairman and later when he was ambassador to the United Nations. Our relationship was not daily, but we were members of the Nixon team and liked each other. When George H. W. Bush became president, he appointed Jon Jr. as US Ambassador to Singapore and later endorsed Jon's candidacy as Utah's governor. It's tough to find much fault in someone with such flawless executive judgment. He did, after all, make the comment: "Everyone who knows Jon Huntsman is aware that he is a man of impeccable character and decency. In sum, he is the best."

I knew Bush the Younger only through his family. Jon Jr. knows him much better than I do. When George W. Bush came to Utah for the closing of the Olympic Games in 2002, he and I met formally for the first time. He told me he grew up in Midland, Texas and knew we had chemical operations there. I wasn't surprised because Huntsman Corporation was at one time the area's largest employer. I give him high marks for his handling of the war on terrorism, for his integrity, and for being a good family man, but he had his blind spots. Specifically, he didn't delegate authority to his cabinet and his administration had no economic or energy policies to speak of. Excuse me if this sounds self-serving, but the lack of an energy program during his administration cost our family's charitable causes hundreds of millions of dollars.

Then, of course, we come to Barack Obama, whom I met when he appointed Jon Jr. as ambassador to China. I applauded that appointment and Jon's acceptance of it, more in service to his country than to a Democratic president. Meeting Obama under those circumstances was impressive. I give him an A grade for public speaking, family values, and a good jump shot in pickup basketball; but his policies on most issues are difficult for me to accept.

I used to complain about US politics and dealing with the federal bureaucracy. I discontinued this practice after I had run-ins with the Soviet government. I made a bit of business history when I decided to make some investments in the USSR, after being mentored by the late oil baron Armand Hammer. It was an experience to remember, even when the Soviet Union came toppling down. But I did help accomplish one thing: getting LDS missionaries behind the Iron Curtain.

9. Tangling with the Soviets

I GREW UP IN A TIME WHEN THE FEAR OF COMMUNISM WAS INGRAINED IN most Americans. The citadel of its dogma was the Soviet Union and its epicenter was Moscow. For decades, to invoke the USSR was to conjure up cold, sinister, war-like, and atheistic images. Ronald Reagan regularly referred to Russia as the Evil Empire, but by the latter half of the 1980s Mikhail Gorbachev had introduced the notions of "perestroika" and "glasnost" as part of restructuring, reforming, and opening life in Russia. To some of us, the Soviet Bear began to represent a potential business opportunity.

As my interest in the Soviet Union deepened, I became more fascinated with the legendary Armand Hammer, chairman and founder of Occidental Oil and its subsidiary, Occidental Chemical, a Huntsman competitor. At that time, no American had the relationships or the business track record with communist countries that Hammer had. His entry into commerce with the Soviet Union and other communist countries during the Cold War was enlightened and insightful, but it put the man under considerable public and political scrutiny. Critics called Hammer soft on communism or a Soviet sympathizer. The Hoover-era FBI maintained a thick dossier on him, especially after he was found to have ferried funds from Lenin to the American Communist Party in 1921. (Armand and I later discussed his relationships with Lenin and Trotsky, how he developed trade as well as controversial relationships between Russia and the US.)

I confess to being one of those who initially raised an eyebrow at Hammer's sympathies, but by the 1980s I began to see him in a more positive light. Throughout his seventy years of doing business with Eastern Bloc nations, Hammer acted on the belief that the way to bring about peace was to keep talking, trading, and interacting with nations ostracized by other governments. During his lifetime, Hammer dealt with every Soviet leader except Stalin and Yeltsin.

When Hammer first went to Moscow to meet Lenin in the fall of 1921, the Soviet experiment was still in its infancy. After years of revolutionary conflict, the economy of the so-called superpower had collapsed. The social structure had been eliminated before a new one took its place, resulting in a devastating breakdown of Russia's manufacturing and agricultural capabilities. In the resulting chaos, its starving citizens received few if any government services. Hammer saw an opportunity to help close the yawning maw of social need. It is also true that he hoped his efforts would be rewarded with economic advantages to Occidental or its predecessor companies. His initial offer to Lenin was to help provide medical assistance, but so critical was the need for food that his offer was dismissed as irrelevant. Hammer countered with offers of food supplies. These were readily accepted, and in recognition of that humanitarian gesture, Occidental received exclusive permits to mine asbestos in the Ural Mountains.

In the late 1980s, the USSR was in the middle of another revolution. As was the case in the 1920s, the Soviet government had swiftly abandoned one economic system for another. Once again, it found itself in a financial mess. Maintaining its military might absorbed financial resources at the expense of the economy, leaving its citizenry disenfranchised and demoralized. Though most Soviets were employed, they were without food and basic necessities because there was so little in the shops to buy. For more than a decade, Gorbachev tried to wean his nation away from socialism and toward private enterprise with his so-called "socialist market economy" and "one-party pluralism." It turns out he had committed the cardinal sin of politics: he raised people's expectations higher than he could boost their living standards. Average citizens of the Soviet Union may have gained freedom of expression, but they couldn't feed their families. Life for Russian consumers was no better than it had been under the ossified Soviet Central Planning system.

I remember thinking younger generations would warm to the new system but worrying that my generation of Russians, indoctrinated on capitalism's evils since birth and programmed to rely on government safety nets, would have trouble switching gears. The country was behind the curve in terms of modern management, industrial progress, and manufacturing know-how. The Soviet-bloc countries needed an entrepreneurial shot in the arm. I wanted to play a part.

The opening came in 1988. The Marriotts called me that summer to enlist Huntsman Chemical's participation in a partnership to create modern in-flight passenger meals for Aeroflot, the Soviet national airline. Under the proposal, Marriott would provide the food and Huntsman would make the plastic trays and plates on which the food would be served, and the protective wrap to keep it uncontaminated. Aeroflot had put out the word it was looking for a catering partner to upgrade its service to Western standards. Already the sole provider of domestic air travel in the Soviet Union, Aeroflot's managers now coveted an international ranking.

It struck me as odd that Aeroflot's director general, Vladimir Nacharov, chose in-flight meals as the place to begin. It was common knowledge the airline had far greater problems to resolve. Aeroflot's planes were poorly maintained, domestic flights often were conditional on whether fuel could be procured, and its flight schedules were as laughable as its spotty compliance with international safety regulations. Soviet airports and runways were in disrepair; pilots essentially acted as their own air traffic controllers and ground crews. Be that as it may, improving food service became Nacharov's focus in mid-1988. Since the Soviet Union was unable to produce plastic packaging acceptable to Western standards for food containment, the contract was up for grabs.

Competing for the contract were Marriott (with Huntsman as its food-service products partner) and German air carrier Lufthansa (partnering with its supplier, Dester). Marriott and Lufthansa and their respective partners were intrigued by the concept of gaining a business foothold in this part of the world. The contract included exclusive rights to serve other foreign airlines landing in Moscow. Following several meetings in which Huntsman was represented in Moscow by Mike Eades (one of our packaging managers) and some outside consultants, Aeroflot chose the Marriott offer.

Fashioning a workable deal ended up being more complex than a SALT treaty. I was happy to join Marriott in the arrangement, but I soon found that I had become the primary roadblock to the negotiations.

Soviet law at the time did not permit a foreign company to own a majority interest in a Soviet joint venture. Marriott didn't mind accepting the minority position, but I flatly refused to play second fiddle and thought it was high time that law was changed.

I was not present for the negotiations, but my team briefed me by phone, which meant, of course, they also were briefing, directly or indirectly, the KGB, which had Eades and outsiders under twenty-four-hour visual and telephonic surveillance. The Soviets were tough negotiators and seemed determined to wear down our team with long meetings in hot, stuffy rooms. Nacharov had developed his own brand of persuasive tactics. He wore dark suits on most days, but once an issue became contentious he would show up in full military dress with an array of gleaming medals plastered across the breast of his jacket.

The Americans were staying in the Mezhdunarodnaya Hotel, nicknamed by Westerners the Mezh, which was built by the Soviet government at Armand Hammer's urging. It was the most modern hotel in the USSR. Even so, faxing documents to me in Salt Lake City took hours because of outdated equipment and a requirement that hotel personnel share the documents with the KGB duty officers at the hotel twenty-four hours a day. Eades knew this because one evening, as he walked the hotel corridor, the door to one room was left ajar. He could see a man wearing earphones, sitting at a desk in front of a wall of reel-to-reel tapes. He realized Eades had spotted him and began yelling in Russian. The only word Eades picked up was *nyet*—he quickly backed away and returned to his room.

Because of the language barrier, Eades engaged Russian interpreter Galena Novosad to help with translations during negotiations. Russian translators worked for the KGB and the US embassy alerted us that Galena would be reporting to KGB handlers after each session. She was a hard worker, but at the end of each day we knew she would file a report to her handlers.

On December 7, 1988, in the middle of the Aeroflot negotiations, I was watching the evening news with Karen in our Salt Lake City home when the anchorman reported that a devastating earthquake registering 6.8 on the Richter scale had rocked the Soviet Republic of Armenia. The extent of the damage was unknown, but it was clearly significant. When the death toll eventually was tallied, the number exceeded forty-five thousand. We sat riveted to the horrific images of crumbled factories and apartments, roads and railways twisted like pretzels, school buildings flattened, and people clawing through the rubble with bare hands in search of loved ones. Given the developing relationship with Aeroflot and my interest in Soviet countries, the death and destruction in Armenia was personal. I turned to Karen and said we had to do something to help.

We already had in place the Huntsman charitable foundation into which we had channeled a portion of the Huntsman business profits. Helping out in Armenia would be a good use of the foundation money—I also thought I might invite the leaders of The Church of Jesus Christ of Latter-day Saints to join in the relief effort. The only question was where these efforts would do the most good or meet the greatest need. The individual best able to answer that question was Armand Hammer, who knew more about the Soviet system than anyone else I knew and I had wanted to meet him for some time.

I telephoned Jack Crouch, a petrochemical industry acquaintance who was vice president of Occidental Chemical, to request an appointment with Hammer. It was possible, said Crouch, but Hammer had just left for Armenia with a planeload of medical supplies and wouldn't be back for a few days. That news took me completely by surprise. Hammer was already off in his private jet to a part of the world where every other American needed a special permit to enter. Hammer fascinated me for his do-it-now attitude and his well-placed connections. Our efforts would be much more effective by joining with Hammer on a project like this.

My next call was to the First Presidency of the LDS Church to arrange a meeting with the three men who ran it. At that time, their offices were across the street from our headquarters building. It seemed reasonable to suggest that the earthquake's devastation gave Mormons an unprecedented opportunity to prove their worth. If the church would step forward to lend assistance, we could show the Soviet Union and other communist republics that the LDS Church is centrally concerned about helping people and rebuilding lives. I proposed working together to arrange a shipment of medical supplies to a hospital in Yerevan, the Armenian capital, and informed them of my plan to join forces with Hammer.

First Counselor Gordon B. Hinckley, who a decade later would become the best-known leader of the LDS Church since Brigham Young, said the matter would be taken under consideration. Within forty-eight hours, Russell Nelson, a member of the Quorum of the Twelve, just below the First Presidency in the LDS hierarchical structure, called to say the church would make a $75,000 contribution, independent of whatever I did. Elder Nelson would fly to Washington to present the check to the Soviet Ambassador to the United States Yuri Dubinin. I was pleased by the church's decision to help the Armenians but disappointed it would not be working with us on a joint project. From that point forward, I decided to do whatever I could to rebuild Armenia on my own.

As soon as Hammer returned from Armenia, his administrative assistant, Rick Jacobs, called me. I told him the Huntsman family would donate as much as $1 million to earthquake relief if I could find the right organization to work through and that I would be grateful if Hammer would meet with me to share his thoughts on how best to accomplish it. Jacobs said Hammer would be pleased to see me, but cautioned that I should not count on Hammer matching my donation. He had just delivered $1 million worth of medical supplies to Yerevan.

Three weeks later, Hammer greeted Ron Rasband and me at the Los Angeles headquarters of Occidental Petroleum, a surprisingly shabby building on Wilshire Boulevard. The building was never updated or improved because Armand Hammer didn't like change. Until the day he died, his New York apartment was the same one he lived in when he graduated from Columbia Medical School in 1921. For security reasons, the elevators in his headquarters building went only as far as the ninth floor. From there, we took the stairs to Hammer's tenth-floor office suite where I was astounded to find one of the most remarkable art galleries in the world.

I was surprised to find the ninety-year-old industrialist spry and full of vitality. Hammer's eyes sparkled with life. This energetic, nattily dressed man charmed us, to say the least, and we immediately understood why he had so many friends around the world. Hammer and his lieutenants, Ray Irani and Roger Hirl, expressed interest in Huntsman Chemical, which six years earlier had existed only on paper.

For two hours, we discussed our desire to help in Armenia and our fledgling negotiations with Aeroflot. Hammer briefed us on the Armenian situation and how to do business with the Soviets. "It's not for the faint of heart, Jon," he said, regaling us with tales of his dealings with Lenin, Trotsky, Khrushchev, and Brezhnev. He cautioned me that whatever I wanted to accomplish with the Soviets would not come easily, but he suggested such efforts were important, badly needed, and ultimately would be appreciated by the Soviet people. As for the Armenian crisis, he recommended concentrating on the housing problem, which was in desperate need of a long-term solution.

Before we parted, Hammer took us on a tour of his private office. The walls were crowded with pictures and mementos from kings and presidents, and the largest, most prominently displayed item on his wall was an elegantly framed expression that read "The Golden Rule—He Who Controls the Gold Makes the Rules." He invited me to accompany him on his next trip to the Soviet Union, scheduled for August. I came away from the meeting excited and optimistic about future charitable and business dealings in the Soviet Union and wondered just how difficult it might prove to be.

Within days of that meeting, Bill Marriott and I walked up the stairs of the stately mansion that housed the Soviet embassy in Washington, DC to participate in the first of two ceremonies marking the signing of preliminary protocols among Aeroflot, Marriott Corporation, and Huntsman Chemical, which established the entity known as Huntsman-AeroMar.

In the six months of meetings with Aeroflot leading up to the protocol signing, a few government ground rules had changed. Most importantly from my perspective was legislation passed by the Supreme Soviet Council that would allow, with certain conditions, foreign investors to hold 51 percent of a Soviet business entity. Within days of its enactment, Huntsman Chemical applied to become a majority interest holder in Huntsman-AeroMar. The application was approved, making Huntsman the first foreigner to own controlling interest in a Soviet business. At one point in the negotiation process, I had almost been convinced to accept a fifty-fifty split because Huntsman Chemical would be managing and operating the packaging plant as well as importing polystyrene from our

Carrington, England plant. By staying the course I was rewarded with a controlling interest.

The cultured Soviet hosts at the embassy, Ambassador Yuri Dubinin and wife Liana, who was half Armenian, caught me off guard. Dubinin greeted me with a polite, soft-spoken demeanor, but his face lit up when he learned I was from Utah. When he discovered I was planning a sizeable contribution, he became positively effusive. Dubinin had seen examples of American generosity, he told me, but having it directed toward people in his own country deeply touched him. He put an arm around my shoulder and told me how much this meant to his family.

Standing next to Dubinin at the Soviet embassy press conference in Washington was US Ambassador to the USSR Jack Matlock, who flew from Moscow for the occasion. Among the comments given to the news media by Bill Marriott, the two ambassadors and me was my statement that "the alliance would allow the Bill Marriotts and the Jon Huntsmans of the world to share their dreams with the Soviet people." The bear-like Nacharov told the crowd, "Aeroflot Soviet Airlines carried more than 118 million passengers last year with approximately 4,000 flights on international routes. We wish to remain competitive in every way with other international carriers, including effectiveness and profitability of our in-flight food service."

During the press Q&A, an American television correspondent asked a question no doubt intended to draw attention to Aeroflot's shoddy reputation for service: "Mr. Nacharov, why do you need Marriott's food and management skills? Aren't you already feeding your international Aeroflot passengers?"

Nacharov paused, then deadpanned: "Sometimes."

We still had months of tough negotiations ahead of us before signing the final deal, but I came away from the ceremonies sensing that cooperation between the two Cold War adversaries was more attainable than ever. This new confidence strengthened my determination to help in Armenia.

Over the next few months, Hammer and I met several times, developing even greater mutual respect as we discovered similar goals and interests. When I told him I would be in Moscow in May for the final signing of the Huntsman-AeroMar agreement, he suggested we rendezvous.

When I touched down in Moscow in May 1989 with three of my children in tow, it was only my second landing in that city. The first had merely been a plane change in the early 1970s during a flight from Japan to Amsterdam. The gray, dreary atmosphere hadn't changed much, although the streets were clean, walls free of graffiti and I saw no homeless people wandering the streets. Subways were a model of efficiency and safety, yet there was a noticeable lack of color or brightness about the place. We were booked at the Mezh whose modern pyramid of glass and steel looked incongruous in the ancient city.

The Huntsman team retired to prepare for the second protocol signing, this one at the US embassy. Securing the embassy for the ceremony had required a minor miracle. Ambassador Matlock initially declined to allow the ceremony to take place there because the embassy was too small to handle it. Neither did he want the embassy to appear to sanction a private US business-Soviet government venture. After I marshaled support from the Reagan White House, Matlock capitulated. I assured him we would cater the event so the embassy would not incur any expense in our behalf. But there would be yet another hurdle before the deal was done.

Two days before the signing ceremony, in an airport conference room, a Huntsman advance party led by Mike Eades, Peter Huntsman, and David Horne met with Aeroflot director Nacharov and Soviet officials to review the pre-agreed deal and ceremony details. Lined up on the table were ten clean copies of the agreement ready for signing. Nacharov pulled out his working copy and began to underline points with which he was not satisfied. Eades stopped him and asked if he had not agreed to the final draft on his last visit. Nacharov said he had, but that he was having second thoughts. Eades looked at him incredulously. There was no way the document could be changed at this point. Even if we did agree to changes, it would take a week to make ten new copies of a one-hundred-page document in the technologically challenged Moscow. Peter and Horne managed to keep their cool, but the exasperated Eades lost his.

"Stop talking," Eades demanded of Nacharov. He ordered the translator to keep up with his words, saying he was going to keep speaking until he was finished saying what had to be said. "I have put up with your tactics for nearly a year. I have gotten precious little rest between trying to accommodate your wishes and being tormented by the KGB. It is obvious you had no intention of going through with the deal." Peter assured Nacharov that what would happen next was that Huntsman would announce at the forthcoming ceremony, with American and Soviet dignitaries and the international press taking notes, that negotiations had failed and that he, Vladimir Nacharov, was solely to blame. Several minutes passed as Peter, Eades, Horne, and Nacharov stared each other down. Nacharov stood up, pushed the documents back across the table, and said he agreed.

"To what do you agree?" Eades demanded.

"I agree to everything. You are a worthy opponent." And Nacharov came around the table and shook hands with Peter, Horne, and Eades.

Still, even that was not the only last-minute hitch. Following a major train wreck in Siberia in which scores of schoolchildren were killed, Gorbachev declared a national day of mourning on the day the signing was to take place. Aeroflot wanted to cancel the ceremony, apparently to comply with the decree. All of us, including James and Jennifer—who came with me on that trip—were scheduled to leave the country in two days, so a delay posed a huge dilemma. The problem was that the Russians could not drink alcohol on an official day of mourning, and they knew Marriott had shipped in thirty cases of expensive French champagne for the occasion. We simply eliminated the champagne, and the event was back on. The Russians polished off the champagne shortly after our departure.

The signing ceremony was held in the auditorium of the commercial annex to the embassy, a huge, ancient building complete with gargoyle downspouts and all the warmth of a bus terminal. A panel of glass was missing from one of the windows and a sheet of plywood filled the void. Fourteen rows of folding chairs were arranged on the vinyl floor. The announcement itself came off smoothly enough and, to everyone's surprise and delight, Armand Hammer arrived to join the celebration. The event received broad coverage in the Soviet news media. No doubt, Hammer's celebrity status in Russia boosted interest considerably.

For our part in the venture, I announced I would build a container plant for the Huntsman-AeroMar facility near the airport. I said we would be taking equipment from our container plant in Spain to England for upgrades, after which we would ship it to Moscow. We vowed the operation would be up and running within a year. At the conclusion of the alcohol-free festivities, Hammer invited us to join with him on his "official" rounds.

Jennifer, James, and I chased Hammer around Moscow in a string of Soviet limos. Hammer wanted to introduce me around at the government ministries, especially those I needed to know if I truly wanted to engage in serious Armenian relief efforts. That night he held a reception in his apartment in an old, elite section of Moscow. The guest list included top professionals and ministers. Hammer explained to each of them my dual purposes in the USSR, our business and relief projects, and suggested to his Soviet friends that I was taking his place as the Soviet Union's business contact and financial contributor from the West. (This was news to me.)

The next morning, Hammer had scheduled one more appointment. This time he would introduce us to Armenian Prime Minister Markaryants in a facility just outside the Kremlin walls, which served as Armenia's Second Presidential Palace. To my embarrassment, Hammer built me up as a figure larger than life. "Whatever you need done," Hammer told Markaryants, "Jon Huntsman is the man to do it." The prime minister responded that his nation's most pressing need was housing, after more than a half a million Armenians had been left without homes. Now the pressure was on me to do something significant.

Beyond my humanitarian efforts in Armenia, I hoped to expand my petrochemical empire into the Soviet Union. After a year of negotiations, I fashioned a joint venture in the Ukraine with one of the smoothest operators I have ever known: Nikolai Yankovsky, general manager of the largest petrochemical company in Ukraine and the wealthiest man in the country. The Soviet chemical industry was centered in Ukraine's Donetsk region and the city of Gorlovka—flashpoint areas of that nation as this is written. Yankovsky was a member of the Ukrainian Parliament and a close friend of Ukrainian Prime Minister Leonid Kuchma. Yankovsky had been scouting the West for a partner and the two of us hit it off from the start, although I found it a bit alarming that the guy had a half-dozen bodyguards with him at all times and told me he kept a gun by his bed.

By the end of 1990, we had located an old factory in Gorlovka that had at one time produced "heavy water" (deuterium oxide) for nuclear bombs. The government was eager to show the world that it was converting factories from wartime purposes into productive, peaceful manufacturing and the low price reflected that motivation. Conditions in the factory were deplorable. What few safety, environmental, or health standards existed were not enforced. Workers lit their cigarettes next to flammable chemicals. Equipment was falling apart. Electricity could be counted on during the day only, and even then it was sketchy. It concerned me that workers lived a frightful existence and received only one meal during their fourteen-hour shifts. Nevertheless, I was determined to build a polystyrene packaging facility that met Western standards.

The venture with Yankovsky was called Huntsman-Stirol. We brought engineers from our British plants to convert the facility. These were unstable times in the Soviet Union, to put it mildly. Materials were obtained through bartering, the chief trading commodity being vodka, the one product immune to devaluation. It took us until 1992 to get Huntsman-Stirol operating adequately. The enterprise was successful, but not wildly so. We trained locals to work at the site and were pleased as they became reliable, efficient, and sober workers.

Five years later, I sold back my half of Huntsman-Stirol to Yankovsky for a paltry $650,000. He runs it to this day. The most meaningful benefit from the Ukrainian experience was the fact that Yankovsky's government approved my request to allow our associates who were building the site, all of whom were of the LDS faith, to hold regular religious services. Later, he supported recognition of the LDS Church in the country of Ukraine, but only after I had presented his daughter with a wedding gift—a shiny, new, Western automobile with a gorgeous pink bow on top and a pink ribbon surrounding the entire car.

After making unprecedented headway in establishing operations in Soviet countries, it was disappointing when the business outlook in Russia took a turn for the worse. After the breakup of the USSR and Boris Yeltsin's decision to levy a 40 percent tax on foreign corporations retroactive to 1992, we pulled out of Russia. Huntsman-AeroMar had never turned much of a profit and I sold my 51 percent interest to Aeroflot in 1999. As corruption had replaced bureaucratic indolence, I ceased to be interested in dealing with the Russian business community.

Helping Armenia was a separate issue—one of great personal importance to me—as well as a controversial endeavor to which I will return later in this book.

My focus on the Soviet Union, later Russia, was temporary and it never had much of an impact on the company's bottom line—acquisitions (mostly in the United States and Western Europe) during the next ten years would have a far greater significance for us. We were about to enter a time of unprecedented growth, becoming the fifth largest petrochemical company in the world with more than sixteen thousand employees. They were heady times, indeed.

10. The Sun Never Sets

I N THE SUMMER OF 1992, THE FUTURE FOR HUNTSMAN CHEMICAL sparkled brightly. As a country, the US had just ended its first military excursion into the Gulf region (Desert Storm), and the Soviet Union was falling apart, but the petrochemical industry was in another down cycle and a number of blue-light specials beckoned, many of which were prime candidates for acquisition by Huntsman.

For my health, things were not as bright. Starting in the fall of 1991, I had to cope with a number of medical ailments, which I will describe in coming chapters. By June 1992 I had recovered, although emotionally I was a bit disoriented. But there was no better cure for that than by getting back to business. After six months out of the deal-making loop, I was suffering withdrawal symptoms and was itching to join the hunt. The resulting buying spree through 1996 tripled our revenues, increased the number of our plants and employees, and significantly broadened the size of our global footprint.

No particular strategy prompted this growth spurt. For an entrepreneur, the most valuable quality is the will to act on a rational impulse that supports one's business objective. With that sort of flexibility, one can hear about a deal today and jump on it tomorrow. Our primary objective since the late 1980s had been to increase revenues—from $1 billion to $5 billion within ten years. Truth be told, going from a $1 billion to a $5 billion operation is not that much of a stretch, employing tried-and-true techniques. The real leap of faith comes when going from zero revenue to $500 million when your techniques are still being improvised.

My primary motivation at this juncture was conquering cancer, not only for my family and me but for everyone. That would take money— a lot of money—which could only come through a worldwide organization. All we had to do was build it.

What follows is not something I talk about readily, as one can imagine. This may be the first time I've ever discussed corporate strategy so bluntly.

The smartest way to increase market share is through acquisitions. I have made billions buying my way into the marketplace, taking advantage of established production volume, existing infrastructure, and employees already in place.

There is always something for sale. That's never truer than during hard times. I delighted in the down cycles in my early days because I didn't have that much to lose and such times produced great bargains. On the other hand, given the current size of Huntsman today, a down cycle now means loss of revenue, which erodes profitability.

There are enormous profits to be made in the chemical industry if one is vigilant. However one must understand its peaks and valleys and be disciplined enough to jump in and out at the proper moments. There is a time and a season for everything.

Since no one can see around economic corners, working with the cycles as they occur is the only way to stay alive. Dealing contrary to the yin and yang of an industry is the route to certain failure. The narcotic effect of acquiring assets drives many CEOs to continue making deals long after the cycle has turned. I blame that on Wall Street. Doing deals is a sure way to excite investors. Given the way most mergers and acquisitions turn out, though, this clearly is not the best way to increase return on equity. For me, that is the bottom line.

Too many decision-makers do not understand the history of cycles and overcapacity; a lot of boards of directors simply go with the flow. When business is strong, they are comfortable approving mergers and acquisitions no matter what they are. They figure the good times will last forever, mistakenly believing that their company's success stems from skilled management rather than from the cyclical nature of the industry. This line of thought can go terribly wrong. To be sure, companies want additional market share but no amount of increased business will compensate for poor margins. Directors typically buy only companies that are doing well, but negotiating deals when values are at their strongest is a mistake. It only drives up prices. The key is never market-share anyway; it is always profitability.

The deeper problem is that most corporate directors don't know enough about the industry they are overseeing to accurately evaluate potential acquisitions. Most boards are weak and hardly ever consider the shareholders. Directors make names for themselves in other arenas before being named to boards for their reputations alone rather than any understanding of the business into which they are being invited. Sadly, such directors can be manipulated easily because, in many cases, their chief concerns are their director fees, retirement benefits, and the prestige of being on a corporate board. He or she typically has invested little, if anything, in the company. A director has nothing to lose by going along with anything the CEO desires. Directors ought to be wary of a CEO's merger and acquisition experiments unless he or she is fully competent in the business' operations. Conversely, directors should not assume that operational excellence guarantees a talent for acquisitions.

Often a company's shrewdest moves are the ones it doesn't make, the investments from which it walks away, or the potential deals it abandons. Passing up deals doesn't happen often enough. Merger and acquisition activity closely tracks the level of market exuberance and confidence among business executives with a disdain for cheap prices. Public companies see inflated stock prices as high-value currency, oblivious to the fact that the properties sought are equally inflated.

Sure I look for cost-saving potential when considering an acquisition, but it's not my primary focus. For me, price is more important than cost savings. Besides, "cost savings" usually translates to "job elimination."

I have engaged in three bet-the-farm acquisitions that doubled or tripled the size of the company. In none of those did we start out operating our newly acquired facilities by announcing wholesale layoffs. We never have to. We did not overpay for the businesses—therefore our backs were not up against the financial wall. We needed experienced employees to run and rebuild the businesses we bought—and because we did not intend to take away their livelihoods, the employees pitched in to make the acquisition work. Often, we were seen as a more attractive suitor because chemical-industry sellers know that cutting jobs is not part of Huntsman's basic strategy.

The strategic goal of any business is to make money. Public companies must continuously generate interest in their stock. To do that, they either have to demonstrate increased profits or promise enhanced value, such as spinning off a nonstrategic division. Often, I am baffled by what parent corporations consider nonstrategic. I have seen divisions sold that were performing well and generating a profit. How can that not be a strategic asset? If a CEO identifies a profitable area of business but declares it expendable because it is not a part of the company's strategy going forward, that is not sound strategy. This is where boards need to pay closer attention and to ask harder questions.

I am a skeptic when it comes to long-range strategic planning. I smile when young entrepreneurs talk about five-year plans. Any detailed plan covering time frames beyond the next six months is nonsense. One can't foresee the challenges and opportunities that will arise in the next twelve months, much less in the next five years. Few corporate strategic plans ever work out as expected. If anything, they make companies more bureaucratic and less opportunistic. Business is unpredictable. Indirectly related to purchases, my long-held rule of thumb is not to build a chemical plant when you can buy one at half its replacement value.

So here is my final bit of soapbox advice in the Huntsman edition of *Business Strategies for Beginners*: too many CEOs focus on how much they can make during good times instead of planning to protect the business on the downside. By all means, enjoy the good times but prepare for the bad. One should be careful that hunger for a deal doesn't cause a memory lapse in the basic economics of the industry.

In September 1991, Huntsman executives were sniffing about for acquisitions. They came up with a number of possibilities, the most interesting being the film products division of Goodyear Tire & Rubber Company of Akron, Ohio. This five-hundred-employee unit produced polyethylene films for pallet shrink-wraps, plus specialty packaging and PVC (polyvinyl chloride) films used by supermarkets around the world for meat, cheese, and produce packaging. Goodyear wanted to concentrate on its core tire business and was eager to sell its packaging operation. Film products sometimes run counter-cyclical to petrochemicals. At the time, it was in a down cycle, but it also happened to be an attractive property that fit perfectly with our strategy of being smarter than just riding out the cycles.

We entered into negotiations with Goodyear President and CEO Stan Gault, who badly wanted to unload Goodyear's packaging unit, but not to just anybody. With most big companies, it's often more a matter of who they are dealing with than the final price tag. They want a level of certainty the deal will go through and that the new owners will take care of the plants and employees. Gault and I hit it off immediately and he was comfortable that Huntsman could be relied upon in those areas. I ended up paying $105 million, half of what Goodyear originally sought. The film business became easy pickings because Goodyear did not consider it a mainstream product. Yet, the deal represented my largest purchase to date. It gave us plants in Kentucky, Georgia, Ohio, Tennessee, California, Germany, Canada, and Australia.

We also added to our portfolio the Performance Films business in Texas and United Films in Indiana. Several other smaller businesses were purchased. These properties, along with our original packaging operations purchased in the late 1980s and our historic Huntsman-AeroMar venture in Russia, were combined into a business unit called Huntsman Packaging. In all, the deals cost us approximately $250 million, but the buying spree was a textbook example of how to increase a business' value through acquisitions. Deals like these don't produce big headlines, but they generate the highest return on equity.

In the beginning, the packaging operations were barely turning a profit. Packaging wasn't a natural fit with the rest of our chemical business, but I was partial to it because it was how I got started. In 1996, son-in-law Rick Durham asked to be put in charge of the division. A gifted leader and a tireless taskmaster, he transformed a lackluster performer into a lucky charm, churning out $800 million annually. I loved mentoring him because he was teachable, eager to learn, and extremely smart. His past experience as Huntsman's CFO gave him the background to produce an efficient operation and pull off quick acquisitions.

By the turn of the millennium, Huntsman Packaging was starting to get noticed. In May 2000, Chase Capital Partners bought it for $1.065 billion. It was a good time to sell, at the tail end of a period when margins were high (and when my philanthropic projects were calling). Unfortunately for Chase Capital, such high watermarks in that business are brief. A month after we closed the deal, the deepest downturn in chemical industry history lowered the financial waterline considerably.

In our chemical divisions, as well, there were a number of acquisitions during this period. Elf Atochem of France, one of the largest chemical companies in Europe with sites throughout the world, let it be known in October 1992 that it wanted to unload an expandable polystyrene plant in Ribécourt, just north of Paris. The company had been on my shopping list for some time because, when paired with our polystyrene plant in Carrington, England, it would greatly enhance our European position. Elf Atochem sold 140 million pounds of product annually to the building insulation and packaging markets. It attracted numerous suitors, but we were the first to pounce. Pat Schwartz, senior vice president of operations for Huntsman Chemical in Europe, pursued the Ribécourt site with admirable creativity and in January 1993 we signed a letter of intent with Elf Atochem's CFO, Jacques Denis. Three months later, though, we were at an impasse on the price.

Huntsman's president, Ron Rasband, suggested moving the discussions to Salt Lake City, hoping a change of scenery might help. But after three days of financial arm wrestling, the deadlock remained. As Denis turned to leave for Paris, he said: "You may see my team again, but you won't see me. You are asking too much of us. You already have a good deal." Seven days passed with no contact and neither side blinked. On the tenth day, an Elf Atochem executive called to say the deal was back on track. By summer, Rasband and Schwartz and the negotiating team nailed down terms favorable to Huntsman.

Our next purchases, two Monsanto chemical plants, came about almost indirectly. Brent Stevenson learned that Monsanto was about to put its linear alkyl benzene (LAB) and maleic anhydride (MAn) businesses on separate auction blocks. LAB is a key ingredient in powdered and liquid detergents and household cleaners. MAn is the major component in an array of consumer products such as auto parts, bathroom fixtures, bowling balls, motor oil, mouthwash, and artificial sweeteners. (Who would have thought it possible to make mouthwash and motor oil with the same base product?) These units would fit snugly into our existing operations. We surprised Monsanto's leadership by tapping them on the shoulder and offering $180.5 million for the entire lot, including inventory but excluding accounts receivable, and Monsanto would continue to operate the plants for us. The deal closed within three months and instantly made Huntsman the world's largest maleic anhydride producer.

That purchase prompted our formation of another business unit, Huntsman Specialty Chemicals and marked our first foray into a new product line.

With the purchasing of the Eastman Chemical polypropylene plant in Longview, Texas in 1994 and a Marysville, Michigan polypropylene plant from Novacor shortly thereafter, Huntsman became North America's third largest producer of that commodity. We already had become the largest polystyrene producer. Perhaps the most interesting development of this period was the formation of a worldwide partnership with Australia's best-known and most eccentric tycoon, Kerry Packer.

In October 1992, Australia's largest petrochemical operation, Chemplex, went under. An auction of its plants had failed to produce a buyer. A South African company was attempting to negotiate a post-auction, fire-sale deal with Chemplex's parent, Consolidated Press Holdings Ltd. (CPH), owned by the Packer family, but the negotiations were not going well. We decided Chemplex would be a nice fit for Huntsman since one of the Goodyear film plants we had picked up was in Preston, Australia. I headed Down Under.

The CEO of Consolidated Press Holdings was Al Dunlap, an American and former-Marine officer who had been labeled by the Australian press as Chainsaw Al for his role in liquidating parts of Consolidated's vast empire. (Dunlap later was hired to consolidate and sell Scott Paper Co. Later still, he applied his tactics to Sunbeam Corp. and eventually paid more than $15 million to settle SEC and shareholder allegations of fraud.) But the man who sat on Consolidated's family throne was Kerry Packer, heir to a communications empire. His current interests included petrochemicals, television, magazines, and agricultural operations. Additionally, he owned half of Valassis Communications, a US company and one of the world's largest publishers of promotional materials. We began our talks in Sydney with Dunlap, who made it clear he had a letter of intent from the South Africans to buy Chemplex for $145 million (AUS).

"That's a good offer and you should go with it," I said without blinking. "You have to do what you have to do. We have to do what we have to do."

"What do you think it is worth?" asked Dunlap.

"About one-hundred-and-ten million (AUS)," I said (at the time about $70 million US). We had thoroughly crunched the numbers. "Please let us know if things fall through with the South Africans, but we would not be interested in matching their offer," I added as our team got up and headed for the door. The bombastic senior Packer burst into the room and introduced himself. He must have been listening to the conversation from an adjoining room because his first question was in perfect context. "How come you don't want to buy my business? I have read a lot about you Yanks and I like you. I don't like the South Africans. Come into my office and let's talk about it."

For the next hour, we did just that. He was all business, but then the conversation stopped as suddenly as it started. Packer told me he had to go exercise, leaving the rest of us to work out a deal. Less than an hour later, he came back and the two of us picked up where we had left off and an intense conversation ensued until we reached an impasse. I looked him in the eye and asked why we didn't become partners? "It won't work," said Packer. "I want out. I need the money for another project."

"You can have both," I countered. "You put up twenty million; we put up twenty million. You then take seventy million AUS, including debt, for half of the company and we'll split the revenues fifty-fifty." (Huntsman would have operational control.) Packer liked the sound of that, but Dunlap brought up the legal obligation to the South Africans who still had six weeks to close the deal. We agreed that if they didn't come through, Packer and Huntsman would own Chemplex.

This was an example of how flexibility, emotions, and personal relationships are key ingredients to a deal. Have the facts, should you need them, but rely on emotions to make the deal. As Rick Durham, who accompanied me on the trip, noted later, "Jon hardly knew who Kerry Packer was when he walked into his headquarters building in Sydney. Yet as soon as he met him, they developed a lasting friendship."

We flew home and nervously watched the clock. For us, the deal would mean obtaining an $80 million loan—a hurdle but doable. Entrepreneurs treat debt as a necessary evil in making money. It is not so much the size of the debt as its effect on the return on equity and operational cash flow. As long as debt does not exceed 4.5 times the annual cash flow of the property, indebtedness does not give me heartburn, much as banks tend to obsess over return on investment.

At the end of the six weeks, the South Africans had not exercised their option. Packer invited me back to close the deal, suggesting I obtain financing from WestPac, one of Australia's largest financial institutions. By February 1993, Huntsman Corporation (a new business unit formed for the purpose) was half owner of Chemplex, which employed seven hundred people at sites near Melbourne and generated $200 million in revenues annually. With management control, we changed the name from Chemplex to Huntsman Chemical Company Australia and began producing ethylene, styrene monomer, benzene, phenol, acetone, phenolic resins, polyester resins, polystyrene, and expandable polystyrene.

I told the Aussie press that ours was a partnership of two families. The beauty of the relationship was that neither one of us actually needed the other. It was an unusual relationship, to say the least. We were approximately the same age, we both had domineering fathers, both were told as youngsters that we had smarter older brothers, and we both liked deal-making on an international scale. The similarities ended there. He had inherited his fortune; I had earned mine. Packer was ruthless in negotiations; I preferred to temper hardball dealings with civility. I personally appreciated Kerry Packer, however, because he was a fun, high-rolling, larger-than-life kind of guy who did nothing in a small way. He was a character for the ages.

Together with others, Packer and I traveled the world on his audacious three-hundred-foot yacht named the *Arctic P*. We had great times and trusted one another like brothers. His only son, James, became close to my sons and sons-in-law. We opened our homes and hearts to James and Kerry, who loved staying in our Deer Valley, Utah lodge. He once told Steve Wynn, the Las Vegas hotel mogul, that our Deer Valley home was "America's best resort."

One anecdote typifies the larger-than-life persona of this tycoon: in 1999, he called to say he would be in Las Vegas and asked if I could join him. We stayed at the Mirage. I would not be playing. This night would be devoted to watching Packer, whose gambling episodes were legendary. I invited my brother Blaine to join in watching the action.

Packer didn't drink, so his gambling was conducted stone sober. By

2:00 a.m., he had won $4 million at the Mirage's blackjack table. Tired of that game, he headed for the baccarat table at the MGM Grand. He played $25,000 chips, lining up his winnings in piles of ten chips each (a quarter of a million dollars per stack). At 4:00 a.m., he had won one chip shy of an additional $2 million. Noting that his final stack contained only nine chips, he asked the three baccarat house players (dealers) whether they would like the uneven stack as a tip or would they rather see him bet the $225,000 in a single double-or-nothing wager and the result would be theirs. They said, "Go for the $450,000." He did, and lost. The three dealers were crestfallen.

Packer went back to playing baccarat while I chatted with an MGM vice president who had been overseeing this high-stakes game. He introduced himself, saying he was the head of the Sunday school at an LDS ward in Las Vegas. That didn't surprise me because about 25 percent of the gaming personnel in Las Vegas are Mormons, valued by casino owners for their trustworthiness. While we chatted, Packer racked up another $2 million in winnings—some $8 million for the night. As fate would have it, the final stack was again one chip short of ten chips. "Okay, mates," said the gregarious Aussie, "one last time, do you want this stack as a tip or would you have me bet it for the chance to double your money." They again said, "Play it." He did—and won. Each of the three house players received $150,000. We called it a night and walked back to the Mirage as the sun was coming up.

I periodically hit the casino tables, too, but small stakes compared to most in my tax bracket. While this activity may shock some people, think about it: it would be ludicrous to believe that a risk-loving entrepreneur would not be drawn to gambling. Betting is what we do. That's who we are. And I am pretty good at it. On the rare occasions when I play, it is purely for the sport of it (except in the early days when I was helping underwrite family vacations). The same holds true with the commodity futures market (oil, natural gas, grains, etc.), small speculative stocks, and other high-risk investments. (I even tried once to corner the cocoa market.) They are all a gamble, but without rolling the dice in my business dealings I never would have triumphed in the areas of philanthropy. Throughout my life, with the exception of a huge natural gas futures trade in 2001, I have broken about even on these small-risk deals. Obviously, I hit the jackpot more than a couple of times.

My relationship with Packer lasted through a second joint venture before we went our separate ways eight years later. During our partnership, Packer became an unlikely minority investor in one of my largest acquisitions: the giant Texaco Chemical Company.

On July 20, 1993, while in New York for a board meeting of Bankers Trust, I received the electrifying news that Texaco Chemical had fallen out of favor with its parent, the behemoth Texaco Oil Company. The latter wanted to unload it and the rumored sticker price was $2 billion. I made my apologies to Bankers Trust in order to have a breakfast sit-down with Ralph Cunningham, Texaco Chemical's CEO. He is a gentleman and a first-class, ethical business leader. I have always respected him. By coincidence, Cunningham was staying in the same hotel, a fact I discovered when I bumped into him in the elevator the night before. I knew him from the time we served together as Chemical Manufacturers Association directors.

Initially, Cunningham and I talked about our buying a small division of Texaco Chemical, but after some preliminary discussion, I took a deep breath and said something that surprised us both: "Why doesn't Huntsman buy Texaco Chemical?"

Cunningham didn't flinch. "That's fine with me," he responded coolly, adding he was on his way to the company's global headquarters in White Plains (New York) to see his boss, Alan Krowe, who would have to approve such a deal. Cunningham called Krowe, vice chairman and CFO of the parent Texaco, to ask about my going with him to White Plains. Krowe had been CFO at IBM and was highly regarded by Wall Street. He didn't know me but must have been curious because he told Cunningham to bring me along. If Huntsman Chemical had been a publicly owned company, I never could have moved that fast.

By evening, Krowe was hinting that Texaco would sell for $1.5 billion in cash. (If you can get the other side to put out the first number, you have an idea of how hard you will need to negotiate or if there is a lower number.) I had no idea where I would get that kind of money but would never let such a minor detail stop the negotiations. Money is always available at some cost if the deal is right.

Texaco Chemical was probably worth every penny of Krowe's proposed price, but I explained to Krowe that I could only manage $1.06 billion. I knew I was risking an impasse that might scotch the biggest transaction of my life to that point, even with Kerry Packer in the deal, but $1.06 billion was my limit. An inner voice told me the timing of this deal was perfect and that the industry would rebound within the year. That, however, did not change the fact that my borrowing line was tapped out. Krowe countered with $1.2 billion but that was *sans* working capital. I held steady at $1.06 billion, which included several million dollars in working capital. I pointed out that Texaco's chemical division had lost $30 million in 1992 and $14 million in the first half of 1993.

Negotiations grew intense. Krowe was a tough negotiator and a rough talker. I knew Texaco had phased out a number of chemical operations with the intent of concentrating on its core oil and gas business. What made this deal so important was that it represented a shift for Huntsman into new areas, producing ethylene, propylene, cyclohexane, and benzene, products that were currently used by Huntsman facilities. Huntsman was among the world's largest buyers of ethylene and propylene, products of the Texaco facilities. A one-cent-per-pound savings on propylene or styrene could mean $25 million added to our annual bottom line. Texaco Chemical was right for us and I wanted those plants during the next several weeks.

I kept at Krowe until he warmed to my $1.06 billion offer, including working capital, for his twenty global plants. I knew I had it made when he went so far as to agree that Texaco would finance $200 million of the purchase price. That detail did not come without intense negotiations. I learned early on that the selling entity, if sizable, would almost always take back "seller paper" which makes the buyer's job much easier in a leveraged buyout acquisition. All my deals were leveraged buyouts because we had no spare change. Equally important, it was a game with me to see how hard I could push before the other side threw me out of the office. Don't forget, Blackfoot, hitchhiking, Stanford Village, and bargaining for engagement rings had all taught me something about playing to win.

Having cut the deal with Krowe, I flew to Brussels to meet with Packer and Consolidated Press Holdings' managing director, Brian Powers. CPH was holding its board meeting there and I had just been appointed a director. There were only four of us: Packer and me; the illusive Sir James "Jimmy" Goldsmith, a British billionaire who was the competitive spirit among the great European financial families; and John Aspinall, noted zoologist, animal collector, and owner of London's major casinos. We would gather for our annual meeting in secret locations, occasionally out to sea on Packer's yacht. Those meetings were great fun. Alas, I am the only one of the four still alive.

Sir Jimmy Goldsmith was quite the character. He was a member of the European Parliament and had eyes so blue he could almost hypnotize you when he spoke. Like all deal makers, he nearly went broke several times in his life. In the late '90s, at one of Consolidated's James Bond-type board meetings, Goldsmith announced to the other three of us (the billionaire's club, if you will) that he had pancreatic cancer and would be dead within six months. Goldsmith owned palatial homes in multiple countries, and spent much of his time at his incredible Mexican villa, which he had built on an impressive estate that covered thousands of acres. When I saw it, I found it nothing short of unbelievable. Mexico had no inheritance laws, and he had stashed $2.5 billion in gold in a vault below his mansion. As his life neared its end, he called together at his Spanish residence his three wives, a girlfriend, and his eight children. (Goldsmith was quoted as saying, "If you marry your mistress, you create a job vacancy.")

It was rumored that he gave each of the women and his children $5 million. The rest was put into trust for fifty years so his great-grand-children would have the wherewithal to carry out a personal goal which he was not able to accomplish in his lifetime: replace the Rothchilds as the most important Jewish family in Europe. Shortly afterward, in July 1997 at his home in Spain, he paid a Spanish doctor $100,000 to inject him with a fatal dose of morphine (or so maintained those closest to him).

While Sir Jimmy Goldsmith was still alive, Packer and I had been looking for a transaction of sufficient magnitude to interest him. The Texaco purchase was just the ticket. My original intention was to split the acquisition fifty-fifty. I presented a study for his inspection that looked beyond the current down cycle. It showed that Texaco's chemical division was burdened with a number of associated costs, the purpose of which was to fortify the parent, Texaco, Inc., and which we wouldn't need to replicate. Packer seemed enthusiastic but his financial stake ended up at only 20 percent in light of Texaco's insistence that Huntsman maintain a major controlling interest. Texaco based the $200 million seller paper on the premise that Huntsman, not Packer, would own at least 80 percent of the business. I had no choice but to negotiate with Kerry, who was unhappy to say the least, but his business was media while mine was petrochemicals. I still needed to float $600 million in bonds to complete the transaction.

On February 4, 1994, I strode into the thirty-fourth floor meeting room of Bankers Trust at 280 Park Avenue in Manhattan, the last leg of a road show to raise the money. Earlier that morning, Federal Reserve Chairman Alan Greenspan cost me millions when he announced a bump in interest rates. Rather than floating the bonds at 9 percent interest, the resulting market confusion left me in the position of paying 11 percent, which translated to an additional $70 million over the life of the bonds. Other banks would have been delighted to lend me the money, but there also would have been restrictive covenants and too many rules on what management could and could not do. The bond route clearly was the way to go.

Just before the board (of which I was a member) took its vote on whether to grant me a sizable $200 million term loan plus $600 million in bonds, I was asked to step outside. The vote was affirmative and it turned out to be a positive investment for the bank; but upon my return to the meeting, Vernon Jordan, a fellow director, my seatmate, and a Bill Clinton confidant, loudly announced, "We have all approved a little walking-around money for our friend, Jon Huntsman." Boy, was that an understatement.

I accepted the higher interest rate, but I engaged in some additional bargaining that got Texaco to finance another part of the deal and grant me a few concessions. They agreed to allow Huntsman to operate the plants even before the sale closed and, because of the higher interest, if any bonds didn't sell, Bankers Trust would hold them in inventory. The sale closed later that month. That left Cunningham, an outstanding leader in the chemical community, out of a job, but he would later become vice chairman for Huntsman Corporation and Huntsman Specialty Chemicals.

Texaco's people showed first-class integrity throughout our dealings. They set up early retirement programs for corporate employees who would not be retained after ownership changed hands. They left no stone unturned in helping us identify costs that could be eliminated. Through this efficiency check prior to closure, we trimmed expenses by $28 million, increasing profitability by 40 percent the first year. We added $100 million to the bottom line the following year, again because Texaco had allowed us to begin cost saving measures months before the deal closed. That sort of pre-closing cooperation was unprecedented. Including the Port Neches acquisition, annual revenues from the newly purchased Texaco facilities eventually would exceed $2 billion.

Here we were, diving into a new business on a grand scale. We did not go into it thinking we knew more than Texaco about running the facilities. Instead, we drew from the knowledge of Texaco's middle managers. They were frustrated and hungry to teach us the business that had fallen out of favor with its previous parent. We approved the engineers' wish lists of initiatives that generated huge returns in the initial years. The deal was wildly successful and put Huntsman Corporation on the map. My son Peter cut his executive teeth on this new business and, operationally, was given free rein.

Kerry Packer and I continued as friends and business partners for several years. Huntsman Chemical entered into a joint venture with Packer's Consolidated Press Holdings in 1996 when we bought the Australian-based Pacific Dunlop Ltd., a polymers and resin maker that complemented the Chemplex operations. We also purchased Deerfield Plastics plants in Kentucky and Massachusetts, Baker Performance Chemicals in Texas, and two polystyrene plants in Illinois from Amoco Chemical. Our relationship was so close and profitable that it remains a mystery to me how this friendship eventually fell apart over a paltry $10 million.

In 2002, economic conditions were in a state of near-meltdown. Packer said he wanted out of our joint holdings before I declared bankruptcy—something he and nearly everyone else was urging me to do. (When I managed to pull the company out of the financial fire a year later to the surprise of all, he wrote to tell me that I was a "Houdini.") Packer, then terminally ill, sent his son James, who by then had been named chairman and CEO for all of Packer's businesses, to negotiate a buyout figure. I felt it was the wrong time to be doing this. Not only were our joint companies not doing well in the depressed environment, Huntsman didn't have resources to spare for a buyout and was having its own near-death experience. But James and I agreed to a $30 million settlement and he returned home with the signed papers.

Not long afterward, Kerry Packer called me from his hospital room to say we had skinned him by at least $10 million. I said $30 million was a fair price to which his son had agreed and that the settlement was legally binding. He said my negotiating with his son was like a "heavy-weight fighting a flyweight," hardly a ringing endorsement of his off-spring's business acumen. Packer was worth $6 or $7 billion at the time, and we argued for weeks over the $10 million. During one shouting match, Packer suddenly said: "Hold it. I'm having a heart attack." I didn't know what was going on, but three minutes later he was back on the line and we resumed heated negotiations.

I didn't budge on my position and Packer eventually died, ending the unfortunate incident. As it turned out, the Melbourne plant was written off shortly thereafter and several lawsuits were settled, costing Huntsman $52 million. The Packers obviously felt better about the $10 million loss, having dodged their half of that settlement figure.

James was much like a son to me for many years. I often offered to intercede whenever he would have a skirmish with the old man. We spent considerable time together in Australia and the US. Since Kerry's death, our family has never heard from James, but I still consider him part of the family and hold him in high respect.

In the early '90s, Huntsman reorganized into four companies: Huntsman Chemical (60 percent owned by the family and 40 percent by Great Lakes Chemical), Huntsman Specialty Chemicals (owned jointly by the family and 50 percent by Huntsman Chemical, which, in essence, means 80 percent of it was owned by the family), Huntsman Corporation (80 percent family and 20 percent Consolidated Press Holdings), and Huntsman Packaging (wholly owned by the family). In 1996, I reorganized again, consolidating everything under a single Huntsman Corporation banner. A few years later, we decided for legal and financial reasons to break off our international holdings from those in North America, and Huntsman International was born. Properties in Huntsman Corporation and Huntsman International all continued to carry the same distinctive Huntsman logo.

Not all acquisitions were successes, and not all came to fruition smoothly. The next few years would witness my best and worst deals ever as well as some of our company's most trying, and finest, hours. Nevertheless, we were on our way to being America's largest family-owned and operated company. We had tripled the size of the company during the first half of the 1990s. In the next seven years, the company would become 500 percent larger than it was in 1990. By the end of the century, Huntsman had sixteen thousand employees worldwide and nearly $10 billion in annual sales.

In late 1996, Texaco was informed we would not be exercising our option on the Port Neches, Texas propylene oxide/MTBE plant that was adjacent to Huntsman operations already there. Under the option arrangement, we had been managing the Port Neches facility for Texaco since its acquisition in 1994. (Having divested its chemical assets, Texaco no longer had technically qualified managers.) We determined the plant wasn't worth the roughly $800 million Texaco sought for it. The facility had the potential to turn a handsome profit, but it also had issues.

Texaco put the site on the auction block and we outbid several other suitors with a $580 million offer—our second largest financial transaction to date—but it only cost us $25 million up front. Our $580 million offer was not quite what it cost Texaco to build such a massive site. In return for a favorable ten-year supply contract for propylene oxide, the chemical giant BASF put up $75 million and Texaco carried a $65 million note (in addition to signing a ten-year supply contract for propylene oxide). I leveraged the remainder. The competing bidders may have been scared off because we had been operating the plant and had let our option lapse. But Texaco favored us as the buyer because the sale time would be shorter given that we already operated it. Texaco and Huntsman also had a history of mutual trust. We knew how to fix its problems and the Port Neches facility became a handsome profit center. In three years, this asset would play a pivotal role in the biggest transaction of my life.

Around this time, we acquired Orica, a surfactants and specialty chemicals business with plants in Melbourne and Botany, Australia. The

$100 million transaction was a perfect complement to our global expansion plans. Orica's two facilities annually produced three hundred million pounds of specialty products with end uses ranging from personal care items to textiles. We were off to a good start and I continued to scan the horizon with acquisition-focused binoculars.

At mid-decade, we began talking about diversifying our product line. Huntsman was the largest producer of polystyrene in America. In this area, size counted against us. Our enormous volume caused us financial heartburn. Not only was the polystyrene business stagnating, but we also had to run our plants at 85 percent capacity. At full throttle, the additional product would have dampened market prices. Small producers of polystyrene could operate at full capacity and at top efficiency because their extra 15 percent was not sufficient to glut the market (which had been our own position only ten years before).

We began to see smaller operations that focused on niche markets as a good balance to the three mammoth "polys"—polystyrene, polypropylene, and polyethylene—known in the trade as "commodities" which, because of volume, produced the smallest profit margins. In the past, I always looked for bargains by seeking out unprofitable operations, usually oriented toward commodity products, which their parent companies wanted to dump. Given the new direction, I saw a "blue-light special" beacon flashing over Rexene Corp., a supplier of high-grade polymers to niche markets such as medical equipment makers. Rexene had caught my eye in the past and there had been informal discussions about some kind of synergy between the two companies, but the vague overtures came to nothing.

Rexene had been purchased in 1988 for $456 million by a banking group but it soon incurred considerable debt. Cash-strapped, Rexene filed for bankruptcy and reorganized under new management and board of directors. Its stock price fluctuated between eight and twenty dollars a share without any value being added. I coveted Rexene for a number of reasons: First, it had considerable potential in the packaging and niche chemical businesses. Second, Rexene's sales in premium-grade polyethylene to specialty markets were most attractive, at 15 percent more than we commodity-grade manufacturers were getting. (Medical supply companies, for example, weren't interested in the cheapest polypropylene on the market. They needed the highest quality and didn't mind paying for it.) Third, CEO Andrew Smith and his team had announced in 1996 that Rexene would invest $300 million to modernize, including $100 million for a small, inefficient ethylene plant in Odessa, Texas that would produce a flexible polyolefin product it had invented using technology previously accessible only to Dow Chemical. Rexene would have a monopoly on this polyolefin. The last reason: my ego. I wanted to show Wall Street that Huntsman had the financial muscle and entrepreneurial moxie to buy an entire New York Stock Exchange company.

On paper, modernization of the Odessa site would increase Rexene's ethylene production by 60 percent while saving three cents a pound on production. (Those two factors represented more than $24 million to its annual bottom line.) Additionally, the site was on the Odessa Oil Pipeline so it held an impressive raw material position. The stock, however, didn't move on the announcement. Equity markets were refusing to give Rexene value for what we felt, at least from a distance, were substantial modernization plans.

In addition to the Texas facility, the Rexene subsidiary CT Films had sites in Clearfield, Utah; Chippewa Falls, Wisconsin; Dalton, Georgia; Harrington, Delaware; and Scunthorpe, England. If we acquired Rexene, we would blend those operations into existing Huntsman Film Products operations. In all, the company had nearly 1,300 employees and more than $500 million in annual sales—at least that is what it was reporting. I purchased a small percentage of Rexene stock and pushed our team to arrive at the best way to acquire the whole company. They concluded we should use a "bear hug" approach: announce our intent to Rexene's board and shareholders, make an offer, and let nature take its course with a nonhostile embrace.

On July 17, 1996, I readied a letter to CEO Smith with an unsolicited bid of $14 a share, an overall $267 million offer, plus the assumption of $175 million of debt. Rexene stock was trading for eight dollars on the open market. I made public my intentions after I first phoned Ilan Kaufthal, an investment banker with Wertheim Schroder and a member of Rexene's board, to alert him about my letter. We had a long-standing relationship and this call was more of a courtesy than to seek his advice. I reached Kaufthal on his mobile phone as he was driving home from

LEFT: *My family promoting our first plastic egg cartons at Von's Supermarket, as Huntsman Container was just getting off the ground in 1970.*

BELOW: *My family's private visit with Richard M. Nixon at Casa Pacifica, San Clemente, 1975.*

To The Jon Huntsman Family
With best wishes for all the good years
ahead — Sin
Richard Nixon
10/14/72

ABOVE: *I served as Utah's GOP National Committeeman 1976-1980. Karen and I also assisted Ronald Reagan during his 1980 campaign for president.*

BELOW: *My family at the White House, during one of many visits there with President Ronald Reagan, 1983. Jon (right) served as Reagan's staff assistant.*

To the Jon Huntsman Family
With appreciation and best wishes, Ronald Reagan

ABOVE: *James Street, President, Shell Chemical Company, and me preparing to sign the multitude of closing documents for Huntsman Chemical's first acquisition, 1983.*

RIGHT: *Riverboat Gambler statue presented to me by executives of Shell Oil Company, symbolic of my reputation in the chemical industry after closing several creative acquisitions.*

LEFT: *Jon M. Huntsman, Founder, President and CEO, Huntsman Chemical Company, 1983.*

BELOW: *Three generations of Huntsmans—my son Jon Huntsman Jr., my grandson Peter Huntsman Jr., and me—attended Pat Nixon's funeral on June 27, 1993.*

LEFT: *This photograph accompanied a feature article in* The Salt Lake Tribune *in September 1999, titled "Billionaire Puts Money Where His Morals Are."*

RIGHT: *Charles Miller Smith, ICI's Chairman and Chief Executive, and me at the closing of Huntsman's $2.7 billion acquisition of ICI businesses, the largest deal in the company's history, in London in 1999.*

ABOVE: *My son Peter and I strategizing at the media announcement in England of Huntsman's $2.7 billion acquisition of certain assets of ICI, 1999.*

BELOW: *Huntsman Corporation's public offering on the New York Stock Exchange in 2005, after 35 years under private ownership.*

ABOVE: *Groundbreaking of medical wing of Huntsman Cancer Institute, 2001. Back row, (left to right): Elder David B. Haight, Utah Governor Olene Walker, LDS Church President Gordon B. Hinckley, US Congressman James Hansen, University of Utah President Bernie Machen, US Senator Orrin G. Hatch. Foreground: Vice President Richard Cheney and me with young cancer patients (left to right) Omar Young, Allison Avery, and Carter Syphus.*

BELOW: *Jon M. Huntsman Center at the University of Utah—largest basketball arena in the Pac-12.*

ABOVE: *With sons Peter and David amid the rubble of the city of Gyumri after the Armenian earthquake, 1990.*

work. He attempted to dissuade me, saying Rexene directors didn't want a hostile takeover. He said I ought to talk to Andy Smith before going public to see if a merger could be accomplished on a friendly basis. I told him my action should not be construed as a hostile takeover attempt but that I did not trust the internal process. After I hung up, we pulled the trigger.

Smith had nursed, coddled, and invested time and money into Rexene and did not wish to see it fail or be sold. He was committed to keeping his pet project out of my hands and his board rejected my offer as being harmful to Rexene's customers and shareholders, contending that Rexene eventually would realize "a far greater financial return to shareholders than the Huntsman offer." Smith knew better, of course, and so did his board. Rexene was on the fast track to bankruptcy. It had eighteen months at best. Part of me now wishes I had let Smith have his way and watched him go down with the ship.

Sniffing an outside interest in Rexene, arbitrageur Guy Wyser-Pratte immediately bought a load of Rexene stock, slightly increasing its value. Arbitrageurs are the vultures of the investment world, circling over potential deals, buying up the stock of the weaker company and accruing value before it is sold. Two weeks later, I upped my offer to fifteen dollars a share, a 62 percent premium over the existing price of its stock. I pointed out that by using this direct route, Rexene's value would transfer straight to the stockholders. I was negotiating with Smith and his board, but I was playing to Rexene's stockholders, confident my offer would be accepted. The company's earnings were a third of what they were the year before and on a downward trend. Five days later, however, on August 5, my offer again was spurned.

I decided to back off and let the stockholders exert pressure to make the deal happen. I kept my relations with Smith cordial and cooled my heels. I announced I was no longer interested in Rexene and showed no interest over the next three months. Then, on October 29, I offered to acquire all shares of Rexene at sixteen dollars a share, along with its debt, for a total of $608 million. That represented $310 million in equity and $292 million of debt. The board unanimously accepted my offer. I erroneously assumed Rexene was ready to negotiate in good faith, had no hidden agenda, and would finalize the deal. I delivered a merger agreement to Smith on November 1. We heard nothing for four days. On November 5, Smith phoned to say our offer had been rejected because of the way we structured the transaction. Rexene simply was fishing for a higher price, even after indicating we had a deal at $16 a share.

Throughout the next week, the sides haggled. Rexene then came up with five unrealistic and outrageous demands:

1. We would pay Rexene a $100 million breakup fee if the deal didn't go through.
2. Huntsman would pay interest from thirty days after the agreement was signed until we delivered the money.
3. Rexene did not have to make formal disclosures of its assets, its legal problems, and the like.
4. Huntsman would commit to the merger even if Rexene violated all of its representations and promises.
5. Rexene would receive an unconditional letter from our bankers affirming that $310 million currently was available at the moment and would be at closing.

Not one of these conditions had been mentioned when Smith accepted my offer, nor would I accept them. Economics 101 spells out that requests like these violate all the rules of competent negotiating and business management. I had been through too many acquisitions to even consider such a totally one-sided proposal.

I went ballistic and began pulling away from the deal. Smith told the industry media his board simply wanted Huntsman to revamp the structure of its offer in order to assure Rexene stockholders full payment for their shares. Smith claimed it was me who was being difficult. This was becoming a Shakespearean tragedy.

Into this high-stakes soap opera stepped Guy Wyser-Pratte, playing both sides of the field. This time he and a second-tier investment firm, Spear, Leeds & Kellogg, headed a dissident group of Rexene shareholders in a proxy battle to remove a majority of the directors. They hoped this would give shareholders leverage to sell to the highest bidder. I had nothing to do with Wyser-Pratte and company because if the Securities and Exchange Commission linked the dissidents to Huntsman, the deal would be stopped and Huntsman may have been put under investigation. The dissidents sent me a letter seeking clarification of our position. That was the last thing I wanted. It forced me to tender a new offer or walk away. The arbitrageurs were also nervous about whether I continued to be a serious suitor of Rexene. They knew that if Huntsman dropped out there was no other interested buyer on the horizon.

On March 17, 1997, I restated my ongoing interest in acquiring Rexene for sixteen dollars a share. At the same time, Rexene shareholders found themselves at a meeting where they would be voting on board replacements. The sitting directors were not Wyser-Pratte's slate. The dissidents knew better than to engage in a costly proxy fight. If they ousted the sitting board and management with no commitment from a buyer, the company would be left rudderless and quickly end up on the shoals. The directors, several of whom already saw my offer as the way to go, stated at the meeting that they would not oppose a fully financed offer at sixteen dollars.

Kimo Esplin, Huntsman's feisty CFO who came to us from Bankers Trust, helped clarify the matter in an April 10 news release and in a subsequent letter to Smith in which he tendered a final bid. Esplin said that, while we were still interested, our offers had thrice been rejected and we did not wish to have further dealings with the current management. Esplin poured it on, noting Rexene's financial downturn that I had predicted the previous summer. Its hunt for other buyers had come up empty handed, and its financial health was deteriorating as the chemical industry was headed into difficult times.

That broadside, of course, was intended for shareholder consumption. While these sorts of quagmires seldom have decent endings, this proved to be the exception. On June 9, 1997, Smith phoned me to offer a brief window to conduct our due diligence on his company. If, after the conclusion of our investigation, we still were willing to offer sixteen dollars a share, Rexene's directors would accept and the company would be ours. We had a deal at last. On August 27, 1997, the yearlong struggle ended when the $608 million merger was formally completed. It soon became clear, however, that not every deal is a good deal.

The underlying rationale for acquiring Rexene was solid enough and remained so. It was an integrated move, save for the level of deception by its management. Far from the usual home run, this merger was barely a single. In fact, if you want to take the baseball analogy a step further, I probably got on base through an error since I ended up paying twice what I should have. The company's infrastructure was in much worse shape than imagined. Its regulatory equipment was not updated as advertised, the modernization was only half completed, and its highly publicized new product was a dog. We had been taken to the cleaners. In the fog of war, I violated my own business rules and the principles hammered into me at the Wharton School and employed over twenty-five years of successful acquisitions. If nothing else, Rexene was a costly reminder to follow time-tested rules of engagement.

In a nutshell, here's what went wrong: I did not buy Rexene at the bottom of the industry's cycle as I had with previous acquisitions. The upswing had peaked in 1995–96 and was only beginning to nose southward, not to hit bottom until 2003. Rexene's owners maintained a charade that they had grand plans for their company and wanted to keep it. The canard was intended to start a bidding war. This would be the first time on a transaction of this size that I was buying the entire company. In the past, I had acquired divisions of large parent companies. That meant there was somebody still around to go after if misrepresentations had been made. There was no liability clause with Rexene because there would be no one left to get our hands on after the purchase (as is the case when one purchases a New York Stock Exchange company in its entirety). We were only allowed two days to perform due diligence and we did not spot the red flags. Normally, we would take two weeks to a month to scrutinize the books, equipment, and facilities. In Rexene's sale, its liabilities and modernization overruns were assigned to the buyer. Rexene would not be held responsible for its plant or product problems. We found the company in worse shape than imagined and had accepted Rexene's faulty financial analysis of what it would take to modernize the site. Most of their audited numbers were inaccurate.

In all, it cost us twice what we had figured to bring the facilities up to snuff. Before the dust settled, we had spent more than a billion dollars on Rexene. It was an okay company on paper, but given its condition it was worth half that, at best. I had wanted Rexene and pushed my people to acquire it. At a meeting with our bankers in late 1997, I took full responsibility, even though privately I was disappointed in our due diligence team for not spotting the glaring problems even in the short time allotted. Rexene would have lasted less than a year on its own. It ended up causing a couple of environmental headaches for us. Live and learn.

Occasionally, after a string of victories, it is important to suffer a defeat, if only to experience the bitter taste of losing. In business, particularly a major high-fixed-cost industry like petrochemicals, one cannot afford many misses. The only way to stay on top, in the parlance of basketball, is by sinking the three-pointers. Sometimes ego, or a sense of invincibility, pushes one to do bad deals. Such was the learned lesson with Rexene. I promised myself it would never happen again—and it hasn't.

I didn't get a chance to dwell on this mistake too long. The granddaddy of all deals was still on the horizon.

Between 1997 and 1999, Huntsman sold most of its polystyrene, styrene monomer, and compounding plants. Polystyrene had been the foundation for the plastics products of the 1960s and 1970s. Nearly thirty years later, it was time to unload. We sold the global polystyrene business to NOVA Chemicals Corporation, the giant Canadian petrochemical company from which we had purchased several properties in the 1980s, for about $840 million. Huntsman probably had $300 million invested in those polystyrene operations, so we did well with the divestiture. Nearly $200 million was in the form of NOVA stock, making us the biggest shareholder of Canada's largest petrochemical company. The stock later was sold back to NOVA at a tidy profit.

Seven manufacturing facilities were covered by the sale, including Belpre, Ohio, our first petrochemical plant. We retained our large North American expandable polystyrene business and styrene and polystyrene plants in Odessa, Texas and in Australia. The compounding plants (where chemicals such as fire retardants are added to polystyrene) originally were acquired in 1985 with the Georgia Pacific purchase. Ralph Andy, who remains the best partner I have ever had, was our CEO. It was a personal fifty-fifty business. I have said it many times: I know of no Huntsman enterprise that outperformed Polycom-Huntsman. The reason: Andy's superb management and the mutual trust and respect that prevailed throughout our working relationship. Andy and I each had about $1 million invested in the business. Eventually, we sold the plants to Spartech, a publicly traded compounding company, for $135 million.

Those two sales netted Huntsman about $700 million. We used the proceeds to reduce debt and to fund modernization at Rexene. We plunked over $100 million into our charitable foundation (most of it earmarked for the Huntsman Cancer Institute). We were debt free and looking for acquisitions.

My philosophy when looking to buy a company is simple—I only want to know two things: Are there areas where efficiency can be optimized through cost cutting? And what is the worst-case scenario on the downside? We were itching for action as the century drew to a close. Boy, did we find it.

The forthcoming deal would equal all previous acquisitions combined. It would make us a world player and transform Huntsman from a traditional commodity-based manufacturer into one that embraced the successors to plastics: specialty and differentiated chemical products. Most importantly, the move would save Huntsman Corporation from what could have been a liquidation sale years downstream.

We restructured into a domestic holding company, Huntsman Corporation, with headquarters in Salt Lake City, and an international division, Huntsman International, located in Brussels and headed by Peter Huntsman. Into Huntsman International we transferred the primo propylene oxide/MTBE plant at Port Neches, Texas, acquired from Texaco in 1997. In two years, we doubled its profitability. It was now valued at around $900 million. (The purchase price was $580 million, although we pulled it off using our own brand of creative financing, which required only $25 million of Huntsman cash.) That facility would provide the equity for what turned out to be the most defining move in the company's history.

Our historic opportunity came in the form of a legendary British company, Imperial Chemical Industries (ICI). With holdings the world over, ICI was once Britain's largest company. At its zenith, it was comparable in size to America's General Electric or General Motors. ICI's industrial output figured mightily in World War II. Over the years, the company had divested a number of holdings, but its history remained fascinating and its name was recognized globally.

ICI had invented many of the industry's most widely used chemicals. In 1933, for instance, two organic chemists working for the conglomerate's research laboratory accidentally came up with polyethylene when a lab test fell apart. E. W. Fawcett and R. O. Gibson had no idea what a revolutionary substance they had created during an experiment in which tremendous pressure forced a reaction between ethylene and benzaldehyde. To them, initially, the experiment was a flop because the testing container sprang a leak and became depressurized. When the pair opened it, they discovered a white, waxy substance closely resembling plastic. Repeating the experiment, they learned that the loss of pressure was only partially due to the leak. The primary reason was that the process of polymerization had occurred, which resulted in polyethylene. From this discovery, ICI developed large-volume compressors that in 1936 made it possible to produce vast quantities of polyethylene. This historic advance revolutionized the world of plastics in consumer products.

Polyethylene played a vital role in World War II as an underwater cable coating and insulating material for military applications. Specifically, because it was thin and light weight, polyethylene met the need for lighter insulation for radar units, facilitating the first use of radar in airplanes. This enabled Allied pilots to detect German bombers in situations of poor visibility. After the war, ICI diversified and grew rapidly around the globe.

In the late 1990s, Charles Miller Smith, the former CFO of Unilever (parent of myriad major businesses including Lever Bros. in the US), became ICI's chairman. Under Miller Smith's direction, the company purchased some $10 billion worth of Unilever assets as part of its transformation to a food processing and chemical manufacturer. In the process, ICI became saddled with debilitating debt, which it was forced to restructure by selling off assets. Among the divisions on the auction block was the titanium dioxide business. (TiO2, as it is known in the chemical industry, is primarily used in the manufacture of paints and coatings.) DuPont tried to buy this division from ICI, but the Federal Trade Commission blocked the transaction on grounds of monopolistic holdings and restraint of trade.

Initially, we were looking at ICI's petrochemical division, its polyethylene and polypropylene sites, and its aromatic products. At the heart of ICI's chemical operations were the crown jewels: urethane plants that made plastic products to replace wood and steel in construction (along with hundreds of other uses), and the above-mentioned TiO2 business.

The former was not on the table, but because of the scuttled deal with DuPont, the latter was. Our appetite was whetted. The commodity petro-chemical sites were scheduled for auction. Following due diligence, Huntsman chose to put in a low-ball bid. In the end, ICI did not accept the bid, but in January 1999 we were back at the table.

Peter Huntsman and Kimo Esplin were the point people for us; Rob Margetts, ICI's vice chairman, represented the Brits. At first, I was leery. The petrochemical plants on the block were in horrible shape and nearly worthless as they currently stood. They were in such disrepair that I didn't want to affix our company name to them. More than two thou-sand tons of trash and used equipment needed to be taken from one of the sites. Moreover, the aromatics division was losing money. Even more troubling, the ICI assets under discussion didn't entirely fit our vision for the company's future.

What was attractive, however, was the thought of purchasing the more profitable polyurethane and titanium dioxide divisions. These represented the future of petrochemicals—and also happened to be the bread and but-ter of ICI's remaining chemical business. I knew we could land the titanium dioxide division and, as the deal progressed, I became increasingly confi-dent we could snare both. The aromatics and petrochemicals operations were ICI's worst performers and the company wanted to unload them in the worst way. It became clear to Miller Smith, however, that we would require more than what was on the table if this deal was to be consum-mated. ICI's jewels would have to be in play. ICI said if we took the money-losers, we could purchase the titanium dioxide division. I said we also desired the polyurethane group. That, too, was possible, came the reply. What started out as an unattractive deal was becoming irresistible.

On the plane ride to London, Peter, Kimo, and I worked out an ac-quisition proposal to present to ICI Vice Chairman Margetts and his team. It was so detailed they must have thought we had worked on it for months. ICI bought in. In fact, the ultimate transaction varied little from the plan devised in just a few hours on the plane. (Historically, our pro-posals are always simple and concise—with a few notable exceptions, such as the Shell-ARCO deal.)

We knew this deal would cost billions, but the tough part was estab-lishing its structure and the exact price. To settle that, Miller Smith and

I personally negotiated for forty-two days. We looked forward to the encounters, each representing something of a legend to the other. Miller Smith needed a smart, fair-value deal to pay down ICI's debt. His stockholders would accept nothing less. He was in the equity market and I was in the debt market. I had to have a bankable deal. If the final price was too high or required too much Huntsman equity, I would not be able to finance it. Yet, we were being driven on by one of our standard rules: if the deal is right, it will get financed. And this deal was turning out to be right.

The camaraderie we built during those long negotiations was nothing short of remarkable. Its depth was unique in my business career. Our friendship—and Miller Smith concurs—was born of mutual respect and the reciprocal recognition that each of us was taking an enormous risk. The experience was mesmerizing.

We allowed no lawyers or aides into our discussions. They waited in an adjoining room. When we finished negotiating a section of the deal, we took it to the legal eagles but we did not permit them to alter the oral agreements we had reached. Peter led our teams in the areas of due diligence, operational opportunities, and management. Miller Smith had impeccable integrity and we became close as the deal proceeded. Neither of us ever considered doing something that would not benefit the other side as well as our own team's interests.

Tragically, Miller Smith was carrying an added burden. His wife, Dorothy, was in the final stages of terminal breast cancer. With the deal close to completion, this marvelous and gracious lady passed away. We suspended talks because he was devastated, emotionally drained, and, understandably, in no position to tackle the final details. There was probably another $300 million on the table I could have squeezed out of ICI, but I let it drop and declared the negotiations closed. We had a square deal, a B+ agreement for each side. A good deal is when both sides feel that they did well and sometimes B+ is good enough.

Huntsman bought 60 percent of the 4 divisions and ICI retained 30 percent. Three banks held the remaining 10 percent. We had to purchase the final pieces by 2003 for $450 million. ICI got the equity market off its back and it cleaned up its chemical portfolio. With the announcement of the sale, ICI shares climbed 23 points. Huntsman doubled in size, acquiring cutting-edge specialty chemical plants around the world and $600 million in additional annual profits. That acquisition cemented our image as a global player. Total cost to Huntsman when all was said and done: $2.7 billion.

I do not know why, but when the deal was announced on April 15, 1999, the British press made much of the fact that I was a Mormon. "Mormons to the Rescue," proclaimed one headline. Another story talked about the "Mormon billionaire" and his "missionary zeal." Stories also hinted at anxiety over job losses and that we might begin massive layoffs. With few exceptions, it was an unfounded fear. In fact, the acquisition safeguarded most jobs. The sale was portrayed in the press as a lifesaver for ICI. Miller Smith received kudos for pulling "a big, fluffy rabbit out of the hat" with the sale of the venerable company's castoffs. I was pleased he got his due, but we did pretty well ourselves. (Charles Miller Smith remains a trusted friend today. Several years after Dorothy's passing, I was deeply honored to be invited to serve as best man when he remarried. And Margetts was named a member of Huntsman Corporation's board of directors).

The price tag for our 60 percent share was nearly $1.8 billion. We also had an option to purchase ICI's $800 million acrylics business but decided against it. Huntsman put up its equity in the Texas propylene oxide plant, which amounted to a steep increase over our $580 million purchase price to $900 million. We leveraged the rest with the 3 banks, which retained a 10 percent share. For this, we had controlling ownership in a company with $3.1 billion in annual sales. In effect, we acquired it with less than 1 percent equity—the $25 million out of pocket we paid for the Port Neches plant that was now worth $900 million. Talk about leveraging. This financing structure was the envy of every private equity or banking firm in the country. Huntsman secured its incredible future with virtually no money down. (It is deals like that which earned us the "Most Creative Financier" award from Bankers Trust.)

The irony of this deal was that, not long before our acquisition of ICI, a British company purchased Kennecott, Utah's largest copper mine and smelter operation, and Scottish Power acquired Utah Power & Light. I had a little fun with the news media on that when I told them, "We, as a

Utah company, are returning the favor by acquiring one of the UK's largest companies." And Miller Smith became chairman of Scottish Power.

With the ICI acquisition, Huntsman assumed outright ownership of ICI's joint venture position in thirty-three plants in the United Kingdom, Colombia, Argentina, France, Thailand, Germany, Belgium, Poland, Spain, Pakistan, Mexico, Canada, India, the Netherlands, Brazil, Italy, Korea, China, Taiwan, Malaysia, South Africa, and the United States (with sites in New Jersey, Louisiana, and Michigan). By 2001, Huntsman had a major presence in forty-three countries. While the corporate flag remained firmly planted in Salt Lake City, we had regional headquarters in London, Brussels, Singapore, Melbourne, and Houston. Peter headed the Brussels office; Jon Jr. went to Singapore to build our Asian business. What was once said of the British Empire could nearly be said of us: the sun never sets on the Huntsman domain.

The number of Huntsman employees had more than doubled, to around sixteen thousand. We increased annual product output to twenty-eight billion pounds from less than nine billion. Revenues doubled. The acquisition enhanced our knowledge of the international business, switching our geographic balance from the US to the world and our focus from commodity plastics to specialty and differentiated chemicals. Besides the basic ethylene and propylene, Huntsman products now included butadiene, performance chemicals, surfactants, maleic anhydride, propylene oxide, performance polymers, polyethylene, polypropylene, polyurethane, paraxylene, titanium dioxide, and aromatics. Nobody reading this is without some household, automotive, or recreational goods made from these products.

For the first time, we were in the research business. While specialty chemicals allow margins of 25 to 35 percent—one is lucky to net 8 to 12 percent from the commodity chemicals—one third of the specialty chemicals product line becomes outdated annually. The amount of R & D that goes into specialty chemicals is staggering, and we were new to it.

We kept most of ICI's plant management. That meant two-thirds of Huntsman managers had not been weaned on the Huntsman culture. Nonetheless, in short order the ICI holdings were making money. It was our fastest turnaround ever. Trade journals noted we were getting a return on equity more than double the prevailing industry levels.

Huntsman Corporation went after three other significant acquisitions during this period. In a move to secure a position as a world leader in polyurethane products, we purchased two manufacturing sites—one in Germany and the other in Illinois—from Rohm and Haas Co. of Philadelphia on September 1, 2000, for $120 million. Six months later, we purchased the European surfactant operations of Albright & Wilson for $200 million, adding some one thousand employees and eight manufacturing and R & D facilities in England, France, Germany, and Spain.

What would become our final acquisition as a family-owned company occurred late in 2002. It was made possible with the backing of a new financial partner, MatlinPatterson Global Assets, a venture capital firm that had invested heavily in Huntsman after we experienced the financial crisis in 2001 (the excruciating details of which are in a subsequent chapter). Vantico, a Swiss-based business, was in epoxy resins, another new product line for us. We were only one of three companies in the world making this hard-coat advanced material.

What we did not fully appreciate at the time, however, was that without the product diversification and manufacturing volume afforded us directly and indirectly by the ICI acquisition, Huntsman Corporation would have sailed over the financial precipice. The start of the twenty-first century also marked the fifth year of an industrial down cycle. What I didn't expect was that the downturn did not bottom out for another two years—an industrial drought of unprecedented duration. High energy prices, combined with OPEC's monopolistic practices, were about to bring down many businesses around the world that relied on energy for their output, including airlines, fuels, agriculture, and transportation.

Huntsman was in trouble—again—but this time it was deeper than any time in its history. Things got so desperate at one point that my staff and many of the family urged bankruptcy. Karen and I responded that this company does not go into bankruptcy. Safeguarding that principle would prove a gut-wrenching experience to say the least, and that story is still to come. But before I do, it seems important to address a subject that is never far from discussions of the chemical industry: the environment.

11. Environmental Issues

THE ENVIRONMENTAL DILEMMA ALWAYS HANGS AROUND THE NECK OF chemical industry. Needless to say, I have strong thoughts about environmental issues—but it is a debate filled with contradictions. Whenever committed conservationists take to the mountains and valleys, oceans and lakes, rivers and streams, forests and deserts, parks and wildernesses, they are carrying gear made from petrochemical products. The four-wheel-drive SUVs in which they often transport themselves to outdoor recreation sites wouldn't exist without plastics and their derivatives.

When many of these same environmentalists—not to mention a good chunk of the news media and general public—think of chemicals, they see life-altering pollution and carcinogens. For instance, they don't think of Gore-Tex, the material that breathes and is widely used in sports clothing. Gore-Tex, named for a DuPont chemist, is derived from Teflon, which, in turn, comes from nylon derived from petrochemicals. Thousands of other products share these fundamental characteristics.

It's a love/hate relationship. People like the end products—and they like them to be reasonably priced. They can't seem to get along without them. At the same time, many are suspicious of chemicals as raw materials. The manufacturing of chemical byproducts is something no one wants in their backyard. The chemical industry is to blame for part of that fear and loathing. We have often taken our lumps rather than promote the responsible behavior and environmentally sound practices adopted by a majority of our members. In fact, most of us go above and beyond what is required. We do not, as some believe, cavalierly spew pollution into the environment. Chemical producers in the US provide vast and essential products in a clean, responsible fashion, and lead the planet in this regard.

To underscore the type of stereotyping attached to chemical manufacturing, one need only look at the fabrics from which clothing is made.

It may surprise you to learn that polyester clothes are environmentally sounder than those from natural materials. The Sustainable Apparel Coalition released its newly created Higg Index in 2012 to measure the environmental impact of clothing manufacturing. It showed that fabrics made of polypropylene and polyester are more environmentally friendly than those made of wool, cotton, leather, silk, and bamboo rayon fabrics when considering such factors as the use of land and water, carcinogens produced, and lower toxic chemicals found in artificial fabrics.

That said, by its very nature, chemical manufacturing is a dirty business. We deal with hazardous toxic products, sometimes made even more so by misuse. There have been notable problems in the past, blunders where chemical companies deserved the black eyes they received. Huntsman and other reputable chemical companies are not indifferent to the environment, or to our employees' health, or to the people in the communities where we have plants.

Huntsman's record is not perfect. No petrochemical company's is. It is impossible to operate a plant today without incurring violations and fines. These are a fact of life, and it isn't because regulations are unreasonable. They aren't. Nor is it because we don't care about the environment. We do. (My son Peter, CEO of the Huntsman operations, has long supported Sierra Club causes. At Peter's urging, for example, our company began producing chemical supplies for UV-reflective paints, insulation foams, and windmill blades—each a "green" end product.)

Occasional violations occur due to the nature of the work. Petrochemical companies handle billions of pounds of chemicals a year under enormous pressures and at extreme temperatures. Chemicals are not only toxic; they often are volatile and flammable. If handled badly, they can cause considerable damage and loss of life.

A fair-size chemical plant will have thousands of valves and pumps and tens of thousands of fittings. In each plant, there are more than one hundred thousand components with the potential of being a leak site. Each of those sites has one hundred possibilities of something going wrong. Surprisingly, leaks are rare, but the potential is there nonetheless. These components are checked monthly, quarterly, or annually, depending on their usage and hazard level. Monitoring equipment measures leaks as minute as one part per million. Any leak registering five parts per million or greater is tagged for repair. A "leak" is not a violation, incidentally, but each leak is recorded and state inspectors note the action taken.

Some violations are unavoidable. A plant can violate an environmental regulation when it is off its specifications for thirty seconds. Sending feedstock or product to a flare to prevent an explosion also can violate regulations. Complex petrochemical manufacturing plants cannot run 24/7 without a hitch and there is no sense pretending they do. Reputable chemical companies, however, do not willfully violate environmental standards. Further, we take responsibility for the times we are not in compliance.

The regulations themselves are stunningly complex; lawyers can differ on interpretations. They are constantly changing and with each change comes another set of interpretations. As complicated as they are, the majority of environmental regulations are neither unfair nor harsh. They are strict, and they need to be. The Clean Air and Clean Water acts produced a sharp drop in harmful emissions. They improved the quality of life for Americans. How can anyone oppose that?

What can be opposed, however, is layer upon layer of regulatory minutia. There is a line that should not be crossed when it comes to regulation complexity, but this country and Western Europe seem to have crossed it. As a result, while several are on the drawing boards, prompted by low natural gas costs, only one new chemical plant is being built in the US; none are being erected in Europe. China, by contrast, has fifty plants under construction. America is steadily becoming an importing nation.

There are times when the volume of "pollution" seeping into the air from chemical plants appears to be enormous. What is visible to the public eye may seem ominous, but it's normally harmless steam. Even with hazardous emissions, perspective is needed. Our Port Neches plants, for example, annually release into the environment a total of nearly ninety-four thousand pounds of butadiene, a raw material for rubber and a suspected carcinogen. It actually represents .001 percent of the plants' production and is within prescribed government limits.

Since 1987, the emission of butadiene has been reduced more than 90 percent, and it took an impressive feat of engineering to do it. In the year 2000, however, the Port Neches plant recorded a major "upset," the industry's term for an accidental emission. More than 40,000 pounds of butadiene escaped into the air when a release valve on the top of a tower reacted to keep the tower from exploding. The butadiene rose to sufficient levels that our fence-monitoring system, which measures down to 1 part per billion, alerted us 3 days later. Nevertheless, we reported the release and became even more vigilant because of it.

Unbeknown to us, the Port Neches plant was under investigation by the EPA when we bought it from Texaco in the mid-1990s. A number of mishaps had taken place on Texaco's watch, and two executives were charged with falsifying environmental reports. After an appeal, the two managers, who were dismissed from the company, pleaded guilty to misdemeanors. There have been no serious environmental problems since Huntsman took over. (Moreover the two individuals' cases were later reversed on appeal.)

Besides the monitoring system, we have installed air-assisted and steam-assisted flares to prevent smoking and to reduce particles. We bought thermal oxidizers to burn vapors more efficiently and new burners to reduce nitrogen-oxide emissions. We invest in technology for better wastewater treatment. Technology offers better monitoring. We can now measure toxic substances as small as one part per trillion, but flaws in the system will continue to pop up.

Our gains on this battle at this point are small and incremental. Here is an example: The chemical used to clean the kettles at one of our plants is a hazardous waste. Our engineers realized that if the products made in those kettles were staggered in a certain order, the kettles would not have to be cleaned after each batch. They also started reusing the chemical. Both changes led to the plant's generating less hazardous waste. We see the goal of reducing waste both as a social responsibility and as a way to save money. Projects designed to reduce emissions often yield unexpected savings. It doesn't take a chemist to figure this out: most emissions are petrochemicals that we could have sold.

All of this led to a unique experiment at the turn of the century. Peter invited the Natural Resources Defense Council (NRDC), the environmental group that signed on to the Higg Index, to help us at the Port Neches plant, our oldest and most troublesome site. NRDC would work with our engineers and make suggestions. We would join in a cooperative effort with an environmental group, one that had been highly critical of the industry in the past. While it was an unusual project, the experiment was semi-successful. It changed the equation for us. Historically, most emissions reductions were achieved by stricter regulations. In this case, it was our company that took the initiative.

Under the arrangement, NRDC hired its own engineer, Charles Czarnecki, to work with us to develop projects to reduce emissions further. Czarnecki came up with several proposals, including this one: at one propylene oxide plant, we annually generated 42 million pounds of spent catalyst, a chemical that triggers the reaction to create the end product. That works out to three railroad tank cars a day. The spent catalyst is a hazardous waste and disposing of it was costing us $3.5 million a year. That's on top of the $7 million expended to buy the catalyst. Czarnecki discovered a way to recover about 30 percent of the spent catalyst, a $3 million annual savings. He also developed other breakthroughs. One permitted recovery of 20,000 pounds of butadiene that we burned in the boilers. Another reduced benzene emissions at our aromatics and olefins plant. Yet another decreased chlorine emissions from our wastewater treatment plant. These suggestions were creative and most entailed only slight changes to manufacturing.

While Czarnecki praised Huntsman's commitment to the project and our cooperation with company engineers, the National Resources Defense Council did not find what it thought it would. Maybe it wanted to see firsthand more polluting practices than it was finding. Feeling it was getting nowhere, NRDC pulled out. Nevertheless, it was a positive experience, and we would like to see industry, regulators, and environmental groups continue the cause of reducing admissions in a less adversarial way. Peter is working on this. It is a high priority for us and hopefully for the industry at large.

I respect the NRDC. Its scientists know and understand the issues. However, that has not always been the case. Too often, a twenty-member, spur-of-the-moment environmental group makes public accusations that end up in headlines. Media people are not scientists. Separating fact from fiction, and recognizing the difference between hard evidence and emotionally charged misinformation, is not easy and the truth sometimes ends up on the cutting-room floor.

The chemical industry certainly shares responsibility for its image. Petrochemical plants were once among the world's worst polluters. One cannot forget the images from Bhopal, India (which, incidentally, was caused by sabotage by a fired employee). The industry has opposed stricter environmental regulations. Who wants to spend hundreds of millions of dollars on equipment that won't increase profits? Yet that's precisely why government regulations need to exist.

The chemical industry also tarnishes its image when it spends more time fighting stricter regulations than it does finding ways to meet them. In the past, industry trade groups have engaged in disinformation—or, at the very least, statistical sophistry. All it does is frustrate engineers and hurt the industry's image. We need to move beyond a defensive response to every new regulation with counter-facts and incomprehensible statistics. Regulations are going to get stricter and we must work harder to reduce emissions.

Conversely, critics ought to be more open-minded. I respect the passion of environmental activists. I have the same compassion for humanitarian commitments. Environmentalists are working for what they believe in, but they, too, can be selective in their information. Oversimplifying complex issues helps build support, as do scare tactics. But if complex issues are reduced to a polarized debate of conflicting assertions, solutions become secondary. Few issues are black and white. More often, the truth is in the objective details. The public needs empirical, emotionless facts to sort out environmental problems. Most news stories simply pass on accusations followed by responses. I understand the media's role in reporting events and statements, but haphazardly giving credence to anything uttered only spreads misinformation. Complicated issues cannot be explained adequately in a headline or a sound bite.

We work hard, spending millions of dollars to meet environmental regulations and to lower emissions. I contend that there are no better environmentalists than the Huntsman engineers and scientists who specialize in this area. Most of them were drawn to the field because of their interest in the environmental movement and, for the most part, have the same passion for what they do as the most committed activist. They do not look the other way when they see something wrong, if for no other reason than their lives, the lives of their fellow workers, and the health of families are at stake. And it isn't just those scientists. Our employees live in the communities in which we operate. The last thing they want to do is endanger their families, friends, and neighbors. Safety is our number-one priority.

We care about our employees, the surrounding communities, and saving jobs and plants from overseas competition. We work hard at being a good neighbor and corporate citizen. A vast majority of our employees and neighbors believe that we are. We spend some $200 million a year on environmental health, safety, and preventative maintenance, but that doesn't necessarily convince the public we are as environmentally friendly as scouts planting trees. However, our employees—who would be the first victims of any chemical accident—know of our concern and appreciate our constant attempts to maintain a safe environment.

When it comes to environmental and safety issues, we have an excellent reputation with the unions that represent our workers. We have thousands of employees and double that number of contract employees around the globe. In the company's history, there has been only one worker fatality, in Malaysia. Statistically, our sites are four times safer than the average home. When we are fined, it is because we have turned ourselves in to federal or state regulators or because we have invited governmental regulation teams to inspect a situation we are concerned about. We average about two to three fines a year, which puts us among the safest chemical companies in the nation. The industry's recognized gold standard for safety belongs to DuPont. Huntsman is just below DuPont.

It isn't just that the industry would like environmental regulations to be painless. People want the cost of those regulations to be absorbed by the companies. Imagine the uproar if Congress mandated that everyone buy a more fuel-efficient car. And this brings me to one of those damned-if-you-do-and-damned-if-you-don't controversies.

Several decades ago, following intense pressure from environmental groups, gasoline producers began to include the additive MTBE in the mix to reduce harmful vehicle emissions by increasing the performance of the gas. MTBE has an oxygen molecule that forces the gasoline to burn hotter. Huntsman is the second largest producer of MTBE in the US. In 1990, this "miracle" additive became the law of the land under the Clean

Air Act. At the same time, the EPA mandated that storage tanks at gasoline stations must be double-lined, but didn't fully enforce the regulation. As a result, only the major gas distributors complied. The mom-and-pop stations did not. As you might imagine, leaks were discovered in those small retail outlets, leaks that got into water aquifers. Because gas and water don't mix, the gasoline could be easily extracted from contaminated water. MTBE, which in its pure form is like alcohol, could not be readily removed. The EPA became alarmed when it first received reports of leakage. In California, rather than force gas station owners to double-line their tanks, the state ordered the removal of MTBE. Humans ought not consume the chemical, but it is considered to be neither toxic nor carcinogenic.

So guess who gets sued? Not the delinquent retail outlets whose storage tanks were deficient. They don't have deep pockets. The class-action lawsuits, naturally, were filed against gasoline producers and MTBE producers, who had done nothing but supply what was ordered under the Clean Air Act. Huntsman and LyondellBasell are the largest remaining chemical producers of MTBE. To show how ridiculous this has become, there currently are environmental groups in California actively lobbying to get MTBE back into gas tanks. I am not optimistic of the long-term prospects for MTBE production. Some one hundred other countries are using the product under safer and less costly regulations. We simply export our MTBE product to some of these foreign markets.

The problem with many environmental causes and environmental reporting is that discussion of costs and inconvenience get skirted. It's easier to build support by finding an inviting target, and chemical companies do make grand targets. The industry once deserved to be a target, but it is different than it was thirty years ago. In fact, the US and Western European chemical industries are the cleanest in the world. That costs a lot of money and at the end of the day you have to compete globally.

Because of public and government sentiment against growing the chemical industry in this country, there are no incentives for new specialty or differentiated chemical plants. That is okay for the moment because we can keep up with current demand and US facilities are in good shape. As those plants age, their efficiencies and output decline. The business will go to foreign producers ultimately and more high-paying

US industrial jobs will morph into minimum wage employment in the service industry.

This does not mean the chemical industry ought not to continue to find ways to lower emissions. We can always do a better job. For my part toward that goal, I made a seven-figure donation to Utah State University almost twenty years ago to help launch an environmental research center. Two of its projects are improvement of air and water quality and recycling of plastics. The technology to help the chemical industry improve the environment will continue to advance; the science of making chemicals continues to show us how to do it with less waste. Until we get there, tradeoffs will be necessary. Some people may not like to hear that, but it's the truth. Environmentalists who do not have a sense of the dual goal of good environmental behavior and improving life for the human inhabitants of this planet will not be effective.

I carry no guilt or shame about being a chemical industrialist just as people ought not to feel guilty or shameful about using the hundreds of items in their lives that are made of plastic. Manufacturing is never a zero-sum game; there is always an environmental impact. The goal is to minimize that impact. More than a dozen years ago, the American Chemistry Council (ACC) adopted principles of responsible care and community awareness and emergency response to which its members must adhere. (Bill Lichtenberger and I were ACC founding fathers in 1991.) The ACC mandates third-party inspections to ensure members live up to the letter and spirit of the codes.

Gregory D. L. Morris, former editor of *Chemical Week* and currently a member of the Museum of American Finance in New York City, described the situation well in a 2004 article in *American Heritage* magazine: "The chemical industry is not a necessary evil. It is more like a high-maintenance friend."

I believe that today more benefits have come about from our industry than harm, and we all want to keep stretching that disproportion in favor of you and me. With every acquisition, Huntsman has improved its environmental record. Period. We have a constant environmental awareness because our name is on the door and because it's the right thing to do.

That's probably why we are often charged with being pro-environment—and we're proud of it.

In the first half of this book, the focus was on growing up, how I built my empire, and how I managed to make a fortune in the process. But there is much more. The second part will look at the more personal aspects of my life: what I have done with that money, how I maintained the company, and how I fought my versions of barbarians at the gates. Yet to come also are stories of family, philanthropy, the building of Huntsman Cancer Institute, my health, one child's presidential bid, the kidnapping of another, the loss of a third, and my goal to make the world a better place.

Part II

GIVING
It
AWAY

12. Kidnapped

AS YOU MIGHT EXPECT, I AM FIERCELY PROTECTIVE OF MY CHILDREN. I would do, and have done, everything in my power to keep them from harm. It is beyond me how I could not have spared one of them a harrowing experience prompted by the notoriety surrounding a simple act of giving or how I could have been unable to prevent the sad and untimely end of another of my children. So emotionally devastating have these incidents been for me, this marks the first time I have publicly spoken about either. This chapter comprises the story of the former experience—the latter I will address later in this book.

By 1987, Huntsman Chemical was rolling in money. Annual sales had broken the billion-dollar mark and our corporate success brought my household greater personal income than any one family should ever expect or need. Of course, philanthropy had long been the family creed and by this point we had made relatively small but frequent grants to charitable organizations for many years. I knew that my dream to help eradicate cancer was closer to inception as the profits from the business began to materialize. By spring 1987, we were ready to make a major gift. The University of Utah was the beneficiary because Karen, my father, my brother, my grandfather, and our college-age children had attended this respected institution. We decided on a $5 million donation to help the university fund a variety of building projects, department chairs, and scholarships.

In 1987 dollars, $5 million was a big deal. University President Chase Peterson announced at a press conference that the school's new special events facility, which seats almost sixteen thousand and is one of the country's premier basketball arenas, was to be named the Jon M. Huntsman Center (which early on hosted the NCAA Final Four where I was lucky enough to watch the likes of Larry Bird and Magic Johnson).

That my name was to be affixed to the structure came as a surprise to me. There had been no expectation of fanfare attached to the gift.

Peterson's announcement generated considerable publicity, which immediately conferred on our family a celebrity status for which we were unprepared. At our corporate board meeting that summer at San Diego's Hotel del Coronado, I suggested the heightened attention might warrant hiring a security person or two out of concern that our children might become potential kidnapping targets for ransom. We discussed the pros and cons, but the idea was dismissed. We lived in Utah, after all, where that sort of thing didn't happen. The conversation was long forgotten by December, when Karen and I embarked on our annual round of our manufacturing site tours to attend Christmas events with employees and their families at different plant locations in the US.

Huntsman Chemical had nearly twenty US facilities with more than 1,200 employees at the time. This, of course, did not include our multitude of foreign facilities. Visiting each site during the holidays took a bit of doing but a corporate plane made the logistics somewhat easier. Because Huntsman Chemical was doing so well, I wanted to share the bounty with those whose hard work had contributed to its revenues. We gave each employee a family gift: their choice of a 35-inch color TV or a 1-week Caribbean cruise. It made me feel like Santa Claus. (What's more, they deserved every bit of it.)

In order to foster a family atmosphere at the plants, we usually took some of our children with us on the Christmas circuit. We had most of them with us on the 1987 tour. Following the Christmas party at the Chesapeake, Virginia facility, Karen and I flew to Belpre, Ohio on December 8. Our sixteen-year-old son James and eighteen-year-old son Paul had to get back to their high school classes, so they boarded a commercial flight for Salt Lake City. They arrived in Utah around 5:00 p.m. and headed home. Paul had a recreation-league basketball game that night and left the house. James was scheduled for a tutoring session in math after which he planned to stop at his girlfriend's home.

Around 6:30 p.m., after the winter sun had set, James climbed into his Jeep Wagoneer, slipped the key into the ignition, and tried to start it. The engine wouldn't turn over, which was not surprising since it had been sitting in the cold for a week. Suddenly the driver's door flew open and an assailant in a ski mask rushed at James. Before he could react, James was handcuffed, his eyes covered with a strip of duct tape, and he was shoved into the passenger side of the front seat. His attacker got behind the wheel and turned the ignition key, but the car wouldn't start for him, either. He yanked James from the vehicle and led him down a trail through our wooded backyard to a side street where a car waited. James was placed in the back seat and whisked off into the night.

The seventeen-year-old person behind the mask was Nicholas Hans Byrd, a casual acquaintance of James's at Highland High School. He had experienced many previous run-ins with the law and was now in immediate need of $500 to repay a debt. Byrd apparently had seen the news of the family's donation and decided that the Huntsmans would be the solution to his money problems. Byrd had been in our home before as part of a large gathering of students we hosted the previous summer, so he was somewhat familiar with the house and grounds.

James would later say the actual abduction was the scariest part of the experience for him. The entire ordeal was paralyzingly frightening for me. James couldn't see his abductor because of the blindfold and the pillowcase that, by then, had been wrapped around his head. Initially, it did not dawn on James that he was being kidnapped. He thought it was a robbery because a cousin had been robbed in a park three weeks earlier. It did not take long for James to discover otherwise.

Paul returned home from his basketball game and noticed James's car in the driveway. He thought it odd when he didn't find James in the house, yet there was nothing especially ominous about that and he went upstairs to shower.

James was taken to Bob's Budget Motel at the northwest edge of downtown Salt Lake City, about a half mile from the state capitol. Bob's was one of those seedy motels that requires cash in advance from clientele of dubious character who prefer not to be questioned at check-in. It was dark when Byrd and James entered the motel room. Byrd pushed James to the bathroom floor and cuffed him to the sink's drainpipe. A short time later, Byrd left the room to make the first of three phone calls to set up the ransom demand. There was no phone in the motel room, forcing Byrd to use the wall-mounted pay phones outside a run-down Safeway store nearby.

Just before 9:00 p.m., our home phone rang and Paul answered. An agitated, menacing voice asked to speak to me. Paul told the caller I was away on a business trip and would not return until the end of the week. Byrd again demanded to speak with me and Paul repeated that I wasn't there. The caller said: "I've got James." The significance of that statement didn't immediately register with Paul until the caller added: "If I don't speak to your dad by tomorrow, the next time you see James he will be in little pieces. If you tell the police or anyone, I'll kill him."

Paul went on full alert, but couldn't help but wonder whether this was some sort of prank. He called James's girlfriend, who said James wasn't with her. Paul quickly began to fear for his brother's safety. Trying not to panic, he dialed my secretary, Roni Whittle, to get the phone number of my Ohio hotel. He then called Brent Stevenson, my lawyer, who called me at the Holiday Inn in Belpre at about 11:30 p.m. eastern time (9:30 p.m. Salt Lake City time), passing along the precious few details Paul had given him. I phoned Paul, who reiterated what had happened, including the kidnapper's demand to speak to me. I told him to stay put and that Stevenson and Terry Parker were on their way to the house. I called an acquaintance in Salt Lake City, Cal Clegg, who was an FBI agent. I caught him at a holiday party and told him my son had been kidnapped. He immediately alerted his superiors.

By midnight in Ohio, Karen and I were hurriedly preparing to return to Utah. I called Ron Rasband, who was staying at the same Holiday Inn, and asked him to alert the crew to prepare for a flight within the hour. What Rasband failed to relay is that he didn't know where they were staying. He opened the Yellow Pages to "Motels" and looked at several dozen possibilities. He scanned the list for something near the airport. One motel stood out on the page and he dialed the number. Miraculously, within seconds Rasband was talking to our chief pilot. (Ron always was a man of inspired resourcefulness.)

James was (and still is) a wonderful, fun-loving, and devoted son. He was the life of any get-together, and his personality was all-inclusive, a blessing to his father and mother. Karen and I reassured each other he would be all right. We tried to stay calm and to comfort Jennifer and Mark, the only children still with us. Getting back to Salt Lake City was all we could think about.

The only kidnapping I knew much about was that of Charles and Anne

Lindbergh's baby, five decades earlier, which became highly publicized and was deemed the crime of the century. I knew it had ended tragically despite the family's cooperation and ransom payment. The twenty-month-old had been murdered and dismembered within hours of his abduction from the nursery of the family home, but his tiny, badly decomposed body wasn't found for two months. James was no baby, but he did not deserve this. A hollow feeling gripped my stomach, and I prayed we would find our boy alive and in one piece.

Back at home, Paul had gone upstairs and located the .38-caliber pistol I kept in my room. He found the ammunition and loaded the gun. Paul worried the kidnapper might return. He wondered whether he could kill if he had to. (One must understand that Paul is a warm, friendly, reserved type of person, gracious to a fault.) Soon he heard the commotion of Stevenson and Parker at the door, along with Paul's older sister, Kathleen, then a student at Brigham Young University. It was around 11:00 p.m. when the four drove to the nearby home of our family's dear friend Russell Ballard, a general authority of the LDS Church, to await our return. (Ballard was and is like a brother to me in every respect. His daughter, Brynn, is married to our son, Peter.)

Alan Jacobsen, an FBI agent assigned to the Salt Lake City office, and his wife returned home from a holiday gathering around 9:00 p.m. on the night of December 8. At age fifty, he was three weeks away from retiring after twenty years of service. Jacobsen had just crawled into bed when he received a call from the nighttime duty officer ordering him to report to headquarters immediately. He threw on a sweatshirt and jeans, grabbed his pistol and badge, kissed his wife good-bye, and drove to the FBI office in downtown Salt Lake City. Such nocturnal interruptions were too common an occurrence for the veteran agent or his wife to be overly concerned. When Jacobsen arrived at headquarters just after 11:00 p.m., other agents were gathering. They were told that one of Jon Huntsman's sons had been kidnapped earlier that evening and were given their assignments. Jacobsen and several agents, including Clegg, arrived at the Ballard home shortly before midnight. They went to our home to secure the crime scene. After interviewing Paul, they asked for names of people who had worked at our residence.

All the while, Karen and I were in an airplane, praying for a tailwind as we streaked westward. The FBI wasted no time obtaining legal authority from a federal magistrate to place a "trap" and recording device on our phone. In the days before caller ID, the phone company could only trace calls with a tracking device installed on the receiving phone, and that had to be authorized by a court order. Before dawn, the technicians had the phone rigged and ready.

At Bob's Motel, shackled in a sitting position on the bathroom floor in the early morning hours of December 9, James slept only in fits. The motel walls were thin and James remembers hearing loud male voices in the next unit, apparently making quite the ruckus. Still blindfolded with duct tape and handcuffed to the pipes, James wondered if they were involved in his kidnapping.

Our plane landed in Salt Lake around 3:00 a.m. and we rushed from the airport on North Temple Street. En route to our destination, we had no idea we were passing within five hundred yards of James's prison. When we reached the Ballard home, Paul and the FBI agents filled us in on what they knew and what they were doing to locate James. Agent Robert Bryant prepared us for the ransom call he expected would come soon. It would be up to us, he said, whether we paid the demand, but he advised us that at least we should go through the motions. He promised that whether the ransom payment consisted of currency or strips of paper, his agents would jump whoever claimed it. We thanked everyone for the help and concern and, at about 5:00 a.m., we went home.

The agents formed several two-man teams on twelve-hour shifts. Jacobsen and Clegg comprised one of those units. Teams were dispatched to all areas of the city in order to be strategically placed when the phone "trap" revealed the caller's location. Other agents stayed at our home and, in the early morning hours, notified the city's police department what was occurring. Generally, kidnapping only comes under federal jurisdiction when a hostage is taken across state lines, which was uncertain at the time, but I had called the FBI first so the agency assumed the lead role in the initial investigation.

Around 7:20 a.m., Byrd left the motel room and returned to the pay phone at the Safeway next door. I have never been as nervous in my life as when I was awaiting that call, rehearsing over and over what I would say. The phone rang at 7:28 a.m. It was the kidnapper, demanding a ransom of $1,000,000–$100,000 of it in used $100 bills. He threatened that if he didn't get the money James would die. I had been instructed to stall the caller as long as possible to give the phone company time to trace the call. I told the caller I would pay nothing until I knew James was unharmed. He had to let me speak to James, I said, to make sure he was physically okay. Byrd and I agreed to a time for a second call when he would put James on the phone, and he hung up. I had managed to keep the line open long enough for the trap to trace the call's origin to one of two pay phones on the front of a supermarket on the corner of 300 West Street and 500 North Street.

Two FBI agents covering that sector of the city raced to the location, arriving only a minute after the call ended, but there was no one at either of the two waist-high pay phones attached, about twenty-five feet apart, to Safeway's front wall. The officers spotted two sets of people getting into parked vehicles. Another FBI team came on the scene within seconds of the first and the agents tailed the two cars only to find the drivers were early-morning shoppers on their way to work. Clegg and Jacobsen arrived at the Safeway at about 7:45 a.m. in a third car. They waited at an old service station, directly across from the store. They backed their unmarked sedan among other parked cars there and began their stakeout as dawn broke over the Wasatch Mountains.

Less than a block from the two agents, Nick Byrd was returning to the motel room with an Egg McMuffin from the nearby McDonald's. He offered it to James, who, with hands taped and eyes blindfolded, didn't feel like eating. Soon Byrd removed James's handcuffs from his swollen wrists, peeled the duct tape from his eyes, and replaced the blindfold with something less conspicuous. Byrd taped one of James's eyes closed and placed tape on the other lens of a pair of sunglasses, which allowed James only to see downward out of one eye. Byrd informed James they were leaving and ordered him to stand up and walk. With Byrd guiding, holding the knife at James's midsection, the two made their way back to the Safeway store.

In their surveillance car, Clegg and Jacobsen passed the time sharing what they knew about James. Clegg had been an advisor to James's youth group at our LDS ward. He knew James could be a prankster and the agents considered the possibility that an elaborate hoax had gotten out of hand. As they talked, two males approached one of the pay phones around 8:00 a.m. It was rush hour, and many people were going in and out of the supermarket, a number of them walking past the two pay phones from all directions. Thus, when James and his captor moved toward the phone, they didn't attract the agents' attention immediately.

At 8:02 a.m., my home phone rang. It was Byrd, who said he had James with him. An FBI agent flashed a signal to the command center. The conversation between Clegg and Jacobsen was interrupted by a radio transmission at 8:03 advising that I was in communication with the kidnapper. Jacobsen and Clegg now noticed the two young-looking males standing at one of the pay phones. Was it possible they were the kidnapper and his victim? One of them had blond hair. They knew James was blond. Clegg was sure it was him.

The agents cautiously drove their sedan to the curb in front of the Safeway store, some seventy-five feet from the pay phones. They nonchalantly got out of the car, trying not to draw attention. Clegg strolled to the vacant phone only twenty-five feet from where the pair were huddled and punched in a phone number. Jacobsen casually walked at an angle that would get him closer to the pair at the second phone, hoping not to draw notice from the kidnapper.

Back at the house, some five miles away, I had no idea what was transpiring. I was nervously engrossed in the conversation with my son's kidnapper who was telling me where to deposit a million dollars in small bills. I told Byrd I could not get that kind of cash until the banks opened later that morning and stretched out my explanation as long as possible to keep him on the line. I demanded to speak with James. He let James talk to me but kept his knife on my son all the while.

"I'm okay, Dad," James said in a brave and relatively calm voice. "Do whatever he says."

I nearly broke down when I heard his voice. I struggled to stay focused. I assured him of my love and promised the ransom would be delivered, that everything would be okay. Suddenly, James stopped talking. The line went silent. I didn't hear a hang-up click and decided the line was still open. Had James dropped the receiver? Had he been hurt? I was nearly panicking and having trouble breathing. After about fifteen seconds, I heard scrambling noises and what sounded like a scream.

As he walked closer to Byrd and James, Agent Jacobsen had spotted what he thought was the suspect's car and wanted to make sure Byrd couldn't get to it. Clegg was still on the other phone; from outward appearances he was having a chatty conversation. In fact, he was talking to his office. As Clegg leaned up against the phone, facing away from the suspect, he quietly informed his supervisor that he was standing right next to the kidnapper and his victim. Within seconds, three FBI vehicles, the nearest only two minutes away, tore out for the scene. Jacobsen had moved to within ten feet of the phone when Byrd glanced over his shoulder and saw the agent. This was it. Jacobsen could wait no longer.

The lawman lunged for the pair, pinning them against the phone. He attempted to pull Byrd away from James with one hand while drawing his pistol from under his sweatshirt with the other. Byrd spun toward Jacobsen and struck him hard in the chest with what the agent thought was a clenched fist. Jacobsen's gun was at his side, aimed downward. He couldn't risk a shot because James was next to the kidnapper. Jacobsen then saw the switchblade in Byrd's hand and realized he had just been stabbed.

After a brief skirmish, Byrd dropped his knife and ran. At the sound of the scuffle, Clegg turned to see his partner struggling with the two individuals. He drew his gun and sprinted over to them just as Byrd started to flee. Clegg ran after the suspect.

As the kidnapper bolted, Jacobsen calmly picked up the dangling phone receiver and spoke the most beautiful words I have ever heard: "Mr. Huntsman, Al Jacobsen, FBI. James is okay. I have to go." Jacobsen ordered James not to move and sped after Clegg to help him apprehend Byrd.

James picked up the dangling receiver and talked to me for about fifteen seconds before dropping it. As he tore off his blinders, he saw two men running toward him, guns drawn. "Are you a cop? Are you a cop?" he yelled at them, not sure whether to stand still or flee. James saw one of them order a hapless male customer, who had just left the store and was walking toward James, to lie face down on the ground and stay there. The spread-eagled customer must have been petrified—though no more so than I was—as I strained to make out what was going on from the muffled sounds coming through the open line.

Clegg collared Byrd about seventy-five feet from the phone. By the time Jacobsen reached the struggling pair, Clegg was wrestling with the kidnapper. Jacobsen pointed his gun at Byrd and barked: "FBI! On the ground!" Clegg handcuffed Byrd and placed him under arrest. Less than a minute had passed. As Clegg started to read the suspect his Miranda rights, three FBI cars screeched to a stop within seconds of each other in front of the Safeway store. Two of the agents had run toward James and accosted the shopper while agents Tim Healey, Kevin Kelly, and Dan Roberts rushed to assist Clegg and Jacobsen.

In the excitement and confusion, no one but Jacobsen was aware he had been seriously wounded. James watched as they placed Byrd in an FBI car. Byrd looked back at him and said, "Sorry, James," as the door slammed and the car sped away.

James rode with Clegg to the FBI office for debriefing, and was then brought home, where Karen and I waited anxiously. We tearfully threw our arms around him as he walked through the door. I realized at that moment we easily could have lost a son—a son for whom our love is infinite. James was shaken but otherwise, thankfully, he was physically fine. Our prayers had most certainly been answered.

Special Agent Jacobsen was not fine. Only after the veteran agent lay down in the parking lot did his colleagues realize he had been wounded. From his training, Jacobsen knew to remain calm. There was little external bleeding from the chest wound, but his mammary artery had been sliced open and he was hemorrhaging internally. An ambulance had been summoned but hadn't yet arrived. Jacobsen was losing peripheral vision and having difficulty breathing. Agent Healey, a former Marine pilot married to an emergency room nurse, had discussed with his wife the previous night the external signs of someone close to death. Watching Jacobsen's face turn gray, Healey saw the gruesome picture she had described.

Lying on the asphalt, Jacobsen felt himself fading. He told agent Kelly, who knelt at his side, to tell his wife he loved her. "He's dying!" Healey yelled to fellow agents. "We can't wait for an ambulance. Get him to the hospital now!"

While agents Kelly and Healey placed their fallen comrade across the backseat of one of the cars, Roberts radioed he was rushing the wounded agent to LDS Hospital, only two miles away as the crow flies but traveling through the congested city streets during morning rush hour it was more like a ten-minute drive—ten minutes which Roberts was certain the wounded agent did not have. Roberts pleaded on the radio for city police to help at the traffic intersections. In less than a minute, police officers had taken positions at key intersections, halting traffic until Roberts's vehicle whizzed through. Jacobsen remained conscious throughout the race to the hospital, feeling increasingly distant from what was going on. But he clearly heard Roberts urging him to hold on. They made it to the hospital in five minutes.

Emergency room personnel and a gurney were waiting as Roberts pulled up. By this time, Jacobsen's lung had collapsed. He managed to tell Kent Richards, one of the ER doctors, to call his wife, who worked at the University of Utah. Salt Lake Police Officer Kim Plouzek, whose patrol car ran interference on the final segment of the dash to the hospital, accompanied the agent into the emergency room. Like Jacobsen, Plouzek was a Mormon and he gave the agent a priesthood blessing while medical staff tore off the agent's clothes. Doctors worked frantically to keep the blood loss to a minimum by inserting a tube to drain the blood between his ribs, running it outside the body through a filtering system and back into Jacobsen through a thigh.

Jacobsen's blood pressure fell to 65/35 and he was only minutes from death when Donald Doty, a cardiac surgeon, rushed into the room. The specialist had been preparing for a surgery that was quickly postponed. He took one look at Jacobsen and ordered him to the readied operating room. Doty said Jacobsen would not have lived another five minutes without immediate surgery. The decision not to wait for the ambulance, the police escort to the hospital, and the good fortune of the available operating room and cardiologist saved Jacobsen's life. The artery was repaired and he recovered. The agents had saved my son and captured the kidnapper in less than thirteen hours, but the ordeal nearly cost one of the heroes his life.

I visited Jacobsen in the hospital to profess my profound gratitude. I also offered him a job as chief of security for our company upon his retirement from the FBI. Later, during his convalescence at home, then-FBI Director William Sessions flew from Washington, DC to commend his bravery.

Jacobsen retired from service in late January 1988, a few days after returning to active duty and about a month later than originally planned. On February 1, he became my chief of security. I later hired his partner, Cal Clegg,
as well. Jacobsen held that position for five years before leaving on an LDS
mission. Clegg took over and eventually left Huntsman for the same reason.
We have maintained security staff ever since that horrific incident.

The criminal case against Nicholas Byrd dragged on for two years. The US
attorney wanted him tried in federal court on a charge of attempted murder
of an FBI agent; Utah wanted him in state court for aggravated kidnapping.
There also was the question of whether to charge him as an adult or a juvenile. In March 1988, it was announced Byrd would be tried as an adult
in state court. What truly stunned us, however, was that the Salt Lake City
School District permitted Byrd to return to Highland High School while
he awaited trial. By this time, we had transferred James to another school.

At his preliminary hearing, Byrd glared at Jacobsen while the agent
testified that the teenager was lucky he hadn't shot him. (Had Jacobsen
pulled the trigger on that December morning, it would have been the first
time the agent had fired a gun in the line of duty during his twenty-year
career.) Amazingly, neither James nor Jacobsen held any animosity toward Byrd. The same could not be said about me. Jacobsen says the experience was the kind of thing that happens in law enforcement. James
chalked it up to a bad experience.

In July 1990, after pleading guilty to lesser charges, Byrd was ordered
to serve concurrently one year in prison for his assault of Jacobsen and
five years for kidnapping James, minus four months served in the deten-
tion center. James relates that his justice side said the sentence was too
light but that his mercy side said it was sufficient.

Byrd was released from prison in January 1995, six months early, at
the age of twenty-five. He was required to leave the state for a year as part
of his probation. James believes Nick would never have killed him; Agent
Jacobsen and I believe otherwise. Byrd now has a family of his own and
one of his children attends school with one of our granddaughters. To his
credit, Byrd is now a contributing citizen of our community and has turned
his life around. James holds no grudges whatsoever against Byrd. In fact,

to my knowledge, James has seldom mentioned the kidnapping outside of our family, and on those infrequent occasions when the matter is discussed, James expresses no ill will or negative feelings toward Byrd. He has never let this kidnapping hold him back. He has handled the entire sorrowful experience in a gracious and dignified manner. He is truly a man of high character and integrity.

As I stated earlier, I have never granted an interview concerning the kidnapping nor have I discussed details publicly before this writing. Just thinking about it again makes me physically ill. The kidnapping became something of a turning point for all of us. Until then, our family had escaped, or perhaps been oblivious to, the dark side of wealth and prominence. Not a year later, daughter Jennifer, who was still in high school, received threatening, vulgar letters, sometimes up to twenty-five a day, from some anonymous, cowardly soul.

Those events, and others of lesser voltage but still of deep concern, evoked fierce loyalty among our family members, and we have dealt with the memories in our own ways. James became more sympathetic to victims of crime and has a higher tolerance for what constitutes bad times. For him, any day is a good day as long as he is free. Incredibly, James has a positive, loving attitude toward all people and possesses a cheerful, always-happy disposition. Today, he is president of the advanced materials division at Huntsman Corporation. By and large, we have put the episode behind us, but since that incident we have full-time security at our offices and residences. We now consider it a fact of life to have electronic surveillance, security gates, guard dogs, and security personnel posted outside. We view them as necessary inconveniences. Karen, who was raised in a home where the front door was never locked, accepts the security at home but strongly dislikes it. I am away so often that the security measures give me peace of mind.

My corporate life has been altered since the kidnapping as well. Now, when I travel around town and on some international trips, a personal security aide usually accompanies me. Do I fear for my life? Not really, but it is surprising how many money-seekers believe that God has directed them to approach me for the gold they seek. Some are belligerent and dangerous, especially at certain church functions. To them, I represent a possible financial lifeline. At times, they get agitated when I don't come through. Karen believes I am a little on the paranoid side, but I once had two ex-convicts come to my church office before I had personal protection. They claimed to be Joseph Smith and Brigham Young and said they had returned to earth to seek money from me. They made veiled threats, but I talked my way out of it, saying I would have to go home and pray about it, which, as Smith and Young, they surely would understand.

Another time, three years after the kidnapping, a man wielding what looked like a knife came to a satellite Huntsman office in Salt Lake asking for me. I did not have an office there, and the startled secretary told him I was downtown at the headquarters building and then gave him the address. When he left, she called the police and alerted me. The guy was arrested as he came up the elevator to my office. The knife turned out to be made of rubber.

I have learned, when staying in another city, to register under an assumed name. I got the idea from the late Kerry Packer, my former partner in several Huntsman enterprises. He and I would stay in the same hotel, yet operators and desk clerks could never locate him when I asked to be put through to the Packer suite. I never did find out what name he used.

13. To Armenia with Love

MY PRIMARY AGENDA UPON RETURNING TO THE CRUMBLING Soviet Union in August 1989 was to establish my financial commitment to Armenia that ultimately amounted to $53 million in contributions over twenty-five years. Armenia had my emotional attention. Before I was finished, my mission had expanded dramatically. While Peter and two Huntsman Chemical executives headed to Yerevan for an on-the-ground inspection of earthquake-related problems, I was returning to Moscow via London, accompanied by our daughter Jennifer, on a chartered Concorde as guests of Armand Hammer. Each passenger had donated $25,000 to Hammer's United World Colleges. We joined with Prince Charles to build schools in underserved countries. The junket was Hammer's way of keeping his international credentials updated and his philanthropy active. Most onboard were heavy hitters.

We were treated royally. From the five-star Claridge's Hotel to a stay with Prince Charles and the late Princess Diana at Highgrove House, their summer home in Gloucestershire; from dining and dancing at the estate of the Duke and Duchess of Marlboro (Blenheim Palace—coincidentally, where former British Prime Minister Winston Churchill was born) to the banquet at the Royal Academy of Arts, it was a whirlwind of elegant affairs, polo parties, and castles. Diana was a terrific dancer to any type of music. She and Charles seldom danced together because the rest of us were constantly cutting in.

Jennifer and I parted company with our fellow donors after two days and flew to Moscow in Hammer's private jet, my second visit to Russia in three months. Russell Nelson, an LDS Church apostle and a renowned heart surgeon, met us in London for the Moscow leg aboard Hammer's OXY 1, a Boeing 727.

Peter, David Horne, Bevan Chamberlain, and Jim Kimball had arrived in Moscow after their fact-finding stop in Armenia, and we gathered at the Mezh in Moscow to discuss the dire situation that existed resulting from the earthquake. I was shocked at my team's grim summary of conditions in Armenia. About a third of the population resides in Yerevan, traditionally a lighthearted city with sidewalk cafes, flowers, parks, and fruit stands. The capital had been spared the wrath of the December 1988 earthquake. The destruction's epicenter was some two hours' drive northwest of the capital, in the Leninakan Valley.

Even eight months after the quake, the area remained chaotic. Peter reported that villages had been reduced to piles of broken concrete. The devastation was so severe that the structures were beyond repair. Officials simply started new villages next to the ruins of those laid to waste. Entire communities had been built almost overnight to shelter the homeless and injured.

The earthquake had struck just before noon. Had it occurred just a few minutes later, the thousands of children who were crushed in their classrooms would have been outdoors on their lunch break and might have been spared. Survivors said that the ground shook violently for 3 minutes, rocking buildings like boats in a storm. Vehicles flew off roads as if they were matchbox miniatures; apartment complexes toppled like rows of dominoes. Soviet builders had not used reinforced concrete with steel rebar, so most structures were reduced to sand and gravel. Spitak, a city of 5,000 souls, was leveled, and 90 percent of the city's population had perished. Most of the victims were never recovered from the impenetrable mountains of rubble. In Narband, a herding village, not a single child survived. When the bells tolled the final tally, some 45,000 Armenians had perished and another half million found themselves homeless.

The disaster's magnitude overwhelmed domestic relief attempts. A heavy fog enveloped Yerevan, forcing thousands of volunteers, medical aides, and foreign doctors to sit for days at the Moscow airport before flights to Armenia could resume. After the planes reached Armenia, more days were lost because neither communication nor travel to the hardest-hit areas was possible. Prior to the earthquake, Gyumri—Armenia's second-largest city—had been the country's most beautiful city, but it was not well built. Within a 30-mile radius, buildings higher than 2 stories fell because of shoddy construction. Peter reported that, at the north end of Gyumri, the army was now constructing a large, high-density apartment complex, completing twelve apartments per day. Under the supervision of Austrian relief workers, another project was producing condo-type housing. (The Armenians were having difficulty comprehending the intended use of these individual units since fewer than 3 percent of them lived in private, single-family homes.)

Given the crucial need for better-quality housing, it was obvious where we should focus our aid. We made plans to erect apartment buildings in Gyumri to house eight hundred families. First, however, we would need to build a factory to produce basic construction materials. Protocols for this humanitarian aid package were formalized at a ceremony in the ornate ballroom of the Armenian embassy in Moscow. Once again, US Ambassador to the USSR Jack Matlock and Soviet Ambassador to the US Yuri Dubinin attended, as did Prime Minister Vladimir Markaryants and numerous Soviet and Armenian officials. I was especially pleased to see in attendance Yuri Khristoradnov, the chairman of the Council for Religious Affairs, with whom I had previously arranged a meeting concerning the status of LDS Church missionaries serving in the Soviet Union.

The presence of Armand Hammer gave the event even greater luster. Hammer's introduction of me was over the top. In his world, I was destined to become the rainmaker and Santa Claus rolled into one—which over time virtually proved correct. I informed the assembly I intended to build a cement plant to produce quality concrete panels meeting Western standards. Huntsman concrete would be reinforced with rebar to better withstand future quakes. Following the start-up of the cement factory, I promised we would concentrate on constructing apartment units and that we would also build a roofing and tile factory. Throughout the country, our objective was to house thousands of families left homeless by this disaster.

Although my humanitarian mission in Armenia was separate from that of the LDS Church, the leaders of the church were in the process of working diligently to gain official recognition by the Soviet Union. For that reason, I also used the event to introduce Apostle Russell Nelson, who spoke of the church's immense resources and the willingness of Mormons to volunteer for reconstruction work.

Later that day, Nelson and I met with Chairman Khristoradnov and his two deputies. For the most part, Nelson carried the ball. He noted the increasing number of new members of the LDS Church in the Soviet

Union and asked whether they might be allowed to gather for the sake of their religion. As was the case the last time this request had been made, Nelson received no reply. When the formal meeting was concluded, Khristoradnov and I went into a nearby room for an informal session where I argued that Mormon relief workers going to Armenia would want to be able to worship together. I offered millions of dollars in reconstruction aid to Armenia, as I knew how difficult it was for the Soviets to obtain Western currency. Khristoradnov reminded me in private that the LDS Church's request for recognition the previous year had been rejected. To my great surprise, he was about to change his tune.

Just an hour later, as we all reconvened, Chairman Khristoradnov announced that henceforth no religion permit would be necessary. The LDS Church would be accepted. At the time, a requirement for a religion permit was that at least twenty members of a church must live in the district in which they desired to worship. I was pleased to report to Elder Nelson that any size LDS group could meet in any apartment, home, or hotel room without pre-authorization. The minister assured us our religion would have no further problem in the Soviet Union. He then promised to arrange for hundreds of hotel rooms if Armand Hammer would bring the Mormon Tabernacle Choir to Moscow. (Ironically, only months before our Moscow meetings, Soviet Ambassador Yuri Dubinin visited our home in Salt Lake City, Utah. During that trip, he announced on our front porch—in front of a gathering of the local media—that LDS missionaries would be welcomed in the USSR.)

Sadly, this would be my last trip with Hammer. Within eighteen months, he was laid to rest in one of the most bizarre funeral services I have ever attended.

In 1991, Karen and I had received an invitation to Armand's bar mitzvah. He was Jewish by heritage but did not practice his religion. Sensing, I am sure, that his time on this earth was nearing the end (he was now pushing ninety-two years of age), he decided to have a bar mitzvah, a rite-of-passage ceremony typically undertaken when a Jewish boy reaches thirteen years of age (similar to a confirmation in some Christian religions). Unfortunately, Hammer did not live long enough to experience the ceremony. His bar mitzvah was replaced by his funeral service at Westwood Village Memorial Park Cemetery in West Hollywood where several film stars such as Marilyn Monroe were interred. The service was conducted in the cemetery's small chapel, two blocks from Occidental Oil's headquarters from which Hammer would have had a splendid view of his final resting place. He had built a modest marble mausoleum among the crypts in this small but prestigious burial site.

Only about eighty-five mourners were invited to attend the services. Among the gathering were several Hollywood celebrities. A rabbi opened the service and five speakers followed including Los Angeles Mayor Tom Bradley, longtime Hammer attorney Louis Nizer, and the new Occidental chairman, Ray Irani.

Toward the end of the service, Hammer's grandson, Michael, rose to speak. Michael had become a born-again Christian and, in turn, introduced his father-in-law, a fundamentalist preacher from Tulsa, Oklahoma. The minister took the microphone, looked toward the heavens, and boomed out: "Hallelujah! Hallelujah! Brother Armand is born again!" Karen and I nearly jumped out of our seats, as did actor Danny Thomas and his wife, seated next to us. The preacher proclaimed in theatrical, televangelist style how less than a week earlier he and Hammer had stayed up until dawn discussing religion. "Around sunrise," blared the minister, "Armand accepted Jesus Christ and was born again!"

You could have heard a pin drop at this otherwise Jewish service. After the preacher sat down, the rabbi hesitated five or six minutes and then mumbled a fifteen-second closing prayer after which Hammer was laid to rest, with Marilyn Monroe for a neighbor. Nobody said a word as we filed out. Karen and I came to the conclusion that, at the end, Hammer must have hedged his theological bets and covered all of his religious bases in the same manner he had handled the Soviet-US relationship: prepare for any contingency. Though it seemed a little odd, I was proud of him.

Peter Huntsman, our point person on the Armenia project, headed to Yerevan after the embassy ceremony in Moscow. In all, Huntsman personnel would make some forty trips to Armenia before the project came to fruition. The team concluded that raising the standards for reinforced concrete production might be the most effective contribution we could make toward easing the shortage of safe housing. Peter brought in a crew of six volunteer engineers to select a site for the cement plant and devise plans for its completion. There already were thirteen concrete plants in Yerevan, each built on a standard design from Soviet Central Planning in Moscow. The equipment inside those plants varied widely. One facility might possess a modern caster but an antique dryer. In the next factory, the opposite would be the case. The lack of efficiency and the absence of any seismic protection standards made us shudder.

By October, we had settled on a rundown building that once had been a concrete plant. Peter flew home thinking everything was moving forward. Perestroika may have been the slogan du jour in the USSR at the time, but Central Planning remained in control of progress.

When Peter returned to Yerevan three months later, with a team of US engineers in tow, he found the plant site far from settled. Mid-level Armenian officials informed the Americans that every plant in Yerevan—or in the entire Soviet Union, for that matter—was locked into a production schedule set in Moscow. Everything had to go through Central Planning. That did not go down well with "get-it-done-now" entrepreneurs.

Under the old Soviet system, individual republics had little control over their economies, and little had changed by 1990. Gorbachev was trying to democratize the Soviet Union, but, without a model, moving the nation was not an easy task. Even if Peter got permission to build the plant, bureaucrats would control the operation. That's just how it is, we were told. That was not how it's going to be, fumed Peter.

We couldn't understand why, if Armenian bureaucrats wanted to encourage the project, they did nothing to contribute to its success. One barrier after another was thrown up. While privately believing it was impossible for an American company to own or operate a business in Armenia, Peter and I nevertheless took another shot at cracking the bureaucracy. After two days of talks, there came a breakthrough. One of the officials mentioned a concrete plant under construction on the outskirts of Yerevan. Because the Republic of Armenia was still building this plant, the facility had not yet come under the auspices of Central Planning in Moscow. If Huntsman were to take over the plant before its completion, the Armenians suggested, it would never come under the suffocating Soviet constraints. Their government would agree to this if Huntsman would equip it. Perfect.

By the spring of 1990, we were ready to commit resources and I made my first trip to Yerevan. The State Department had advised us not to fly into Yerevan but, as in so many other episodes of our life, we went where our hearts led us and forged ahead with a Soviet navigator on board. Vazgen Manukian, recently appointed prime minister of the Soviet-controlled Republic of Armenia and a man of strong physical stature, greeted me at the Yerevan airport with a bear hug I did not soon forget. At least three of my ribs felt as if they had been seriously injured.

I was excited to see that progress was being made. One of our initial concerns was finding an adequate supply of sand and gravel. There was a large sand and gravel pit located near Etchmiadzin on the Turkish-Armenian border. A railroad ran between the pit and Yerevan. To ensure reliable delivery, I bought the entire railroad—the tracks, engines, rail cars, gravel pit, rock crusher, washing facility, trucks, and loaders—for $80,000. Who could pass up owning your own railroad at that price?

At the time Armenia was an armed society with its share of Mafia-style gangs. In the first half of the 1990s, violence was a fact of life. My safety during my visits seemed to be of paramount importance to Armenian officials. On both President Levon Ter-Petrosyan's and President Robert Kocharian's orders, I was afforded head-of-state status, which meant twenty-four-hour security. Whether their concern for my well-being was designed to protect the source of major reconstruction funding for their country or simply out of courtesy, I never quite knew. But they made sure that four heavily armed bodyguards accompanied me everywhere I went, either on foot or in an automobile along a carefully monitored motorcade route. When I chose to stay at a hotel rather than at the Presidential Palace, the adjacent rooms and the one opposite mine on the corridor were purposely left unoccupied. Four guards with AK-47s stood watch outside my door, talking with each other and smoking so heavily that I coughed throughout the night.

To make matters even scarier, since there was no reliable banking system in Armenia at that time, all transactions had to be in cash. Each time one of our executives returned to Yerevan, he carried hundreds of thousands of US dollars. The money for salaries and materials was kept in a plant safe or other hiding spots even though there are no secrets from the Soviet KGB, which undoubtedly was monitoring this American incursion.

We were operating in Armenia just as the breakup of the Soviet Union began. Gorbachev survived a coup in 1991 but the end of communism was at hand. It was also about this time that hostilities flared between Armenia and Azerbaijan over the disputed territory of Nagorno-Karabakh, a Soviet autonomous region located inside Azerbaijan but adjacent to the Armenian border. Nagorno-Karabakh had been in Armenian territory before the forced breakup of the country in 1920 and it contained a sizeable Armenian population. Armenia eventually was victorious, but the fighting was fierce and costly.

Peter asked his brothers James and David to accompany him and David Horne, our resident engineer who spoke passable Russian, on one of their many trips to Armenia. Horne was overseeing construction of the concrete plant, while the Huntsman brothers were going to Yerevan to coordinate the distribution of relief packages we had shipped by rail and truck through Turkey and Iran. The Iranian participation was particularly remarkable. We had committed to a 5-year food distribution program. In late 1993, we arranged for a 750-ton shipment, via Iran, through an Iranian consulting firm. Relations between Iran and the United States had been untenable for at least 2 decades, but Peter had nothing but praise for his Iranian counterparts, calling them as fair a group to deal with as anyone with whom he had done business. The US State Department advised us not to deal with Iran, but Iranians were on the border with Armenia and possessed the only food available in the region. We did our usual thing and made it happen.

By February 1994, however, the 1.5 million pounds of Iranian food we had purchased—rice, sugar, chickpeas, spaghetti, lentils, cracked wheat, red beans, and sunflower oil—had not arrived at the border locations where Armenian trucks were to pick up the 50,000 cases of food for distribution. Iran, an ally of Azerbaijan, was getting heartburn over shipping food earmarked for the enemy. It took a while, but an alternative route was devised and the supplies eventually arrived. Armed trucks from Armenia went to the border and brought back thousands of loads to be warehoused in Yerevan.

The Huntsman boys' journey ended up being a hair-raising adventure. The trio had flown to Moscow and transferred to a domestic Aeroflot flight to Yerevan—no simple matter on the notoriously unreliable airline. For openers, there was no reservation system. Even when I flew on my private jet into the country, communications between planes and air controllers was haphazard at best. Pilots routinely circled airfields before landing to make sure the unpaved runway, usually chock-full of potholes, was clear of vehicles, other planes, animals, and debris. As long as we had a Russian navigator in the cockpit, the Huntsman jet was cleared to fly over most of the Soviet Union, the exception being sensitive military installations.

In Moscow, Peter found that Aeroflot only had room for one passenger and baggage, or all three of them without their baggage. They weren't about to leave their luggage behind, so Peter flew on to Yerevan alone. James and David waited 48 hours in the airport for the next flight to Armenia. Finally, they boarded an aging Tupolev jetliner only to find a goat in the passenger compartment and luggage in the aisle. The plane did not take off. Passengers spent the night in their seats as the plane sat on the tarmac while the crew rounded up sufficient fuel for the flight. The flight left in the morning and David and James eventually made it to their destination. Food was scarce in parts of Armenia. Desperate crowds pushed and shoved their way to where my sons handed out parcels at a number of sites. We spent the next 2 years transporting thousands of tons of food from Turkey and Iran into Armenia by rail and truck. The president later told us we saved the lives of 250,000 elderly who otherwise would have succumbed to starvation.

In due course, Peter decided he wanted to see the Nagorno-Karabakh border fighting first hand. David and James agreed it would be exciting and the trio sought to catch a ride into the war zone on a dilapidated military helicopter. Peter argued with then-Defense Minister Vazgen Manukian, the former prime minister who knew me as a friend and was anxious that nothing happen to Jon Huntsman's sons. It was not an especially dangerous flight, even though the nation was at war, but Manukian knew that at least one helicopter a month ended up getting shot down as it flew to the front. All the choppers were chronically short of spare parts and flew on a wing and an Armenian prayer.

From the moment we met, I liked Manukian, a brilliant mathematician and native Armenian. Many Armenians thought of him as a hero, and I was deeply honored by his trust and friendship. He had advanced to the prime minister's seat directly from a prison to which he had been sentenced for political dissent. One day, out of the blue, a group of men walked into the prison and escorted him, without explanation, to a waiting government limousine. Still wearing his prison garb and carrying his worldly possessions in a brown paper bag, he was driven to the prime minister's mansion where he learned he was the new prime minister. When hostilities broke out with Azerbaijan, he became defense minister. I had met him on my first trip to that nation. He and I spent many hours strategizing over issues important to Armenia, including a possible peace treaty with Azerbaijan.

For two days, Peter pestered Manukian, assuring him he and his brothers would not expect the government to guarantee their safety. Peter asked only that Manukian not report this trip to me. As an incentive, he said they would bring food packages to the soldiers. Manukian relented. The next morning the young Huntsmans found themselves staring dubiously at a decrepit Soviet military helicopter. They were not reassured when the pilots were unable to start the engine. After waiting another day for mechanics to arrive, Peter, James, and David finally arrived at the battlefront at Stepanakert, capital of the disputed Nagorno-Karabakh autonomous region, some 150 miles northeast of Yerevan. They intended to return to Yerevan that afternoon, just an up-and-back look at the fighting. Following a visit with troops and a tour of a POW camp of badly abused Azerbaijanis, they returned to the landing site where they were informed their helicopter had been called away on another mission. They would have to spend the night at the front, sleeping in a bombed-out hotel.

During the night, Azerbaijan launched a major offensive. Explosions and gunfire only a few miles away kept my sons alert and on guard. The Armenians were now in control of an island of territory, surrounded by Azerbaijani troops. When the next day dawned, my sons were told the choppers were being diverted to transport wounded soldiers from the battlefield and the next flight couldn't accommodate "sightseeing" Americans. Peter feared the chopper, gearing up to leave, would be the last out of the stronghold for a while.

Without authorization, Peter, James, and David leaped into the helicopter as it was about to lift off. They sat among the maimed and the dying and were struck by the horrors of war. The chopper's engines belched smoke and roared to life. It flew at treetop altitude as it made its way back to Yerevan because the craft had been fired upon earlier that day. The boys never told Karen and me about that episode. It was Manukian who finally got up the nerve to inform me of the harrowing trip four months later. When I passed it on to Karen, she nearly had a stroke.

The border war, a disintegration of the USSR and the resulting political dramas, and frequent power outages were slowing construction of the cement plant. Secessionist movements, with the Baltic nations and Armenia at the forefront, were near a boiling point.

With assistance from the ambassador's wife, Liana Dubinin, and her Children in Crisis Foundation, tons of medical equipment and supplies were donated by Utah hospitals at our request for the Leninakan hospital. By May 1991, the cement plant was near enough to completion that we could install the machinery. We had purchased modern pre-cast machinery for several million dollars from Spancrete of Milwaukee, Wisconsin, but with that came a new problem: How do you transport 240 tons of machinery to Yerevan? The only plane large enough to do the job was the gigantic Antonov An-124. There was only one in the world and the Soviet Air Ministry owned it. It took three months of intense negotiations with the military to obtain permission to use it in our humanitarian effort.

On May 22, 1991, the Antonov became the first Soviet military plane in history to fly over the United States. Its size staggers the imagination. With a crew of 14, a wingspan of more than 240 feet, and 24 wheels, it could land on rough airstrips, snow, and ice. It dwarfs the Boeing 747. NATO had code-named it "Condor." The An-124 first flew to Milwaukee to pick up the majority of the equipment and returned to Yerevan. A week later, it swooped into Utah for a load of medical supplies—from X-ray equipment to hospital beds to microscopes—and spent an extra day on the Salt Lake City International Airport tarmac to allow public tours. (I can just imagine the meltdown among communist-conspiracy types when this gigantic craft with the red star on its tail passed overhead.)

More than 20,000 open-mouthed Utahns turned out to view the behemoth. Its final stop was Milwaukee, where it picked up the rest of the production equipment and returned to Armenia.

By June, the Mormon Tabernacle Choir had been invited to perform in Moscow's famous Bolshoi Theatre. We scheduled the dedication of our Yerevan plant to occur 2 days prior to the performance. I invited 120 of Utah's civic, political, religious, and business leaders and their spouses, along with a handful of journalists, to attend both events. The plan was to fly them from Paris to Yerevan to Moscow and back to Paris in the most modern Aeroflot jet I could charter. Events did not unfold according to plan. When the guests got to Paris on June 23, they found no Aeroflot plane awaiting them. It had not left Moscow because Aeroflot had not received the rental for the plane in cash. After we negotiated with Aeroflot's Moscow manager (involving a hefty bribe plus the rental costs), the airliner arrived in Paris 5 hours late.

On June 24, 1991, a large delegation from the Armenian government; the sizable Utah contingent; and a gaggle of American, European, and Soviet journalists surveyed what our efforts had wrought. I was proud of Peter, David Horne, and others who diligently worked to create one of the most modern, efficient concrete and construction plants anywhere in the world. The facility had cost many times more than the $1 million the Huntsman family initially had planned to donate to earthquake relief. I was certain it would never turn a profit, but that was not the goal. We were keeping our promise. We came to know the Armenians as friends and neighbors and were committed to provide housing, irrespective of the substantial costs involved. Afer all, the entire project was for humanitarian purposes. I was the last to speak at the dedication ceremony. My words were heartfelt and passionate but landed me in the doghouse with the two LDS general authorities who had accompanied me as guests.

The weather was scorching in Yerevan on June 24, the day of the dedication. Having rehearsed my remarks, the speech came off without a hitch—as far as the prepared text went. At the end, I paused, looked out at the thousands of Armenian faces in the audience and overflowing into the streets, and decided to add something from the heart. I may have been prompted by the presence of Prime Minister Manukian, who had spent part of a brilliant teaching career in jail for opposing Soviet repression. It might have been my experiences with the rapidly dissolving Soviet Union. Or it could have been my moral compass. Whatever the genesis, I segued from discussing victims of earthquakes to victims of oppression to Armenia's long struggle for independence. In the two years I had observed Armenia, the unrest became overpowering. I closed with a prayer and an emotional expression of hope that Armenia might soon gain its independence from the USSR, escaping the oppression it had endured for so long. Armenians in the crowd responded with cheers and applause.

Following the ceremony, Henry Nagy, the eighty-seven-year-old founder and chairman of Spancrete, who had been on site since 6:00 a.m. to ensure nothing went amiss with his company's equipment, threw a switch. A bright yellow sixty-five-ton overhead crane moved slowly up and down its track, signifying that we had succeeded in building the most modern facility in the country. The crowd went wild. To everyone's amazement, nothing went wrong. My spirits were high; things appeared to have gone well. But in short order the wind was knocked from my sails.

I was pulled aside by two senior leaders of the LDS Church. "You must make it very clear," they warned without elaboration, "that when you are speaking, you speak for yourself only and not for the church." I was confused. Had I said something wrong? "You must be clear that your sentiments concerning independence have nothing to do with the LDS Church. You are speaking only for yourself."

Who else would I be speaking for? The LDS Church was all but unknown in Armenia. It had never been recognized in Armenia as an organized religion. Its only involvement was through a delegation invited by me to attend the formal opening of our family's humanitarian project. Armenians knew me as an individual; I was a known entity to them. No Armenian would have viewed my comments as representing the LDS Church. (In fact, a church official from Switzerland, who was one of my guests, was asked to leave the country by Armenia's foreign minister because of his negative comments and attempts to order people around.) "As you know, the political situation here is very difficult," they continued. "It must not be construed that the church is taking a stand."

More than anything else, elections on Gorbachev's reforms had resulted in an outpouring of nationalist sentiment across the crumbling Soviet Union. People wanted to be free of Moscow. The issue of Armenian independence would be put to a vote in a matter of days. Armenians have always been fiercely independent, almost from the time when the Christian disciples Thaddeus and Bartholomew took the message of Jesus Christ to this barren and faraway land. Armenians wanted freedom and dignity and I had felt moved to speak on the subject.

The LDS Church, on the other hand, was in the USSR solely by the grace of the Soviet government and my humanitarian efforts. I fully understood why it needed to be seen as neutral. The LDS Church's Twelfth Article of Faith states: "We believe in being subject to kings, presidents, rulers, and magistrates, in obeying, honoring, and sustaining the law." Revolution is not part of the church's theological equation. As an individual, though, and an American entrepreneur conducting business in a foreign land, I was not required to be neutral and felt entirely justified exercising my right to speak freely.

"I am neither an official representative of my church nor of my government," I told the church officials. "When I speak, I speak for myself and my family alone. That surely was quite clear to everyone."

It amazed me that, as sensitive as these church leaders were on the subject of independence, the two seemed comfortable aligning themselves with me in the humanitarian realm, even to the extent of overshadowing our efforts. Shortly before the dedication ceremony at the Children's Republican Hospital in honor of those who donated medical equipment, they ordered last-minute changes in the program, rearranging the order of speakers. The result was a discernible shift in the ceremony's emphasis, turning the day's program into a church-sponsored event.

I was stunned. This was the culmination of two years of hard work and tens of millions of family dollars. I recalled that my January 1989 suggestion to tackle the humanitarian aid effort in tandem with the LDS Church had been quickly rebuffed. The Huntsman family had been urged to go it alone, while the LDS Church gave a modest gift of $75,000. For this trip, we had invited friends from Utah and elsewhere, including the two LDS leaders, to join us in celebrating our accomplishment as a courtesy, and for no other reason. This was a Huntsman family affair, not a church event. Yet, the program suddenly was being restructured to infer that our relief effort had come about under church guidance and stewardship.

During the special luncheon in Prime Minister Manukian's mansion following the dedication, I was seated at the head table and shown considerable deference. No doubt my remarks earlier in the day had something to do with that. Manukian presented me with the Armenian Medal of Honor that contained the following inscription: "Your personal support and generous commitment to us will always remain engraved in our memory." I was the first and only American ever to receive such an honor. It was an emotional moment; I could not speak for several minutes. Finally, I managed to choke out: "Thank you. I believe in your future. Our family will honor its commitment to help the Armenian people for many, many years to come." I reiterated my admiration for the Armenians and wished them success in their struggle for independence.

In the plebiscite a few days later, the people voted almost unanimously—96 percent—to leave the USSR.

A press conference followed the award presentation. By that time, several Utah journalists covering the dedication had picked up on the fact that Mormon officials were distancing themselves and the church from my political comments. One reporter asked point blank if I could freely express my position on independence. "Of course I can," I responded, adding that I vehemently supported Armenia's liberation. "They should have the independence they desire." Pressed further, I stated: "When my mind tells me something is right, it doesn't matter if I am in the minority. If it's right, it's right. Armenia deserves its independence, as does any law-abiding country."

I hoped that would end it, but I was yet again called aside by church leaders. They wanted to be "absolutely sure" I was speaking for myself. I did not want to have this conversation again, but I repeated the same assurances. They kept at me and I reassured them that if I were a general authority in the LDS Church I would not have said the things I did regarding independence. I was respectful to them but resented being chastised.

Yet a third discussion of the matter ensued, this time initiated by a Swiss-based LDS Church official with responsibility for that area of the globe. He had flown to Armenia for the occasion as my guest. About the same time, I heard reports that an overzealous, full-time church attorney who had accompanied him had engaged in a heated luncheon discussion with the head of the Armenian Parliament and the minister of religion, men with whom I enjoyed good relationships. They had made matters worse by getting pushy in requesting missionary housing concessions. It was neither the time nor the place for such demands. The earthquake left an extreme shortage of housing. Residents were still living in container boxes, yet these mid-level church leaders had the temerity to seek special privileges for LDS missionaries. It was unconscionable.

Moreover, in a land where the Armenian Apostolic Church had been the dominant religion for 1,700 years, one ought not to expect overnight changes. Doors had been opened to the LDS Church, property had been made available for a chapel, and the church was presented with an opportunity to be involved in the new republic. We had worked the church into sort of an "acceptance package" which hinged on my friendship with the Armenians. I could envision this carefully cultivated rapport eroding through thoughtless words of clueless people who had no idea the price of what they requested. The irony of this episode was that the final event on the day's schedule, just before we took off for Moscow, was the dedication of the site for the first Mormon chapel in Armenia. The land was donated by the Armenian government to our church as a way of expressing gratitude for our family's "relief efforts" as stated by Minister Manukian.

During the Aeroflot's return flight to Moscow, the Americans experienced firsthand how things worked (or didn't work) in the Soviet Union. Either the plane's air conditioning broke down or the Russian crew had learned of my independence comments, but the result was a miserable three-and-a-half-hour ride to Moscow. Exactly ninety minutes before the Mormon Tabernacle Choir was to perform in the historic Bolshoi Theatre, the Aeroflot plane carrying the Utah delegation of leaders, their spouses, and members of the news media pulled up to the Sheremetyevo Airport gate. The wrung-out Americans rushed to the newly rebuilt Metropol Hotel to freshen up before the concert.

The choir performed magnificently. That portion of the evening was a resounding success. A banquet followed to which some two hundred guests were invited. The high spot at the event was an announcement by the vice president of the Soviet Union that henceforth the LDS Church would be recognized officially and would be allowed to proselytize in Leningrad (soon to revert to its historic name, Saint Petersburg) and

Moscow. This was electrifying news to the LDS in the audience. At last, LDS missionaries would be permitted in Russia.

Unfortunately, things went downhill from there. The Huntsman family had underwritten the $35,000 dinner, but it was clear we were not considered in the events of the evening. When we arrived at the hotel ballroom, there were no name cards on the tables. Confusion reigned while people tried to figure out where to sit. Karen and I ended up in a corner behind a potted palm.

Neither was the affair efficiently executed. It quickly descended into the dinner from hell. While the food was passable, the service was excruciatingly slow. The featured speakers—all LDS Church officials—seemed unaware of time and droned on for nearly four hours into the steamy night. There were far too many of them, and each talked way too long. That mind-numbing experience was mitigated in part by poor acoustics and a sound system that didn't work. What was worse, they spoke as if the Soviet Union had just been discovered, much to the embarrassment of other Americans present. One church representative pointedly praised the absence of ashtrays and alcohol at the tables. This was not well received by the Russian, Ukrainian, and Armenian guests, who were accustomed to having vodka and cigarettes with their meals and who were not amused about having their vices disparaged by people they had just invited to the table. It really didn't matter much because most guests were using their salad plates as ashtrays anyway. And to my personal dismay, not one of the attending senior government officials from Russia, Armenia, or Ukraine (where we were about to launch a polystyrene joint venture) was acknowledged from the podium.

The hours dragged by and the discontent became obvious. Members of the news media were particularly cranky. Virginia Clark, my personal guest from the Wharton School in Philadelphia, stopped by my table to ask why the church speakers were pushing so hard. After all, she correctly noted, they were only guests at this dinner. US Senator Jake Garn later told me it was the single worst event he remembered attending in his twenty-four years of public service. On top of this confusion, our son David became violently ill after eating whatever "mystery meat" was in the hors d'oeuvres. His breathing virtually stopped and the medics were called. Thankfully, he eventually recovered.

In spite of the years and millions of dollars I had invested in Russia, it was troubling that there were some who thought my efforts had been made with the LDS Church in mind. It's true that one of my goals was to help my church find a foothold in the Soviet Union, using a path the Soviets would accept, but my underlying goal had always been to help the Armenians.

I left the banquet at midnight, with the speakers still droning on. I had a press conference scheduled early the next morning in the US embassy at which I would announce an expansion of the Huntsman-Aero-Mar plant in Moscow and a formal protocol for the joint venture with Styrol in Ukraine. These were historic events since, as I earlier mentioned, no American firm, up to this time, enjoyed a 51 percent ownership of a Soviet business.

Back in Salt Lake City, the news coverage focused, as I had feared, on the division between my position and the LDS Church's on Armenian independence. Two days after my return to Utah, one of the senior church officials called me to smooth things over, assuring me that "there was never any problem between us. It was just that we had to take our position and you had to take yours."

My response: "We have already discussed that. I thought it was unnecessary for the church to say anything because clearly I was not speaking either for or on behalf of the church any more than I am speaking for or on behalf of the American government. I am not a spokesman for either body. I am a private citizen and businessman." I said it would have been better had the church allowed us our dedicatory ceremony and allowed me to speak what was in my heart. "After all," I concluded pointedly, "you were my guests."

Shortly thereafter, a note came from a gracious church leader, warmly thanking me for all I had done in Armenia, and I put the matter behind me. He later joined me for lunch in my Salt Lake City office and brought a lovely gift. We have always been friends. To my mind, that matter was settled, but I was worried things were going downhill in Armenia. In an attempt to assess the damage and to make amends where needed, I returned to Armenia within a month.

Other than the Armenian Apostolic Church, the LDS Church was the first Christian church allowed to conduct services in Yerevan since the

Soviets took control in 1920. Armenians' initial contact with Mormonism came between 1886 and 1890 when a missionary, Ferdinand Friis Hintze, traveled throughout Asia Minor, although most LDS preaching since then had occurred in Armenian communities in what is now Turkey. There is little evidence Mormon missionaries ever set foot into present-day Armenia.

On my return to Armenia, I met with the leader of the Armenian Apostolic Church, Catholicos Karekin I (Armenia's equivalent of the Roman Catholic pope). His feathers were ruffled that a Mormon beachhead was being established in his territory. The government was again limiting visas for representatives of foreign churches. The progress we had previously made was eroding. On June 8 I was to meet with Karekin I and the archbishop who would succeed him as Karekin II, who also oversaw his church's post-earthquake reconstruction programs. I walked into the meeting room to find a number of bishops, priests, and monks already assembled. No one was smiling and the tension was palpable. When Catholicos Karekin I entered, I shook his hand and he invited me to sit across the desk from him. I used an interpreter, but the Catholicos spoke broken English.

I acknowledged the Armenian Church's firm Christian foundation over the last 1,700 years and, though others had tried to destroy it, it never wavered. I stated how humbled I felt to be in the presence of his holiness. I explained The Church of Jesus Christ of Latter-day Saints was young compared to his church, and that it could learn much from the experience and history of the Armenian Church. I invited him to come to Salt Lake City where I would introduce him to his Mormon counterparts. The atmosphere immediately changed. The clerics began smiling and shaking my hand. I was invited to tour the grounds of Etchmiadzin, and was shown precious artifacts and relics.

Later the same day, at the Presidential Palace, Armenian President Kocharian and ministers Darbinian, Oskanian, and Felix Pirumian, governor of the Shirak Region, recognized our contributions to Armenia's reconstruction. After a related press conference and a private luncheon with Kocharian, the presidential delegation, which included Huntsman family members and Armenian and US diplomats, flew to Gyumri for the groundbreaking of our Huntsman Village apartments and school.

The day was a succession of emotional experiences for me, especially in light of the challenges we had overcome in getting to that point and the lives lost in the process.

Things got markedly easier for the LDS Church in Armenia after my meeting with the Catholicos. His holiness Karekin II, at a chance meeting sometime later, told one of my executives in Yerevan that "Mr. Huntsman is my friend." (Today, Armenia has among the fastest-growing LDS populations in Europe. On June 16, 2013, the first LDS Stake (similar to a Catholic diocese) was created in Yerevan, which was welcomed by approximately three thousand members of the LDS faith who now reside in Armenia. I was not present for that event due to serious health challenges, but Elder Nelson read a letter from me to the Armenian people acknowledging our love for them and referring to our twenty-five-year relationship with the country.)

To obtain official recognition of a new faith or religion in many countries is awkward and difficult. Typically, national leaders are not interested in dealing with religions that have an eye toward missionary activity in their nation. It is often much easier for an industrialist, who is willing to invest millions of dollars in a country, to be granted an audience on religious matters. Most countries are interested predominantly in the creation of more jobs for their people. The fact is that Armand Hammer had as much to do with getting Soviet officials to allow formal LDS services and missionaries into Armenia as anyone, beginning with his endorsement of my business venture and humanitarian efforts in the USSR. The LDS Church was established in Armenia through our family's humanitarian efforts and not in response to official requests from the church. The LDS Church historical record does not reflect this interplay, nor does it accurately reflect our years of effort, at significant humanitarian cost, to help the church gain recognition in various Soviet republics.

I never push my religion on others. I have always felt comfortable with other beliefs, maybe because I had contact with other religions as a child. I don't criticize or belittle another's faith. Making religion a peripheral topic rather than central to a discussion helps keep it nonthreatening. *By the way, would you mind if we established a house of worship here at some point?* I have always found people to be most accommodating that way. Hammer told me something once that resonates as I look back on all of that: "The most effective spokesperson isn't always the one in uniform."

The project manager in Armenia, as I said, was David Horne, a retired homebuilder from Utah. He and his wife, Jean, gave up a comfortable retirement, time with their family, and the comforts of home to relocate in Armenia for much of the Huntsman project. As it turned out, he made the ultimate sacrifice, which tragically marred an otherwise exhilarating experience in that country. I kept an apartment for David in Yerevan. He spent long periods overseeing the cement plant's construction and operation. (We soon added a roofing business to our concrete facilities.) In January 1996, Horne left again for the nation in which he had spent the better part of half a dozen years. It was to be his final trip, during which he would turn over plant operations to Armenian management, under Huntsman supervision.

It gets cold in Armenia in January and electricity is intermittent, so he had two backup propane heaters in his apartment for reliable warmth. Upon his arrival, after twenty-four hours on planes and in airports, David wanted to take a shower. The electricity wasn't working, so he lit his propane heaters, leaving one in the living room and placing the other in the bathroom. While he was showering, the flame in the living room heater went out but propane gas continued to spew into the room.

When David stepped from the shower and opened the bathroom door, the propane gas floated into the bathroom where the flame from the heating unit there ignited the fumes into a deadly fireball. The explosion blew out every window in the apartment and burned over 75 percent of David's body. In spite of the pain and shock, he put on a bathrobe and drove himself to the nearby home of a friend, Zhirayr Zabunian. He honked the car's horn and screamed for Zabunian and was almost unconscious when Zabunian came running to the car. He placed David in the passenger side and with his cell phone called a friend, who was chief of staff at a local hospital. When they arrived at the hospital, doctors began to work on David, but they did not have the proper equipment or medication. Zabunian was asked to drive to other hospitals and pharmacies to collect what was necessary to treat Horne. The victim was moved to the only specialized burn hospital in Armenia in the only Western ambulance in the country. A French doctor, who was working with the Red Cross, was summoned to assist.

When David was stable enough to be moved, I arranged for an air ambulance from France, loaded with French doctors, to fly him to Lyons,

France, where I had assembled a team of specialists from the University
of Utah Hospital's famed burn unit would be waiting. We brought him
back to Utah under their care. Morphine kept him as comfortable as possible. I spent hours on board with a hand pump to help him breathe. On
the flight home, we stopped in Pontiac, Michigan, where Dr. Roy Wirthlin performed a tracheotomy in a desperate effort to save David's life.
But his condition was deteriorating.

David Horne died January 21, 1996, a few days after returning to
Utah and his family. He loved the Armenian people. He told me that if he
didn't make it he would be content that his last act was in service to the
people of that great country. He carried twenty-five thousand pairs of eye-
glasses to Armenia on his last trip because we concluded that many people
there had trouble reading due to eyesight issues. He was a devoted servant
of the Lord and a hero to all Armenians, as well as to our family.

During a 1998 visit to Armenia, I invited the country's newly elected
president, Robert Kocharian, to visit Salt Lake City. The Armenian leader
accepted the offer in October of that year. His trip drew criticism from
his detractors at home, who pointed out the folly of his associating with
someone who was not Armenian and who had strong ties to the LDS
Church. (I was taking flak from both sides on this issue.) Kocharian arrived with Foreign Minister Vartan Oskanian, two assistants, and a slew
of bodyguards. As a head of state, he was entitled to Secret Service protection, although one can waive the extra security if desired. At the last
minute, Kocharian accepted the US protection team. The decision to add
the Secret Service led to two amusing incidents.

The agents set up a command post in one of my garages at our Deer
Valley compound where the Armenian delegation was staying. I took the
president and foreign minister on a tour of our classic antique automobile
collection stored there. When I told them the cars were all in perfect running order, they asked if they could drive them. "Sure," I said. The head
of the Secret Service went berserk, saying there was no way his agents
could provide proper protection while their charges were attracting attention in high-profile cars. Earlier, I had noticed this same lead agent
drooling over one of the Ferraris. I told him if he could figure out a way

to let the president and foreign minister drive the cars for a short time, he could take the Ferrari out for as long as he wanted after the two had finished their drives and he went off shift. He hesitated, knowing full well that if anything happened to the pair, he could lose his job. Still, he always had wanted to drive this particular Ferrari and he took the chance. They all drove my cars and had a delightful, incident-free experience.

Kocharian also was a basketball fan. I arranged for the delegation to visit my friend Karl Malone, the former power forward for the Utah Jazz, voted the NBA's most valuable player that year, and an Olympic gold medalist. His home was something else. It had an indoor basketball court, a workout room, an extensive wine collection, a shooting gallery, and an oversized version of everything.

To these visitors, the most impressive attraction was Karl's shooting gallery and gun collection. Before becoming president, Kocharian was a military leader in the Armenia-Azerbaijan conflict and a longtime pal of Russia's current president, Vladimir Putin. (Here it is 2014 and another war has just broken out over the disputed land between Armenia and Azerbaijan.) Kocharian was familiar with several of Malone's guns and asked to see one in particular. He disassembled it in seconds. Malone challenged the president to a shooting contest.

The Secret Service people went ballistic (no pun intended) and refused to allow the use of live ammunition. I calmed the agents, assuring them no one would get hurt. Kocharian is an excellent marksman and Malone is as good a shot with a firearm as he is from inside the paint. As it turned out, Kocharian hit five perfect bull's-eyes. Malone hit one. Then Malone invited one of Kocharian's bodyguards to shoot at a target, using his Armenian-issue service pistol. The security man emptied his sidearm, but failed to hit the target, let alone hit the bull's-eye. Malone tested the weapon and found it wasn't sighted properly.

The Mailman, as he was known in the NBA, ended the tour by presenting his guests with signed basketballs and jerseys and a box-load of NBA souvenirs and memorabilia worth a small fortune in Armenia.

For several years following the collapse of the Soviet Union, Armenia was plagued by political and economic turmoil. Armenia's housing problems in particular continued to trouble me. Our cement factory was turning out quality concrete building panels and the government was making progress on the housing shortage, but whenever I visited the country I continued to see people living in metal shipping containers. Shortly after Kocharian's visit to Utah, I returned to Armenia and asked the Huntsman people there how far $10 million would go toward alleviating some of the persistent housing problems. They estimated that much money would build five hundred apartments which would house up to four thousand people. When I announced my decision to do just that, Kocharian became emotional. He said I had done more for the country than any other living person. The foreign minister said no non-Armenian was more familiar to his nation than Jon Huntsman.

We decided to locate our apartment complex in the city of Gyumri, in the northwest Shirak region, close to the epicenter of the quake. The local governor, Felix Pirumian, agreed to supply the land, but the sites he offered were problematic. I asked to see alternative sites the next morning. Upon returning to the governor's office, I spotted a large parcel of land directly across the street. It was an abandoned factory site. Pointing to it, I said, "We would like that property." The governor said no. It was a great site and I quietly asked Armenia's minister of town planning, David Lokyan, who was accompanying us, to see what he could do. Immediately, a heated argument broke out between Lokyan and Governor Pirumian. For an hour, they yelled back and forth to the point of stalemate. I suggested that Lokyan set up a meeting with President Kocharian in whose presence I would ask the governor why this abandoned property could not be the site of our apartment complexes. This led the governor to reveal that he had intended to sell it.

We held firm. If the apartments were to be built in Gyumri, I insisted, they would have to be located there. The city needed apartments more than money, so we eventually got the land.

I brought in a seismology expert and a Swiss construction team. That we didn't hire Armenians for the work caused some contention, but we didn't have confidence in their skill levels and wanted to build a structure that could withstand future earthquakes. It was crucial in rebuilding Armenia to utilize Western building standards and quality-assurance management. Armenians were still building by the traditional Soviet standards. We would use the "base isolation system," widely used in Western construction in earthquake-prone cities because it employed rubber bearings, allowing foundations to move. Once again, the fight over who would be awarded the construction contract went all the way to the president's office. The government capitulated.

The rebuilding problem in Armenia was clearly illustrated by an incident with the American Red Cross (ARC) on whose board I served. Bernadine Healy, then president of the agency, had received a disturbing report from the ARC's engineer that he could not certify the quality control used in the construction of twenty high-rise Red Cross buildings under way in Armenia. The engineer reported the apartments (forty units to a building) might not meet international standards and recommended they be rebuilt with Red Cross money.

This evaluation was causing angst within the Armenian government and ARC lawyers, as well as in the mind of billionaire Armenian-American Kirk Kerkorian, whose charitable organization, the Lincy Foundation, had underwritten the first set of buildings. The dilemma was that ARC had promised hundreds of families living in those metal containers they would have permanent quarters before the onset of winter. The Armenian government feared that delaying the move-in date would cause a riot that could destabilize the country. Lawyers for the ARC worried the relief agency could be held liable if there were another quake and the homes collapsed. Lincy Foundation officials were in a dither over the possibility its reputation would be tarnished because it was their project. Their tax-exempt status could be in jeopardy.

I asked my team in Armenia to evaluate the situation. It found that, in terms of meeting specifications, the cement panels ranged all over the map. Some were reinforced with concrete rebar, others were not. Contractors used recycled steel with no pretesting. The Huntsman plant produced prestressed concrete panels, but local contractors would not accept our product because we refused to pay kickbacks. Ultimately, our seismologists determined that ARC buildings were no worse than the others recently built in Armenia. Certainly they would be safer than the *domeks* in which earthquake victims still were living. I counseled all parties it would be best if they did not destroy the buildings.

The ARC lawyers, however, were not persuaded, although Healy deferred to me, the only board member with experience in Armenia. I would be the legal middleman between the Red Cross and the Armenian government. I would indemnify the Red Cross and obtain a full indemnification from Kocharian's government. He trusted me, and thousands of Armenians were housed in these new apartments. The Red Cross was off the legal hook and the buildings were allowed to stand. I would be responsible from this point forward. It was a risk I was willing to take. It would have been devastating for them to see these new high-rise apartment buildings ripped down only because of building code violations by the American Red Cross. That was why I insisted on having our own contractors for the construction of our apartment complex at Gyumri.

The abandoned factory building on our apartment site presented another bureaucratic mess. The government did not want it torn down, but the structure wasn't suitable for apartment units. With extensive reinforcement and design work, we thought we might be able to convert it to a school building, and that's what we did. We erected the most well-equipped, modern educational facility in Armenia and obtained used computers for the school.

About a year after the school opened, the city of Gyumri held a dedication celebration. When my plane carrying President Kocharian and several ministers touched down, it was the first such private plane ever to land in Gyumri. Even after a year's occupancy, the school looked brand new. The children took pride in it. It was exquisite. Much of the city turned out to celebrate the occasion. More than twenty thousand residents filled the streets to cheer the new school's opening. The apartment complex, named Huntsman Village, was dedicated in 2004.

Armenia was suffering from donor fatigue by the late 1990s, even though much of the country still remained in shambles ten years after the quake. Our Gyumri project was one of the few humanitarian efforts still in place. I met several times with a Kerkorian lawyer, Jim Aljian, to offer use of our land and designs for an apartment complex building of its own, but he declined. Part of the problem was the Huntsman project was receiving constant play in the Armenian press. President Kocharian mentioned it every chance he got. Kirk Kerkorian, the world's best-known Armenian outside of the country—and certainly the wealthiest—noticed this. But in 2000, Kerkorian's Lincy Foundation announced its intention to inject millions of dollars into the country, and they proceeded to construct apartments on land we had offered them. Kerkorian was a lifesaver to his native land. I revere him immensely and we remain friends. In 2010, his charitable foundation donated $5 million to the Huntsman Cancer Institute in Salt Lake City. It was his way of thanking me.

Yerevan was being refurbished and the country was making progress toward recovery. That was good because by the dawn of 2001 I had infused hundreds of man-hours and massive sums of money into the Armenian effort and was facing my own economic challenges. We honored our commitments but could do little more. I had been made a full-fledged citizen of the country, complete with voting rights. There can be no greater honor.

Today, we continue to provide Armenia with limited humanitarian aid. The concrete and roofing business was donated in 2011 to one of the country's largest charities. In order to offer better education to its young people, I provide twenty-six full scholarships annually to Utah State University for the benefit of the country's top students.

One would think that dealing with crises for years—family, natural disasters, political, religious, and business related—would steel me for almost anything. It didn't. And I would be left to cope with a crisis of a different kind: my life.

14. Facing Mortality

NOT COUNTING MY SHAKY BIRTH, A MILD HEART ATTACK WHEN I was running the early plastics business, and a nearly disastrous 1967, my health throughout my first fifty years was fairly robust. Things haven't gone all that well since. Within the 1967 calendar year, I cheated death three times. That's pushing one's luck with the Lord, but I am here to write about it and that beats the alternative.

In the first incident of that fateful year, I decided at the last minute to change my flight and, instead of flying from Dallas, Texas to Houston, I boarded a plane for San Antonio to visit one of my dearest friends at Wharton who owns H-E-B Supermarkets. My associates, two close friends, took the Houston flight. That plane was struck by lightning en route. The resulting crash killed all aboard. In the same year, one morning at dawn just outside of Fillmore, Utah, my vehicle was hit head-on by a gasoline tanker loaded with jet fuel. The car rolled three times and was demolished. Miraculously, I walked away with only a knee injury.

Shortly after that, I signed up for volunteer work at the LDS Temple in Los Angeles and was pulling a double session when, at about 8:30 p.m., I doubled over in agony and headed home. My doctor saw me twice during the next ten days. Throughout the first five days, he treated me for stomach flu. At that point, he acknowledged a misdiagnosis and began treating me for a duodenal ulcer. After another five days of suffering, I decided he still had it wrong. In severe pain, I nearly crawled on hands and knees to the emergency room of Providence Saint Joseph Medical Center in Burbank, where the chief of surgery told me I was lucky to be alive. My appendix had burst ten days earlier and I had been suffering from a deadly case of peritonitis. It took doctors six weeks to drain the poisonous fluids from my body.

That was it, except for a hemorrhoid surgery in 1980 (I lost thirty-five pounds), a pair of cracked vertebrae in 1983, a bout of phlebitis in 1984, and the onset of Addison's disease in 1986. Most of that can be written off to the luck of the draw. The real body blow came in 1991.

The banks were pressuring Karen and me to jointly purchase $100 million in life insurance, which wasn't a bad idea. The children would be the beneficiaries and it would assist with inheritance taxes should anything happen to us. The children would be required to pay the premiums, however, which came to nearly a half million dollars a year. I worked out a generous bonus plan to help them cover the annual fees. It was the largest individual dual-survivor policy ever written in Utah to that point and, for all I know, that could still be the case. Three insurance companies joined to underwrite the policy but insisted Karen and I submit to comprehensive physicals before issuing the policy. In August, we underwent physicals and passed with flying colors. The policy was issued and our lenders were happy.

During the fall, quite coincidentally, Salt Lake City's LDS Hospital invited me to tour its new highly touted Fitness Institute. It was difficult to fit a tour into my schedule, so I kept putting it off. Hospital Administrator David Wirthlin was a friend, so in early November I finally found time for a one-hour walk-through. "I have no time for tests," I told the doctors. Besides, I'd had all the testing I wanted during the insurance physicals. Near the end of the tour, Frank Yanowitz, the institute's medical director, asked me if those insurance physicals had included a prostate-specific antigen (PSA) blood test, which measures levels of a protein generated by the prostate. Cancer swells the prostate, he explained, which then makes more protein and raises the PSA count.

I was 54, an age when one had to start thinking about such things. After all, my father died of prostate cancer, the most common form of cancer in males. Statistics show that about a quarter of a million men annually are diagnosed with it. One in 2 men and 1 in 3 women will have cancer in their lifetimes. Since the early 1990s, the prostate cancer survival rate—which was already better than that of many other cancers—has increased significantly. In fact, the Huntsman Cancer Institute just announced technological advancements lifting the survival rate from 90 to 95 percent. The highest percentage of diagnosed cases is found in men between ages 65 and 74, but about 1 percent is diagnosed in 45 to 65 year olds, my age group at the time.

In any case, I told Yanowitz that a PSA had not been part of the insurance physicals. It would only take a minute, he said. *Why not?* I thought. The decision probably saved my life. Within a few hours, the PSA results came back: 4.6 nanograms of protein, which placed me in a danger zone. About half the men with a 4.0 count or above have prostate cancer; a higher count increases the probability. (To illustrate the precision of the test's measurement, a nanogram weighs a billion times less than a gram, and almost a trillion times less than a pound.) A few days later, I visited urologist Ned Mangelson, a friend, who drew 6 prostate biopsy samples with a needle and sent them to the lab. The day before Thanksgiving, Mangelson called me at my office with a message that hit like a sucker punch: "Jon, you have prostate cancer."

It was like receiving a guilty verdict for a crime I didn't commit. Hadn't my comprehensive physical exams in August given me a clean bill of health? I was stunned—terrified, actually—and confounded. It was as much an issue of control as anything else. All my life, at least in business, I had some level of control over the situations in which I found myself. This was different. I had no control whatsoever. At fifty-four, I was the same age my mother had been when she learned she had breast cancer. Fewer than five years after her diagnosis, she was dead.

Mangelson scheduled more biopsies to determine the extent of my cancer's development. He took eleven samples. Cancer showed up in two of them. The good news, according to a full-body scan, was that the cancer had not metastasized to the bones. If it had, I would have been a goner. My cancer appeared to be localized and he recommended surgery. Prostate cancer treatment at the time followed one of two routes: surgery (invasive, radical surgery with major side effects but which produced a solid chance of long-term survival) and radiation (offering better post-treatment quality of life but with less assurance of survival). I chose the radical prostatectomy involving complete removal of the gland, the seminal vesicles, and the nerves on both sides. Unfortunately, I made the decision without a full understanding of what the postoperative ramifications would be.

I launched a search for a top prostate surgeon and I didn't have to look far. The name Robert Stephenson, a urinary oncologist who had been associated with Memorial Sloan Kettering in New York City and later with Houston's MD Anderson Cancer Center, was mentioned often during my search. I phoned Shell Oil CEO Frank Richardson, who was on the MD Anderson advisory board in Houston. He confirmed that Stephenson was everything his reputation suggested he was but he told me that, to their disappointment, Stephenson had been hired away just a few months before.

"Where is he now?" I inquired.

"About a mile from your office," responded Richardson. Stephenson had moved to the University of Utah's School of Medicine. He was a Utah native and had returned to the mountains.

Radical prostatectomy is no simple procedure, but I was told it would remove my cancer cleanly and provide relative assurance of long-term survival if the cancer was in fact confined to the prostate gland, which, at that time, was nearly impossible to confirm prior to surgery. What I didn't know was that the price of that assurance would be incontinence and impotence. The former usually becomes controllable in time; the latter almost never does. Therein resides a dilemma: a significant percent of prostate cancers won't kill you, especially if you are over the age of seventy-five when detected. Generally, radiation is more frequently recommended as the treatment for men between the ages of seventy and seventy-nine. Radical prostatectomy is the usual choice for men under sixty-five. Watchful waiting often is recommended today for men over the age of seventy-five because something else will likely take you out before this slow-moving cancer does. You don't die *of* prostate cancer, you die *with* it. But determining who needs treatment and whether it should be surgery or radiation is sometimes faulty science.

A debate rages even today over the value of routine biopsies and a finding that PSA tests are not all that conclusive. One camp argues any PSA reading higher than 2.5 ought to be biopsied. Other medical scientists counter that watchful waiting to see what develops is the more prudent route. They say any PSA reading below 10.0 will lead to the discovery of at least microscopic carcinoma cells, which are not fully understood. The majority of them are not life threatening, but others are dangerous and there is no current way to distinguish which is which. This group says PSA screenings, using the standard 4.0 benchmark, have led to too many biopsies and subsequent unnecessary treatments. Others warn that too many men die waiting for the PSA level to get above 4.0. In 1991 there was no such debate and, for me, the decision was clear.

I have since spoken to large groups of prostate cancer survivors who belong to the organization Us TOO. For the most part, they are angry and disillusioned because their treatments robbed them of control of basic physical functions. What upsets them most is that doctors did not properly inform them of the consequences prior to their operations. Even if there was informed consent, such as in my case, they were so scared that they did not listen closely to the oncologist regarding the after-effects.

My surgery was scheduled for the first week of January 1992. Shortly after I learned I had cancer, I began to grasp the important lessons of vulnerability and mortality. My emotions were on a roller coaster, but I made the transition from the initial stunned reaction to a determined resolve to beat the disease.

One of my sources of strength came from an encounter the previous Christmas when Karen and I attended the annual Festival of Trees fundraiser for the Primary Children's Hospital. We had been cochairs of its foundation for nearly a decade and came to know a beautiful nine-year-old patient, Becky Bair, who had a deadly form of leukemia. Her cancer had gone into remission when she was four, but it reasserted itself five years later. Becky was chosen to turn on the hospital's holiday lights that year and, before pulling the switch, told the audience why she was in the hospital and revealed her greatest wish: a trip to Disney World. After the ceremony, I went over to her mother, introduced myself and told her that getting Becky to Disney World would not be a problem. Pick a date when you and her brothers can join her, I said, and we will meet at the stairs of my jet.

Five months later, Becky, her parents, and her four older siblings flew with me to Disney World in Orlando. We had a ball together. Just before we landed, I gave each of the children a one-hundred-dollar bill for spending money. I could not stay through their three-day vacation, but I covered their hotel, meals, and Disney World expenses. When I picked them up three days later, they bombarded me with tales of all the fun they'd had at the park. It was a memorable experience for all. As I contemplated my future, I thought about that trip and about Becky's courage as she fought for life. Through it all, she maintained a wonderful, sunny outlook. She was a marvelous role model, and I vowed to adopt her faith and optimism. Becky wrote to cheer me up during my eleven days in the hospital. (Today's robotic surgery involves a stay of only two or three days.) About a year later, sadly, sweet little Becky lost her battle.

Two days before my surgery, I called our family together to help keep things in perspective. Our children were adults at that point, but some of them were frightened and may have been thinking the worst. A family meeting seemed like a good idea. I reminded them we had been blessed far more than any family had reason to expect and suggested they were not to entertain the idea that my having cancer was somehow unfair. I told them I was certain I was going to be fine and that this issue was a mere blip on the radar screen in an otherwise blessed life, certainly so when compared to the burdens many people face on a daily basis. Even if I ultimately should not survive the ordeal, I told them, it would not be a national tragedy and they should devote their time to thinking of others and giving thanks for what we have received in life. There were a few tears and sniffles, but everyone felt better having acknowledged the elephant in the room. I invited them to go with me on a little side trip the next morning. If submitting to surgery turned out to be my final act on this earth, I wanted my next-to-last act to be meaningful.

On that snowy January morning in 1992, I drove to Russ's Barber Shop in Salt Lake City for a trim, the first of five stops I would make before checking into the hospital that afternoon. A few of the children and grandchildren met me at Russ's. We joked and talked during the haircut; neither my cancer nor the next morning's surgery was mentioned. From there, we drove as a convoy to the Travelers Aid homeless shelter (since renamed The Road Home) where we gathered in the parking lot. The shelter's administrators had been warned the Huntsman clan would be calling. Over the years, we had been contributors to Travelers Aid so the staff probably thought this was a donor visit to witness how the money was being used.

Shelter Director Patrick Poulin took us on a tour. The shelter was housing more homeless people than usual because of the bitter-cold temperatures of the previous few nights. We asked that he gather his staff in the conference room where I handed him an envelope with a note inside that thanked the center for its good work. Accompanying the note was a check for $1 million. The family filed out as Poulin and his staff stared in disbelief. Talk about a fun event. The ability to do things like that is the greatest benefit of being wealthy.

We only had to walk across the street for stop number three, the St. Vincent de Paul soup kitchen and distribution center. The Reverend Terrence Moore, then head of Catholic Community Services, was overseeing preparation of the noon meal as we barged in. We joined him for lunch, partaking of the food that would be served to the center's clients, and asked if he could join us in the small chapel near the front entrance. "I would like to read you this letter," I began when we were all assembled. The charity had received several donations from us in the past and Moore probably figured the latest gift was being hand-delivered. The note commended the priest for his devotion to the needy and for the good work being done at St. Vincent de Paul. In closing, I told him the Huntsman family would like to play a larger part going forward and handed him a check, also for $1 million. He stared at it for a moment and promptly teared up. I hugged him and we took our leave. Years later he told me he had never received a check with so many zeroes in it. "I couldn't count them all," he said.

The next visit was the Fitness Institute at LDS Hospital where I had taken the PSA test nearly two months earlier. I presented director Frank Yanowitz with a $500,000 check for the institute's work in early cancer detection. (I later gave the hospital another $2 million.) Overwhelmed, he nevertheless found words to express his gratitude. My final destination was the University of Utah hospital. My whole family was with me as I checked in for the next morning's surgery. It was standing room only at the administration desk.

Word of our $2.5 million excursion reached the news media. On the next day's *Good Morning America* program, Moore portrayed me as "The Millionaire" from the old TV series of the same name. Host Charlie Gibson asked Moore if I had sampled the soup that was to be ladled that day. Moore said I had, although he had not realized that I was on my way to major surgery. "I was very glad St. Vincent's was preparing something healthy that day," he told Gibson. I, however, was unable to catch the program or read the newspaper accounts that morning. I was on an operating table undergoing a radical prostatectomy.

I spent the next ten days in the hospital, floating in and out of the effects of the sedatives and painkillers. During my lucid moments, I was buoyed by swarms of well-wishers and hundreds of get-well cards and telegrams (which people still sent, even in 1992). The floral arrangements became so numerous that Karen had the children deliver them to other patients throughout the hospital. I had no idea we had so many friends. Cards and letters came from people in high places, from Huntsman employees and friends, and from grateful people our charity had helped over the years, directly or indirectly. Karen or the children had to read most of them to me. I was out of it much of the time, but my heart was deeply touched by the concern.

Chase Peterson, then-president of the University of Utah, sent a particularly touching note saying, "The granite of the Wasatch Mountain Range is not supposed to ever chip or erode—at least not in our lifetimes. So do what you need to do, buoyed by the love that surrounds you, then get back to building more empires . . ." A different but no less appreciated note arrived among the others, sent by a recipient of the Travelers Aid shelter: "I was warm and dry and out of the cold last night. Maybe this will not mean much within the vastness of the universe, but it means a great deal to this homeless woman." Senator Bob Dole, the GOP presidential nominee in 1996, had undergone prostate cancer surgery a few days ahead of me. He and Elizabeth have been friends throughout the years. After learning of my surgery, he called twice to tell me what to expect.

With Karen's help, I compiled a list of nurses, operating room technicians, dieticians, orderlies, and maintenance personnel who came and went from my fifth-floor hospital room during my stay. It became the guest list for a party we would throw for them and their spouses a month later—nearly eighty people in all—at our Deer Valley home. I brought in the Utah Opera Company to entertain them and each guest received a color TV set. For surgeon Robert Stephenson, to whom I owed my life, I endowed a $1.5 million chair at the University of Utah medical school on the condition that he be the first to benefit from it. Ned Mangelson, who had taken the biopsies, received what could be called a most noteworthy surprise.

It took me six months to regain my mental, emotional, and physical strength. After a radical prostatectomy, however, a man never truly returns to normal. I have talked to others who have undergone the operation and, as I indicated earlier, every one of them was upset about the aftermath. None had been told the full story of the side effects, which often included incontinence and erectile dysfunction. In my case, the former was overcome within a few months but the latter was permanent.

I don't worry anymore about being a he-man, but it was frustrating and disheartening for both Karen and me to lose that part of our lives forever. Most men don't like to talk about this aspect. Some will tell you everything is okay, but I suspect that is half-truth at best. Even many doctors then didn't know the extent of post-surgery problems because their patients couldn't bring themselves to share the whole story.

After his prostate surgery, Bob Dole became the closest thing we men had to a national spokesman for ED, or erectile dysfunction. He put on a positive face for the television commercials but during one private conversation in which we frankly discussed our respective experiences he declared: "Yeah, it's the shits." There have been some breakthroughs in postoperative treatment since then, but the National Cancer Institute still acknowledges that, unlike many other side effects of cancer surgery, loss of function is a problem in more than 80 percent of those who undergo radical prostatectomy.

Women face similar emotional feelings following radical mastectomies after breast cancer (which took my mother) or treatment for ovarian cancer (which took my stepmother), and when chemotherapy results in baldness. That's why, in our Huntsman Cancer Institute (more on that amazing facility in a later chapter), we created a "femininity" center that offers wigs, prostheses, grooming techniques, and counseling so a woman can come out of treatment feeling as beautiful and feminine as when she went in. It is one of only two or three such programs in the nation. The Huntsman Cancer Institute has a similar program for men that benefits them physically and emotionally, restoring self-confidence and enhancing their quality of life.

I am not embarrassed to talk about prostate cancer or its side effects. Men ought to understand what's involved before making such a life-altering choice. Within months of my surgery, I was discussing the subject in television interviews. I occasionally write and give speeches on the subject. My overall goal, however, is to encourage early detection and to ultimately defeat cancer. Sadly, too many American males stay away from diagnostic procedures and potential treatments, purely out of fear. Early detection allows for a number of options that a late-stage diagnosis does not. And researchers are investigating the possibility of drugs that would keep latent prostate cancer from becoming active.

Would I undergo the radical surgery if I had it to do over? Yes, because, above all else, I wanted to keep on living. I watched my mother wither away with the cancer that invaded her bones. My father's prostate cancer had moved to his bones by the time he died. The downside of radical prostatectomy notwithstanding, my surgery just about guaranteed that my father's fate would not be mine. There were a lot of tears on the pillow that first year, but I decided to take charge of my new life and become a better human being. "Ironically," I wrote in the foreword of a 1999 book on prostate cancer survivors, "the disease that many characterize as a threat to their manhood demands those very qualities traditionally associated with manhood: strength, courage, decisiveness, and dignity. The values and lifestyles of [the survivors profiled in this book] were altered; their spirituality, humility, and feelings of love were enhanced. After cancer, they conclude, a man realizes what is really important."

I was determined to manifest masculinity in other ways. When I physically recovered in midyear, I sought with a renewed and mighty vengeance to expand the company, tighten the family bonds, and create a world-class cancer center. This self-renewal gave me the focus and energy to do what had to be done. Through it all, Karen was my guiding light.

While the prostate cancer has never returned, it didn't take long before I faced another form. The disease was far from finished with me, as it turned out in the intervening years. It was the start of a plethora of other health problems that made me a walking medical textbook over the last fifteen years.

In the late fall of 1992, I was bothered with a canker sore inside my lower lip. It wasn't a major incident compared to prostate cancer and the distractions of the mammoth business deals I was lining up in the latter half of 1992, but it was worrisome. I tried over-the-counter canker remedies, but it wouldn't heal. In mid-November, the doctor took a biopsy as a precaution.

On the day before Thanksgiving, precisely a year to the day after I had been given the prostate cancer news, I received a call informing me I had mouth cancer. Specifically, it was a squamous cell carcinoma, a mid-level type of skin cancer. It carried a ten percent mortality rate. I slammed down the phone receiver. This time, I wasn't scared, bewildered, or in shock. I was ticked off. I promised myself I would beat this cancer into submission. I met with Gerald Kruger, an oncologist at the University of Utah medical school (the predecessor to the Huntsman Cancer Institute). He said the traditional treatment was removal of the cancer by cutting out the tissue areas surrounding the canker. That would mean cutting away a sizable chunk of my lip and chin. He said plastic surgery would mask the disfigurement. I wasn't so sure. Further, if it turned out the surgeons didn't get all of the cancer cells, they would have to remove more of my face.

The brother of a friend of mine had the same type of cancer, only his was in the nose. I went to see him to discuss the results of the surgery. He looked terrible. He told me he frightened his young grandchildren. The man's cancer later came back and he lost his entire nose with the second surgery. He died not long afterward. Needless to say, I was apprehensive.

The doctors assured me plastic surgery could do wonders, but I knew no matter what they came up with I would not look like the original article. (This situation, however, is changing dramatically. Last year, for example, the Huntsman Cancer Institute perfected artificial body parts that are almost impossible to differentiate from the real thing.)

Seeing no option and resigned to my fate, I checked myself back into the University of Utah hospital for another operation. I knew it would not affect my body the way prostate cancer had, but I wasn't looking forward to the way I would look for the rest of my life. Almost as I was being wheeled on a gurney into the operating room, my doctors had second thoughts. They decided at the last minute to try an experimental drug that was in the clinical trial stage—a high-powered salve that would eat away the skin, layer by layer, until the cancer was eliminated. It would do a number on the inside of my mouth, but it would raise even more havoc with the cancer. The two specialists decided to give it a try before surgically dismantling my mouth.

Twice a day for six weeks, I applied the anticancer balm. The family and I were on an extended vacation in Hawaii during this time. Business-wise, it was our slow time and I thought the Hawaiian beaches might make the course of treatment easier. It didn't. It was awful. My mouth bled continuously during those six weeks. My food intake was restricted mostly to liquids. But it worked.

We returned from Hawaii the second week of January 1993. I went back to work as good as new, although my cancer specialists told me it may only stay in remission for up to eighteen months. I am happy to re-port they were wrong. While I have had small, routine basal cell cancers removed from my face several times since 1993, the squamous cell car-cinoma reared its head again and had to be removed from my ear, neck, and head. In 2010, I had to have a dangerous melanoma tumor surgically removed from my back. Just prior to that, my nose had to be recon-structed by Dr. Bhupendra Patel, a renowned plastic surgeon, after re-moval of a deep cancerous growth. Similar surgeries have also been performed by Dr. Patel on my hand, eyes and head.

On top of those health issues, I survived four minor (if there is such a thing) heart attacks between 2001 and 2008. I've undergone a long list of surgical procedures, including a rotator cuff operation on the right shoulder and another procedure some years later on the left one. I had eye surgery, carpal tunnel surgery on my right hand, and the replacement of one knee and several operations on the other. A colon problem in 1980 required surgery followed by several months' recuperation. Two broken vertebrae in 1983 that involved a painful recovery over four years, and a fall in 2008 caused a 5.5-millimeter separation between my head and neck vertebrae. Polymyalgia rheumatica was added to the mix, which at-tacks the body's joints and has been excruciatingly painful.

I have had shingles, stomach ulcers (four times), asthma, osteoarthri-tis, neuropathy, and a torn Achilles tendon followed by twelve months of recovery. Recently, a painful hernia required surgery, which was com-plicated by the presence of scar tissue from an earlier incision made to extract that ruptured appendix. My recovery from these procedures may never be complete because my compromised state of health and my lack of a functioning immune system leave me unable to heal properly. The heavy prednisone dosage required to help treat pain and swelling during the past six years has exacted a heavy toll in terms of side effects.

It's hard for Karen to watch me suffer and I sometimes get a little fatalistic about my life, but I bounce back quickly. Considering all I have been through, I suppose I am lucky to be alive. My history of maladies notwithstanding, I manage to travel extensively, work long hours, and maintain a positive mental attitude, and I can say that I feel terrific. I expect to enjoy a long and productive future.

The problem with me is that I strive for excellence and remain a stickler for detail. You could eat off the floors of our headquarters building and our products are first rate. Each site in the Huntsman organization is clean, beautifully landscaped, and well maintained. Our name is on the door of our businesses and quality has been our hallmark from the beginning. All this fussing takes a physical toll, sometimes without my realizing it, but it personally creates enormous pressure and stress.

During parts of the year, my therapeutic base of operation is the Pritikin Longevity Center in Miami where, as *Business Week* magazine reports, "the A-list goes" to recuperate. Time spent there is a great pressure valve. Pritikin also is a refuge from the debilitating air inversions that typically plague the Salt Lake Valley the first three months of each year, which are not only ugly and depressing but make breathing difficult for me. Last but certainly not least among my stress remedies are Peter and David Huntsman; David Parkin; Rick Durham; our sons Paul, James, and Jon Jr.; and so many others who I thank for their gifted leadership of our businesses over the years. Their assumption of much of the day-to-day responsibility has reduced the pressure considerably and leaves me more time for thinking up better mousetraps.

My doctors tell me I will not die from one horrific physical assault. My demise, they point out in a chipper assessment, will be "death from a thousand cuts." How's that for positive news? Be that as it may, I am blessed with the grit and determination to get going every morning and a zest for tackling the challenges before me.

So, is it worth all this effort at my age? Of course it is. My whole life is about taking risks. I love and enjoy my job, making deals, building my charitable foundations, and expanding our renowned cancer institute. What would be worse is to not have the drive or the opportunity to make a difference. Will I get cancer again? I am beyond worrying about that. Karen and Markie are my constant inspiration.

The thing that drove me to recover as fast as I did following the prostate surgery was that I had to expand the company and to make more money. We had to build a first-class cancer research center and hospital from scratch in Salt Lake City. Our hospital would have to be a magnificent structure—an unparalleled cathedral of optimism where cancer patients would come to be given world-class care, treatment, and hope. That dream would come to fruition in less than a decade and only after I had the business infrastructure and more profits to support this massive undertaking.

15. Making Good on "The Promise"

I COULDN'T WAIT TO GET OUT OF BED ON OCTOBER 28, 2011. THE DAY was bright and crisp, my spirits brighter yet. I knew I would be making another step toward fulfilling the vow I made to my mother over four decades earlier. This was the day on which I would officially dedicate the hospital expansion of the Huntsman Cancer Institute. For me, the occasion marked the culmination of an achievement that trumped all my business deals combined, even though those triumphs had made this one possible.

My excitement notwithstanding, getting to this point had required Herculean effort: circumventing restrictive bureaucracies, surviving turf wars among regional medical facilities, struggling with a state government reluctant to accept its funding responsibilities, finding alternative funding for corporate contributors who backed out of financial pledges, and taking out personal bank loans to cover my own pledges in the face of business downturns.

This milestone came twelve years after we first opened the doors to the Huntsman Cancer Institute, a combined facility that houses a world-class hospital, massive research labs which are second to none, and one of the country's best cancer education centers. Together, they comprised nothing short of sophisticated and successful war rooms in the fight against cancer.

In attendance at the dedication were US senators, state and local officials, university presidents, religious leaders, members of the news media, and, most importantly, my guests of honor, cancer survivors. Karen and I were showcasing the expansion of a five-star hospital with some two hundred inpatient and outpatient rooms and clinics, individual chemotherapy units, the latest advances in medical equipment and technologies, and a cadre of physicians and researchers recruited from the most prestigious institutions in the nation.

In my remarks, I pointed out that the expansion included a Center for

Infusion and Advanced Therapeutics for patient relaxation and comfort during chemotherapy treatments whose rooms featured sweeping views of the surrounding Wasatch Mountains. The new imaging technologies included the only intraoperative MRI in the Intermountain West, a scanner that moves on ceiling-mounted rails into the operating room during surgery and enables surgeons to be certain that no tumor tissue remains.

The final phase on the drawing board—at least I speculate in my lifetime—is the expansion of the Institute's research arm. And in that regard, I am delighted to report that we had the pleasure of announcing on November 1, 2013, that the family will play a leading role in creating the Primary Children's and Families' Cancer Research Center. Our foundation came up with nearly half of the $100 million project; the remainder came in the form of gifts from individual donors and major contributions from the Utah legislature, Intermountain Healthcare, and The Church of Jesus Christ of Latter-day Saints. (The latter, according to a *Forbes* story on this most recent HCI turn, said the donation from the Church "is circling back to its history . . . it opened a children's hospital in Utah over 100 years ago." That caregiving center was called Primary Children's Hospital, which is now run by the University of Utah Health Sciences Center, and it became the name of our new wing.) This specialized research facility within the Cancer Institute, which opens in 2016 and includes a tumor imaging suite that will reduce the often six-month wait to determine if tumors are spreading, will focus solely on childhood cancers and fits perfectly with the genetic research already being done on inherited cancers. We know now that the risk of siblings getting cancer is double that of the general population. So what happens to their children? Do the odds go up for the next generation? Nobody knows—yet.

The motive for sending me in this direction was witnessing my mother die and other family members succumbing to this killer and a concern for giving to those in need. The formula for success is entrepreneurial in nature: innovate and get it done. I engaged in this humanitarian project the way I tackle business acquisitions: with audacity and with gusto.

The early planning for this project began in 1992 and 1993, but it wasn't until 1995 that I had the financial wherewithal to put my wallet where my heart was. That was the year I announced our first $100 million commitment to build Phase I of the Institute, the research laboratory component. By 1999 HCI's research operations were underway.

Before HCI, the Intermountain West had not been particularly well served by cancer facilities. As a result I have worked hard to make HCI the largest, most advanced, caring, comfortable, and prestigious specialized cancer center there is. And on September 13, 1999, with Karen and Jon Jr. flanking me and with other family members close by, we dedicated the Institute's 6-story, 225,000-square-foot research building that immediately was filled with more than 150 medical investigators, clinicians, and researchers. At its dedication, I underscored 3 goals: scientific cancer-cure breakthroughs, clinical care with an emphasis on comfort and dignity, and education. Those 3 power points could well be encapsulated into 1 overall mission: Helping people escape death and the suffering from cancer and extending the quality of their lives. It is this that makes HCI unique.

On April 26, 2000, Karen and I announced our family's additional $126 million donation for the first phase of the clinical research hospital. At the announcement event, University of Utah President Bernie Machen predicted "countless human lives . . . would be affected." He said the gift was among the largest investments by an individual in US higher education. Superlatives notwithstanding, precious little in the way of help followed. The Institute became the only cancer research and treatment facility in America where a single family provided the major source of funding.

Four years later, on my birthday, June 21, in 2004, we dedicated the new hospital, which extended magnificently from the research building. With the hospital in place, discoveries from trailblazing medical research at the companion research institute could be instantly conveyed down the connecting corridor, directly to patient bedsides. Research drives the clinical discoveries, and some 16 percent of our patients choose to participate in clinical trials, more than 3 times the national average. (In 2011 alone, the year of the hospital's expansion, HCI investigators received more than $79 million in research grants, putting the facility at the top in a competitive field for diminishing private and public grant money.)

Our family created and constructed the Huntsman Cancer Institute. But once it was built and equipped, we deeded the brick and mortar and ongoing operations to the University of Utah and, thus, to the state of

Utah. Our family neither owns nor operates the facility, which may come as a surprise to many since I am the face, primary financier, and founder of the center. The original plan was that our family and private donors would build the facilities and fund its research needs. Federal grants would help with research costs. The state, operating as the University of Utah Health Sciences Center, was to cover the upkeep, maintenance, and other operating costs. To my everlasting frustration, it hasn't always worked out that way. The state's approach has been: no need to worry about it, "deep-pockets" Huntsman will cover whatever the university and the legislature does not. Every lawmaker and university administrator knows I will not let care levels erode or the research deteriorate. And, so far, that promise has held up.

These frustrations notwithstanding, my enthusiasm for and commitment to the fight against cancer have never wavered. My commitment was reinforced over the years as I watched my parents, brother, relatives, in-laws, friends, and colleagues die of this equal-opportunity killer, striking without regard to race, socioeconomic status, gender, age, nationality, or religion.

The Institute represents the fruition of a personal crusade that absorbed the last two decades of my life. Despite naysayers, our perseverance and a lot of help from generous donors large and small brought about its completion and a sense of fulfillment. Ultimately, the Institute will have received more than a billion of our family's dollars and pledges. Almost half of that amount has been donated so far and another $800 million came from grants, donations, and every other conceivable source. Thus, the total investment in HCI as of 2014 is approximately $1.4 billion. If you believe nothing else, believe this: the challenge was worth every day, every frustration, every dollar it took to make it happen.

On the hospital's dedication day in 2011, the morning dawned inspirationally clear and calm. The scene in front of the hospital's sparkling, three-story glass lobby, however, was anything but serene. A thunderstorm had hit during the early morning hours, unleashing a freak microburst of wind onto the mountainside dedication area. An upended stage and a shredded tent lay in disarray. Chairs and mini-grandstands that had been arranged in advance of the one thousand guests' arrival for the 9:00 a.m. dedication ceremony were strewn hither and yon. Security

officers noticed the devastation around 5:00 a.m. and called Cancer Institute personnel, who formed a brigade to tackle the chaos, and order
was restored with ninety minutes to spare.

The emergency cleanup effort following the predawn havoc was symbolic of the Huntsman Cancer Institute's purpose: to shepherd patients
through adversity to a place of hope and wellness. Those entering this
towering complex with cancer-ravaged bodies would leave with spirits
healed and minds at peace, and with new and powerful allies to battle
the disease. The storm's destruction was merely a momentary distraction
from the architectural and scientific marvels of the towering center, a
medical cathedral of faith, hope, and love. The green-tinted glass panels
that clad the research and hospital buildings gleamed like emeralds in the
sunlight. At its hillside elevation, it is the highest commercial structure
in the historic Salt Lake Valley, standing as a beacon of comfort and healing on the foothills of the Wasatch Mountains.

Nature's curveball was all but forgotten by mid-morning when I
looked out from the dedication stage at the swell of civic, business, and
religious leaders; medical staff and news media; the curious; and well-
wishers from every walk of life. Some in the crowd may have understood
the statistics applicable to the individuals in that gathering alone: one in
two males and one in three females would need this facility or one like it
sometime in their lives. The hospital is located at the end of a street
named Circle of Hope, and hope is indeed reflected everywhere. It was
emotional for me, but I wasn't the only one shedding a tear.

Those assembled for the ceremony marveled at an edifice that from
the outside, or viewed from inside the warm expansive lobby, resembles
a five-star hotel rather than the old-fashioned, austere, hermetically sealed
medical facility. I remembered my stay at a traditional hospital following
cancer surgery two decades earlier. I was scared and lonely. When I did
get visitors, there was a single chair on which they could sit and visit. I
would not permit my hospital to be so inhospitable. That's why, in the
mid-'90s, I hired a senior oncologist and former head of St. Jude Children's Hospital in Memphis, Joseph Simone, from Memorial Sloan Kettering Cancer Center in New York to conceptualize a hospital that would
inspire patient confidence and offer the latest technology and medical
care in a pleasant, peaceful, inspirational environment. Cost was not to

be a consideration. Simone and his team, with input from more than two hundred healthcare professionals and hundreds of cancer patients, presented final recommendations to architect Don Finlayson (whose daughter had been struggling with cancer for a number of years). He created an architectural masterpiece. Truly, Simone is a brilliant oncologist as well as a master planner.

As its proud parent, nothing pleases me more than showing off the amenities of this facility. First, there's free valet parking awaiting patients and visitors when they pull up to the entrance. Upon entering, one stands in a three-story lobby/atrium, whose tinted-glass walls embrace an integration of live trees and a healing garden of plants. The design draws the eye skyward to a ceiling where fiber-optic lights shine like stars in the heavens, radiating optimism. Every part of the hospital is easily accessible. Whisper-quiet doors, luxurious carpeting, and sound-suppressing acoustics minimize noise.

Patient/family-only elevators whisk them to private rooms larger in size and with four times the window area than in traditional hospital rooms. Those one-way windows assure patient privacy while allowing them to view gardens, patios, and mountains. Each room offers a sofa sleeper for loved ones should they wish to stay the night. A family kitchen, a lounge, a business center, laundry and shower facilities, and a library make extended visits convenient and free of stress. Two magnificent restaurants offer subsidized meals for the public, exquisite and varied cuisine, and a view of the Salt Lake Valley unmatched by any commercial restaurant in Utah.

In terms of technology, the center is unique in the Intermountain West. It combines stereotactic radiosurgery and radiotherapy, two full-field digital mammography units, combined PET/CT (positron emission tomography and computer tomography, today's most accurate and powerful imaging technique to detect cancer and characterize tumors), fluoroscopic imaging in pancreatic endoscopy (the sole way to diagnose pancreatic cancer in early stages), and facial prosthetics for those who have lost features to cancer, birth defects, or accidents.

When we first announced the PET/CT addition to the hospital, several new media outlets inquired if we also would be treating animals. But the PET/CT truly is a lifesaving, space-age machine. I had learned of this groundbreaking technology through my General Electric Medical Systems contacts. It enables doctors to locate and identify cancers years sooner than was possible using conventional methods and equipment. For assistance in obtaining this equipment, I called Jeff Immelt, now chairman and CEO of GE but at the time GE's medical division president, with whom I had a close relationship. With his help, the Huntsman hospital rose to the top of the waiting list to receive complex, portable scanners. At the time, the closest PET/CT for Intermountain West patients was at UCLA. That is no longer the case.

In most cancer hospitals, the radiation therapy suite is in dark, isolated basement space because of safety requirements for radioactivity. The Huntsman Cancer Hospital, however, is built on a hillside so the radiation unit resides on the first floor, partially tucked into the mountain. The result is an abundance of natural light and a warm and soothing ambiance. Four large, sophisticated surgical suites, centrally located, foster collaboration among specialists. (After our recent expansion, HCI now features nine top-of-the-technological-line surgical centers.)

All this was on display at the hospital's grand opening in 2004. A most telling moment in the ceremony came when Dr. Steve Prescott, the Institute's second medical director, opened the program with a request: Would members of the audience who are cancer survivors stand and remain standing? About one hundred individuals rose. Prescott then asked attendees with a loved one or an extended family member who had cancer to stand. This time, nearly every seat was vacated.

In her remarks before the crowd that day, Karen said that one has to believe passionately in something before it can happen and that many times adversities along the way will persuade you to abandon "impossible" dreams unless you are truly committed. "The timing and forces (for such a momentous project) are never right," she said, warning that if one waits for precisely the right time, it won't happen. She was absolutely right, as usual, but her point that there is never an ideal time to begin any task of significance was right on target.

For me, the cancer hospital's and research center's administrators, doctors, researchers, and staff, who in 2013 numbered 1,500 dedicated professionals, are the real heroes. They are the purveyors of hope. "Those who have cancer will cherish the names of each and every one of you," I told the staff at the 2011 hospital dedication. "Each cancer patient will find kindness and solace within these walls. They will be treated like kings and queens." I promised from day one, in 1995, we would build the finest and most up-to-date, state-of-the art cancer research center and hospital, and by 2011, we were delivering on that commitment. The 2011 dedication marked the opening of the world's most elaborate and comfortable chemotherapy center, serving 108 patients simultaneously, in lovely, modern, and private individual comfort areas. When our current construction of the Primary Children's and Families' Cancer Research Center is complete, our center will be the largest genetic cancer research institute in the world, with over 2,000 professionals on staff.

Cancer is hideous and deplorable and must be conquered, and it will be, as any evil eventually is defeated. An institute such as this must stay at the technological forefront. The latest equipment is generally termed state of the art, but today's hard fact is that, at the speed by which technology now advances, a piece of equipment is no longer state of the art once it is on line. "State of the art" is what is being conceptualized, prototyped, and tested at a given moment, and that process' appetite for dollars is insatiable. Cutting-edge research is crucial to effective patient care. It costs more than $100 million a year to operate HCI (nearly all earmarked for the research given that the hospital is self-financing). If it takes my last dollar—and I expect that will be the case—I will see to it that the Huntsman Cancer Institute and Hospital remains a model of medical excellence, the research continues unabated, and that patient care is first and foremost.

I believe the cancers that assaulted my parents and me were as much hereditary as environmental, although my mother and grandfather were "downwinders," a term for Utahns who resided downwind of nuclear bomb testing in Nevada in the 1950s and who later contracted cancer. Utahns consider the testing an act of betrayal by the US government, which deliberately and silently chose to let the fallout drift eastward into Utah. For years, government scientists denied any relationship between the testing and the inordinate number of cancer deaths in Utah. This legacy of deceit continues to cause bitterness in many Utah families whose tragedies were only recently acknowledged by the government. Indeed, in recent years, we are witnessing soaring cancer rates in many counties throughout the western US into which weather patterns blew heavy doses of the radioactive fallout five decades ago.

Today it is within our capability, through education and lifestyle precautions, to reduce our exposure to environmental cancers. But, until the last decade, one could do little about inherited cancer genes. Between 35 percent and 60 percent of all cancers are inherited, depending on the age of the patient. Colon, breast, and prostate cancers are the most susceptible to genetic transmission. (I have a trusted assistant whose father, two sisters, and nephew died of colon cancer and a brother and two nephews currently have it.) Early detection and development of an anticancer drug to prevent an inherited gene from generating cancer cells are priorities of the Institute's research, which relies on a colon cancer registry through which offspring of colon cancer patients are alerted to hereditary danger signals.

The companion mission of the Institute, as I said, is the elimination of suffering accompanying the disease. We generally hear of cancer victims one at a time—a relation, a friend, a colleague, a loved one. Overall, however, the cancer toll is much more ominous: one in five of us, as this is written, will die from the disease. We want that figure to be reduced to one in ten, then one in one hundred, and then zero. We are moving in the right direction. The number of cancer deaths has not receded in the last thirty years, not because there haven't been significant breakthroughs but because survival rates in other, less pathologically complex diseases, such as cardiovascular disease, have greatly increased. People who suffer from other diseases are living longer, thereby increasing their odds of cancer forming in their bodies.

With early diagnosis, however, one soon may be taking a pill or a vaccination to keep a certain protein in the blood system from turning, say, into colon cancer. In my excitement, I tell anyone who will listen that we want to cure cancer. That is perhaps too idealistic and broad. Practically speaking, with roughly two hundred kinds of cancers involving more than one hundred individual pathologies, I know that creating an overall cancer vaccine, such as Jonas Salk did for polio, isn't likely in my lifetime. Even so, cancer no longer is the death sentence it once was. Reasons for optimism steadily increase as more cancers become treatable.

(We can block, for instance, some varieties of adult leukemia and a rare form of colon cancer.)

The keys to treating and controlling cancer are early detection and cutting-edge intervention therapies. What medical science did with infectious diseases at the dawn of the twentieth century it can do for cancer in the twenty-first century. Cancer tumors rarely kill if they remain localized. Conversely, when the cancer spreads, or metastasizes, it is often fatal. The Institute is working on ways to keep the cancer localized, but that demands early detection. And there have been encouraging breakthroughs in early genetic changes, known to be the origin of cancer. Hereditary research led us to the first damaged gene.

Part of the complexity of a potential vaccine is that cancer is nature at work, albeit on an abnormal course. Nothing foreign, such as bacteria, necessarily has to invade the body. Cancer happens when something goes awry as cells divide, and cells are dividing constantly. The longer we live the more our cells divide. That, in turn, provides additional opportunities for something to go wrong.

HCI already has earned a national reputation in genetic research and has discovered more mutations for inherited cancer than any other cancer center in the world. One secret to the Institute's success is that it is the steward of the Utah Population Database, the world's most comprehensive population registry linked to medical and health records. This database has enticed many of the nation's best and brightest researchers to our facility. At the core of this marvelous tool are the world-renowned genealogical records of the LDS Church, a treasure trove of demographic and personal information from two-thirds of Utah's population for researchers mapping the patterns of cancer-causing gene mutations and their subsequent interactions with other genes. Data are used under conditions of strict confidentiality and informed consent.

Medical researchers are poised to make great discoveries in the next several years. Unfortunately, in much of today's biomedical research community (the cancer field being no exception), the process, rather than the results, is what brings grants and earns merit badges among peers. The view at the Huntsman Cancer Institute is the opposite: the focus is on advancing discovery of precancerous conditions and acting upon those findings with appropriate urgency.

The Institute's process is entrepreneurial science, an approach which, historically, has been resented in the scientific community and earns us occasional chiding from peer reviewers. I love the term "entrepreneurial science." It makes some scientists nervous, probably because it carries accountability, but that's just tough. People who have cancer don't have the luxury of time. I give money and expect results. I dote on HCI's scientists, but I won't bankroll mediocrity. Fortunately, National Cancer Institute director Andy von Eschenbach, himself a three-time cancer survivor, understands this approach. HCI is the only NCI-designated cancer center in the region.

Another problem encountered at HCI is that Utah does not have the population base to support certain clinical trials. Part of our research must be farmed out to cancer centers in large metropolitan areas for trials. Trial results are important in the recognition game, and recognition is important when it comes to funding and staff. Here's an example: Our diagnostic test for early ovarian cancer was given to MD Anderson Center in Houston for trials. It was successful and the cooperative testing venture will save many lives (ovarian cancer has a 90 percent cure rate when diagnosed early, but is 75 percent fatal when discovered in late stages). The Huntsman Cancer Institute won't get credit because the test was conducted at MD Anderson. We were all overjoyed by the results—and complimented MD Anderson for its assistance. The scientific-community mindset of keeping it in your own shop is not always the most effective way of doing something. Progress is looking up, though. We were the site of a controlled study released in 2011 and are making progress in this area each year. In 2013, we announced the next phase of expansion, which will double the size of HCI's research facilities, thus permitting hundreds of additional clinical trials each year.

HCI's reputation has grown throughout its fifteen years in operation. I particularly am proud that one of the Institute's focuses is an education program for underserved populations, including four Native American tribes in the region, and that all of HCI's materials are printed in Spanish and English. HCI's education center offers patients and the public information on specific cancers, treatments, risk factors, prevention guidelines, and screening. Additionally, we provide the Huntsman Online Patient Education (HOPE) website with resources and documents about the disease, a toll-free telephone service staffed by specialists who can provide personalized information on all aspects of cancer, and the Cancer Education Outreach Program which provides public presentations. The Institute exists for everyone. Our goal is that no one be turned away simply because he or she does not have the means to pay for services.

I am optimistic HCI's efforts will continue to produce dramatic results. We have several researchers hitting home runs in their labs every day. One such example: viewing inflammation as the possible catalyst to cancer's spread could mean that by reducing inflammation the tumor might remain localized. Another example: by looking at tissue samples of prostate cancer cells removed in surgery, the hypothesis is that finding a way to stop them from adhering to various surfaces will slow or halt certain cancers from spreading.

These were the highs that sent me to cloud nine during our dedication ceremonies, especially as I considered the future. But the road that brought me to this point hasn't always been so uplifting. Jealous competitors, unhelpful bureaucracies, financial challenges, and funding double crosses provided frustrations and unnecessary challenges. In the 1970s, 1980s, and 1990s, I concentrated on building a business empire with earnings sufficient to launch a prestigious cancer center. After my bouts with cancer in the 1990s, the family was ready to commit a major gift that would lead the way, confident that our industrial colleagues would be eager to join with us in this endeavor. As it turned out, we overestimated the potential pool of donors.

Our initial donation of $10 million was to get the contribution campaign rolling. The family was planning to pitch in a total of $100 million, but we were hoping corporate giving would broaden the contribution base. I had received serious approaches from the University of Pennsylvania and Duke University to build HCI on their campuses, each school promising matching funds for private donations. But we opted for Utah, our home and the home of our ancestors. At the University of Utah, the Institute would be helping loved ones, friends, and neighbors. As Brigham Young's ragged band of Mormon refugees looked out over the Salt Lake Valley in 1847, he declared: "This is the right place." It was the right place for my pioneer ancestors, and it is the right place for me. (From my headquarters office, I can see the Huntsman Cancer Institute, gleaming in the sunlight about a mile away.)

Setting out to build a leading cancer-research facility in Utah was not a quixotic undertaking. Aside from the financing component, we recruited from far and wide to bring our team together. Ray White, a globally respected molecular biologist and a pioneer in mapping the human genome at the University of Utah, was HCI's first director. In 1980, White, along with David Botstein of Stanford, Ronald Davis of Stanford, and Mark Skolnick of the University of Utah, published a landmark paper outlining a method for mapping the human genome that is considered the manifesto of the revolution in human genetics. (Skolnick would later discover the gene whose mutation causes a form of hereditary breast cancer.) The paper was an outgrowth of a scientific meeting in 1977 in Alta, Utah where Davis and Botstein proposed the idea.

White, with a doctorate from MIT and having done postdoctoral research at Stanford, had come to Utah to gain access to the LDS Church's genealogical records for his research. He was affiliated with the Howard Hughes Medical Institute at the University of Utah, which had established a laboratory specifically for the legendary recluse. White later directed the Eccles Biomedical Institute on the same campus before moving to the Huntsman Cancer Institute in 1995. Ultimately, White moved on, and was succeeded by Stephen Prescott, a brilliant administrator and medical doctor, who in turn stepped down to focus squarely on research. The third and current CEO is Mary Beckerle, one of America's preeminent scientists and a truly gifted leader. She is unquestionably America's most outstanding scientist/CEO combination. But I am getting ahead of myself.

When I laid out my dream for the Institute, then-University of Utah President Art Smith was surprisingly only lukewarm. He felt the university was not large enough to support such a facility and doubted we could raise the sufficient funds to build and operate it. He opposed my plans at every turn. At South Carolina State University, where he had been provost and interim president, Smith always had relied on state funding and had no experience working with a wealthy donor focused on a specific project. His skepticism and negativity remained steadfast to a point that it hindered progress toward realization of the facility.

Worse, Smith plainly did not see the need for an institute of this nature in Utah, no matter what the funding mechanism. All I could see were the thousands of people dying from cancer in the Intermountain West who had no treatment center on a par with those serving larger metropolitan areas on both the East and West Coasts. My argument was supported by the fact that we had available to us the largest set of genealogical records on the planet to use in the genetic tracking of cancer. It became clear that either Art Smith or the cancer center had to go. As it happened, the presidency of the University of Houston became vacant, and Smith jumped at the chance to move back to a southern school.

The university's next president, Bernie Machen, a dentist by discipline, was personally supportive of HCI, although precious little funding came our way on his watch. He left to head the University of Florida and was succeeded by Michael Young, whose time as president did not mark an improvement to the funding situation. Perhaps it is understandable that the main focus of each succeeding president was the University's Health Sciences Center under whose domain reside the medical and dental schools. Nevertheless, it was frustrating that under each of those presidents—Smith, Machen, and Young—a portion of National Institute of Health (NIH) funding intended for the Huntsman Cancer Institute was skimmed off by the university for purposes of "overhead charges" that ended up in Health Sciences Center coffers.

When I personally solicit a donation to HCI, the check intended for the Institute must be made out to the University of Utah, which, at least initially, kept 30 percent of it for "overhead." What overhead? I paid for the buildings and all other costs. The university did not lift a finger to obtain this donation so no cost there, either. But only 70 cents on the dollar ends up in cancer research. The university does little, if any, fundraising for HCI. Its philosophy: leave that to Jon Huntsman and his foundation. It's plain frustrating and I don't appreciate it.

The last three presidents told me repeatedly they would help and they all cheered me on—yet behind the scenes, each in turn redirected what could have been HCI money to some other use. Notwithstanding all of this, we try hard to work together, taking care to keep Huntsman Cancer Institute aligned to the university, much in the manner MD Anderson Center does with the University of Texas.

Hopefully, things will improve under David Pershing, who was installed as president in 2012 when his predecessor, Michael Young, left for the University of Washington. Pershing is home grown, having been dean of the College of Engineering; a university vice president; and a longtime friend. He is as good as it will get. He is open-minded and seems to understand my nature. He sees the advantages of having a world-class cancer facility on campus and works well with us toward maintaining the integrity of its contributions. All grants and contributions received currently are directed to HCI entirely.

Other frustrations and obstacles have surfaced along the path of good intentions. After announcing to the world we were building a cancer research institute in Salt Lake City, I had to raise $140 million above my $10 million to begin the initial phase of construction. For an anchor donation, I turned to a leading global pharmaceutical company Glaxo-Wellcome of London. (Following a merger, it became GlaxoSmithKline, or GSK, as it is known today.) Bob Ingram, its president, felt comfortable about the project when Senator Orrin Hatch of Utah and I discussed it with him in 1994. Sir Robert Sykes, the company's chairman and CEO, based in London, also was encouraging (although, in retrospect, his support was more a matter of not wanting to say no to Hatch, a great congressional friend of pharmaceutical companies). Sir Robert made an oral commitment of $100 million from Glaxo during our visit in London. Six months later, Ingram notified me that "negative business trends" would force them to back out of the $100 million pledge. The company offered $5 million instead.

When others, too, began to squirm, the prospect of a broadly funded institute began to fade away. The family met and agreed to sell off assets in order to raise the necessary cash. If necessary, we would build it ourselves, but I wasn't through putting the squeeze on others. On October 2, 1995, under a sprawling tent at the groundbreaking of the Institute, Karen and I announced we would donate $100 million of our family's money toward the center. Eventually, another $100 million would be donated or pledged from private sources, including Consolidated Press Holdings Chairman Kerry Packer, Intermountain Health Care, the American Trial Lawyers Association, and Zions Bank. The most crucial donations came in the form of $10 million checks from the

LDS Church; the late Jazz owner and automobile magnate Larry H. Miller; and Ira Fulton, an Arizona home builder known for generously plowing profits into philanthropic endeavors. My friend Wayne Reaud has proven to be a major contributor for many years and has assisted in bringing additional funding to the Institute. Elder M. Russell Ballard has made a huge difference for the Institute in his personal zest to assist with fundraising.

HCI has been incredibly fortunate to have the goodwill and support of three individuals in particular who, while disparate politically, are dear friends of mine: Senate Democratic Leader Harry Reid; Republican Senator Orrin Hatch; and talk-show host Glenn Beck, a tremendous cheerleader in the cancer fight who has raised millions of dollars during his time with CNN, Fox News, and now GBTV. His commitment to help us solve the staggering mysteries of this dreaded disease is second to none. He has been to HCI several times. He believes the food served there is the best in America. I agree. Our patients deserve nothing but the best. (They are served their meals any time they feel inclined to eat, morning, noon, or night.) Beck is a big-picture guy. His often-controversial stands on political issues notwithstanding, he has a huge, charitable heart.

Cancer research has benefited immeasurably from the support of these remarkable individuals, notwithstanding their vastly different approaches to public policy and politics in general. Former Senator Max Baucus, a Democrat from Montana who was named US ambassador to China in 2014, for example, has been a marvelous supporter. He would say when he saw me walking through the Hart Senate Office Building, "Here comes the cancer guy again. Get ready for another sermon on the need for more money for cancer." But he often has come through. And I would be remiss if I left my old fishing buddy, former Vice President Dick Cheney, off the list of politicians who have helped. Cheney has dedicated some of the HCI facilities alongside our family and was most helpful in passing pertinent legislation. Isn't it interesting how these individuals enter the political spectrum through different doorways but are united in this cause? That's what makes America great.

Cancer research must be relentless, and it is done at enormous cost. In spite of the challenges, we are making it work, mostly because of the first-class leadership of Dr. Mary Beckerle and Dr. Randall Burt at the hospital. Working with others, Dr. Burt helped prove the theory that genetic inheritance is a crucial risk factor for colon cancer. In his capacity as senior director of prevention and outreach, he is a leader in genetic testing and promoting awareness. He continues to make significant strides toward the goal of earlier detection and improved outcomes.

In the interest of doctor-patient confidentiality, names cannot be mentioned but suffice it to say that rich and poor, young and old, famous and infamous, along with thousands of "average" people have been treated at the facility. Each receives the same level of care.

Many of HCI's successes are not understood by the media, and discoveries are not always found in the headlines. Our researchers have made pivotal discoveries relating to gene modifications that greatly enhance cancer research in the area of gene mutations. (For his contribution to this research, one of our standout researchers, Dr. Mario Capecchi, shared a Nobel Prize in Medicine in 2007.) They have also discovered how patients with an inherited basis for cancer should be evaluated, how DNA tests should be used, and which diagnostic tests are best (and how often to use them).

Even more impressively, our researchers have mapped key molecular stops in how genes are turned "on" and "off." Made public in the spring of 2005 in the *Proceedings of the National Academy of Sciences*, this breathtaking discovery could possibly halt a gene mutation believed to be responsible for nearly a third of human tumors. The gene with cancer-causing properties is found in cancers involving the pancreas, colon, lung, and thyroid, as well as leukemia. (The Institute's second director, Steve Prescott, worked on this breakthrough. Scientific work is Prescott's first love and the pull proved so strong that, in 2005, shortly after the gene mutation discovery, he resigned to return to the labs as a senior scientist.)

If that is not already enough, our team created a promising new compound for the potential treatment of aggressive leukemia, identified a gene that causes increased breast cancer risk when mutated, and invented a lifesaving lung cancer screening technique in 2011 that shows a 20 percent reduction in deaths from this cancer. They also created the world's largest computerized database with genealogical research, a vital step toward discovering the genetic basis of many cancers.

LEFT: *Greeted by Pope John Paul II at the Vatican, 1993, to express appreciation for providing relief for human suffering.*

BELOW: *Jon Jr. and I visit with His Majesty King Bhumibol Adulyadej of Thailand, 1995, where he expressed gratitude for our assistance during the heavy floods in his country.*

ABOVE: *Former British Prime Minister Margaret Thatcher and Sir Denis Thatcher with my son Jon Jr., my wife Karen, and me on the occasion of Thatcher's dedication of Huntsman Corporation's new headquarters building in Salt Lake City in 1996.*

LEFT: *Gyumri school children and some 20,000 Armenian citizens thanking me at dedication of Huntsman School, the country's most modern K–12 school in Gyumri, Armenia, 2000.*

ABOVE: *Lighting the Olympic torch, as both a financial sponsor and one of many participating cancer survivors, at the Salt Lake City Winter Olympics in 2002.*

LEFT: *With my fishing buddy, Vice President Richard Cheney, on the south fork of the Snake River, 2001.*

BELOW: *With President and Mrs. George W. Bush and Chinese President Hu Jintao and wife Liu Yongqing at the White House in 2006.*

ABOVE: *Fishing with my wife, Karen, at the South Fork of the Snake River, 2008.*

RIGHT: *Catching the big one at Huntsman Springs with LDS Church President Thomas S. Monson, 2009.*

ABOVE: *With my wife Karen and our children at the Utah Governor's Mansion, 2009.*

ABOVE: *Our sweet daughter Kathleen, just weeks before her passing in 2010.*

LEFT: *Karen and me, 2010.*

ABOVE: *The gathering of the clan for the Christmas card photo, 2013.*

ABOVE: *Visiting with a cancer patient at Huntsman Cancer Institute, 2012.*

A cancer diagnosis gives rise to hundreds of personal questions that range from "why me?" to "will it kill me?" The inability to find good answers to these questions can be more frightening than the disease itself. HCI is working to change that.

I told a British newspaper reporter in 1993 that I had three primary focuses in my life: family, business, and a cure for cancer. Uttering those words was easier than facilitating the cure. It will take big money, and we were determined to move the company into a position where it could make the mega-dollars to do just that by increasing the value of our Huntsman stock holdings. I want the Huntsman Cancer Institute to be the Mayo Clinic of cancer research and humane treatment. (When I said as much at our 2011 cancer hospital Phase II dedication, John Noseworthy, president and CEO of the Mayo Clinic, called to thank me for mentioning them, and to say they admired our efforts.)

While the mood at each of our three dedication events was festive and upbeat, part of me wanted to cry out that the Institute was not doing enough, that we needed to become more effective, to move faster in producing battle victories in the war with cancer. But we managed to set those concerns aside long enough to drink in the dramatic, humbling moments of each dedication. The experiences of those milestone events touched me more deeply than I can relate.

No one else in the audiences on those occasions would have noticed her, but there was one person in the crowd whose quiet presence meant so much to me. As I gazed out in the sea of faces, I caught a fleeting glimpse of Kathleen Robison Huntsman. I was sure I saw Mom there, about thirty rows back, toward the left side. I would recognize her smile anywhere. Scanning the sea of faces further, I caught a glimpse of my father . . . my stepmother . . . my grandfather . . . my brother, and other relatives who, too, were victims of this disease. And there, sitting on the top row of the bleachers, barely visible from the speakers' platform, was Becky Bair, the brave little girl I took to Disney World a decade earlier who was my inspiration while I battled the disease. She gave me a shy, little wave, as if to say, "Remember me?" How could I ever forget you, Becky? All of them were with me in spirit and I knew each of them was pleased that we were opening and expanding a facility that would treat the soul as well as the body.

While there is still much to be done, our vision for the Institute is being fulfilled. For example, my longer-range goal for HCI is for it to be the research hub for a network of global hospitals that can't afford the expense of a research center. (Dr. Randall Burt is already heading up an experienced international team for this very purpose.) Medical teams would train in Salt Lake City and take the knowledge, findings, and discoveries back to their hospitals. And we know for a fact that HCI is making a difference in the lives of patients and their families. Just pick up any of the letters we receive from people who have been impressed by its atmosphere of reassurance and hope. The wife of a patient treated there for esophageal cancer wrote, "I want to thank you for what you've created. I've spent many dark days in other hospitals with one of our sons. What a contrast Huntsman is!!! Looking at the mountains from [his] room, and seeing the wildflowers, bikers and blue skies made me feel *hope*. What a difference you made in our lives at this critical juncture."

We are honored to have been in a position to sow the seeds from which the Huntsman Cancer Institute has grown. Karen and I, and our entire family, are enormously proud of this inspirational facility, which welcomes patients into an atmosphere of hope and optimism.

Our greatest heroes today are cancer researchers, clinicians, and medical specialists. They are the ones responsible for our enormous progress and for the feeling of hope that permeates throughout the entire institute. I feel humbled at our good fortune to make money and our drive to give back.

16. Giving Back

FORBES MAGAZINE NOTED THAT IN 2011 THE WORLD HAD MORE than 1,200 living billionaires. Of that number, only 19 had in their lifetimes donated, through actual contributions or pledges, at least $1 billion. I was one of them. I say this with a deep sense of humility. My enthusiasm for charity has led me to harass certain others in my wealth bracket to step up to the plate and give more. During discussions of this nature, I think of one of my oft-used expressions, "Let no person, but you, be the captain of your own destiny."

The Chronicle of Philanthropy tracks the most generous American donors every year. The year I added my name to a list that included Bill Gates, Warren Buffett, George Lucas, Boone Pickens, Paul Allen, Michael Bloomberg—all signers of the $600 billion Giving Pledge—I am ashamed to say that less than 2 percent of the *Forbes* 400 richest Americans joined us. The Giving Pledge obligates signers to give away at least half of our fortunes.

I was happy to sign, but I had one complaint.

"The only thing wrong with this," I told the group, "is that it's the wrong formula. It should be 80 percent." Why not? If a family has $5 billion, why should it only give away $2.5 billion? Surely it wouldn't require the remaining $2.5 billion to live a full and productive life. We can't take it with us, but we can direct it toward helping others in significant ways.

Buffett knows this well and, in truth, believes the 50 percent pledge sets what he called a "low bar," when we talked about it. He is one of history's great humanitarians. In 2006, he pledged to give all of his estimated $47 billion to charity through the Bill & Melinda Gates Foundation. Warren, along with Bill and Melinda, are my real heroes—not for what they make, but for what they give. My fortune is nowhere near the size of theirs, but whatever the sum I have at the end, I want to leave this world with the same amount of money in my bank account as it contained the day I entered it.

Philanthropy ought to be the basic ingredient in everyone's recipe for financial success. In his book *The American Dream*, former CBS news anchor Dan Rather said something about philanthropy I found completely accurate: those who earn rather than inherit their fortunes retain an acute sense of what money can do. "What matters is not that you made it, but what you do with it once you make it," he wrote. Earned wealth makes one acutely aware of economic inequalities and just how many American Dreams remain unfulfilled. Rather may as well have been talking about me, and not only that, from my personal observation, generosity is not an exclusive trait of the originator of the wealth. Many who inherit are at least as giving as the parent who amassed the fortune. It's where one's heart is that determines how much should go to lifting the lives of the underserved.

People are charitable for many reasons. Mine is simple: no one is self-made. All of us received help, breaks, and opportunities along the way, and our good fortunes and blessings must be returned by helping others. The cycle must not be broken. I never have forgotten from whence I sprang, or the lean early years, or the stigma of poverty in high school and college. The terrible feeling of having nothing, through no fault of one's own, is indelible.

But there are other drivers of the philanthropic spirit. A 1997 *Time* magazine story examined the nation's top twenty-five philanthropists, looking for commonalities. The investigation found we shared such traits as being self-made, religious, and long in the habit of giving without tax deductions as a motivating factor.

Religion is certainly important to understanding what motivates me to give. The Bible warns about the love of money being the root of all evil—a line that refers to greed and the worship of money, rather than the good it can achieve. Money earned and earmarked for philanthropy, for example, can be the root of great benefit. A scriptural rule of life I keep posted behind my desk reads as follows:

"But before ye seek for riches, seek ye for the kingdom of God.

And after ye have obtained a hope in Christ ye shall obtain riches, if ye seek them; and ye will seek them for the intent to do good—to clothe the naked, and to feed the hungry, and to liberate the captive, and administer relief to the sick and the afflicted."

In his book *More Than Money*, Fox TV business editor and host of *Your World* Neil Cavuto did a grand job of summarizing my feelings: "(Huntsman) doesn't think much of fellow billionaires who wait until they're dead to give their money away. There are too many people in desperate need of help now to justify hoarding vast piles of cash. It's selfish and unintentionally cruel for billionaires to hang on to their money until death finally loosens their grip." I think it's sad when a person with great wealth regards charity only as an afterthought in a will and selfishly holds onto it until after his demise. In all likelihood, he would have left nothing in his will for charity if he knew he could live forever.

In the pages that follow I hope to demonstrate that I practice what I preach, discussing the kinds of charities that interest the Huntsman family and why. I am aware that I am in peril of appearing self-serving—I hope only that the reader will remember that this isn't personal: giving back is a sacred duty for anyone of means.

My most satisfying moments occur helping others in need—especially "the least of these, my brethren." I grew up with little but we were never homeless or without love. For that, I am eternally grateful, but my appreciation of such a background begat a higher sensitivity to the suffering, the shoeless, the lonely, the homeless, and those who are otherwise struggling. The greatest number of Huntsman dollars has gone to cancer research; to educational causes; and to the hungry, homeless, and victimized.

As previously noted, quiet, spontaneous gifts produce an unequalled high—they represent giving in its purest, most satisfying form. However, because the Huntsman Foundation and the Huntsman Cancer Foundation are 501(c)(3) entities (charitable entities registered under the US tax code), much of our philanthropy must be preplanned and becomes public. Publicized giving has its rewards and advantages, not the least of which was underscored in a 2004 *BusinessWeek* article on the nation's top fifty philanthropists. It prompts others to do likewise. But giving a spontaneous, unheralded donation is more fun.

If my mission in life was simply to build a great chemical company, I could have stopped years ago. With the help of others, we have built that empire. But the company was the means to an end. It provides the wherewithal to do something substantial for mankind in direct proportion to the material blessings we have received. The greater the profit, the greater the gift. That's why the relief of human suffering is embedded formally in Huntsman's corporate mission statement. Giving back is plain good business. Philanthropy prevents a company from becoming complacent. Besides earning profits, the company also must focus on philanthropy. Such a mandate imposes fiscal discipline. Once you make a charitable commitment, you can't let those people down. As old commitments are fulfilled, new ones are made. We constantly raise the bar. Such progression is healthy. If you don't stretch, you stagnate. There have been years when I have given away more money than I should have, and then I had to work both harder and smarter to make up the difference.

My most controversial contribution—or failure to contribute, as some perceived it for a time—involved the Winter Olympics held in Utah in February 2002. The saga began in Birmingham, England in the summer of 1991 when Utah lost the bid for the 1998 Winter Games to Nagano, Japan. It became obvious that many voting delegates of the International Olympic Committee (IOC) had been influenced by Japan's brazen use of lavish gifts and cash. Let's call them what they were: bribes.

Corruption among some IOC delegates had become a way of life. An atmosphere of arrogance permeated the IOC in the 1980s and 1990s—IOC head Juan Antonio Samaranch insisted on being addressed as Your Excellency. In the resulting culture of outlandish perks and payoffs, naïve little Utah was outgunned, outspent, and outmaneuvered. While we offered IOC delegates taffy from the Great Salt Lake and Mormon Tabernacle Choir CDs, the Japanese delegation slipped them Toshiba laptops.

By all accounts, Utah should have gotten the nod at Birmingham based on objective criteria. Japan brazenly bought the winning votes. Somewhat embarrassed by what had transpired in Birmingham, the US Olympics Committee recertified the near-perfect site of Salt Lake City as its approved 2002 site for IOC delegates to consider when they again met to vote in Budapest, Hungary in 1995. Tom Welch, leader of Utah's Olympics bid committee, vowed not to be "outbid" for the 2002 Winter Olympics.

I had issues with the bid committee's numbers from the start. Salt Lake City bid leaders Frank Joklik, then head of Kennecott mining operations in Utah, and the late Jack Gallivan, publisher-emeritus of *The Salt Lake Tribune*, projected a ludicrously low initial budget of $400 million for the Games. Two revisions later, it rose to $800 million. As I studied the numbers in the early 1990s, I became disenchanted with the plan to host the Olympics and believed the projected costs were scandalously low.

The two men came to me for a sizable donation. I had forked over $100,000 in 1988 as Utah opened its ground-floor campaign to snare the Games. This time, however, I told Joklik and Gallivan to forget it, warning their unsupportable plan would push the state over the financial precipice. I asked whether they had figured inflationary factors into their calculations. They claimed that they had, but I knew there was no way $800 million would cover the Olympics price tag. I told them it would almost certainly cost over $1 billion.

A few weeks after meeting with Gallivan and Joklik, I accepted an invitation to speak at the Rotary Club in Salt Lake City to explain my negative stand on the Olympics. I told the group the bid committee was grossly underestimating costs and warned that the state could be left holding a $300 million to $400 million bag by the time the Olympic torch was extinguished. Utah taxpayers would be saddled with the debt for decades. The Games had to be weighed solely as an economic investment, I said, rather than as a means of putting Salt Lake City and the state of Utah on the map. If that was the primary reason we sought the Olympics, I cautioned, the bid effort would turn out to be a bad investment. When the news media reported my remarks I found myself in hot water for raining on the Olympic parade.

Nevertheless, in the mid-'90s, we had the pillars of the state, not to mention much of the news media, acting as unabashed cheerleaders for the Games. They spun the facts, sugarcoated the finances, and generally misled the public. (The LDS Church remained neutral until after Utah won its bid.) My biggest complaint was that nobody was leveling with the taxpayers. Worse, many bid committee members had conflicts of interest and stood to benefit, directly or indirectly, should Utah be awarded the Games. I started raising these issues in 1991 and kept harping on them until 1999 when the financial matters were supplanted by a bribery scandal that made the Japanese payoffs look like chump change.

Many believed Utah won the 1995 vote in Budapest because the IOC was on a guilt trip over what had occurred four years prior. Not even close. IOC delegates were supping at the trough as never before, and Salt Lake City had become skillful in satisfying those insatiable payoff appetites. Bid Committee executives lavished IOC delegates with gifts, perks, college scholarships for their children, medical care, and out-and-out cash bribes. Anyone following the Olympics knew many delegate votes could be bought. When this international den of iniquity was exposed in late 1999, a few months shy of two years before the opening of the Games, I was not surprised at the scope of corruption.

The scandal caused me personal and corporate heartburn. Huntsman employees, suppliers, and customers across the globe increasingly became concerned. For years I had been battling allegations, perpetuated by the foreign press, that the LDS Church owned Huntsman Corporation and that everyone in Utah was a polygamist. Now the state was being portrayed as the bribery capital of the world and Huntsman was the highest-profile international corporation based in Utah at the time. Because of this geographic coincidence, the first question I got wherever I traveled was whether I was involved in the bribery. Headlines in the foreign press depicted Huntsman and the Salt Lake Olympics as one and the same. We tried to distance Huntsman from the Olympics, but the specter of guilt by association cast an unavoidable shadow.

The nominal head of Utah's Olympics effort was Governor Mike Leavitt, yet he remained publicly oblivious to the problem and flatly refused to accept, even in the spirit of "the buck stops here," any responsibility for the conduct of his Bid Committee. Leavitt insisted he knew nothing of the committee's shenanigans—although polls consistently showed the public did not believe him. I recall walking into the office of an LDS Church official one morning to find Leavitt sitting there. I told the governor that something had to be done about this Olympics embarrassment, that our company was being hurt because of the scandal. He dismissed my concerns: "Jon, these are my Olympics. I will determine if anything needs to be done."

The personal extravagance on the part of Bid Committee leaders was stunning. I witnessed firsthand examples, most of which were eventually documented by the news media. I remember one like it was yesterday. I was in a five-star hotel in Wiesbaden, Germany conducting company business. The hotel's rates were so extravagant that I was uneasy about costs. As I headed to my room that night, I passed the presidential suite. A room service waiter was knocking on the door. As I passed, the door opened and Alma Welch, wife of Salt Lake Bid Committee president Tom Welch, told the waiter to bring in the full-course meal. She saw me and turned beet red.

Bid Committee chairman Frank Joklik, a most competent former Kennecott executive, resigned in 2000 in the wake of bribery revelations. Nobody ever offered an apology for the embarrassment Utah suffered, nor did anyone accept responsibility. In their best imitation of Sergeant Schultz of *Hogan's Heroes*, organizing committee members and Olympic officials announced "I know nothing" and ran for cover, blaming everything on Welch and his assistant, Dave Johnson, who also was forced to resign. It was not Utah's proudest moment. (Felony charges against Welch and Johnson were filed by the US Department of Justice though both were eventually exonerated—and rightfully so.)

With less than two years until the opening ceremonies, corporate sponsors were bailing right and left. There was talk of canceling the Games altogether. I was one of those publicly calling for Utah to return the bid to the IOC. Meanwhile, the Salt Lake Organizing Committee (SLOC) looked for a "white knight" to save the day. Certain SLOC representatives called to inquire if my son Jon Jr., then a returned US ambassador to Singapore and our corporate vice chairman, was interested. Jon is a gifted and natural leader, as the people of Utah eventually witnessed when he twice sat in the governor's chair. Jon said he would be happy to step in and, if selected, would serve without pay. They told him he was the leading candidate.

The other candidate was Mitt Romney, the Bain Capital venture capitalist in Boston. While in the Nixon White House, I had worked with Romney's father, George, who was secretary of Housing and Urban Development and a fine man. Mitt's sister Jane was Karen's college roommate at the University of Utah. Mitt had gone to school at Brigham Young University and did exceptionally well with Bain. (We all know the rest of the story, as Mitt went on to be governor of Massachusetts and a presidential primary candidate in 2008 and the Republican Party's unsuccessful nominee in 2012.)

The very week the committee executives contacted Jon, I had a chance to phone Romney during a refueling stop in Halifax, Nova Scotia, en route to Europe. I wanted to determine his level of interest in running the Olympics. He was keen on the idea, as I immediately discovered.

"I can pull Utah out of the mess," he told me. "I can save Utah."

I nearly choked on my Altoids. I told him that Utah did not need a savior. What it needed was a leader with vision and good business sense. Romney was brash and arrogant during the conversation, and his political ambitions were apparent. It was not a pleasant conversation.

A day or two later, Governor Leavitt, at the behest of SLOC, selected Romney. Truth be told, he already had been offered the job when I talked to him. I had been led to believe Jon Jr. was the nominee, but we realized he was actually SLOC's fallback candidate should Romney decline.

The governor had not leveled with us. I had seen this sort of thing happen before in the Nixon White House. But this was Salt Lake City, where I had assumed I was dealing with hometown friends. If SLOC had been forthright with Jon and me from the start about its interest in Romney, it is unlikely that I would have become as estranged from the Olympics as I did.

Romney announced that he would take no salary unless the Games turned a profit, then surrounded himself with predominately Mormon administrators. I groused in a news media interview that more diversity was needed in his top echelon, noting the 2002 Olympics were becoming the "Mormon Games." This perception gained traction as the LDS Church generously filled some critical funding voids via land donations and in-kind contributions. Major sponsors had pulled their underwriting in the aftermath of international publicity over the bribery scandal and a financial crisis was evolving.

As if things couldn't get worse, the 9/11 tragedy seventeen months before the Opening Ceremonies brought incredible global pressure and focus on Utah. The 2002 Olympics would be the first gathering of nations in the wake of the terrorist attacks. Anxiety over security was off the charts. Some leaders wanted to cancel the games altogether, but level heads prevailed, arguing the US must not let terrorists deter us from living our daily lives.

A desperate but determined Romney and members of SLOC approached me for a donation. Romney, SLOC chairman Robert Garff, and Governor Leavitt arranged a meeting in my office in which they acknowledged that seeking the Games may not have been the best idea but, given all that had transpired, our state had a duty to follow through. I agreed, but I wasn't of a mind to chip in any money.

I soon relented, however. I lifted my donation boycott and contributed $1 million, but I insisted that it be earmarked for the Paralympics, the worldwide winter sports competition for physically challenged athletes. Under the auspices of the International Olympic Committee, the Paralympics operates in the shadow of the Olympics. It runs for a week following the Olympic Games and has difficulty drawing sponsors because it does not receive much media coverage. The Paralympics also better fits our giving philosophy. From that point, I put the "episode of deceit" behind me and focused on making these Games a success.

As it turned out, the presentation and running of the 2002 Winter Games were the smoothest in IOC history and they turned a record profit. Romney and his staff scored a ten in the court of public opinion. But credit ought to be given where it is due: more than thirty thousand volunteers and numerous sponsors never received the recognition to which they were entitled. The Games were the rave of the planet. (Okay, there were two brief flaps. The French skating judge rigged her scoring so that the Russian skaters received a gold medal instead of the Canadians. Then there was the brouhaha over whether the prim and proper Romney used the "f-bomb" in chewing out a security guard who wouldn't let Romney's bus through the gates. He says he didn't; the guard and a half dozen members of the press corps heard otherwise.)

Aside from Romney's political reasons for wanting the job, he came through as a most capable leader and deserves his share of the praise. Tom Welch and Dave Johnson, in my opinion, deserve just as much credit. They did a terrific job of building the Games infrastructure, their part in the scandal notwithstanding. Romney did not extend them that recognition.

Through 2013, the Huntsman family has given in excess of $1.3 billion to worthy causes during the previous 20 years. In the 2 years prior to this writing, I have parted with some $130 million (though admittedly I don't keep that close of a record). While that ranked me number 22 in actual dollars given, *Forbes* says I gave away 7 percent of my net worth in 2012 which puts me in the top 5 when considering the percent of net worth. If lifetime giving is the benchmark, I am in the top 10, according to *Forbes*.

Nearly 50 percent of my giving for the last fifteen years has been earmarked for the Huntsman Cancer Institute. I have no reliable record of our gifts prior to 1984. About 80 percent of my donations and pledges are to Utah causes. In 2007, I pledged $700 million in stock from the sale of our company to the Apollo-owned Hexion Chemical. *The Chronicle of Philanthropy* noted that this was the second largest single donation of the year. However, that amount was based on the per-share value of $28.50, the price at which Apollo said it would purchase the stock. Unfortunately, the deal fell apart nearly a year later and the company did not sell (details of that sordid affair are to be found in a later chapter).

I am ecumenical with my overall contributions to religious institutions. I give a lot of money and in-kind services to the LDS Church, including the use of my two Gulfstream IV private business jets, a full tithe, and donations to Church-owned BYU, but Karen and I have also supported Catholic institutions to the tune of more than $4 million. The year after I gave $1 million to St. Vincent de Paul Center, then-Cardinal Roger Mahony of Los Angeles called to comment on the irony that the largest single donor to Catholic charities in 1993 was a Mormon. I also had an audience with His Holiness, the late Pope John Paul II, who thanked me for my philanthropy and informed me I was the first Mormon he had ever met. (That made us even; he was the first Catholic pontiff with whom I had come in contact.)

After a tour of the Pope's apartment, I was escorted by several cardinals and the Swiss Guard to "the balcony," not knowing exactly what that meant. When two of the accompanying cardinals asked me to step outside, the applause from tourists below in St. Peter's Square began with gusto. I wasn't the person they expected to see and beat a hasty retreat from view. One can only imagine the smiles on the faces of all the Vatican folks. Other Catholic organizations which have been recipients of Huntsman philanthropy include St. Joseph's Villa's assisted-care living services and the Cathedral of the Madeleine restoration project where I served as fundraising vice chairman. The Huntsman family also has donated over the years to the Unitarian, Episcopal, and Presbyterian churches, as well as to non-Christian faiths.

For years, the Salt Lake YWCA struggled to provide shelter for abused women and their children. Until the late 1990s, the YWCA was the only domestic violence shelter for the metro area's nearly 1 million residents. Some 1,500 families were being served annually. It was a crisis shelter only, with a 30-day limit on stays. When that month ended, many mothers and children, without the means to pay for separate housing, had to return to abusive households. The shelter clearly needed more living space. I am sensitive to abusive home situations having come from a home where some occurrences fit that description. Karen and I decided we would be the lead donors, giving $1 million toward a 36-apartment complex on the YWCA campus, where each unit would house a mother and up to 4 children for as long as they needed to stay. They are beautiful, furnished, turnkey residence apartments. The complex was named after my mother.

Several years later, the facility tripled in size and we donated an additional $2.5 million to that end. Utah's homeless causes have received some $4.5 million from our foundation and another $1 million went to United Way. The Special Olympics and the National Ability Center each got three-quarters of a million dollars. Higher education is another charitable focus, to the tune of some $100 million, given among others to the Wharton School for its Huntsman Hall, Utah State University, University of Utah, Brigham Young University, Weber State University, Snow College, Southern Utah University, Idaho State University, and Utah Valley University.

One of the great joys has been getting to know Douglas Anderson, dean of Utah State University's (USU) business school, and the institution's president, Stan Albrecht. I had a keen interest in working with them to develop a unique Wharton-style business school at USU, so that young adults from Utah, Idaho, and elsewhere could receive one of the best business educations in America. After some discussion, we donated more than $35 million for programs, faculty, scholarships, and a new building for the newly named Jon M. Huntsman School of Business. More than

$4 million of Huntsman money has gone to public libraries in Utah, and there my enthusiasm got me into a spot of trouble. I gave $500,000 for a new library in a low-income area of Salt Lake City. At the dedication, I was so impressed with the facility that I said—somewhat figuratively—that I would help with any library project in the state. You can imagine the number of requests that materialized on my desk within the week.

Huntsman is the lead sponsor of the World Senior Games in St. George, Utah, having contributed roughly $6 million as of this writing. In 1987, we became the benefactors of this growing event for two reasons: First, it is important for seniors to be in good health, to stay in shape, and to prove the theory that getting older does not necessarily mean losing one's edge. Second, it established an economic engine in southern Utah. Annually, thousands of athletic seniors from around the world flock to the Games. Visitors bring an estimated $50 million to the region's economy. Zion National Park, the Grand Canyon, and other unique and grandiose sites are visited by our participants.

One restless night in 1993, I began thinking about how public school teachers, a group that included my father, grandfather, and grandmother, traditionally have received insufficient recognition. Raised in an educator's home, I feel empathy for public school teachers, knowing they are underappreciated, underpaid, and under great pressure. Karen and I discussed how remarkable it is that teachers, who have extraordinary capabilities and could earn more money in another field, choose to serve children. That's how the Huntsman Awards for Excellence in Education program was born. Each year since, we have conducted an annual search for ten educators statewide who are models of such merit and recognition. In addition to front-page media attention for the recipients, the ten honorees are invited to an all-expenses-paid banquet in Salt Lake City where each receives a check for $10,000. Past recipients are also invited to attend subsequent annual banquets. Marking the twentieth anniversary of the program in 2012, we expanded the number of recipients to eleven and presented the first Mark H. Huntsman Award to an educator in the field of special education. I have no intention of discontinuing this tradition. Currently, there are four other similar programs in other parts of the country.

The arts in Utah have received a few million Huntsman dollars, although I am hardly what you would call a connoisseur of the classics. When I became chairman of the Utah Symphony Board of Directors years ago, the musical director asked me if I had a favorite classic the orchestra might play on opening night. Giving it a moment's thought, I said, "Certainly, my favorite and most memorable classic is 'Blue Suede Shoes.'" The director informed this uber-Elvis fan the orchestra did not have that piece in its repertoire, but being good sports and not wanting to disappoint a benefactor they rocked Abravanel Hall with the first Elvis slam-bam.

Primary Children's Hospital in Salt Lake City has been another family favorite. Over a period of many years, we have provided countless cancer screenings for employees and residents of the communities surrounding various Huntsman manufacturing sites, and thousands of college scholarships were presented to children of Huntsman employees. The Wharton School and the Republic of Armenia (through our post-earthquake reconstruction effort) each received more than $50 million.

In the first decade of this century, the health of the chemical industry has been precarious enough that the primary sources of our giving have been sales of assets and personal loans. As the economy rights itself, the scope and depth of our contributions will only increase. Cancer research will always be paramount, but the homeless, food banks, domestic abuse centers and the like will continue to be on our philanthropic radar.

And, because there are those who love to know these things, Karen and I also "give" roughly two dollars in every five dollars of income to the government in the form of taxes. I don't mind paying taxes—indeed, they are the obligation of every capable citizen worthy of the name—but I don't like it when I hear that wealthy individuals don't pay their fair share or the government is tossing so much money away, which is normally the case.

But enough trumpet blowing. Suffice it to say giving has and continues to be a priority which brings me to a crucial philosophical point: Karen, the children, and I do not do this for self-aggrandizement. Giving is a humbling experience. The Huntsman name has been attached to a minority of our contributions. In specific cases, such as the Huntsman Cancer Institute, we do take pride in the name recognition. When people see our name on the door, we want there to be a feeling of hope that the disease which brought them there will one day be eradicated. For most of our charity, though, I don't care about credit. The average person knows little about the extent of our involvement in scores of other philanthropic endeavors, nor should he or she. Some of our largest and most significant gifts remain unmentioned.

There was a time when I considered charitable giving a matter of individual discretion. About twenty-five years ago, I realized that giving back ought not to be voluntary and that any person of means is obligated to return in a constructive way what he or she has been given. We are but temporary trustees of our fortunes, no matter the size. How much should rich folks give? There is no set formula, but I would hold that the excess over and above whatever it takes to enjoy a respectable quality of life is reasonable. For each individual, each family, that level is a moving target. I have given this a great deal of thought. What does it take to enjoy a desirable quality of life? How much is enough for shelter, food, medical care, clothes, vehicles, insurance, entertainment, travel, and rainy-day funds? Once that's decided and the budget is met, the remainder should be given back to society. As I said earlier in this chapter, I hold that more than 50 percent of the excess must go to charities. For a wealthy family not to give generously is disgraceful.

I certainly concur with Pope Francis when, toward the end of 2013, he denounced the "idolatry of money" and called on the rich to share their wealth. "Just as the commandment 'Thou shalt not kill' sets a clear limit in order to safeguard the value of human life, today we also have to say 'Thou shalt not' to an economy of exclusion and inequality. Such an economy kills. How can it be that it is not a news item when an elderly homeless person dies of exposure, but it is news when the stock market loses two points?" Francis called for support from more people of influence who are disturbed by the state of society, the people, and the lives of the poor. I echo that call.

The people of Utah, according to *The Chronicle of Philanthropy*, are the most generous folks in the nation, giving away nearly 15 percent of their discretionary income. In large part, that is the result of the state's population being predominantly Mormon. The LDS Church requires tithing of members in good standing. Churches of many stripes urge members to tithe. The magazine's survey mixes church and secular giving. I have never counted what I gave my church in the tally of my charitable giving. Church donations and public philanthropy are two different duties. Putting money in the collection basket, be it a weekly offering or an annual tithe, is expected from everyone who practices a religion. In my opinion, it is the duty of each member of any faith to pay a tithe to offset expenses, charitable causes, and other costs incurred by their religion. Churchgoers often are theologically reminded that giving is a spiritual plus, if not a must. In the case of LDS Church members, tithing is a requirement for temple admission and other forms of ecclesiastical privilege. Without pressure from the pulpit, I doubt if churches would collect the money they need.

Not everyone has the wherewithal to spread his or her wealth in the community, but that does not mean philanthropy is the franchise of the rich. Giving is available to all income levels. Indeed, the poor are probably more generous than the wealthy if measured by the percentage of what is available or how much it hurts. Giving is supposed to be voluntary, but I would like to see everyone experience the sort of pressure to give back that churchgoers feel when it comes to the collection plate.

At the end of the day, my favorite form of giving remains that which is spontaneous. This ranges from acts as small as giving a coat to a homeless man on the street (yes, I truly did) or as large as the time I acted on impulse during my commencement address to the Class of 2000 at Weber State University. Weber State is an institution that reflects the hardworking, mostly blue-collar demographics of its host city, Ogden, Utah. It is a fine school that probably serves its constituency better than any other four-year institution in the state. A majority of its students are nontraditional, and all age groups and family backgrounds are represented in the student body. Though a few are wealthy, most are middle class or those with next to nothing. If any school has important services to provide, it's Weber State.

From my seat on the commencement stage I looked out over the large audience of students, children, parents, siblings, and grandparents proudly looking on. I knew many of these students had held full-time jobs while managing heavy course loads. It was clear also they had better things to do with their evenings than listen to a series of speakers. I had prepared a speech, a version of one I had given the previous year at the University of Southern California where, thirty years earlier, I had earned my MBA at night school and this day I was receiving an honorary doctorate degree. The text centered on the duty of each of us to render service to those in need.

As the program progressed, babies began fussing, youngsters fidgeted, and adults seemed distracted. The last thing anyone needed, just before an endless line of seniors climbed the steps to receive their individual diplomas, was another wordy commencement address. I took out my pen and started truncating the speech. With each successive speaker, I pared my remarks a bit more. By the time it was my turn at the microphone, my speech had been whittled to a single, central sentence. It was a short philosophical gem by physician and author John Andrew Holmes that succinctly expresses my own philosophy. And if that was to be the sum total of my remarks, I thought, it better be followed by a significant punch line, something I was still formulating even as I was being introduced.

I walked to the podium and gazed out at the mass of students, who had worked so hard to pay their way to their diploma and who appreciated the value of their education. They greeted me with polite, please-let-this-be-short applause. I smiled and pointedly dropped my formal address onto the floor, except for the one page containing the Holmes quotation. "If you graduates take away only one thing from this commencement," I began, "let it be this simple thought. Please stand and repeat after me."

The audience rose, and I slowly read Holmes's fifteen words: "No exercise is better for the human heart than reaching down and lifting another up." I had them repeat it a couple of times, all of which took less than a minute. For the punch line (and, believe me, the fun part), I turned to then-President Paul Thompson and declared: "The Huntsman family wishes to provide two hundred scholarships of five thousand dollars each to be awarded to promising students who might not otherwise be able to afford college. We are giving one million dollars to Weber State University."

Thompson's jaw dropped. Administrators, graduates, parents, friends, and faculty sat in stunned silence for several seconds before reacting to the surprise gift. What began as a smattering of applause increased to shouts and whistles and ended in an ovation that shook the arena as if a buzzer-winning basket had just secured the conference championship. Those scholarship recipients, whoever they would be, could care less about the Huntsman Corporation—what struck home with each of them was two hundred students would get that lucky break and an opportunity for a degree and a promising career.

As it turned out, CBS News host Bob Schieffer was giving a commencement address at the University of Utah the same night I gave mine at Weber State. In a segment on *CBS News Sunday Morning* the following day, Schieffer noted he had given the "second best commencement address in Utah" that weekend, comparing it to my brief remarks and spontaneous $1 million gift. Twelve years later, at a commencement address at Louisiana State University, Schieffer recalled the event. "I thought I had delivered a profound address, but it was bested by a fifteen-word speech," he laughed. It's hard to say which of our graduation addresses was the more profound. Surely, mine was more fun.

The experience produced such a personal high that I pulled a similar stunt at Idaho State University's graduation ceremonies the following year—with the same exhilarating result. (Those two events prompted a marked increase in invitations for graduation addresses, I might add.)

I want to share my good fortune. I need to give it back—all of it—before I leave this good earth. And to give away a lot of money, I have to earn a lot of money. Before our company went public, my son Peter, our CEO, said that the challenge for Huntsman executives was to make money as fast as I gave it away. Memo to Peter: you are quite right. And I can't wait to start spending again.

That line of Peter's got some laughs at the time, but it was no laughing matter as we said good-bye to the twentieth century and headed into the twenty-first. The industry was buffeted by the longest downturn in its history, the cost of energy went through the roof, the company was out of money, and I was drowning in charitable obligations. On September 11, 2001, things got a whole lot worse.

17. Heading for the Lifeboats

A S THE SUN ROSE ON THE TWENTY-FIRST CENTURY THE CHEMICAL industry was in trouble. Oil and natural gas prices were heading in the opposite direction from our bottom line. The dot-com frenzy had burst, plunging the stock market to frightening lows, and for all my painstaking planning for bad times, I had not foreseen the financial maelstrom that was now upon us.

The worst crisis in the chemical industry's history didn't make landfall on a single, cataclysmic morning. It sneaked up on us over time with a vengeance, affecting different sectors to varying degrees. The industry didn't overreact—its players had weathered downturns before and learned to expect them. Typically driven by excess supply, these down cycles would hang around for two or three years and then the market would head north again. This time was different. It was a cyclone that took almost seven years to spin itself out. I didn't recognize its scope and lasting effect until it was too late.

In the thirty years after I started Huntsman Container, the business had become a remarkable empire, primarily through intricate debt-financed acquisitions. I nearly went bankrupt twice during that time, but things worked out—and for the better. An entrepreneur must keep a finger in every aspect of his business. In the earlier years, I was a one-man band, trying to be all things to all people and relying mostly on my own counsel. I believed I knew the market better than anyone, that I was the company's best salesman. I made the daily decisions in finance, sales, manufacturing, and product line. In the more technical areas, I deferred to our top managers. We always had a first-rate team, but those who put up the gold take the brunt of the beating when things go south.

Over the previous three decades, I had three management teams. The first, from 1970 to 1982, directed a regional company. The second, from 1983 to 1992, took us to national-player status. And the third, from 1993 to the present, provided the direction for a global operation. In my capacity as CEO, I called the shots and determined how to change direction when the need arose. I made sure we operated effectively in all three periods. Senior management sometimes found it difficult, if not impossible, to roll with these changes. When that happened, I had to remind them I was the quarterback. This sets the stage for what happened in the initial years of the twenty-first century. Ironically, my roots as an entrepreneur nearly cost me the company.

In 2000, Huntsman enjoyed its highest revenues up to that point, $7 billion. In July of that year, we closed the sale of Huntsman Packaging to Chase Capital for $1.1 billion. We were at our zenith. Charitable giving, particularly with respect to the Huntsman Cancer Institute, was at record levels.

Edging its way into this rosy picture was a fivefold increase in energy prices. It caused concern, but no one panicked. I turned sixty-three that summer and decided to surrender to Peter the chief executive title, a position I had held for thirty years. He had been president and COO since 1994. Upon the CEO's shoulders rests the mantle of ultimate responsibility for the entire company. I would become chairman of the board, with a view to clearing more of my time for church responsibilities, civic service, and philanthropy. I had become chairman of the Wharton School's Board of Overseers, a member of the American Red Cross (ARC) Board of Governors, chairman of the ARC's Blood Services Board of Directors, as well as a leader in the church globally. Additionally, I had served five NYSE company directorships. I wanted to devote more of my focus to the cancer fight. I also hankered to do some fly-fishing, and even though giving up day-to-day control caused me anxiety, witnessing the second generation taking over was a joyful occasion.

I signed retirement papers on July 1, 2000, which removed me from the payroll and from eligibility for company benefits. Karen remained a vice president of Huntsman and I became a dependent on her health insurance. That was fine with me. My take from the sale of Huntsman Packaging put an extra $350 million in my wallet. Additionally, the family held millions of shares of Huntsman Corporation stock, plus other assets. I remained chairman of our family board of directors. Even though pulling out of Huntsman's day-to-day oversight would be a paradigm shift, it was a logical transition.

I had purchased a $2.5 million ranch home on the Teton River in Eastern Idaho where, from the porch, you can cast a line for trout. With time and cash on my hands, I was investing in stocks and real estate while giving money to charities left and right. I told everyone retirement was great. The truth is, the fishing gig would only last about five months. By the end of the year, it was clear that my leaving had been ill-timed.

An unprecedented mix of factors conspired to create a crisis of historic proportion for the chemical sector—only 5 things can go wrong in our industry, and by 2001 all 5 had done so. Europe and Asia watched as the price of American petrochemical products rose. Demand for US goods dropped 10 to 20 percent in less than a year. In addition to a drop in demand and a rise in natural gas and oil prices, the country was heading into a recession. In the 1980s, chemicals had been this nation's number 1 export. We sent 15 percent more product abroad than we sold domestically, but by early 2001 industrial exports were going down the tubes.

In our case, the higher cost of doing business and a strong US dollar meant the product was becoming too expensive for many emerging players, such as China, which turned to the Middle East for chemical imports. Exacerbating matters, the industry had invested much of its profits from the good times (1995 through 1996 and the relatively profitable years of 1997–98) into a construction surge of new facilities that were set to come on line in 2001. We had a diminishing market and more production capacity, especially in the critical commodities sector. Plant utilization rates dropped below 80 percent.

These were the pieces of the jigsaw puzzle. By March 2001, there were already signs Huntsman operations in the US were in trouble, although we still didn't realize the full extent. As the year unfolded we were losing more than $1 million a day—a figure that caught our attention. Even so, there remained a false sense of long-term security. We had weathered 1- or 2-year downturns before. Besides, Huntsman International, separately financed and owned, remained relatively healthy, although it, too, began feeling the pressure, especially since 20 percent of its asset base resided in the US.

The picture grew uglier by the day. By May, we would be unable to make our interest payments to bondholders. In July 2001, a year after my "retirement," I had to put $30 million of my own money back into the company to meet those payments. That we might default on our corporate bonds was a real possibility. By midsummer, we couldn't imagine that it was possible for things to get any worse. Was I in for a surprise. It turns out we weren't even close to the bottom. The downturn that had actually started in 1997, we would painfully learn, and would not bottom out for another four years.

Looking back, it was terribly unfair to Peter that he was positioned as CEO just as all these forces began to conspire against us, but nobody previously experienced or could have foreseen the hurricane-strength headwinds that hit the industry at that point. Many of our competitors were in no better shape and were teetering on the brink of bankruptcy.

In early August, Peter and the senior staff came to my office and unloaded a bombshell. They announced we had run out of money and our financial experts could not see how we could generate enough to even meet payrolls—a situation I had not faced since starting the business thirty years earlier. They proposed we hire a Los Angeles law firm and New York financial consultants should the need arise to declare bankruptcy.

Bankruptcy? I was incredulous. This was the first time I had heard that word with regard to our situation. During the last year in which no one had been formally reporting to me, Huntsman had suddenly become financially devastated. I felt out of the loop and it was time I got a grip on what was happening.

Huntsman International, based in Brussels, was doing okay, although a financial downturn was beginning to hit Europe, too. Having journeyed so high, it was inconceivable that our company, my creation, was foundering. I had been in this exact spot in the early 1970s when I faced a board that wanted to call it quits, but I had been able to convince them to hold on. I said then, and still held firmly in 2001, I would have no part of a bankruptcy. As far as I could tell, the family name was still on the door. If it killed me—and it nearly did—I would lead this remarkable company through another recovery. As captain, I would not be going down with my ship because there was no way I would allow it to sink.

I headed off to New York to meet with officials of Deutsche Bank, which had purchased Bankers Trust, a longtime primary lender on whose board of directors I had served for many years. This time, however, I would be dealing with its German leadership at Deutsche Bank. Its senior vice president Tom Cole, Huntsman's CFO Kimo Esplin, and our attorneys at Skadden of New York believed that if we continued on the present course, the company would go under in six months. By the end of 2001, we were down to $50 million in liquidity. Technically, they said, we were at a point where lenders could force bankruptcy whether I agreed to it or not. Our senior staff, led by Tom Cole, maintained there was no way out. They underscored the merits of declaring bankruptcy on our terms, where the family might retain control of the company.

I would have none of it. With the exception of Peter, all of them thought I was off my rocker. He, along with Karen and the other children were the only allies. It was a lonely existence. Jon Jr. unfortunately had left to accept the position as deputy US trade representative in the Bush-Cheney administration and was residing in Washington. I missed his creative mind. When I returned to Salt Lake City, I called everyone into the boardroom, including the bankruptcy lawyers and consultants, and announced I was coming out of retirement to take charge. I was furious.

If Huntsman had been a public company, we could have sold more stock to raise cash. As a family-owned business, it was painfully evident that private financing was our only route. We already had $800 million in bonds outstanding and we were tapped out with the banks. The people around the table were unanimous. They thought I was unable to face reality. It became a defining moment of my life. "We will not go bankrupt!" I exploded. "It is not an option. I will never sully our name." And I ordered everyone out of the room.

The situation facing me was emotional, all consuming, and close to deadly. As a result, my health went completely out of whack. Nobody will ever know the extent of the emotional and physical toll this crisis took on me. The past challenges of losing my mother, dealing with Haldeman, James's kidnapping, and fighting cancer paled next to this. In past business crises, I was fighting outsiders. This time I was doing battle with my executives and consultants. This was an entirely new scenario, and it was deeply personal. For me, bankruptcy was synonymous with failure.

In the midst of the melee, I was hospitalized twice—once for a mild heart attack and again for a form of Addison's disease that had cropped up, which eventually turned into polymyalgia rheumatica (PMR). (Karen now jokes that if I had not been hit with PMR, I probably would have started four new companies in the midst of all this.) My blood pressure was terrible. But I had to ignore all of that and press on. All that mattered was salvaging the company.

The first step toward rescuing the company was to change the opinion of every bank that carried Huntsman paper—a daunting challenge considering how many there were. One of the financial institutions closest to me, Bank One in Utah, couldn't wait to call its loan. I had been one of its first stockholders, yet it was bailing out on the strength of a rumor that Huntsman was going down the drain. Citibank also clamored for its money. *The New York Times* featured me on page one as one of three Americans who had lost a fortune in 2001, from $3.9 billion to significantly under $1 billion.

We thought we had Bain Capital, Mitt Romney's company, on board with about $560 million for 20 percent of the company. By late summer of 2001, Bain had agreed to terms. The money would be split between paying down debt and purchasing the minority interest ICI still owned after the giant deal 2 years earlier. This infusion of capital would not have resolved the long-term problems, but it would have bought us time to come up with a permanent fix. Bain eventually balked and left us to die.

Though we reduced our workforce through early retirements of some seven hundred associates, including more than one hundred at the corporate office in Salt Lake City, Moody's downgraded our bonds from B+ to D. Despite our personal assurances, suppliers were becoming anxious about extending credit. Could things get any worse?

I wondered just that as I headed back to the Marriott Hotel at the World Trade Center on September 6, 2001, after rendering my second passionate presentation to Deutsche Bank officials. I sensed I had not made much headway, but I was certain I had spotted a glimmer of possibility in some of the faces of those financiers sitting around the table. Perhaps it was just my eternal optimism and refusal to accept cold facts. Either way, I was left with the notion that I had experienced the worst, that nothing else could go wrong.

Five days later, on September 11, 2001, the skies over Lower Manhattan exploded in a fireball of unprecedented terror.

I was in a meeting that morning with the leaders of my church in Salt Lake City, briefing them on the new Alliance for Unity which I had helped to create four months earlier. The hope was it would bring together high-powered civic, religious, and political leaders as a forum for airing contentious community issues. The LDS hierarchy had asked one of its twelve apostles—my close friend, Russell Ballard—to be part of the group. The late LDS Church President Gordon B. Hinckley inquired at this particular meeting if Ballard's presence had been a positive thing. As I started to explain that indeed it had, Hinckley was handed a note from his secretary. A second airliner had struck the Twin Towers. President Hinckley stopped the meeting and one of his counselors, Thomas S. Monson, turned on a television set in the office. We watched in horror as the two skyscrapers crumbled and the Pentagon exploded in flames in Washington, DC in the murderous assault that would be recognized as the deadliest act of terrorism in US history.

The entire world was stunned. The resulting economic fallout turned Huntsman's descent into a tailspin. Overnight, Huntsman's chemical plants were shut down in anticipation of more terrorist acts—chemical facilities are high on the list of potential targets—and hundreds of millions of dollars in additional plant security was added to the expense column. A well-placed explosion at a chemical plant could be disastrous to nearby communities.

The chemical industry now found itself in a perfect, catastrophic storm. Huntsman was no longer isolated in its paralysis but had something in common with all manufacturers: we were at war.

The rest of September and October were a blur. We weren't sure what to expect for the company, but we did notice that natural gas prices were moving downward. Demand was off due to industry shutdowns and curtailment in the 9/11 aftermath. That was the only good news. The price of oil was starting its long, steady climb to more than sixty dollars per barrel when the stock market crashed, taking my investments with it.

This was the point at which Bain Capital pulled out of our refinancing deal. Dr. Robert Gay, who replaced Romney, gave us the axe. The banks were going crazy. I figured that any progress I may have made with a few of the banks in early September had vanished. The nearly unanimous voices for bankruptcy became ever more strident. In the business world, there is a basic principle: when corporate bonds trade at fifty cents on the dollar, prepare for bankruptcy.

The banks would be first in line if it came to dividing up the spoils and there would be nothing left for the bondholders after the banks applied assets to the debt. Some of the banks sold these discounted rates to other financial institutions. (Bankers actually encourage a company to declare bankruptcy—and can force it to do so—because it allows the company to walk away from those who have extended credit, such as suppliers and bondholders, but not from banks.) Bankruptcy rules ensure banks get their money first, at one hundred cents on the dollar. It's a federal law, naturally, passed at the prompting of the banking lobby.

Our management team and consultants told me they respected my determination and my attempts to prove the company could be saved, but now it is over. All is lost. Huntsman must lower its flag and declare insolvency. And doing so would be in my best interest, they said solemnly, because the family would be able to retain 10 to 15 percent ownership.

"All is never lost," I told them. "Shove it."

I vowed that our bondholders would get 100 percent of value one way or the other. The fact that no one in US history had ever pulled off such a thing didn't concern me. Karen believed in me. She and my children had witnessed past comebacks achieved by my magic tricks, but those scenarios were nothing like this one. Karen steadfastly maintained Huntsman would not go under. Her affirmation gave me the strength to survive the first 2 years of this century and to prove with certainty there was at least 1 more rabbit in the old top hat.

As the dust of 9/11 cleared and the nation regained some equilibrium, the troubling picture of private industry became crystal clear. *Maybe*, I thought, *Huntsman's dire situation will be seen as part of the whole picture*. After receiving a special blessing from LDS Church president Hinckley, I set off to convince banks and others to stand by us. To do so, I had to win three consecutive hands in the highest-stakes poker game of my life.

I tried first to persuade my Australian partner, Kerry Packer, to help me refinance. He screamed bloody murder and told me to opt for bankruptcy, which, he pointed out, would fend off creditors. I told him I could bring Huntsman back without bankruptcy; he responded I didn't understand life. I countered that my name was on the door and I would not see it besmirched by bankruptcy. That argument had no impact. Packer simply didn't understand; he had inherited $200 million from his father and was the wealthiest man in Australia. That was the real difference between us. He wasn't an entrepreneur. As it turned out, he wasn't even the gut fighter I thought he was.

At this point, my team approached the Blackstone Group, another New York private equity firm, about purchasing a stake in the company in return for working capital. An old friend from our White House days together, Peter G. Peterson, was chairman of Blackstone. Blackstone President Steve Schwarzman initially agreed to put up enough money to keep the banks at bay in return for a stake of the company. The next day, Schwarzman came back and asked for a larger percentage. This back-and-forth behavior put me in a bind. I would tell our suppliers on one day that financing had been resolved and on the next that the deal would be off because Blackstone wanted another 3 to 4 percent. Schwarzman ultimately asked for 75 percent. I told him to forget it and that I would never work with him again.

Nobody comprehended the depth of my commitment to turn things around. For a while, it was a surreal, lonely world. I quickly learned who was a true friend and who was more comfortable with a fair-weather relationship. Everything I had spent a lifetime building was in danger of imploding. I had established a reputation as a man of my word and I had made charitable commitments it appeared I could not fulfill. Over the years, I had been extended more credit than most because I was someone the banks trusted. But the banks were no longer trusting; some were hedging, big time. I called suppliers, pleading for more time to pay. Because of their long histories with me, I was granted extensions others might not have gotten.

Meanwhile, we had broken ground on the hospital phase of the Huntsman Cancer Institute, to which I had pledged $125 million. University of Utah President Bernie Machen suggested we hold off until the economic picture improved. I countered it was the time to go forward with the hospital portion of the cancer center. I would find a way to fund it and my other obligations, including my million-dollar contribution to the 2002 Winter Olympics, which I had reluctantly promised to help bring some peace to Utah.

In order to finance charity commitments, I personally borrowed millions of dollars, which drove my bankers nuts. "How can you borrow to give to charity?" they asked. I told them a commitment was a contract that could not be broken. They never quite understood, but I eventually fulfilled every charitable commitment and repaid every bank in full, with interest.

It was clear to me that the ultimate financial solution would be to pull off three little miracles that would be excruciatingly difficult. First, we financially had to restructure by persuading bondholders to accept equity in the company in exchange for nearly worthless bonds. Second, and assuming we succeeded with the first feat, we had to persuade 87 institutional lenders around the world to extend lines of credit which were set to expire between 2003 and 2007 and beyond and to increase our credit limits. Finally, there was the matter of Imperial Chemical Industries. ICI still had 30 percent ownership of the giant operations we had bought in 1999. We were obligated to buy the remaining piece by 2002, but the deadline had been extended to 2003 after Bain jumped ship in the summer of 2001. My friend Charles Miller Smith had been replaced as ICI's head and the new CEO was in no mood to extend the sale further. I would have to win this hand another way.

With annual raw material and energy expenses running close to a half billion dollars more than previous costs and with Huntsman perhaps a month or two away from insolvency, 2001 came to a nerve-wracking close. As a young father with a growing family, our vacations were underwritten with an hour or two at the blackjack tables during overnight stops in Las Vegas. To save my company, I would play the most crucial poker game of my life. Winning it would involve a colossal bluff for a pot worth billions.

The first of those three miracles, which eventually would grow to four, was to persuade several hundred Huntsman bondholders to convert interest-earning investments to equity in the company because we didn't have the money to meet the semiannual interest payments. At stake were some $800 million in bonds. The amount hadn't changed much for more than a decade and we had three tiers of bonds: Huntsman Polymers bonds inherited from Rexene when we bought the facility in 1996; Huntsman Corporation bonds tied primarily to the US piece of our business; and Huntsman International bonds that financed the acquisition of a majority interest of ICI in 1999. (ICI, however, held claim to valuable assets of Huntsman International if the minority interest was not purchased by 2003.)

In July 2001, we used $30 million of my personal money to make the interest payments, but it was clear that that would have to be a one-time stopgap. I had just committed $125 million to the hospital phase of the Huntsman Cancer Institute and had some $40 million in other obligations, including a sizable commitment to a new building at the Wharton School. I told my financial staff and the banks that Huntsman would have to default on the December 2001 interest payments, which, in turn, would trigger a default on my bank loans. It was definitely a gamble.

With a private company, any bond rating below B is considered junk. When we missed the year-end interest payment, the rating fell to D. We were lower than junk. Historically, when a private company was rated D, it meant bankruptcy. Even the so-called "vulture" investors who prey on struggling companies were scared away from Huntsman, mostly because they could not figure out the complexities of our capital structure. As might be expected, the value of the bonds themselves had deteriorated drastically. The Huntsman Polymers bonds plunged to a range of ten to twenty cents on the dollar; the Huntsman Corporation bonds fell to twenty-five to thirty-five cents on the dollar; and the Huntsman International bonds dropped to seventy-five to eighty cents on the dollar. Bank debt was trading in the range of seventy to eighty cents on the dollar, but some loans traded as low as fifty cents, indicating that the market expected us to go under.

If I could persuade bondholders to convert to equity bonds, which would make them co-owners and partners, it would give us time to work out loan extensions with our more than eighty lenders. When the company returned to health, the bondholders could sell their equity shares. This option required that we persuade a highly skittish group of people that this was an opportunity, and most of them knew only too well that never before had a private company recovered when its bonds were trading below fifty cents on the dollar. We had the six months until July 1,

2002, the deadline for the next interest payment, to pull off this impossible act. As Kerry Packer later said, "Even Houdini could not have pulled off a stunt like you did."

Missing a single interest payment is one thing, missing two is quite another. Bondholders could have bolted to the nearest bankruptcy court themselves since they held the power to force the issue. My first priority had to be holders of Huntsman Polymers and Huntsman Corporation bonds. They were in the worst shape. Then, just as we were beginning our quest, a "white knight" came knocking.

Huntsman CFO Kimo Esplin received a telephone call in December 2001 from David Matlin, CEO of a division of Credit Suisse First Boston that dealt in distressed debt. He had a proposal Esplin thought was worth exploring. Matlin was a Wharton School alum and a successful if little-known investor who within a few months would be starting his own firm. Matlin knew we were saddled with too much debt and that the industry was on a down cycle, but he also knew me and the history of the company. Matlin said he would put up $350 million to buy up to two-thirds of the Huntsman Polymers and Huntsman Corporation bonds at the current fire-sale prices. It was a risk, but he felt that even if we did go bankrupt he could double his money in any settlement. He actually liked the idea of converting the bonds to equity status. All this and we hadn't even met. He didn't know it at the time, nor did I, but his interest in Huntsman Chemical would end up being the deal of a lifetime—for both of us. To be sure, Matlin had his agenda and the cost would be high, but we fashioned a deal. In the end, Matlin turned out to be a decent, stand-up partner.

In return for purchasing the bonds and converting them to equity status, Matlin's new company, MatlinPatterson Global Advisers, owned 62.5 percent of the restructured and consolidated Huntsman Corporation, which now became the umbrella name for our operations. The family would retain a 37.5 percent interest. Technically, the deal gave Matlin the right to place the company into Chapter 11 bankruptcy proceedings at any time. I insisted the deal allow the headquarters building in Salt Lake City to be transferred to our charitable foundation and I would receive, as a loan, $27 million for my immediate charitable obligations. (I repaid the debt with 15 percent interest in 2005.) The family was given a route to increase its minority ownership stake. Based on positive levels of future performance, ownership could return to a 50-50 split, which is what happened in 18 months.

"We had to do the most complicated valuation we have ever been involved in," Henry Miller, chairman of a bank specializing in restructuring, later told *The Wall Street Journal*, "and at a time the chemical business was in the doldrums." Miller noted that bondholders viewed Matlin as a "lunatic," but that Matlin saw an enormous upside, both to buying in at a low valuation and being associated with Huntsman.

Temporarily losing control of my company was emotional for me, but I could not dwell on that. Under the laws of business-friendly Delaware (where Huntsman and a sizable portion of industrial America file their articles of incorporation), it takes only 3 bondholders to force a judge to set a bankruptcy hearing. It was imperative we had a united bondholder front, and at least a third of the holders of the high-yield bonds did not wish to sell to Matlin. Most of those bonds were in the hands of a group that had organized to take over the company. These investors didn't want to work with Matlin, even though he was offering to buy the bonds at an average of 35 cents on the dollar, a rate well above what they were trading for on the open market. The dissenters felt they would get more out of a bankruptcy settlement and they hired a legal firm, Houlihan Lokey, to force us into bankruptcy court. There also was a small group of bondholders who simply wanted to hang on, true believers who lashed themselves to the mast of the Good Ship Huntsman as it tossed about in the typhoon. (For their loyalty, these hardy souls were paid back in 2004 when they received 108 percent of full value plus interest.)

As spring arrived the situation had become desperate. Banks would not lend us another dime and I had no more personal money to infuse into the operations. The list of chemical companies going under during this period was not short. I had fewer than three months to pull the rabbit from the hat. It would not be with sleight of hand but with a bluff. It would require Houlihan Lokey recommending its bondholding clients sell to Matlin at his current offer.

In March 2002, I requested a meeting with Eric Siegert, a senior partner in Houlihan Lokey and a direct representative for bondholders on the verge of legal action. Siegert was vacationing in Baja California, Mexico. He said I could come to his home in Cabo San Lucas if I wanted to talk. The inconvenience notwithstanding, I flew with Sam Scruggs, then head of our corporate legal department, to Cabo San Lucas and we drove to Siegert's spectacular residence perched on a mountainside overlooking the Pacific Ocean. Everyone but me thought it would be a wasted trip.

As Scruggs and I walked to the front door and rang the bell, I told Scruggs not to say anything, not a single word. I didn't want the survival of the company, which would be decided that very day, to depend on a conversation between lawyers. Settlement is the only thing attorneys understand and there was to be no settlement. Siegert had arranged a sumptuous buffet lunch to greet us on our arrival. But he seemed a less than gracious host when his opening line was, "Let's eat lunch together so I can tell you how we are going to take over your company."

"I've got a hell of an idea," I retorted, my anger rising. "Let's skip lunch and I will let you know why I came to Cabo San Lucas. If you haven't sold your bonds to David Matlin by the end of this day for thirty-five cents on the dollar, at eight a.m. tomorrow I am calling the chairman of Exxon Mobil Corp. and the chairman of Shell Oil to tell them I am leaving the company and that I would be very grateful if they would immediately suspend further credit to our company." That would mean Huntsman would cease to operate and, under the circumstances, to exist.

I watched as it dawned on him that my calls would have the effect of dropping the bondholders' valuation to zero. All that would be left would be the scrap value of our pipes and property. That, I concluded, would not even come close to satisfying the lenders, who would get everything from a liquidation sale. Siegert's eyes went wide and he seemed to have lost his appetite.

Mustering the look of a crazed man, I told him it would be the biggest mistake of his career to think I was kidding about trashing the company. "I didn't build this business to turn it over to shysters like you," I said. I continued the bluff by pointing out that I had enough personal money that I could care less what happens to the company. "I assure you your investment will be worthless." I wheeled around and left, steam spewing from both ears. I hoped he was convinced he had just met someone who was nuts enough to destroy his own business and take everything down with him. A somewhat rattled Scruggs and I drove to the plane and flew home. *Buenos dias.*

I was bluffing, of course, but it worked. The performance drove Siegert and his bondholders into the arms of David Matlin by nightfall. Siegert called Matlin to tell him he was throwing in the towel all right, but not without one last bit of chiseling. He told Matlin it was public knowledge he had paid as high as 40 cents on the dollar for the Huntsman Polymers and Huntsman Corporation bonds. Siegert wanted that rate for his clients. Matlin didn't quibble. The transaction would give MatlinPatterson 90 percent of the bonds, which it could convert to equity at will.

On to the second miracle: convincing the bankers.

Dealing with the bankers was no simple matter. The Huntsman financing structure was complicated given that we had a lending consortium of more than eighty banks. To deal with the delinquent Huntsman account, this group had formed a special credit committee comprised of six representatives to act in a nonbinding fashion for the consortium. Tom Cole, an on-again-off-again friend at Bankers Trust and now at Deutsche Bank, chaired the group, which was fortuitous for us. Cole had been a Huntsman supporter (although he later turned against me) and one of the few key holdovers from Bankers Trust after it was acquired by Deutsche. He had been Kimo Esplin's boss when the latter was at Bankers.

My task was to prove to the bankers that Huntsman was still alive and that converting high-yield bonds to equity bonds would be a sound decision. If we could persuade them, it would stave off financial ruin long enough for us to regain a footing. At face value, we had $2.5 billion in outstanding bonds that, effectively, were now the equivalent of stock ownership. We owed the banks another $3.5 billion, most of which was about to come due. We sought an extension to 2007 and an additional line of credit. For the next few months, I met continuously with the credit committee, concentrating nearly all my waking hours on the lender crisis.

Meanwhile, Peter Huntsman initiated drastic but effective cost-cutting measures, including some two thousand layoffs—a painful move for a family culture that had never before done such a thing—and implementing product price increases and plant consolidations. Gradually, we made headway with the committee. Its makeup could only be described as cautious old men. By this time, Huntsman operations had ceased hemorrhaging and the market had improved from dismal to bad. By year's end, things were noticeably better. Finally, the committee voted four to two to recommend to the other seventy-four banks that we be given loan extensions.

By January 2003, natural gas prices had spiked to $10 per million BTUs and we had only gotten fifty of the eighty-two banks to extend credit. I hit the road to visit the holdouts, but more often than not I ended up meeting with the banks' bankruptcy specialists instead of the senior officers. Part of the problem was that a number of the holdouts were French banks. In February 2003, America descended on Iraq against the advice of much of Europe. US foreign policy strained relations with France, in particular, which hardly helped me. I did convince some of the lenders, and Deutsche Bank pressured the remaining holdouts until we reduced the number of naysayers to five: Wells Fargo, U.S. Bank, Crédit Lyonnais (France's largest bank), BNP Paribas, and Bank of Montreal. I pulled in every chit I had with powerful Wharton alumni, asking them to lobby on my behalf with the holdout banks, but the five financial institutions remained adamant.

It was now time for my second theatrical performance. I essentially pulled the same bluff with these banks as I had with Eric Siegert in Cabo San Lucas. "I'm pulling the plug," I announced, with eyes as glassy as I could manage. "You will end up with nothing. Think I'm bluffing? Try me." And I stormed out. Lo and behold, Wells Fargo and U.S. Bank came aboard. Finally, Deutsche Bank's pressure brought two more into the fold. Crédit Lyonnais, with whom we had only a $3 million loan, was the last sheep into the pen. By March 2003, the second miracle had been wrought.

The final challenge was to raise enough cash to buy out the remaining Imperial Chemical stock. The new management of the British company had refused to extend the deadline a year, believing that my friend Charles Miller Smith had been too accommodating when he had originally cut the deal with Huntsman years before.

ICI's directors wanted their money. Unfortunately for them, ICI stock had dropped considerably in the interim so the purchase price would not be as steep. Unfortunately for Huntsman, we had no money no matter how attractive the price. If we didn't pay up this time, ICI would essentially get the rest of Huntsman International as a penalty. To come up with the $360 million we needed, we decided to issue warranty bonds, a rare type of financing that paid 15 percent interest and were convertible to stock. Few thought there would be a market for such bonds, but hedge funds did take an interest. In particular, Och-Ziff Capital Management bought half the offering, betting we would make it. (Their trust paid off. Eventually, Och-Ziff made a $100 million profit on the investment.) Daniel Och is one of the few honorable men left on Wall Street.

Confidence was building that Huntsman would survive. With the money we raised through the sale of warranty bonds, the flabbergasted directors of ICI were paid off. Its managers were relieved because ICI lacked the experience and personnel to run the Huntsman International properties should it have been forced to exercise the penalty clause. By this time, our bonds were selling at eighty cents on the dollar and the bank debt hovered at ninety-five cents on the dollar. Things had improved to the point that by late 2003 we were actually in a position to make an acquisition. It would be Vantico, the Swiss specialty chemicals company that turned out to be a terrific property. Because MatlinPatterson fronted the money, we acquired it without affecting the Huntsman balance sheet. Its profit was well over $200 million the following year. The Vantico purchase completed in early 2004 turned out to be the cherry on the sundae—the sundae in this case being the first profitable year for Huntsman in the last four. I have Peter and Kimo and their teams to thank for that one.

The sun was breaking through. Our earnings before interest, taxes, depreciation, and appreciation (EBITDA) were $1.25 billion. We were on track to turn a profit in 2005, quite a feat at a time when energy prices were at an all-time high. My management team had come through like World War II veterans. Peter was maturing and the experience led him to become a skilled leader and tough competitor. He had earned the equivalent of twenty PhDs. Kimo Esplin, our CFO, while at first reluctant due to his early bank training, was turning into a hard-hitting negotiator and a strong financial leader. Each management team member deserved a Bronze Star for valor. Karen deserved the Medal of Honor. I was ready to claim a Purple Heart and head for the south fork of the Snake River in Idaho to fly-fish with Dick Cheney.

Please humor me if I call what we accomplished the greatest comeback in the chemical industry's history. Those who believed in us were repaid and then some. MatlinPatterson Asset Management would end up tripling its $500 million life-raft investment in 3 years. By mid-2005, MatlinPatterson's equity stake in Huntsman Corporation was down to 35 percent. In spite of the turnaround, however, the debt load on the company remained a problem. No matter how black our ink, there would still be more than $6.5 billion in loan repayments coming due in 2007. On top of that were my charitable commitments, which were in the red. I could not walk away from my pledges. I gave my word.

Huntsman Corporation had been restored to health. By Labor Day 2004, the resuscitators had been turned off for nearly a year. We had been financially restructured and we were cruising toward one of our most profitable quarters ever.

For a year, the chemical industry's fortunes had been on the upswing and our options as we plowed into 2005 were three: sell/merge, go public, or go under. To provide the cash to meet both debt and donations, we had to raise more than a billion in capital. It was time for the most profound, and the saddest, transaction of my life. There was no avoiding it any longer: we had to take America's largest family-owned-and-operated business public.

As it turned out, the timing for our IPO couldn't have been better. The move would reduce the debt, provide steadier financing for the Huntsman Cancer Institute, and ensure that Huntsman Corporation would never again find itself in the financial straits from which it was emerging. We had landed in trouble because of our debt load amassed through gifts to charities and acquisitions, complicated by a market downturn. Had we not become the company that turned approximately $12 billion in annual sales, investors would not have been interested. Two years prior, our corporate health had been declared terminal and we were given Wall Street's version of the last rites. Through cost savings, an upswing in the market, and an incredible amount of shoe leather and arm-twisting, our corporate pulse was returning to healthy levels. Not only had we risen from the ashes, we were a vibrant company. Either selling or going public would provide the capital to reduce our debt load and ensure long-term financing for the Huntsman foundations, most especially my commitment to the Huntsman Cancer Institute.

We entertained a sale to Dow Chemical and considered a merger with Lyondell Chemical, but not for long. Going public was the proper course—even though I hated the idea. It was the third time we had considered this route and this time we all were in agreement—and, by "all," I mean Karen, nine children, and grandkids on the scene in 2004, each of whom had trusts of their own.

I even brought up the possibility of Warren Buffett buying the company. I asked Buffett, a philanthropic trooper after my own heart, if I could bring Peter by for a talk. He said he would love to and we flew to his office building in Omaha. No guards, no security. Finally, we asked someone if he knew where Buffett's office was. Up the elevator to the top floor, was the response. There was a nondescript door twenty feet from the elevator that said "Berkshire Hathaway." A small sign said "Ring bell." He and his secretary opened the door and greeted us warmly. He took us to his relatively small office with a sofa that seated two. I got around to telling him about our great business and that he ought to own it.

"I am going to teach you a great lesson," he responded, and explained that his company buys only "simple" businesses they understand. "The chemical business is too complicated." He said he would ask his partner Charlie Munger if Berkshire Hathaway ought to buy Huntsman. "If his answer is a firm 'no,' that means 'yes.' But if he responds with 'hell no,' then he really means 'no.'" He called me back a few days later and merely said, "Charlie said 'hell no.'"

The move to go public would represent the final company decision we would make as a family. While I have grave reservations about a public corporation's ability to simultaneously honor charitable obligations and satisfy investors' appetite for profits, selling stock on the open market does allow a corporation to cover its financial exigencies. I became convinced the hard way that, given the volatility of our industry, a privately owned company as large and as leveraged as Huntsman simply could not survive such onslaughts. We ultimately were defenseless when faced with a critical need for a large infusion of capital.

It was fall 2004, the right time to go public and for the right reason. In its present condition, Huntsman was the ideal candidate. We would offer 30 percent of the company, more than 60 million shares of stock, for $1.5 billion. As it turned out, the offering brought more than that. The goal was to give up as little as we could in the way of equity while bringing in as much cash as possible. In our case, our CFO wanted to reduce debt to about $4.5 billion, which would bring the debt-to-earnings ratio into an acceptable range.

After making a decision to take your company public, the next step in the process is referred to as a beauty contest. You become the judge deciding which investment bankers will underwrite and manage your IPO. For this, the twelve banks and half dozen minor players received a total of $75 million in fees. Before it was over, the price tag of going public was $100 million. These bankers provided tremendous balance and did a terrific job backing up Peter, Kimo, and me at institutional presentations throughout Europe and the US.

Each of us headed a team. I took the foreign countries and parts of the US. Stops included London, San Juan, Milan, Frankfurt, New York, Boston, Bermuda, San Francisco, Jakarta, and Austin. Peter remained in the US. For two solid weeks, our two Gulfstream IVs crisscrossed the skies in a series of dog-and-pony shows. I enjoyed the encounters, but we were lucky. There were two of us who knew the company inside and out which allowed us to double-team global markets. We not only had to sell the company at each presentation, we also had to sell ourselves. At the end of the day, we were not the Huntsman CEO and chairman, respectively. Peter and I were salesmen. We had come full circle.

Here's how Deutsche Bank analyst David Begleiter described our comeback in a post-IPO article in the May 18, 2005, edition of *Chemical Week*: "Before the IPO, the more bearish creditors framed the company as a classic example of a spending spree leading to excess leverage, flirtation with bankruptcy, a shotgun marriage, renewed discipline and possibly a more productive future . . . We think that the comeback tale underestimates the impact of Huntsman's near-bankruptcy experience. In part because of that, we expect Huntsman to ride this cycle the right way, using the cash flow from its commodity businesses to deleverage, and as importantly, strengthen its position in more differentiated growth businesses."

As we circled the globe, Peter and I assured each institution that, not only was Huntsman out of the woods and engaged in a well-paced, long-distance race, it was also the leading global manufacturer of polyurethanes, advanced materials, and paint pigments. We emphasized our broad geographic customer base and management experience. The institutional investors liked what they heard. At the end of the first go-round, we had initial orders for $5 billion in stock. We were oversold three to one. Of course, we hadn't as yet set the price of the stock and initial indications were that it would be in the range of eighteen to nineteen dollars a share. Because of the enthusiastic response, the investment bankers went for the high range—twenty-three dollars a share. That produced $1.65 billion, most of which went to our lenders.

Reducing our debt to approximately $4.75 billion allowed us to tweak the due dates of some of the remaining loans to as far out as 2009. There is a fine line between obtaining a good opening price for an initial public offering (IPO) and getting greedy. If you set the IPO price too high, investors turn around and sell it immediately. Investors have to see potential for growth. And that is what they saw in an IPO at twenty-three dollars a share.

Analysts were predicting the stock would hit thirty-two dollars within a year. On Friday, February 11, 2005, at 9:30 a.m. eastern standard time, Huntsman Corporation shares hit the floor of the New York Stock Exchange, trading under the ticker symbol "HUN." It was one of the ten largest IPOs in the history of the exchange at that time and the largest IPO in the history of the chemical sector. Shares immediately rose to thirty dollars before settling back to twenty-six dollars. In the coming weeks, as with most IPOs, the price came down, settling just below nineteen dollars a share—a reflection of the rest of the chemical industry—before starting a slow climb back into the twenties.

The Huntsman family gathered on the balcony overlooking the floor of the NYSE on that opening day, poised for the ceremonial ringing of the opening bell. As I looked down at what collectively would now be my "bosses" in the open market after three decades of being sole captain of the ship, I did not feel much remorse. I was swept with a feeling of relief that never again would I have to go through what I had endured during the past four years. That very day I would pay off $75 million in personal loans (including the loans that financed my charity commitments) and would walk away with $25 million in cash in my pocket.

Standing next to me, Karen, too, was relieved. She commented that the day I handed over the day-to-day operations to Peter five years earlier had been a far more emotional experience. She, too, was at peace with the family business turning into a public company. We were proud of Peter. He came through like the true champion he is. We all believed the heartache was behind us.

On that miraculous morning, as I surveyed the chaotic trading floor of the New York Stock Exchange, I found myself looking forward to chairing a company for others as well as the family—nearly 70 percent of the business was still privately held—and to concentrating on our struggle to defeat cancer. I vowed to myself that as chairman of a publicly traded company, I would safeguard the corporate duty to give back to others, at least with my own shares.

I keep my word. But as I'll explain in the pages to come, not everyone has the backbone to keep his or her word. As a result of other people's dishonesty in the years that followed, Huntsman made a couple of billion dollars.

18. The Double-Cross

IT WAS EARLY 2006, AND WITH THE DEBT EQUITY MARKET HEATING UP, Huntsman found itself the target of acquisitions interest. None of us anticipated the wild ride that was to come. The three years that followed were filled with high-speed action and capped off by a surprise conclusion.

The first nibble came in February, when the takeover group Apollo Global Management sent its calling card. Also interested were Basell, a Dutch conglomerate owned by US-based Access Industries, and Lyondell, a Houston-based polymers manufacturer. We informally had approached Lyondell about a merger possibility in 2005. It hadn't gone anywhere then, but Lyondell returned with renewed interest.

Huntsman at the time was the fourth largest US chemical maker with nearly $12 billion in annual sales. Its earnings were healthy and the stock price was within striking distance of twenty-three dollars a share. Many analysts felt the actual share value was around twenty-six dollars, even though profit levels had softened in 2006. Most of our divisions were considered excellent buys and the six units comprising Huntsman could be broken up by a new owner.

The only weak link was the commodity chemicals business, which was under increased pressure from new sources of competition in China and the Middle East. The increased worldwide production of various polymers was sapping the life out of that division. It seemed prudent to listen to what these potential suitors had to offer. The new board of directors, formed as we went public in 2005, authorized the prerequisite legalities of the bid process. My own philosophy was: if the time and price are right, we will sell. Above all, a sale must be the right move for all stakeholders.

I sold a small slice of my personal stock to pay down loans for philanthropic donations during the IPO but was waiting until we could assure maximum value for the company before selling any substantial amounts. Early in 2006, Peter announced at an investors meeting in New

York City that we had the strongest balance sheet in our history. He was bullish, pointing to the sustainable financial model we employed. We had reduced operating expenses by 15 percent, primarily by closing several unproductive plants. Debt had been reduced from $6.4 billion to $2.7 billion, saving us some $350 million a year in interest. As *Chemical Week* had noted, Huntsman's progress truly was one of the industry's great, dramatic turnaround stories.

Even so, Basell and Lyondell were hesitant about our asking price. Apollo's people, on the other hand, liked what they saw. Josh Harris, one of Apollo's three principals and president of the group, met with us in Salt Lake City in late February 2006. Apollo's chairman was my old friend, the Wall Street tycoon Leon Black. He had helped develop the junk bond market in the 1980s along with Michael Milken, who eventually went to prison for his Wall Street sleight of hand.

Prior to meeting with Harris, I warned him he needn't bother coming to Utah if he wasn't willing to offer us twenty-five dollars a share. He assured me he would not enter a lower bid. Our stock was trading at just under twenty-two dollars. It had been at twenty-six dollars a week earlier, but there was moderate downward pressure after a fourth-quarter 2005 earnings report showed us short of projections. The Port Arthur, Texas operations had not come back on line since Hurricane Rita's storm surge inflicted considerable damage.

On the strength of Harris's assurances, our board's executive committee—David Matlin, Peter, and I—met with him. Harris revealed that Apollo planned to sell off the cyclical commodities business, combine the specialties divisions with Hexion, and float an IPO for the new venture. The committee was receptive to the twenty-five-dollars-per-share offer. It seemed like a done deal. Harris excused himself and we worked into the evening to craft a working sale agreement. Around 11:00 p.m., Harris returned to announce that, upon reflection, Apollo would have to lower its bid to twenty-four dollars a share. He said they had reviewed Huntsman's most recent earnings data—numbers they had seen prior to committing to twenty-five dollars—and decided the lower price was accurate. Harris and whomever he had talked to in the interim apparently hoped we were so far past the point of no return that we would swallow a 4 percent price reduction.

Apollo's backtracking should not have surprised us. Matlin had had bad experiences with them in the past and his dislike of the firm was intense even on the best of days. When Harris dropped this bomb, Matlin went ballistic. He stormed out of the room, slamming the door behind him. I went over to Harris and put my hand on his shoulder. "Josh," I said calmly, "how can we trust you now? We're done here." I showed him to the door. He returned about a week later offering $24.50 a share. "Our deal was for twenty-five dollars," I reminded him. With the board's concurrence, I showed Josh the door for the second time. His boss, Leon Black, tried a third time during a dinner in Washington, DC, but we wouldn't budge. Our earlier experiences with Bain and Blackstone proved there is no honor among thieves or among most Wall Street shops. Apollo was no exception.

Matlin had warned us Apollo would attempt to shaft us and Apollo did not disappoint. Little did any of us realize how bad it was going to get. Apollo eventually would create for Huntsman the most profound setback in its history.

With Apollo out of the picture for the moment, Peter pointed out we could do the same thing Apollo had planned to do, and spin off the commodities piece of our business. He estimated the move could create as much value as the failed deal's purchase price. The board gave Peter's plan a thumbs-up.

In 2006, we closed on Texas Petrochemicals' $275 million purchase of our old Port Neches butadiene facility, part of the business we had acquired from Texaco in 1994. We also sold our European commodities piece for roughly $800 million to petrochemical giant Saudi Basic Industries Corporation (SABIC). In the same year, we sold our entire US petrochemicals segment to a subsidiary of Koch Industries, the world's largest privately held enterprise led by my close friend Charles Koch and his brother David (known also for their sizable contributions to conservative candidates and causes). That sale would bring Huntsman another $800 million, give or take a couple of million. The good news: the eventual proceeds from these sales would reach almost $1.9 billion. The bad news: just as we were about to close the deal with Koch, disaster struck at the heart of the business it was about to buy. A massive explosion and fire devastated our Port Arthur, Texas plant. The sale to Koch was contingent on restarting it.

Rebuilding cost us $600 million, not counting lost business and property damage. Our insurers were shell shocked, saying they would only cover about two-thirds of the claim, so we were forced to take them to court. Our claim ended up in arbitration through which we managed to recover an additional $110 million.

It was also about this time that oil prices began their historic ascent, eventually reaching $147 per barrel, and they began to retreat only because the Great Recession crippled manufacturing. Huntsman's annual sales dropped by the end of 2006 from $14 billion to $9 billion, primarily because we were operating fewer business units after our divestitures. Yet overall, Huntsman was a tighter, more focused operation than it had been and its share price rose as a result.

The next wrinkle in our game plan came in March 2007 when David Matlin served notice that MatlinPatterson intended to sell its 40 percent stake in the company. He wanted us to put the business up for sale. The other directors were not excited about that option, so Matlin hired UBS to help him unload his holdings, which were worth more than $1.5 billion. UBS' bush-beating raised outside interest in our company once again. And, at an investor presentation in New York in February 2007, we let it be known a deal might be in the making. Matlin's goals were a quick turnaround and cash; our goal was to maximize shareholder value. It was a frequent conflict in our partnership. Private equity versus management or public ownership.

While in the city, I stopped to visit Josh Harris at his office overlooking Central Park, curious to see whether Apollo was still interested in acquiring Huntsman. Harris was indeed interested, most particularly in the advanced materials and polyurethanes divisions, which would mesh nicely with Hexion. On the spot, he made a strong offer of twenty-five dollars a share. A week later, and before our board could even consider that bid, Harris had lowered his offer to twenty-three dollars a share. Why was I not surprised? I told him to forget it.

By June 2007, we were in discussions with three potential buyers: Access Industries, once again, and its Dutch chemical subsidiary, Basell; The Blackstone Group, an investment company with which we had dealings in the past; and, believe it or not, our "old friend" Apollo Global Management, who had returned with yet another proposal for a Huntsman-Hexion marriage. We were also in communication with Reliance, the largest chemical company in India. Blackstone lost interest quickly because of the competition, and the discussion with Reliance went nowhere, but Basell and Apollo remained in the chase.

Our sparring bouts with Apollo earlier in the year left Huntsman directors with a bad taste in their mouths. I had additional concerns about the fact that Hexion was a major competitor in the epoxy business. Access' bid was $25.25 a share; Apollo bested it with a $26 offer. The board leaned toward Access because the sale could be consummated in three months since the European-based Basell would not have antitrust issues in the US or Europe. A Hexion merger would undergo careful scrutiny by the FTC and the European Commission. The deal would take a year to close. Much can happen in a year, as we ultimately—and painfully—discovered.

From the get-go, we were as uncomfortable with Apollo's financing plans as we were with the firm itself. We felt somewhat reassured when Apollo produced strong financing commitments from Credit Suisse First Boston (CSFB) and Deutsche Bank—European banking giants with whom we had enjoyed a long and positive history. What did not bode well was that Hexion would be swallowing a company three times its size consisting of six separate businesses: polyurethanes, advanced materials, textile effects, performance products, pigments, and petrochemicals. (The commodity chemicals piece was still in the process of being sold.) Even worse, it would be financing the entire deal with debt. Because of this risk, we asked Apollo to improve its bid. Apollo would not budge.

On June 26, 2007, the board followed its gut instinct and unanimously accepted Access/Basell's bid of $9.6 billion ($5.9 billion plus the assumption of $3.7 billion of debt). The purchase agreement imposed a $200 million fee for backing out of the deal before closing. Apollo apparently had not seen that coming. Josh Harris and Leon Black went berserk when they learned their twenty-six-dollar bid had been passed over in favor of Basell's lower offer. Within hours, they raised their bid to twenty-eight dollars and, within a few days, Black and Harris were on a plane to Utah.

At our spacious Deer Valley home, they confirmed the twenty-eight-dollars-per-share offer. Apollo further agreed to pick up half of the breakup fee to Basell for our failure to consummate the original deal. So far, our shareholders were gaining mightily. All of this took place in the presence of Utah's two US senators, Orrin Hatch and Bob Bennett. I had invited them to join the board meeting for this discussion because the board remained suspicious of Apollo after experiencing their previous shenanigans. We wanted Harris and Black to look two US senators in the eye, shake their hands, and tell them it was a done deal. I hoped that might bind them more firmly to their offer. Black assured us of Apollo's "100 percent commitment" to the price and Harris repeatedly said the deal was "rock solid."

After all of that, the board still faced a dilemma. Selling to Apollo ran afoul of our basic instincts. Matlin's dislike for Harris and Black was a serious consideration. On the other hand, to ignore a far superior bid—with a three-dollar-a-share premium—could have prompted class-action lawsuits by investors, which would delay the sale for two or more years. Furthermore, we were informed that Apollo had signed a financial commitment package with Credit Suisse and Deutsche Bank to put to rest our doubts that it could finance a $10.6 billion deal.

Apollo's Hexion Specialty Chemicals, when combined with Huntsman, would become the world's largest producer of specialty chemicals. In addition to the $10.6 billion sale price, which included assumption of debt, Apollo/Hexion agreed to an 8 percent increase in per-share purchase price if the sale was not closed by April 5, 2008, some 270 days from the date of the agreement. That clause put pressure on Apollo to obtain an antitrust exemption from the US Justice Department sooner than later. Getting a waiver is not difficult, but the process is time consuming. Finally, we knew that the sale contract contained a "material adverse effects" clause which allowed the buyer to cancel the deal should certain factors substantially change between the deal's announcement and closing.

On July 12, just sixteen days after our initial agreement, we formally notified Access/Basell we would be exiting its earlier deal to take Apollo's higher offer and that we would be paying the $200 million breakup fee. Even Matlin concluded Apollo's superior offer merited pursuit. Shortly thereafter, Matlin exited the board and separately sold his shares at a slight discount before closing. Access, understandably, was not pleased with our decision but chose not to match or raise Apollo's bid. Instead, it used our $200 million penalty toward the acquisition of Lyondell (which soon went bankrupt).

Apollo's higher bid notwithstanding, Hexion was leveraged to the gills with an estimated $3 billion in debt on only $4 billion in annual sales. For that reason, we crafted a no-contingency contract allowing Hexion an exemption for a narrow range of deal stoppers not of its doing, such as being turned down for an antitrust pass from the Justice Department. Even then, Apollo would have to pay a three-quarters-of-a-billion-dollar penalty. I privately felt Hexion had overreached with its bid, which included more than $4 billion in debt assumption.

A stockholders' meeting was called to ratify the merger on October 16, 2007, in the Marriott Hotel in The Woodlands, Texas. Only two stockholders—an elderly couple—showed up to meet with a contingent of company officers, banking executives, and lawyers but, through proxies, the shareholders ratified the directors' decision and overwhelmingly approved the merger. As I observed these proceedings, reverie overtook me. We had acquired thirty-six separate entities up to that point in my career and had sold them all through five major deals: Huntsman Container, the styrenics business to Nova, Huntsman Packaging, Huntsman Polymers, and now the entire company in a deal that would dwarf them all. Peter and I almost felt as though we were selling a family member. I alone had been at the helm of each Huntsman venture at its genesis. Each had attracted professional and capable management and loyal workers whom we respected and enjoyed. That was coming to an end.

Or so I thought.

It could be said that the Huntsman-Hexion merger symbolized the exuberance of the market and the heady days of 2006 through early 2007. It was a time of expansion, growth, easy money, a booming housing market, and tremendous leveraging. Only a year later, under President George W. Bush's administration, we were in the worst US economic meltdown since the Great Depression. In fact, it may have been worse than the historic Depression. Only an elite few went down with the stock market when it crashed in 1929. Neither the Securities and Exchange Commission nor the Federal Reserve Bank was created until 1934. This latest recession—or depression, depending on your outlook—occurred in spite of regulatory "safeguards" and government oversight, which were nonexistent in the 1920s when the nation did not have the enormous wealth it had in 2008. This time, everyone was affected—pensioners, middle-class families, public companies, philanthropies, even Wall Street and its denizens—and all would have to claw their way back from financial Armageddon. Unfortunately, the route Apollo chose for saving itself was duplicity.

With the promise of liquidation of our corporate holdings only weeks away, there was sufficient confidence to start making plans in 2007 to build new enterprises and diversify my holdings. I committed some of my expected sale proceeds to start a new venture with partner Bob Gay, which we cleverly called Huntsman Gay Global Capital, a private equity firm that would be based in Palo Alto, California. My participation in this enterprise would be another mechanism for earning money to channel into the Huntsman Cancer Institute and Hospital. To fund our humanitarian aspirations, some $700 million in Huntsman shares—about half of what would be generated personally from the Hexion sale—was donated to the Huntsman Foundation, our conduit for philanthropic injections to HCI and many other charities we supported. Another charitable entity named Huntsman Cancer Foundation (HCF) was established to raise money specifically for cancer research at HCI from outside sources and to receive more than $50 million worth of Huntsman Corporation stock.

Late in 2007, we gave $26 million to Utah State University's business college, with the promise of more to follow. Our gift funded scholarships and business programs centering on ethical leadership and entrepreneurship. Shortly afterward, Stephen R. Covey, best-selling author and recognized authority on ethics-based leadership principles, agreed to join the faculty and became the first to hold the Huntsman Presidential Chair in Leadership. A new, spiffy, technology-loaded business school building was scheduled to be constructed, and the institution would soon become a top twenty-five business school. I was as proud of USU's president, the dean, and the faculty of the business school as I was humbled by the words of former Wharton dean Thomas Gerrity when he declared at the announcement ceremony that USU's Jon M. Huntsman School of Business and its programs would not only carry my name but would promote "the values of an individual known for his vision, integrity, and humanity." In the months to come, it would become clear that those attributes were hard to find among our would-be owners and financiers.

As the Great Recession tightened its economic chokehold in the latter months of 2007, the once-dauntless banking institutions began to tremble. Huntsman reported soft first-quarter results that did not meet projections. Falling commodity prices and the sliding value of the dollar produced earnings less than those of the previous year, as reported in the second below-forecast quarterly report in a row. It didn't take long for Apollo to signal anxiety. In its January 2008 notification letter to Huntsman, the company announced it would exercise its right to extend the sale's closing date by ninety days, from April 5 to July 4, 2008. What Apollo really wanted, of course, was a way out of our deal. The material adverse effects clause in our contract was the obvious straw at which to grasp but, as court depositions would later show, that threshold was not breached. Not even close. So Apollo's officers and board devised an insidious maneuver on which to base an exit justification.

Independently and surreptitiously, Black commissioned Duff & Phelps (D&P), the firm that did much of Apollo's valuation work, to study Huntsman's situation. In the resulting report, D&P declared the combined post-merger entity (Huntsman-Hexion) would be insolvent if the deal went through. Relying solely on that flawed and self-serving document, Hexion and Apollo filed suit on June 16 in Chancery Court in Delaware where Huntsman is incorporated. Apollo/Hexion asked the court to cancel the merger agreement because of negative financial circumstances it alleged had come to light since the agreement was signed. It further claimed the bleak D&P analysis made it impossible to obtain financing from Deutsche Bank and Credit Suisse, whose commitments were contingent on a certificate of solvency.

When Wall Street got wind of this erroneous, self-serving analysis, Huntsman stock slid to thirteen dollars a share. It would tumble much lower before the smoke cleared.

Apollo's double cross knocked the wind out of my normally stiff sails. Flying back from Washington, DC to my summer home in Driggs, Idaho in May 2008, I remember wondering how this episode would end. However it unfolded, it would not—could not—be the last chapter for our company. Yet, I was tired. It had been a long year. I was down. The stress nearly cost me my life. It was necessary to undergo a knee replacement, and the surgeons had a hard time keeping my heart pumping during the operation. They had to pack me in ice to keep my body temperature down. I emerged from that procedure only to be diagnosed with polymyalgia rheumatica, a painful disease for which I began taking fairly large doses of prednisone just to keep functioning. The side effects of that drug exacted a toll of their own that limits much of my emotional and physical endurance—even today. Following this development, the need for a bladder operation arose. The affair left me with heart problems and high blood pressure. Shortly thereafter, I underwent operations for cancer on my nose and a malignant melanoma tumor on my back.

Without question, I was hit hard. I had been down rough roads before, but when the other side intentionally plays dirty, it is infuriating. In its effort to back out of the deal, Apollo was willing to destroy me, the company, and our values—to gut the worth of our stock and, by extension, to hobble our charitable projects. For me, this would be the test of the ages. I would not let Apollo and the banks win under any circumstances.

Because we are headquartered in Utah, the sophisticated big boys often look at us as hicks. As soon as they see signs of decency, openness, and straightforwardness, some take it as a sign of weakness and think they can take advantage of us. Some have found out the hard way that when cheated or threatened with an unfair set of playing rules, there is another side to Jon Huntsman, a tough side of which advantage can't be taken. These New Yorkers had underestimated the country boys.

The rapid unfolding of the devastating turn of events had left me, as *Forbes* magazine accurately described it, "sputtering, flabbergasted and litigious." We returned fire on June 23, 2008, with a lawsuit in Texas courts.

Our civil complaint charged the defendants, including Apollo, its partners Josh Harris and Leon Black, and Hexion Specialty Chemicals, with slander and tortious interference with the merger agreement. The damage figure was not fixed because it represented the difference between Huntsman's then-present value and what the stockholders would have gained had we sold to Basell at $25.25 a share. As it turned out, that would represent in excess of $4 billion.

Credit Suisse and Deutsche Bank were but months away from being added to the Texas suit for withdrawing financing and forcing our stock to plunge. Hexion's "made as instructed" appraisal of our value amounted to little more than a conspiracy to damage the company's image where the market instantly reflected the body blow. I was determined to make Apollo and the banks accountable for this vandalism. First, we had to get Apollo's attention.

Huntsman's board of directors voted on July 1 to extend the termination date for the merger from July 4 to October 2 and quickly set about building a model for the trial showing the company was not only solvent but poised for earnings growth, as the cost of oil and natural gas eased and the dollar strengthened. We hired David Resnick, a business valuation expert with Rothschild, Inc., to review the Duff & Phelps report and create one of his own. We weren't surprised that while the D&P report found a funding *deficit* of $858 million, Resnick reported a surplus of $124 million. Where the D&P report listed a negative net asset value of $1.9 billion, Resnick showed a positive net of $3.7 billion.

On July 2, we filed a counterclaim against Hexion/Apollo in Chancery Court in Georgetown, Delaware, the judicial arena in which we were required to litigate contractual issues. Each side essentially charged the other with knowingly breaching the merger contract. Fox Business News, *The Wall Street Journal*, *The New York Times*, and numerous business magazines followed the unfolding drama closely. I used every opportunity to publicly charge Black and Harris with unethical conduct in their scheme to woo us away from Basell, to show how Apollo made promises it never intended to keep in hopes of trapping us into renegotiating the merger at a fire-sale price, and to demonstrate how Apollo's statements injured Huntsman with suppliers and customers. Despite this turmoil, the company remained profitable and fared better than most chemical companies at that time, but Apollo's mischief eroded several billion dollars of our company's value.

On the strength of our airtight contract, I was determined Apollo's tactics would not prevail. I was confident about our case for three reasons: First, Chancery Court had never found a material adverse effects clause to be sufficient grounds for backing out of a merger. Second, financial and legal media noted that if Apollo prevailed other future merger agreements would not be worth the paper on which they were written. Finally, the facts and our good faith efforts to close were on our side. Apollo had nothing to rely on but the bleak and distorted Duff & Phelps report speculating that the combined companies would not be viable, which we knew we could prove was inaccurate.

The next step in our legal shootout was to exercise the right to extend the merger agreement by ninety days—to October 2, 2008—and seek a fast track in the court proceedings to enable us to complete the merger quickly despite Apollo's acute case of buyer's remorse. Hexion/Apollo opposed both actions, but on July 9 we were granted an expedited trial and later received approval of the extension.

Hexion's argument focused on three points:

1. Apollo was not obligated to close since the combined company would be insolvent, per the Duff & Phelps report, and therefore should be allowed to pay the $325 million breakup fee and bow out.
2. Since the contracts were signed, Huntsman's earnings had diminished and its debt load had increased, i.e. constituting "material adverse effects," and justifying its exit.
3. It had no liability to Huntsman per terms of the agreement.

Our counterclaim was also three-pronged:

1. Hexion deliberately breached the merger agreement.
2. We had not suffered a "material adverse effect" and the Duff & Phelps evaluation was flawed.
3. Hexion was obliged to complete the deal and should be ordered to close or pay damages.

The Wall Street Journal summed it up nicely: "The gloves have come off." Outside the courthouse, other events helped our case even as our stock dipped below 10 dollars. Two other chemical mergers were announced: Dow Chemical acquired Rohm and Haas, paying a premium for the latter's stock, and Ashland bought Hercules at a premium price. Those sales provided a benchmark for how Huntsman might be valued. In a July 15 court filing, we presented financial reports showing projected earnings for the year at 11 percent above street estimates. Our second-quarter results were released the following day, showing 10 percent greater earnings than the previous quarter along with improved sales volume. A day later, on July 17, the price of a barrel of crude oil, which had reached $147 the week before, started downward, easing expenses for our petro-dependent industry. And, last but not least, a Huntsman shareholder had filed a separate suit against Hexion for defrauding Huntsman investors. Our stock value jumped past 13 dollars a share.

The judge, Vice Chancellor Stephen Lamb, set the trial for September 8. Lamb said he would render a timely decision that would give Huntsman sufficient time, should we prevail at trial, to conclude the merger by the October deadline. This was not a positive beginning for Hexion and its Apollo handlers. Our attorneys—nearly two dozen of them hailing from four law firms—had less than ten weeks to prepare for the biggest, most pivotal legal trial most of them had ever experienced. Through depositions and trial witnesses, evidence emerged which our lawyers stitched into a seamless cloak of bad-faith behavior. At trial, they laid out scenarios that read like a John Grisham novel.

Among the tidbits they revealed was the fact that Apollo and Hexion were unquestionably excited about the deal at first. Apollo partner Jordan Zaken testified that the "industrial logic" for such a merger was "very strong," and that a Hexion/Huntsman merger would have created the largest specialty chemical company in the world. Their enthusiasm dampened when Huntsman reported first-quarter numbers on April 22, 2008. Apollo revised its merger model and concluded the deal would produce lower returns than expected, at which point Apollo began to look for ways to break the deal and came up with the material adverse effect claim.

Evidence also showed that on May 9, Apollo Global Management discussed with its attorneys whether the contractually defined material adverse effects had occurred, but applying the facts to three subsequent hypothetical models had not produced an outcome of Huntsman's insolvency. Realizing its material adverse effects argument was not strong, a case based on insolvency of the combined companies and/or lack of financing was contrived. From there evolved the scheme to obtain an outside insolvency opinion, publicize it to erode lender confidence, and use it as the basis of its claim that Hexion did not breach its contractual obligations.

An Apollo e-mail proved that the banks, Apollo, and their lawyers conceded the merger agreement was as tight as a legal document could get, and that Apollo told its attorneys to "find loopholes." It was then Apollo chose the outside appraiser Duff & Phelps.

Notes dated May 16 taken by Duff & Phelps' Allen Pfeiffer showed Apollo hired the firm specifically to create grounds for its intended claim of insufficient capital to close the deal. This, in itself, was a problem for Apollo because Duff & Phelps knew its opinion was being readied for a legal proceeding and, therefore, had lost the aura of objectivity. Duff & Phelps, using overly pessimistic earnings forecasts to show an unrealistic funding gap, reported a combined Hexion-Huntsman would be worth only $11.35 billion—$4.25 billion less than Apollo had originally estimated and not enough to maintain solvency. Further, Apollo suddenly added a $102 million advisory fee to the Hexion expenses that was not included in earlier models.

Perhaps most damaging to Hexion's case was evidence that Duff & Phelps did not seek input from Huntsman management for its financial analysis. Apollo specifically had instructed Duff & Phelps personnel not to talk with Huntsman management because making such inquiries might have compromised the termination objective of the Hexion board.

By filing its lawsuit, Hexion made the D&P report public and sent copies to Credit Suisse and Deutsche Bank the next day (in case the financial institutions had missed the news) for the sole purpose of prejudicing funding decisions. The banks had never questioned the solvency of the combined company prior to reading the report. Hexion CEO Craig Morrison testified at trial that publication of the Duff & Phelps report effectively killed the financing.

Finally, we showed that Apollo's duty to obtain antitrust approval from the FTC had been breached. After an initial application in August 2007, little follow up had occurred. Apollo never intended to obtain FTC permission for a merger.

On August 28, 2008, a group of Huntsman shareholders offered to finance $500 million of the merger. Hexion's Morrison rejected the offer within two hours of its issuance, stating in a press release: "We are not seeking to renegotiate this transaction. We are seeking to terminate it." Later, in the middle of the trial, Hexion conditionally consented to this proposal but noted it did not believe it would solve the problem. Judge Lamb saw, as did we all, that Apollo simply wasn't interested in closing under any circumstances.

As the trial progressed, we became more and more optimistic. Lamb took the case for consideration on September 19. Ten days later, he ruled in Huntsman's favor, handing down a stinging rebuke of Apollo's tactics. It was a well-deserved slam dunk.

On the claim of material adverse effect, Judge Lamb found that disappointing quarterly performances are short-term issues. A buyer must assume a long-term strategy. Huntsman's missed projections were a "short-term hiccup" and did not constitute a substantial defect.

He also found that the merger agreement explicitly holds Huntsman harmless for any estimate, projection, and forecast that did not meet target. Had Hexion wanted this to be part of the sale agreement, it ought to have included that in the contract.

On the claim of increased indebtedness ($4.1 billion by closing, versus $3 billion forecast for year-end 2008, and which subsequently was reduced after selling three divisions), Judge Lamb held that Apollo's debt projection in its own pre-signing models was $4.1 billion.

On the reciprocal claims of intentional breach of contract, the court found Huntsman did not breach the agreement but that Hexion had, in several particulars: Hexion was obligated to use its best effort to obtain financing; there was no clause allowing Hexion out of that obligation because of the lack of solvency of Huntsman or the combined Hexion/ Huntsman entity; Hexion was obligated to inform Huntsman of substantial activity concerning the status of the financing and to give notice within two business days if Hexion believed it would be unable to obtain full funding for the merger.

On Hexion's argument that it was only protecting itself and did not knowingly breach the agreement in bad faith, the judge used the example of a man taking someone else's umbrella from the stand. "It is no defense to say I did not realize that stealing was illegal, nor is it a defense that his purpose was not to break the law but simply to avoid getting wet.

Contrary to Hexion's contention, mistake of law virtually never excuses a violation of law."

Lamb also ruled Hexion had dragged its feet getting antitrust clearance (which would have been easily obtainable since the company was planning to spin off those areas where there might have been a problem). Lamb's order justified our moving the closing date to October 2 and extended it five business days.

On the matter of damages, Lamb's ruling was not quite as clear a victory for us. The breakup fee was required and Hexion was ordered to proceed with obtaining financing and FTC approval by October 2. But Lamb refused to act as a "referee" as to whose appraisals were the most accurate on the grounds his court was not the proper forum. He stopped short of ordering Hexion to close the deal, but he warned that if Hexion backed out, they could be held liable for damages beyond the contract's $350 million penalty. Lamb further ruled that Hexion was under an obligation to pressure the lending institutions to perform on funding obligations but that it was not under an obligation to close if that did not occur. Again Lamb made it clear that Apollo could be held liable for damages—uncapped and potentially sufficient to sink Hexion—if it did not embrace the merger and proceed.

Lamb didn't go easy on the banks, either: "If the lending banks refuse to fund," he wrote, "they will, of course, be opening themselves to the potential for litigation, including a claim for damages for breach of contract," which is exactly where Credit Suisse and Deutsche Bank would soon find themselves with our Texas lawsuit. The judge forbade Hexion from doing anything to materially delay, prevent, or harm financing arrangements, and to take all necessary steps to gain antitrust approval by October 2.

The lead of the *New York Post* story on Apollo's stinging defeat summed it up beautifully: "Leon Black's experiment with the chemical industry blew up in his face."

Hexion/Apollo and Huntsman agreed to a closing date of October 28 at which time Huntsman was to produce a certificate of solvency acceptable to the buyers. Our October 23 report from American Appraisal Associates, Inc. confirmed the combined Hexion/Huntsman operation would be solvent, backing up a similar report by Kimo Esplin, our CFO, which also was presented.

Our shareholders, too, took steps to assure the financing. After the Delaware decision, a group of Huntsman investors decided to help turn up the heat on the two European banking giants. They promised to preserve $416 million in Hexion after the merger. Apollo, desperate to show it was trying to go through with the sale so it could avoid another devastating lawsuit, added to this figure $540 million. Nearly a billion dollars, we all thought, surely would assuage the banks' concerns about the combined companies' solvency.

But no. On the day before the October 28 closing, Credit Suisse and Deutsche Bank said, via letters, they would accept neither of the verification documents nor had they any intention to fund the merger. Even after Apollo answered by certifying that both documents were in traditional and acceptable form for Apollo portfolio transactions, the banks were not persuaded. They were, we assume, looking at the specter of a deepening banking crisis and the world economic turmoil that would cast a dark shadow over their hallowed headquarters. To cover itself, Apollo brought suit against the banks in New York in which they sought, among other things, a restraining order against the banks from terminating their letters of commitment.

Huntsman's board sent a letter to Apollo on December 13 terminating the merger agreement and served notice we would be seeking a settlement. The meeting took place in New York City a few days later in the law offices of Vinson & Elkins, one of the firms on our legal team. Key participants from our side included our board's litigation committee chairman Wayne Reaud, CEO Peter Huntsman, Kimo Esplin, Sam Scruggs, and me. Josh Harris and Leon Black were there for Apollo. Although the meeting was cordial, the sides started out far apart: Apollo was looking at $200 million to $300 million; we saw it closer to $2 billion. We settled on a billion dollars in cash and preferred notes.

Had we gone to court, back in Delaware, we could have received a judgment in excess of that. But the company was in the midst of a free fall in profitability, with business down some 30 percent. If we could get a reasonable settlement now, we could weather the Great Recession and see the stock return to 20 dollars a share. Extracting the last possible dollar in a court battle that could last up to 2 years just wasn't worth it. Settling where we did was the best deal for stockholders. Besides, Black acknowledged that our court victory gave Apollo the largest "black eye" it ever had received and noted that damage to its franchise's reputation was more costly than the financial settlement.

In return for cooperating with us in the Texas suit against the banks, we agreed to drop Apollo as a defendant in that suit. This move permitted Apollo to drop its New York litigation against the two banks because we would be addressing those claims in the Texas tort action.

We used the billion dollars to reduce debt and as working capital to provide a cushion for future flexibility. Apollo's partners, clearly worried about another issue, exacted a promise in the settlement that I would not publicly say, write, or cause to be published anything negative about Harris, Black, or Apollo. (This book reports only those facts that are in the public record. I further honored my promise by retaining two of Apollo's three founding partners on various Wharton boards on which, until recently, I served as chairman, and by turning down numerous invitations for speaking engagements or media interviews in which private equity's shortcomings or Apollo's tactics might have been discussed.)

Now it was time for us to take on the banks—in Texas.

The day after our victory in Delaware, we filed an amended lawsuit for $4.5 billion in Montgomery County, Texas against Credit Suisse and Deutsche Bank, alleging the banks conspired with Apollo to interfere with the original merger deal with Basell and nearly ruining us in the process. Our list of claims ran the gamut: civil conspiracy, tortious interference, unjust enrichment, and common law fraud. In Texas, state courts retain jurisdiction in matters of fraud. Otherwise, the case would have returned to Delaware, something the defendants desperately desired. Texas state courts are an entirely different animal than Delaware's Chancery Court. As a harbinger of things to come, District Judge Fred Edwards ruled in our favor on a series of pretrial injunctions and maintained jurisdiction of the trial, a decision the Texas Court of Appeals quickly upheld.

The jury trial was set for June 8, 2009, in Conroe, county seat of Montgomery County, which is home to Huntsman's operational headquarters and a performance products plant. Only a few miles north of

Houston, Conroe is less cosmopolitan than its urban neighbor to the south—as the defendants soon discovered. When the judge entered the courtroom, everyone rose and recited the Pledge of Allegiance facing the US flag on the front wall. After the pledge, the defense lawyers started to take their seats. The veterans of the Texas judicial system, however, remained standing and pivoted to face the rear wall of the courtroom, on which hung the Texas state flag, and recited the state's pledge of allegiance. Some of us northerners, who likewise did not know the words to the Texas pledge, merely stood respectfully facing the state flag until the pledge was completed. The New York lawyers never quite got the hang of that routine. Judge Edwards, the jury, and everyone in the courtroom watched wearily each morning as the throng of New York lawyers mumbled incoherently through the Texas Pledge of Allegiance, or remained seated in what the Texas court perceived as a sign of disrespect. I would say they lost the gunfight before a shot was fired.

Texas lawyer Wayne Reaud, a big man with an even larger reputation, was lead counsel for us. He was and is chairman of our board's litigation committee. Wayne's approach was made clear on the first day of trial: "Jon, we are going to f- these guys and we are going to make a lot of money doing it." Reaud and I, along with Peter, who throughout this legal unpleasantness continued to run the business from our Houston headquarters, never missed a day of trial action. We developed strategy as each day progressed. Reaud and I were inseparable during this time. A formidable legal whiz, Reaud championed our side and was my head coach and cheerleader. The two of us were like alley cats when we got into these lawsuits. It could be said that Wayne's trial experience and my fighting spirit made us the perfect team.

I had been dealing with lawyers for nearly a half century, most of them corporate attorneys who are hardwired from law school to settle. Few corporate lawyers have the stomach to go the whole nine yards. After all, a lawyer working for the plaintiff today may well be working for the defendant tomorrow on a separate legal matter. Opposing counsel play golf together and meet socially. Litigation settlements are routine. Win or lose, billing hours and rates remain the same. Corporate attorneys seem to lack Wayne Reaud's passion. Most find loathsome a take-no-prisoners approach to winning. They embrace as facts of life two basic tenets: a company requires representation, and lawyers must be compensated handsomely. When Reaud takes you to court, be assured you are going all the way and that there will be blood. He has been an incredible friend over the years, trusted and loyal. He has protected the company and our family. To my mind, he is the finest lawyer in America today.

When the logistics for our two trials are tallied, some two hundred lawyers, staff, and researchers were on the clock. Our legal costs for the two suits came to $103 million. But this regiment of lawyers could not have achieved the settlement we reached, especially in Texas, without the strategy and tenacity of Reaud (who charged us nothing for the hundreds of hours he spent on these cases).

Wayne and I developed a strong union with a common purpose, establishing an iron wall between us and the legal team and discounting three-fourths of what they recommended. We knew we had a good poker hand and we wanted to call the opposition's bluff. We would not accept token offers, only a settlement commensurate with the damage caused.

The trial was scheduled to take five weeks. The banks initially attempted to downplay the devastating memos and e-mails that surfaced in the Delaware trial, portraying such communications as typical loose talk between lenders and clients. It was a weak defense and the banks knew it. They had been signaling a desire for an out-of-court settlement since jury selection. We ended up having four negotiation meetings with them. In the initial meeting, held at the historic Houstonian Hotel in Houston, the banks' lawyers offered $50 million. I am not kidding. We were seeking $4.3 billion in compensation for the difference between the value of the stock at the time of trial and the twenty-eight dollars a share offered by Apollo/Hexion. Our stock had fallen to as low as two dollars at one point in 2008. We sure as blazes weren't going to settle for six cents on the dollar.

Peter and I told the bankers we didn't think they understood the problem. They had harmed our shareholders severely. They had conspired with Apollo and there was empirical evidence to show it. We were referring to the e-mails entered in evidence at the Delaware trial and they knew that. Their arrogance, at first, was astounding and may have blinded them to the realities. But as they became more familiar with the Texas court environment—and its pro-plaintiff reputation—their swagger became somewhat restrained. With nothing in hand to refute the evidence submitted in Delaware and in the Texas pretrial proceedings, even the vainest Wall Street lawyer would take a serious second look at his hole card. They had to consider the perspective of a jury made up of townsfolk.

Here was a case of Wall Street bankers—who were deemed bad enough in ordinary times but in 2009 were held in utter contempt by people whose retirement accounts had been ravaged by Wall Street's greedy shenanigans—versus one of the area's largest employers that had been a good and charitable corporate citizen.

The second exploratory settlement meeting took place in New York City. The banks upped their offer to $100 million. Some of our attorneys were in favor, but Peter, Wayne, and I would not hear of it. We loved the sport of this. One thing helping us take the starch out of defense counsel collars was the impeccable manner in which Huntsman's management gave testimony—knowledgeable, smooth, and effective. In the first two weeks of the trial, we out-lawyered, out-strategized, out-evidenced, and out-testified the defense. In both the Delaware and Texas trials, Peter in particular was phenomenal—poised, prepared, and persuasive. His team followed the leader and rendered exceptional performances. The defendants could read the tea leaves: they were going to lose, big time.

All this prompted a third settlement meeting, this time in Reaud's Beaumont law office. It was quite a sight. Two large SUVs, crammed with lawyers for Credit Suisse and Deutsche Bank, pulled up in front of his law office. They piled out and marched in. During the talks, they would run back to their SUVs to make cell phone calls to their bosses, who in turn had to call their bosses at the banks. We stood firm. Pretty soon, the frustrated defense team aborted that round of talks. Our lawyers also were terrific, a rare comment coming from me. Wayne and I went into his office and played a little blackjack. Our unexplained absences made the bank attorneys decidedly nervous. This turned out to be great strategy. The other side was sure we were brainstorming, examining numbers, trying to triangulate some settlement figure when all we were doing was killing time with cards and enjoying the idea that it rattled the New York boys.

To no one's surprise, the banks sought a fourth meeting, this one on June 22. The venue was the conference room of Atlantic Aviation, the fixed base operator serving executive jets at Bush Intercontinental Airport in Houston. We got there first, and before long a parade of SUVs and limos swarmed through the yawning hanger doors and the talks resumed. Once again, lawyers for the banks would run back to their vehicles to privately discuss demands. Back and forth, to and fro. It was entertaining to watch. We had them on the run and, at last, the banks got realistic. We ended up settling for more than $1.7 billion—$632 million in cash and $1.1 billion in loans at highly favorable rates that would save us $50 million annually in interest over what we had been paying.

The banks and Apollo had thought they could get away with treating us like mangy dogs but, in the end, they learned a costly lesson to the contrary. From the combined court actions, we received more than $2.7 billion in cash and favorable financing in the largest out-of-court settlement in the history of American business. Apollo's nearly $1 billion settlement was, by itself, the third largest. The combined proceeds brought some $2 billion in added value to the company.

I stated in interviews afterward that the settlement symbolized a reward for the integrity with which our company conducts its business. Privately, I was thinking about the Latin adage that Virginia adopted as its state motto: *sic semper tyrannis* ("thus always to tyrants").

While the victories were exhilarating, I was exhausted. Heavy daily doses of prednisone, blood pressure medications, and heart medications, along with powerful pain pills, were taking a significant toll on my shattered body. My faith kept me going. During all of this, I was spending twenty hours per week fulfilling a calling by my LDS Church to serve as an area seventy, a volunteer assignment involving preaching and teaching before a number of large congregations most weekends each month. It was terrific therapy for me because, as always, I remained committed to my faith and it gave me strength.

As it turned out, and as surprising as it may sound, Apollo's besting Basell's bid, only to renege, turned out to be the best of all possible scenarios for Huntsman. Had the Huntsman board proceeded with the Basell offer at $25.25 a share in 2007 and merged into a Basell-Huntsman chemical giant, the coincidental economic downturn would have bankrupted the US operations, as indeed turned out to be the case for LyondellBasell, which ended up in Chapter 11. The Huntsman name would have been associated with a corporate bankruptcy, something I said I would never allow.

Likewise, had Apollo and the banks honored their agreements and purchased Huntsman as first agreed, the $15 billion in bank loans would have blown Hexion-Huntsman apart, in all likelihood taking Apollo down with it. Nobody could have survived 100 percent leverage in the environment of the Great Recession and Apollo was not in a position to put up more equity. Alone, Huntsman would have made it, but together with either Basell or Hexion, given the amount of debt a merger would require, there would have been no hope. Sure, the family would have had our money, but the Huntsman business name would have been forever besmirched.

Without question, Apollo had figured it correctly. It could not have survived paying us what ultimately would have been twenty-nine dollars per share, factoring in the delay penalties. Unfortunately for Apollo, that was beside the legal points being argued in Delaware. The issue was the solvency of Huntsman. We were solvent and Apollo's allegations to the contrary did Huntsman substantial harm. Moreover, Apollo had given its word it would buy Huntsman no matter what contingencies emerged. Its word, and our ironclad contracts, apparently meant little to the company.

On reflection, what we ended up with after our painful ordeal was the best possible outcome considering what was going on with the economy. The original sale would have netted us $5.9 billion after debt repayment. The settlement moneys from Apollo and the 2 banks brought us more than a third the value of that sale price, and we still owned 100 percent of the company.

I have put behind me the ill will I had harbored toward the defendants and replaced it with friendship. My motto is: get mad, not even. Long-term grudges waste so much time and are so unproductive. Just move on. We have since solidified relationships with Apollo and the two banks. To be totally up front, I still have affection for both Leon and Josh. (I wouldn't mind another attempt at some type of joint venture with them because I know we have a genuine respect for one another.)

No need to cry for Leon Black and Apollo, in any case. In 2013, the media reported that the equity firm took in $2.5 billion. As chief executive, Black pocketed more than a half billion dollars of those earnings, according to *The New York Times*, up from the quarter billion he made the year before. Tim O'Hara from Credit Suisse turned out to be one of Wall Street's superheroes for whom I have enormous respect, and CSFB's Eric Varvel is unquestionably the most admired CEO on Wall Street. He is a man of ethics and high integrity.

At one time, I thought selling the company was the thing I wanted most. Through the subsequent course of these events, I was reminded of another adage: be careful what you wish for, you just might get it (and it can produce considerable grief). That said, I continue to support selling at the right price and the right time.

19. Legacy Projects

URING THE YEARS 2011 THROUGH 2013, HUNTSMAN CORPORATION had fifty-seven sites globally with more than eleven thousand workers and some twenty thousand contract employees. Notwithstanding our growth and success in the petrochemical and related businesses, my mind often shifted back to entrepreneurial thoughts and possible new investments. This time the focus was on something previously not on my radar screen: developing land.

Karen and I owned a decent-sized ranch in Idaho's Teton Valley, on the Teton River near the high-plains community of Driggs (with an elevation 4 times its population of 1,500 souls), guarded by the breathtaking peaks of the Grand Tetons. We call it Markie's Ranch after our youngest child.

The Teton Valley is not far from my humble birthplace, and we acquired the ranch there as the result of our search for a getaway that Karen and I both liked. For some time, we had owned a second home in Deer Valley, Utah. I loved it and Karen was fine with it—at least in the beginning—but she gradually began to spend more time in our spacious home in Salt Lake City, which was closer to the families but still surrounded by spectacular mountain terrain. She also loved the exquisite beauty of Lake Powell in southern Utah and decided she would like a houseboat there. I bought her one, after presenting a scale model of it to her as a birthday present. We eventually ended up with two houseboats, but I never got back my navy sea legs and seldom ventured onto either one.

Thus, the Teton Valley ranch was a place we both could appreciate and it still brought me back to my roots. We love it there—it's a place to unwind (to the extent I am able to do that) and spend pleasant interludes fly-fishing the adjacent Teton River or the South Fork of the Snake River. We even purchased white buffalo to roam the property.

Fly-fishing has been a passion of mine from my first experience with it as a boy in Pocatello. I suppose it appeals to my zeal for competition—me versus the trout. Rainbow and native cutthroat trout are tough catches.

It is almost impossible to outsmart the big ones. I compete against myself for a couple of hours in the late afternoons whenever I'm in Driggs. Those fish I do manage to nab are released to compete with other like-minded fishermen another day.

LDS Church leader Thomas S. Monson and I have fished the Teton and Snake Rivers for many years together. Among the small lakes we own near our ranch is one we affectionately named Monson Lake. A small dock at the water's edge supports a couple of chairs in which President Monson and I sit, casting our flies and talking about whatever comes up. When we opt to fish from a boat, we are usually accompanied by John Pehrson, our trusty fishing guide, who knows every inch of the Teton Valley's rivers and always provides access to successful fishing.

President Monson and I have a particularly close relationship and have always found it easy to confide in one another. Our families love Utah Jazz basketball and for years we have shared our Huntsman suite with him and his guests for the Jazz games. With mutual respect for each other's approaches to life, we compare notes on the world from our respective seats in the industrial and ecclesiastical front rows. Our relationship is candid and dates back 34 years ago when we first worked together on the president's task force for religious leaders in Washington, DC during my days as mission president there.

In July 2010, about a year after he ascended to the role of president of the LDS Church, President Monson and I spent the day in a float boat, catching native cutthroat and rainbow trout, mostly in the two- to three-pound range. Then he caught a whopper of a rainbow that about pulled him into the water. The fish was a fighter and Monson stood to reel in his trophy. Pehrson and I were hollering advice and wildly gesturing as he fought to keep his footing. The powerful trout broke his pole, but this was a conquest that could not be abandoned. President Monson grabbed the line and started dragging it in by hand. He was slipping toward the water, so I grabbed hold of his belt loop with one hand and attempted to grab the line with the other. Pehrson hollered instructions. Anyone watching us might have thought we were looney.

President Monson finally maneuvered his prize catch near enough that we could net what must have been a ten-pounder. "No one is going to believe this," beamed Monson, who was eighty-three at the time. Our practice is catch and release, but not that day. This beauty was caught, baked, and consumed with great enjoyment.

Perhaps because I felt guilty to be fishing so often while others were at their labors, it seemed important to look for a plausible excuse for my extended stays and to legitimize them as productive. While floating the river, I imagined the development potential of this tranquil valley. Some visionary person one day might create a natural wonderland in these miles and miles of pristine territory. That person would have to respectfully integrate that which would be man-made into the idyllic surroundings God and nature had wrought. The more I thought about it the more it seemed that person ought to be me.

The adventure into land development began with a casual conversation with our sons David and Paul about buying more land in the Teton Valley. We mulled it over and within a week tendered an offer to purchase a thousand additional acres. Sadly, the land had been sold on the very day we made the offer. Undaunted, we continued to look around. The Lowell Curtis Ranch near Driggs became our next target. Things fell into place this time and within 2 weeks we were proud owners of 500 acres of the Curtis spread. We soon purchased 3,000 contiguous acres plus a separate 1,500-acre parcel, originally naming the combined acreage Blackfoot Farms after my birthplace roughly 80 miles to the southwest.

Our five-thousand-acre purchase qualified as big news in Driggs. The community buzzed with speculation about our intentions. At the time we had none to report. I sent David to assure then-mayor Lou Christensen that, notwithstanding the absence of concrete plans, whatever we ended up doing would be first class. The Huntsmans are good citizens of communities in which we operate, David told him. We continued to buy land from ranchers who wanted out—thousands of additional acres that provided ideal growing conditions for potatoes, barley, and alfalfa. We let the farmers continue to keep the profits even after they were paid in full for the land. We paid $3,000 to $25,000 an acre in 2005 and 2006, a good price, considering those values tripled by 2007 but not so thrilling a year later when the real estate market tanked.

About this time, the Teton County Commission decided it needed a new courthouse to replace the historic structure that had served as the seat of county government for nearly a century. The commissioners also coveted some of Huntsman's choicest acres as a perfect location for the courthouse. They proposed a swap: some of our Curtis Ranch property nearest town for a few parcels the county owned farther out. We would be doing a great service to the community, intoned the commissioners, and "Oh, by the way, could your family help out with the construction costs?"

We soon came to realize the parcels they were trading were smaller, less desirably situated, and not as valuable as our part of the property exchange. In fact, they were almost worthless, but to make good on our promise we decided to be accommodating. Our land allowed the courthouse's construction to be exactly where the commission wanted it and we threw in about $5 million for a new building. We were therefore surprised when during the courthouse ribbon cutting the native-son commissioners smiled proudly at the cameras, cut the ribbon, and took full credit for the structure.

So be it. Our support was never about recognition. We were satisfied we had done it for the right reasons, even in tough economic times. The folks got a courthouse and we were true to our word. Huntsman money also went into the creation of a new football and track complex at Teton High School in Driggs. Funds in Mark's name, to the tune of about half a million dollars, underwrote new sod for the field, bleachers, game lights, and a track. The school folks were more appreciative than their commissioners. Mark was thrilled when he received the game ball and his own special jersey at the first game played at Mark Huntsman Field.

Now that there was a public building on the best piece of our central land in the City of Driggs, we went back to figuring out what to do with the rest of our acreage. In 2007, we met Canadian George Gillett, who owned the Grand Targhee Resort a few miles east of Driggs (in addition to another resort in Vail, Colorado). He asked what we thought about building a world-class golf course. It would be a summer draw for the Teton Valley, he figured, dovetailing nicely with Grand Targhee's winter recreational activities. It would keep the community active year round. My position has always been that Jon Huntsman doesn't play golf. He makes deals. Still, we considered the idea. After all, the Huntsman family was back in Idaho where I was a native son and it was important to the entire family to contribute to the economic development of the area we love in a responsible and meaningful manner.

Among our goals for the future was the ability to enjoy the rewards of our hard work over the past half century. Yet, while raw land is a solid investment, development of property can be risky. Most developers I knew had gone broke. On the other hand, the only other development in the Teton Valley similar to the one we envisioned had sold out by 2005. If we are to do this, I counseled the family, we should do it prudently. Start small, primarily for the experience, and, if it works, then expand. That seemed to be the right approach financially, since we really didn't know what we were doing when it came to this sort of venture. Proceeding cautiously was important, especially because any return on investment was earmarked for the Huntsman Cancer Foundation. It was imperative we achieve the best possible outcome.

Building a golf course didn't seem a viable project on its own, which suggested that our adjacent property would have to be developed into residential parcels. A substantial number of homes would have to be sold along the fairways and on other sections of the property if the Huntsman Cancer Institute was to profit from the investment. It would take a decade or more to put it together. Contrary to this prudent advice, I followed that inner instinct which has driven me over the years: "Think no small thought; do no small deed. Life is too short to proceed in measured increments."

Much discussion went into the resort's name. We made a lengthy list of possibilities. One was Lucky Pierre, named after a rare albino buffalo in our ranch's herd. (The beast was named for Pierre Tivanitagon, a not-so-lucky French fur trapper killed in 1828 by Blackfoot Indians.) In the end, we decided on Huntsman Springs because our family name was relatively well known in the West and because much of the property is comprised of wetlands and natural springs, so much so that we had about five hundred acres officially certified as a wildlife refuge. The development also has eight small lakes, all brimming with large native rainbow and cutthroat trout. We stocked the land with more than ten thousand pheasants, although hunting would not be allowed.

The financial wherewithal to embark on this venture was to come from my share of the proceeds of the Hexion merger. At that point, Apollo had agreed to buy Huntsman Corporation for $10.6 billion including assumption of debt. My holdings in the company would be liquidated, providing me with ample capital to invest. I was confident enough the merger would close on schedule that the golf course project became the first order of business in the Idaho venture. I placed David in charge of day-to-day oversight and Paul oversaw the finances.

The Teton Valley is an environmentally pristine area. Unfortunately, past developers had cut corners and made little effort to create harmony between nature and what and where they were building. David considers himself more aligned with environmentalists than with developers, and we were not about to let that kind of thing happen on our watch. Our vision was to create a family sanctuary in a spectacular setting at the gateway to year-round recreational opportunities. Its success would depend on preserving a rural, open feel. David and Paul made a point of maintaining relationships with community and environmental groups. They listened to antidevelopment advocates and promised to work with them, incorporating many of their suggestions in the planning. In fact, most of their primary concerns already had been addressed. About 70 percent of our holdings, including the wildlife refuge, had been set aside as open space.

The initial hurdle was to identify a first-rate architect who could design a course that would attract players and be a compatible centerpiece for the residential sector of the project. We contacted the ever-popular Jack Nicklaus team, which must have fifty courses under construction at any given time. One of its architects surveyed the layout and told us the company was working on an installation in Colorado whose design, with minor tweaks, would work perfectly on our site. Not wanting a cookie-cutter course, we passed. There are plenty of paint-by-numbers outfits who specialize in pre-designed layouts that can be shoehorned into a site regardless of terrain. We were interested in the exact opposite: a course designed around the natural landscape to the fullest possible extent.

Enter David McLay Kidd. We heard that Kidd had designed and built

Bandon Dunes on the southern Oregon coast. He and his DMK group had designed or remodeled courses in Scotland, South Africa, Morocco, and Fiji, each known for a unique personality dictated by the peculiarities of its habitat. The harsh, unsheltered landscape of his native Scotland influenced Kidd to design courses that would blend oceans and dunes, rocks and grasses, wetlands and pines into a golfer's dream. That's what we wanted for Huntsman Springs—originality, natural convergence, and a layout geared to challenging superior players yet affording the average golfer a pleasant experience.

We invited Kidd to Driggs in December 2006 for a candid evaluation. Unfortunately, by the time he arrived, the temperature had plunged to twenty below, and candor we got. Squinting against the cold, Kidd scanned the flat, snow-blanketed cow pasture, turned to David and Paul and said, "Good luck." The land, he said, wasn't suitable for a golf course. There was nothing to work with. He departed, leaving us wondering what to do next.

I have long held that *no* is just the beginning of the conversation, so we coaxed Kidd back for a second opinion in February. It still was the dead of winter, still bitter cold; he still saw a desolate, snow-laden landscape. Kidd grimly traversed our field of dreams. Then he stooped and cleared the snow from one spot and piled it onto another, forming a mound. "You know," he said slowly, "if we could play with the elevation, say thirty to forty feet, and make the most of the wetland features, we might just get a terrific golf course." Never before had he moved as many tons of soil as he would have to at Huntsman Springs. The topography of his other courses had always been natural. The Huntsman landscape would have to be gently and artfully sculpted.

As he discussed it, Kidd became increasingly animated. One would need a lot of water for wetlands and hazards. Water we have, we countered. We promised to let him paint with his own brush, unconditionally. For Kidd, the blank canvas of a featureless landscape was the selling point. He accepted the challenge.

By the time the dirt and dust settled, four million cubic yards of soil had been moved and shaped into graceful mounds resembling the rolling dunes of Scotland. Huntsman Springs turned out to be Kidd's most ambitious project in terms of sculpturing. It also was his most expensive. The

Scottish-links style course cost considerably more than a million dollars a hole. We had no idea what a hefty cash infusion this project would require, especially during a recession, but we worked through it. The surrounding infrastructure, roads, homes, and the like were costly, as well. Before the year ended, the tab for this investment topped $100 million.

The Huntsman Springs course opened for limited play in the summer of 2009. It takes two years for a golf course to mature, thus the course didn't officially open to the public until the summer of 2010. We hired greens keeper Guy Johnson, who had held a similar position at Steve Wynn's Shadow Creek Golf Course in Las Vegas. Johnson was recommended by Kidd's father, who was himself an agrarian expert, who termed Johnson the best in the business.

We soon learned that our location involved unique and unexpected quirks of golf course management. The land teems with coyotes, foxes, sandhill cranes, whitetail and mule deer, moose, bear, trumpeter swans (the largest swan in North America and an endangered species), geese, and skunks. Moose like to walk on our greens and lick the flagsticks made salty by golfers' hands. The foxes love to burrow into our fairway bunkers. We dug up one burrow and found more than one hundred golf balls. That fox no doubt wondered why these eggs were impossible to crack.

The national media discovered Teton Valley during the first decade of the twenty-first century and the accolades rolled in. *National Geographic* ranked it one of the ten best recreation areas in the nation. *The Wall Street Journal* termed it one of the best locations for vacation homebuyers. *Men's Journal* proclaimed Driggs the number one small town in America. The golf course and subsequent development caught the eyes of the golfing media, as well. *Executive Golfer* magazine zeroed in on Huntsman Springs, specifically, with an article in 2008. Our philanthropic goals for the resort appealed to its publisher. He gave the course a great review and titled his story, "Golf Has its Place in the Gospel of Giving." *Links* magazine placed it among the top one hundred courses in 2012. *Golfweek* dubbed it the best residential golf course and best modern golf course in 2012 and the best new private course two years earlier. It was *Golf Magazine*'s best new private course in 2010. And the *Robb Report* presented its Best of the Best Award to Huntsman Springs in 2011. In 2014, *Golf Weekly* ranked Huntsman Springs the number three residential golf course in America (out of almost 11,000 courses). Many other national and international awards were presented to David and his team for this project. So far, the golf course is our best marketing tool. We had double the membership and players in 2012 than the year before, which had double the participation of the opening year. It is a challenging course. A golfer must figure it out. To help on that score, we provide experienced caddies. But let me warn you, you will never hit the same shot twice.

Overall, selling the 650 Huntsman Springs parcels has not been easy. Huntsman Springs began in a tough economic environment. We launched the project a year before the real estate bubble burst and splattered trouble all over the nation. Most of the other projects in the western region were shut down or suspended. Many had been operating for years but were forced to declare bankruptcy. Unlike traditional developers, we didn't wait for "better times." We pushed ahead, employing hundreds of area people at a time when the national unemployment rate rose. Yet our project goals have either been met or soon will be in spite of the fact that the anticipated funds from the Hexion merger never materialized. Huntsman Springs' revenues continue to grow. David and Paul accomplished the impossible and did it in spectacular fashion. They have been pivotal to the successes we have seen to date.

Paul jumped into the learning process with both feet and visibly grew as a businessman. He later went on to a senior vice presidency in Huntsman Gay Global Capital. Paul performed admirably in all respects and has made me proud. He is naturally gifted in financial analysis, particularly where the industrial sector is involved. He was a quick study in our private equity business. He is now president and CEO of our Huntsman family investments, including our charitable foundations and trusts. Here again, the lion's share of the profits go to the Huntsman Cancer Institute.

I am pleased that David remained with Huntsman Springs. He demonstrated increasing leadership and, whether or not he knows it, he impressed his father with his professional maturation. As a manager, leader, visionary, and human being, he developed gracefully, in the same manner as the land. He oversees not only the now vast Idaho property, but also our family charitable foundations and other significant investments.

Karen's deft hand with interior design assured that the residential floor plans and specifications were practical and comfortable for family living. This venture has been a family project. I am convinced history will show we made the right move. It has been a tremendous struggle but the project inches ever closer to a break-even point. The project is paid in full—and now homes and businesses are beginning to blossom.

It is my belief that sales drives ultimate success in any undertaking, whether one talks about petrochemical products, soliciting donations to fund the Cancer Institute, or lifting Huntsman Springs to self-sustaining status. That train of thought brought us to the decision that controlling the sales operation is what is required in a tough market. Deciding it was advisable to handle sales in-house, we bought Sotheby's International Realty offices in Jackson Hole, on the other side of the mountain bordering Idaho and Wyoming, and Sun Valley. Sotheby's International controls 60 percent of the market share in the area and the relationship has sparked an even greater interest in Huntsman Springs.

Huntsman Springs is a twenty-year, multigenerational project. The intent has always been to create a legacy project for the family. Someday, it will surpass Sun Valley and perhaps Jackson Hole as a resort destination. There are not many places of such beauty and tranquility.

There is another chapter in my life I have not yet discussed: the occasionally controversial, often effective, and always inspirational interfaith, multiethnic legacy organization called Alliance for Unity in Utah which I formed in 2001. Having bounced around in different churches as a child, I have always felt comfortable accepting the religions and philosophies of those who believe differently than I do. I have tried to act as a bridge between religious, cultural, and community chasms. That philosophy was formalized with the Alliance.

Because Utah is so heavily LDS—70 percent of the state's population is at least nominally Mormon and between 80 percent and 90 percent of its legislative seats, public offices, judicial appointments, and much of its judiciary are held by LDS men and women, there is bound to be friction with those not associated with the predominant religion. It is more a cultural than a religious problem, but since Utah's dominant culture is faith-based, the minority cultures often grumble about not having a say in how their lives are regulated. Liquor and other so-called blue laws and various church-state issues long had been traditional flash points for much of the debate.

This Great Divide, as it has been termed, was coming to a head in the run-up to the 2002 Olympic Games. Overall, 2 out of 3 Utahns polled, and nearly 90 percent of the non-Mormon respondents, said they experienced the tension. In 2001, I asked Salt Lake City Mayor Rocky Anderson, who became a voice for non-Mormons (especially inside the city limits of Salt Lake City where the LDS are in the minority), to join me in forming the Alliance. We convened a group of influential religious, business, and civic leaders whose stated mission would be to promote acceptance of diversity among other faiths, cultures, and values, and to provide an environment in which all residents of the state would benefit.

Religion wasn't the only rub. Two Utah banks were feuding bitterly at the time over a merger gone sour. I included their two presidents. *The Salt Lake Tribune* and the LDS Church-owned *Deseret News* were at war over the latter's intervention in the *Tribune*'s ownership battle, so I included the editors of those newspapers as well. I also invited the bishops of the Catholic and Episcopal Churches, the pastor of Utah's oldest and largest African-American church, a member of the LDS Church's Quorum of Twelve, and, later, a representative of the Jewish faith. Representatives from the Latino and Asian-American communities, the president of the University of Utah, and an advocate for the homeless and low-income households accepted invitations to become members. Two key community-at-large figures rounded out the group.

Within a year, the Alliance was in the thick of a boisterous and divisive struggle over a downtown block of Salt Lake City's Main Street that Mayor Anderson's predecessor had sold in 1999 to the LDS Church. The street ran between two important features of its campus, separating its headquarters building from Temple Square. The church sought to convert the roadway into a park-like setting that would link the two areas. On the face of it, the sale seemed straightforward and innocuous, but the devil—no pun intended—is forever in the details. Because it involved closure of a main thoroughfare, the city retained a public easement. The public right-of-way and the collateral freedoms it entailed collided with rules the church imposed governing speech and behavior on what it considered sacred grounds, rules identical to those in place for the gated temple area where they traditionally had been accepted. This created a dilemma. Non-Mormons saw free-speech issues; Mormons saw the right to establish the ground rules in their own backyard.

Because a public easement was at issue, the ACLU and others argued that the rights of free speech and behavior that pertained to other city sidewalks and parks in downtown Salt Lake City extended to the LDS plaza. Following a divisive lawsuit, the Tenth Circuit Court of Appeals upheld the First Amendment rights. That decision prompted fundamentalist religious protestors, who held a theological grudge against the LDS Church, to take the court ruling as a statement that civilized behavior was no longer required. They screamed, taunted, and belittled Mormons who were there for weddings, church activities, and conferences. The situation was nothing short of dreadful. Protestors made a mockery of sacred rituals and shouted at young brides and grooms, posing for their wedding pictures in the plaza, that they were condemned to hell.

The situation was a test of constitutional principles. While acknowledging the legal right to do so, religious leaders of all stripes, as well as the news media and civic leaders, condemned this behavior as boorish, bigoted, and counterproductive. Mormons and non-Mormons alike were appalled at the conduct of a few fanatics.

Yet many who were not of the LDS faith were still upset with the city's original sale of the block of Main Street in 1999, complaining the city council, voting along religious lines, had caved to the wishes of the dominant faith. To a number of people, the idea of simply turning over—or selling—the public easement to the LDS Church, as was then under consideration as a means of allowing it to control behavior in the plaza between its temple and church office buildings, was unacceptable in principle. To do so would have divided the community even further and the ACLU said giving up the easement would not be legal. For its part, church leadership had already paid $8.3 million for the block and was in no mood to pay any more for what it believed it already possessed. The resulting stalemate was a religious, cultural, constitutional, legal, and political nightmare.

In late 2002, the Alliance for Unity hammered out a land-for-peace compromise: the city would extinguish the easement in return for a parcel of LDS-owned land in a struggling, low-income Salt Lake City neighborhood where the Alliance would build a "Unity Center." The complex would offer educational programs, legal aid, health clinics, college extension classes, and a small business support center. The Alliance raised $5 million for the construction of the Unity Center.

The ACLU initially bought in, reasoning that as long as the easement was exchanged for something of value the problem was solved. That stand didn't hold for long. When the compromise was announced, many felt relieved the city would be moving on to more pressing problems. Others believed the Alliance (whose membership is predominately non-Mormon) had caved to LDS Church wishes. What wasn't known is how much inside diplomacy took place to get church leaders to have anything to do with this potential solution.

LDS Church President Gordon B. Hinckley, who had purchased the land in 1999 and felt the church could do what it wanted with it, was not an easy sell, and understandably so. Just hours before the compromise proposal was to be announced at a press conference at City Hall, the Quorum of Twelve refused to sign off. It had called a rare meeting early that Monday morning to discuss the proposed agreement, but things were moving too fast. Church leaders did not have a good grasp of the compromise. The deal was falling through.

I called President Hinckley's office at 10:30 a.m. and got an appointment to see him immediately. I told him the issue was dividing the community and time was of the essence. I sold it as a positive resolution for the church and suggested he needed to acknowledge a courageous move by people on each side to bring peace. The ACLU had tacitly approved, I added, as did the major plaintiff in the initial First Amendment lawsuit. We needed to go forward.

Hinckley reluctantly allowed Presiding Bishop David Burton, head of the church's property arm, and Elder Russell Ballard, a member of the LDS Church's Quorum of the Twelve and an original Alliance member, to attend the press conference "if they stood in the back row," but insisted that the "agreement" had to be explained carefully as a proposal only. There was no sense of agreement or partnership on the part of the LDS Church on something it did not help create. We unveiled the historic "proposal" two hours later. The church, after careful study, eventually signed on. The ACLU, however, changed its mind and brought a second, this time unsuccessful, lawsuit over the relinquishing of the easement. The ACLU pursued that claim through yet another appeal, which was resolved in October 2005 when the Tenth Circuit Court of Appeals dismissed the suit.

After many complications and delays, the city had the Unity Center up and running by 2007. Elder Ballard told me I had "pulled off a miracle" with President Hinckley. "I have never seen him change his mind like he did with you." Elder Ballard himself is a rare breed. He can bring people of all faiths together and make them feel at peace and comfortable. He has unique experience in business and as an arbitrator is always fair and reliable. He was of tremendous help in settling this conflict and has been a marvelous leader in our community.

The Alliance for Unity weighed in on a number of other community issues and we remained a cohesive body throughout many controversial moments. There is one cute anecdote that underscores this: As fate would have it, my son Jon Jr. and Scott Matheson, the son of my seatmate on the Alliance board, Norma Matheson, faced each other in the 2004 race for governor. A gracious and revered woman in Utah and the widow of the late Governor Scott Matheson Sr., she and I remained good friends throughout the campaign. When Alliance members volunteered to deliver food from the Utah Food Bank to shut-ins in early October 2004, Norma and I teamed up in the same vehicle. TV news crews had a field day shooting video of the parents of the two gubernatorial candidates delivering food parcels in tandem. It demonstrated how Alliance for Unity members check biases at the door.

As this chapter is being written, the Alliance meets semiannually after undergoing renewal at its ten-year anniversary. Utah's cultural divide is not as wide as it once was—in that, at least, we were successful—but some frustrating challenges required different approaches. We took a stance of opposing storage of nuclear waste in Utah and supported legislative reforms, focusing on lawmaker conflicts of interest and transparency in lobbyist influences. Half the board's makeup has changed since its inception, ensuring vitality and a range of perspectives.

In the middle of the first decade of the twenty-first century, I was asked by Wharton School Publishing (an arm of the world's largest publishing firm, Pearson PLC) to pen a nice-guys-really-can-finish-first type of book. It would stress ethics and leadership. Wharton Publishing was intrigued by my belief that corporate executives ought to be people of their word and that corporations and wealthy individuals had a moral obligation to contribute to philanthropic causes. The book was entitled *Winners Never Cheat*. CNN's Larry King graciously agreed to write the foreword and Fox News' Neil Cavuto offered to write the afterword, as did attorney Wayne Reaud, my close friend.

We completed the manuscript in four months, which was somewhat miraculous given the timing. I had to check proofs on my plane traveling between IPO road show engagements. I was fortunate to have Jay Shelledy, the former editor of *The Salt Lake Tribune*, at my side— he assisted me in this endeavor. As a first-time author, I was hopelessly insensitive to deadlines. I am sure Pearson Editor Tim Moore had nightmares of me wrestling with his press operator to halt production so I could make just one last change. The book was in its tenth printing when, in 2009, we did a revision to discuss the pressures of the Great Recession. The second edition's reception overwhelmed me. This time, Glenn Beck wrote the foreword. He did a masterful job. A rough estimate of nearly 250,000 copies (there is no accurate way to measure in some countries) have been printed, including editions in Chinese, Korean, and Arabic.

The basic theme of *Winners Never Cheat* holds that the rules we learned as children are as relevant in the boardroom as they were on the playground. The book was not hard to write. All my life I have maintained the philosophies that my word is my bond, that getting even is a waste of precious resources and focus, that liars will eventually find their pants on fire, that it is right and just to treat others how you like to be treated, that fudging on the rules ultimately makes you a loser, and that you always help those who are in need.

Life is simple; life is good.

I have saved the best of my life, my family, for the last. They have been central to my existence and success in business and an inspiration of immeasurable depth. As you will soon discover, the joy of writing such a chapter is tempered with the loss of a family member. What would have been a delightful task now comes with a serving of indescribable grief. I struggled with that part. Still all eight of the others and my dear, dear wife, Karen, and the memory of Kathleen provide me with strength and a deeper sense of blessings. Everything is based in family. It is, indeed, all in the family.

20. It's All in the Family

THE STORY OF MY LIFE WOULD BE INCOMPLETE, AND INDEED EMPTY, without a discussion of the importance of Karen and our family. Karen and I are parents to six boys and three girls. The events that have brought the greatest joys and the worst of heartaches in life have all involved our children. We share their victories and grief. We are only as happy as our unhappiest child. Karen and the children mean more to me than life itself. It is difficult to imagine that people nurtured under the same roof could evolve into adults with such disparate goals and personalities. But they did, and it has been exhilarating to witness. Ours has been, and will forever be, a deep, loving relationship. The significance of that in my life cannot be understated.

There are a few things for which the Huntsman family will be remembered. I fear that among them is the holiday greeting card we have sent out for more than fifty years, growing in size annually, to friends and business acquaintances. But I don't mind that, because the card, while it has lasted, was symbolic of many wonderful times and feelings.

It has been, as some have described it, the Christmas card read round the world. Our holiday tradition of sending a card with our faces on it was no different than that of any other family, albeit on a larger scale. Richard and Pat Nixon sent out twenty-five thousand Christmas cards while he was president. The Huntsman mailing list exceeded thirty-three thousand at its zenith.

Karen and I began the tradition in 1960 with the arrival of Jon Jr. From there, it took on a life of its own. As our group grew to include spouses, grandchildren, and great-grandchildren, the annual greeting card presented the entire clan in matching attire, with scrubbed faces and our trademark toothy grins. In terms of its scope, the scene could have been mistaken for a yearbook class picture. It is often the first thing friends, relatives, and particularly our company's customers, suppliers, and associates mention when they see us.

It is virtually impossible to gather over ninety men, women, and children in one place. To put squirming toddlers in starched dresses and pressed trousers and expect them to freeze until several cameras clicked rivaled the intricacies of the Hoechst-ARCO-Shell deal. As some of our adult children moved out of state and their children started producing great-grandchildren, the adults grew tired of responding to the command performances to appear before a "firing squad" of sweating photographers, especially when they knew that the size of the crowd would result in individual faces too tiny to be identified. We increased the card's dimensions to overcome that, which became a problem in itself. Bob Reid, former Shell CEO and later head of British Rail, told me his wife once complained that if the Huntsman family Christmas card got any larger she would have to get a bigger mantel.

We finally put an end to the logistical nightmare in 2010, only to resume the tradition in 2012. That 2012 holiday card represented how central and precious the family is for Karen and me and reflects the family unity and loyalty that we have tried to instill in the hearts and minds of its members. In 2013, the Huntsman family Christmas card was even larger. Measuring ninety square inches in size and containing the ninety smiling (and faintly smiling) extended family faces, it represents four generations. I figure one more generation and we will have to send out the greeting card in two volumes.

Our family has been likened in the news media to a dynasty. While many families in the business world end up suing and backstabbing each other, we get along great. Karen and I have always fostered sibling competition, tempered with playfulness, forgiveness, and cohesion. No matter how many Huntsmans the family eventually includes, we are a unit. When you deal with one, you deal with the multitudes. It is this unity that has given Karen and me the strength to get through life's trials and challenges. Above all else, I am rooted in family.

Throughout those years when our nine-member brood lived at home, I tried to be there for them and to teach them what I could. They learned to be competitive but always to cheer for each other. When someone was out of sorts, the others would coax him or her back into the circle. To this day, they are incredibly interactive with one another. Kindness has been the common thread binding the second generation. When they gather, there is good-natured ribbing, but no backbiting or jealousy. They genuinely like each other.

Thus far, we have escaped the second-generation conflicts that sometimes arise among siblings and in-laws in family businesses. The traditional thought among children of many families is that "the old man" doesn't know what he is talking about. Let's do it our way. Not a bad thought I have often said—and many times they are right on target.

There are occasional differences between our children and me. I walk a fine line between the father and chairman roles. During the 1980s and 1990s, I spent about eight hundred hours a year in our Gulfstream aircraft, circling the globe. Usually, a few of the children, and sometimes Karen, traveled with me. Love is essential in our family, and I tried to make sure each child felt its embrace. Each of our children will tell you he or she is my favorite. I tried to make everyone feel special. Karen has been the perfect partner. Always supportive of me and our children, she is the model wife and mother. But make no mistake: Karen runs the home front; I make only a few proposals—and those are timed well.

It has been so much fun to watch each child blossom and mature. They learned to overcome adversity. If confronted with trials, they worked through them. Their collective and individual development were wonderful blessings to witness. Karen and I have attempted to fashion the Huntsman household, whether in California; Washington, DC; or Utah, as a place of peace, unity, love, bonding—and fun. I worked hard to make every outing an adventure, every activity a memorable experience. As testament to this, when we lived in Washington, DC, our home was in close proximity to the Bill and Richard Marriott families, our dearest friends. The Marriott children always wanted to come along with the Huntsmans, even it was only a trip to the mall. We often seemed to be an integrated family, as our children always felt welcome when accompanying the Marriott clan.

I am frequently asked whether growing up wealthy affected the Huntsman brood. First of all, not all of them grew up in affluence. Jon Jr., Peter, and Christena remember how tight things were when we barely qualified as middle class. By the late 1970s and early 1980s, our home and lifestyle were upgraded as we moved up the food chain. Yes, we had a big home (worth $200,000 at the time), but some of the rooms weren't furnished.

Our children knew how close to the brink of bankruptcy we came at times, during the downturns of the early 1970s, the early 1980s, the worst of all meltdowns, the post-9/11 scenario when together we peered into a financial abyss and again in 2009 when Apollo pulled the plug on us and our stock plummeted to $1.97 while the country went into a significant recession. The business was run on borrowed money and there wasn't a whole lot of money in the bank.

The first significant infusion of cash came from the sale of Huntsman Container. Everything opened up after that. In a two-year period in the late 1980s, I went from just scraping by to being one of the wealthiest individuals in America. The kids had no idea what was happening to our finances, nor did others close to us. Heck, for that matter, it took me years to fully realize what was happening.

David says he didn't know the family was wealthy until he came home from his LDS mission in Taiwan. As a surprise, some of his brothers and I met him at the Portland International Airport and we flew home in a private jet. It perhaps was a bit harder on the younger children who grew up when we had a great deal of money. Jennifer remembers schoolmates saying to her, "Oh, you're a Huntsman. You live in that big house on the hill." I told her to be gracious to all and to remember that we used much of our money to help others.

The 1990s, however, were fabulous times in the chemical industry, a period when I could have written a personal check for $100 million—several times over. Becoming wealthy produces an interesting phenomenon: cost no longer matters. Whatever you want, you can buy. No wonder some people with newfound wealth go off the deep end. For the Huntsman family, however, it was the decade in which we instituted our charitable giving to some forty groups or causes, with cancer being the prime recipient.

On the other side of the coin, wealth can vanish overnight. In 2001, which marked the start of what I call the petrochemical industry's Dark Ages, the corporate purse strings tightened considerably. We were hardly starving, but the spigot on the money pump had all but rusted shut.

Karen put the kibosh on our household spending. That a family worth $2.5 billion would put itself on a budget may seem like a non sequitur, but that's what we did. My wealth at the time was all on paper. To be sure, we weren't going without. Our personal property was paid for and my income was steady. Where things got tricky in those tough times was on the philanthropy side of the equation. I always made charitable commitments during the good times and then had to scramble to meet those pledges during bad times. When the post-9/11 downturn enveloped us— the worst ever in this business—I had some two dozen ongoing charitable commitments. I ended up selling company properties, borrowing from the bank and going into personal debt to meet my humanitarian obligations. As one's handshake is one's bond, likewise pledges to charity must be honored above personal discretionary spending.

Throughout all of our child-rearing years, our offspring were better off materially than I was at their age. My own childhood poverty instilled in me a level of ambition and a determination to be successful. I vowed I would never again live in a Quonset hut and have only two shirts to my name, and neither would my children. I have made good on that promise. Having worked hard for everything I had as a young man, I admit to splurging shamelessly on my family when I had the wherewithal to do so. My philosophy has been that you can go broke making bad business decisions, but it's never bad business to provide a comfortable home, to spend time and money on your family, to provide those in your care a decent quality of life. It doesn't cost that much when they have their priorities straight.

I know our children's notions of success are different than mine. Each became a millionaire at an early age through trusts and stock ownership, yet each was and continues to be hard working and dedicated. I doubt any of them ever realized they didn't have to work. I am not sure if I, as a child, could have handled the kind of money my children received. Their generation rolled with us through the pitfalls and pleasures of wealth and handled the agony and ecstasy with equal aplomb. On the other hand, it never got so bad that they experienced the scars that truly doing without can leave. The truth is that Karen receives the credit for their being balanced and well-rounded.

While I may be the founder of our family business, Karen has always been CEO of the household and she nurtured our children with a firm and consistent approach—the same approach she uses with me, by the way. The little family secret is that I am not much of a disciplinarian. While I often share business concerns with her, she has made it clear she does not want to be involved in the day-to-day responsibilities of running the business. Always steady and practical, Karen has never second-guessed me; she is a rock-solid partner and supportive counselor. I often introduce her as the chairman of the chairman, a title *Forbes* originally bestowed on her in an article. She knows her mind and tells it straight. Throughout our family, she is known as the Queen Mother.

Yet Karen has managed to spend much of her time serving outside the home as well, in community service and, at one point, as a regent for Utah's system of higher education. She has served on a hospital board and on a major bank board. She gives numerous speeches, at times in my behalf, and she is a hit with audiences. For one thing, she knows me and tells it like it is. People love that.

Karen's influence on me is unmistakable. She is the truest of friends and confidants. In an age when it is popular for women to seek fulfillment professionally, Karen chose to apply her intelligence, skills, and energy within the home and at my side. While I tend to make decisions from the heart, Karen makes them from the head. She has a knack for a logical, unemotional analysis of problems. She also can be more skeptical than I am. She has watched too many people try to take advantage of me. Even though she cautioned me hundreds of times about people meddling in our business ventures, at times I did not listen—always to my detriment.

In many small ways, Karen and I are opposites. I like my meat cooked well-done; Karen likes her meat on the rare side. She is more comfortable in a cool room; I like it warm. Karen feels strongly about healthy eating; I like sugary things. We do not differ, however, when it comes to goals, desires, and the larger picture.

My love and respect for Karen and each of my children and their spouses knows no bounds. Their encouragement has meant the difference between success and failure. They are my personal heroes. During their formative years, I was away from home more than half the time as the business grew from domestic to global. I tried to remain close to home, but often that wasn't possible. I focused on quality over quantity in our time together. My older children saw much more of me. Jon Jr. and Peter, for instance, had me around most of the time. I coached their baseball teams and Paul's and David's basketball teams. By the time James reached that age, coaching was out of the question for me and he excelled in individual sports. Yet I took advantage of every moment I had at home and made those times count.

Every Saturday, while other dads mowed the lawns, I devoted my time to daylong activities with the kids. Granted, I had the luxury of hiring a person to take care of the lawn, but I tried to make the most of my days at home and to never miss an important event in one of my children's lives. I caught many red-eye flights to get home in time for a recital, someone's graduation, or a band gig. I remember several times flying all night from London or Tokyo to ensure I made it to a ball game or a picnic.

Even while I was in the White House and working constantly, I attempted to make time for the kids on weekends. Later, Jon Jr. would say it meant the world to him that I stood by him while he practiced for track and field events at an oval near our home. But each of them will tell you they would have preferred to have had me around more, that they didn't have enough time with me. They also acknowledge that they hardly were abandoned. Paul would tell you he and his siblings wanted more one-on-one with their father, but that they also understood that when running a business empire with a family as large as ours, there is only so much time.

Coupled with heavy LDS Church leadership responsibilities, as a bishop (branch president), stake president, mission president, and eventually a member of the Seventies Quorum, another twenty hours or so per week were required outside the home. I simultaneously served on five Fortune 500 boards of directors and served in many community and charitable leadership functions. Nevertheless, I tried to make a positive impression when I was home and to leave the stress of the business at the front door. "Dad may have been juggling chainsaws," remembers Peter, "but he never came home uptight."

As a family we loved engaging in discussions, games, and "I-beat-Dad" contests, where each child had to pick a sport in which they would try to best their father. When they succeeded in surpassing my ability level, as eventually each of them did, they received a plaque commemorating the milestone. It started with Jon Jr., who is a natural athlete, but he was eleven before he finally nailed me—in billiards, no less, a game in which I considered myself to be talented. During dinner and as I tucked each child into bed, we would discuss what we had done that day. As they got older, I would seek their input on business decisions.

Often on a weekend, we would hop in the car and go places, especially to pet stores. I never saw a pet store I didn't like. Karen complained that our home was a menagerie. You name it, dogs, cats, rabbits, hamsters—and snakes. I hate snakes. Jon Jr., Peter, David, and James each had a pet python. (To me, the phrase "pet python" is an oxymoron. Pythons don't like being pets.) Some were passed down from one to the other. Occasionally, one of these hideous, slithering creatures would escape from its cage. I always suspected it was no accident because my fear of snakes was well known among the children. No one had informed me of the fugitive reptile as I blithely ran around the house at night with bare feet. I would have gone through the ceiling had I ever stepped on one.

Once, a python got loose and couldn't be found, even after a lengthy search. A few weeks later, something began to smell in the heating vents. Karen called a furnace expert to crawl into the duct and retrieve whatever had died there. The guy nearly had a stroke when he came face to face with a seven-foot python, quite dead, as it turned out. Another time, one of James's snakes was loose for a month. It was found alive, among the strings of our baby grand piano.

Our children were not perfect, by any means, but they had happy childhoods. They got into their share of trouble because they were rambunctious and loved pranks. (Being a founding member of the Bremmer Park gang in Pocatello, I could relate.) Some of the pranks were funny. Some were not, such as the homemade bombs they exploded in the canyon behind our home. One was loud enough to draw the attention of the police.

I was always an easy target for their shenanigans. I have a hard time sleeping and always keep a bottle of water beside my bed. One night, before I retired, James replaced half of the water in the bedside bottle with vodka. At about 2:00 a.m., I took a long swig of what I thought was water. My next thought was that I had just swallowed butane. I nearly choked to death. I refused to acknowledge I had fallen for the ruse. They would still be wondering if Karen hadn't told them a couple of days later.

I have no one to blame for their pranks but myself. The children know me as world-class prankster. What goes around comes around, I suppose. One of the legendary stories the children tell was once on vacation I had bought ice cream cones for everyone. As I drove the station wagon down the road, James plopped his cone on top of my head. I didn't react. I just stopped the car, retrieved my comb from a pocket, and calmly combed out the butter pecan from my hair. James quickly adds when this story is told that I started it all, earlier in the morning, by pouring orange juice over his head, to everyone's merriment.

Some of the children believe I am funny, at times bordering on goofy. Jennifer loves to talk about how I, in my bathrobe, make my way to our sugarless kitchen in search of a sugary snack nearly every night about eleven o'clock, cracking jokes (which they think are corny) and making up my versions of nursery rhymes. What's so goofy about that? Says Jennifer: "The best time to catch the funny side of my dad is around eleven p.m. in the kitchen. And bring a spoon."

I wouldn't have missed one minute with any of my children. Each holds a special place in my heart; each is loved unconditionally.

To outsiders, the life of the Huntsmans may appear glamorous and trouble-free, as if everything we touch turns to gold. To be fair, some of our youngest children were born with the proverbial silver spoon in their mouths and with a bit more potential to jump ahead of the pack. The downside of that scenario is that no matter what they accomplish in life there will always be some who say it was because of the family-status advantage and not their abilities. Our children and in-laws during the thirty-five years we were a private business have been part of the corporation and have had to earn peer respect. I can assign job titles. I can pay them hefty salaries. What I cannot do is ensure them peer approval, and that is what each of them values above all.

All our children have experienced the heartaches, stress, and challenges of our business. They have been observant students of life, brutally aware from the start that there is no such thing as the Midas touch. The only realities in life are hard work, preparation, determination, honesty, and charitable giving. The children have been a part of the building process. They skated along the financial precipice right beside me. They know what it is like to be fenced off from the outside world. They also see what goes on in that world and cannot stand by and watch others suffer. Our progeny have not lost sight of the big picture. They comprehend it because they are—and have been from the start—founding members of the Huntsman Corporation. Indulge me while I talk about each individually.

Our firstborn, Jon Jr, was a model for obedience and integrity. I never remember hearing him utter an untruth or deflect responsibility for something he did. He is a talented musician and a fearless competitor. He won his age bracket at the Utah Motocross Championship at sixteen. At age eighteen, he was in a heavy-metal rock band, long hair and all, playing keyboards. Elvis's music was more my speed, but I would show up at Jon's gigs to hear him play. No one could have guessed the individual futures of the band members then, but they all turned out to be highly successful.

Jon loved to explore and to take part in spirited conversations. He found everything interesting, from motorcycles to the White House. He is articulate and thoughtful, equally at ease talking with Alice Cooper and the Dalai Lama. He thinks outside the box and reaches into its deepest corners. It was assumed, I suppose, that he would go into the family business, since he started out accompanying me on my glamorous egg route. But for Jon Jr., foreign service was always his first love. Before he jumped for keeps (ambassador postings, governor, and presidential candidate), though, he made a conscious decision in 1983 to spend some time helping build the business. His wife, Mary Kaye, is his soul mate. She is at once regal and gentle, solid and loving, loyal and independent. From my vantage point, she has been Jon's best friend and partner on every step of their remarkable journey. Karen and I love and admire her enormously. Their children reflect all the best qualities of their inspiring and intelligent parents.

Next in line is Peter. From the time he was a baby, Peter's trademarks have been tenacity and integrity. Born in 1963, he loves the outdoors, hunting, fishing, and the mountains—anything that takes him into the wild. An energetic, keen competitor with a corresponding physical agility and strength, he also is an avid reader, especially of history. Peter's determination is unmatched. I used to send him out to sell the leftover inventory from my Christmas album business. Peter would not return until he had sold every album. He knew how to close a sale.

School, however, didn't move fast enough for Peter. During his second year at the University of Utah, he stopped attending classes and declared his entrepreneurial intentions. I turned over to him a small company to run, called Top Stop, which consisted of seventeen convenience store/gas stations in Utah. Peter became its president and CEO before his twentieth birthday. He did such a terrific job that, when he was twenty-one, I put him in charge of our small oil distribution business. He is a born businessman, evidenced by his gifted leadership as he became a major corporate CEO in 2000. Well versed and self-taught, Peter is one of the best chemists we have in the company, and we have thousands of them. He learned everything there is to know about petrochemical products and the workings of the industry. The president of Dow Chemical once referred to Peter as the most outstanding CEO in the industry.

The three toughest jobs in any business we own are chief operating officer, the lead attorney, and the lead media person. Peter and I butted heads in his early days as our chief executive because we didn't always see things the same way, but in the end we always supported one another. Today, I am, quite honestly, in awe of his administrative talents and how he operates the company. He and Brynn have eight children, and she is his ideal match. Brynn is beautiful, intelligent, capable, and an outstanding mother and role model to their family. I can't remember seeing her without a smile on her face. We love and cherish Brynn as a daughter.

And speaking of daughters, it is time to admit publicly that I have a soft spot in my heart for our girls. As each of them is well aware, they are my pride and joy. Perhaps that is because I had no sisters, or because I so dearly loved my mother, who always smiled and had nice things to say about everyone. My father was quite the opposite. No doubt about it, I favored the girls. I get teary-eyed just talking about them. Not one of them went into the business. They certainly were sharp enough to earn a seat at the table had they wanted it, and they always were part of the discussions at home. But they chose the appeal of being a full-time mother and homemaker over business careers. They chose Karen as their role model. Who could possibly question that?

Christena, our oldest daughter, was born in 1964. A one-time championship diver, she could well be the best athlete in the family. From the start, she was driven, competitive, and smart. I used to call her Little Miss

KIA (Know It All). She simply had to keep up with her older brothers. Under no condition would she let go of her end of the rope. Christena reminded me of myself as a child. She is a leader and much like her mother in that she is a natural beauty who can run a large household and entertain with ease. With charm and forthrightness, she speaks her mind clearly and with candor. She is a people person, drawn to individuals of all walks in life. She is the last one to leave a room full of people. Unlike me, she is not sensitive to criticism.

Christena attended the University of Utah and Brigham Young University and married Rick Durham. They brought seven beautiful children into the world and are now grandparents (as are Peter and Brynn and Jon Jr. and Mary Kaye). Rick, who attended Columbia University before transferring to the Wharton School where he was nearly a straight-A student, played a critical role as the company's CFO during a key period of time before becoming CEO of the packaging division. *Forbes* magazine referred to him as "the Clark Kent of the Huntsman clan."

Rick grew up near us. He lost his father when he was a teenager and began spending time at our home. He said he liked coming to our house because he noticed that I participated in some of the antics kids normally do when the parents aren't looking. A remarkable and gifted individual and an investment banker by training, Rick started his own venture capital business and a number of other businesses after we sold Huntsman Packaging. At first, he was reluctant to join our family business because he saw the size of our family perhaps limiting his opportunities in the company. I told him I loved my business and my family and that he was definitely part of both. What's the problem? Besides, the business was so big by then there was plenty of opportunity for all. His expertise has earned him respect as one of the most astute businessmen in the nation.

David, born in 1967, is the Rock of Gibraltar. Smack in the middle, he is even-tempered and athletic, having climbed nearly every mountain peak in North America. He literally runs up those mountains. Pragmatic, positive, and conventional, David attended the University of Utah for two years before transferring to the University of Pennsylvania for his degree. I have never heard David utter a negative statement about anyone. Not a day passes that he doesn't come into my office to ask what he can do to help.

David has been a source of great strength for me, having served in several corporate positions. He currently is president of the family's foundation and CEO of the Huntsman Cancer Foundation. He truly gets what giving is all about. He empathizes and connects with people with an ease that is inspiring. David also is the driving force behind our latest enterprise, Huntsman Springs, in Idaho. David and Jon Jr. speak Mandarin Chinese and love to confuse me by speaking in that language.

David and Michelle, his first and only love, have eight children and their home is near Karen's and mine. Michelle is a trooper—an unflappable problem solver who is ready for anything. She is an exceptional mother who shares David's gift for humor. Their home always seems to be a happy place. He asked me once if I ever wanted to get off the treadmill some of the time. I told him I don't have an off switch. He and the other children do, and I respect that. When they are home sleeping at night or on vacation, they can leave work behind. Wherever I am, I'm dreaming up new ideas or ways to improve on earlier ones—at least until my sleeping pills kick in.

Paul is handsome and dignified, although perhaps the shyest of the bunch. Born in 1969, Paul is the last one to speak, but when he does his input is thoughtful and articulate, so simply expressed that everyone wonders why they didn't think of that. Paul runs in many marathons, one of which took him up and down the mountains of Switzerland. He is determined, competitive, and loyal—and would give you the shirt off his back. He reads me better than anyone and is surprised how poorly some people understand me. As reserved as Paul is, it is ironic that he, like me, makes deals based on emotions and tries to avoid conflicts and calculations.

After graduating from the University of Utah and working for our company in Australia and Texas for a few years, Paul returned to school and earned an MBA at the Wharton School. He recently was senior vice president of Huntsman Gay Global Capital and has done a remarkable job putting together petrochemical acquisitions. He is currently president and CEO of our family financial office and our investments.

He and Cheryl have eight children, to whom Paul is a marvelous father. Cheryl is a strong, creative, caring person who is as much a supportive helpmate to Paul as she is a gracious mother to their family. She is one of seventeen children born to Dr. and Mrs. Roy Wirthlin. She grew up knowing how to work and she understands what leadership is all about. A remarkable woman.

James, born in 1971, is spirited, fearless, and fun-loving. I know of no one who doesn't like James. He lives each day to the fullest. He embraces the outdoors, is a gun collector, and would spend his entire life in the mountains if he could. But he can't, because he is president of Huntsman Corporation's Advanced Materials Division and takes his responsibilities seriously. James is hard working and not afraid to get his hands dirty. For several years, he donned blue overalls and worked at one of our manufacturing plants alongside the maintenance crews so he could learn how it was done from the ground up. He would work all night, trying to restore a lost generator. He became one of the crew and his coworkers loved him.

Everyone wants to be around James. He will phone me often just to say, "Dad, I love you. I just want to tell you what a great guy you are and how lucky I am to be your son." James will tell you that he got his prankster genes from the old man. I like that. You can't take life too seriously. But he also has other traits that I try hard to follow, such as accepting others with different views, forgiving and forgetting, and treating people with respect. James is hardly the only child of ours with those attributes.

James graduated from the University of Utah. He spent a few years as a moviemaker, joined the Screen Actors Guild, and produced two films to his credit. He even talked me into playing a cameo role in both of them—as a Walmart greeter and later as a professor. He and his imperturbable spouse, Marianne, have five children. Marianne is a terrific wife and mother, as sweet as the day is long. Thankfully for James, she was blessed with a well-developed sense of fun. James continues to pull pranks on his dad. Marianne rolls with all the activity and fun. She is just great.

Jennifer, our youngest daughter, came into our world in 1972. She is the consummate blend of Karen and me. Jennifer loves everybody. She is patient and kind, with a delightful mix of humor and compassion. Her patience and steadiness were a great help to Karen as her mother managed the household and took care of Mark, our youngest.

She caught how I juggled my love and attention among such a large brood. Jennifer was quoted once as saying: "In any large family, each child thinks he or she at times has fallen through the cracks. But Dad has this incredible ability to make everyone feel special. Once, while we were on a family vacation, I felt disconnected with the family. I was young, married, and we had moved away. Dad and I went for a walk and he made me feel that I was the most special among the children. And I have felt that way ever since."

It was hard to see Jennifer leave the nest, but leave us she did to marry David Parkin, whose father is a noted physician and his mother a poised and organized woman who led the LDS Church's Relief Society for many years. Jennifer attended the University of Utah. Dave graduated from the same institution and has worked in several leadership positions in Huntsman Corporation. He has earned my respect as a husband to our Jennifer, father to their six beautiful children, and recently a partner in Huntsman Gay Global Capital. He later cofounded a very successful private equity business with three partners—and what a legacy he is building.

As she was growing up, Jennifer always told me she would end up leading the company. Perhaps one day she will. Meanwhile, she enjoys leading her family as an admirable homemaker while serving as PTA president. Dave is an all-American in nearly every sport. He works hard and is tough and gracious at the same time.

Mark, or "Markie," as we call him, is our youngest child. Mark was born on January 20, 1975, several weeks early. I was out of town when Karen reported becoming immensely tired and that her water had broken. Her doctor told her to stay in bed. The next day, sensing all was not as it ought to be, Karen again called the doctor. His advice was the same: "Stay down. Your only danger is the chance of infection."

Thankfully, one evening, a physician friend stopped by the house and found Karen feverish. He recommended she immediately be taken to the hospital because he suspected infection. Her own doctor was notified and he said he would check with her later that evening. He didn't see Karen until the next morning. Exhausted and frightened, she asked the doctor to take the baby by caesarean section. He did not think that was necessary and delivered the baby by natural means—through an infected birth canal. It was a difficult delivery, to say the least, and the consequences, of which we were unaware at the time, were infinitely more stressful.

It was a full year before Karen recovered her strength. We were deeply concerned that Mark was listless and slow to respond to stimuli. Within his first year of life, his medical evaluation revealed he had suffered severe brain damage at birth. We were told he would never be able to speak, read, write, or behave normally. The prognosis turned out to be partially correct. Mark is an active, cheerful, handsome young man. His vocabulary is quite limited, but he loves to be around people. Karen bore the majority of the challenges of Mark's upbringing, assisted to a great extent by his sisters. It was by watching Karen deal with Mark in those early years that cemented our daughters' determination to be a mother like their role model.

Mark's behavior was uncontrollable in the early years. Having no sense of memory, obedience, or logic, he consumed Karen's every waking moment. I did my best to help, but she was his mainstay. Slowly, he learned acceptable behavior, developed speech at the level of a four-year-old, and began to approach each day with childlike wonder. He loves cars, costume jewelry, key chains, orange slices, cowboys, and, most especially, people. He strides purposefully through the corridors of our business headquarters in his official capacity as corporate messenger.

Markie has been the glue in our family. He judges everyone by their hearts. He is a gift from God and lifts my spirits daily as he spreads his brand of joy. He works alongside the staff and the property management guys, loved by all who have the privilege of knowing him. He still calls me Jon or Horse Biscuit (I am not certain why), but we blend well and love one another greatly. He is another of my heroes.

Kathleen, our dear, dear second daughter, has left us. We lost our precious Kathleen at the tender age of forty-four for the most terrible of reasons. No pain in the world—from disease, famine, war, or poverty—is as great as that felt by a parent at the loss of a child. Nature structures generations so the oldest will pass on before the youngest. It's not supposed to be the other way around. A parent in Afghanistan weeps as sorrowfully as does a parent in America when a child dies first. No parent in the world either expects or is emotionally equipped to witness the death of a child. The death of a spouse, parent, friend, or sibling is painful and emotionally devastating, but when a parent watches a child leave this world, the trauma can be insurmountable. Kathleen's story has been too painful for me to discuss outside the family. This is my first attempt.

Born in 1966, between Christena and David, Kathleen probably was the most like me in looks and in the desire to give back. Tall, blonde, perpetually tanned, she was every underdog's best friend. She would give anything she had to her children, neighbors, friends, or someone in need. Everyone loved Kathleen. She reminded me of my mother, for whom she was named, and because of that our relationship was special. She had the Robison genes and was kind and thoughtful, devoted, and gracious.

When I was called to be mission president in Washington, DC, Kathleen never fully accepted our move. When she was on her A-game, she was fun to be around, but she missed the friends she left behind in Utah and showed her unhappiness by acting out.

I did not want to see the signs that our child was headed in the wrong direction. Kathleen and I had such a special bond. I could not bring myself to get tough with her and had a hard time saying no. I did, however, say no to one young man who was seeing her. He was a bad influence on her and I told him I did not want him around the house. As I had feared might happen, she became pregnant out of wedlock. We sent her to live with Christena and Rick who were residing in New York, where Rick was attending Columbia University. Kathleen had the child and gave it up for adoption. I was right there with her at Mount Sinai Hospital in New York City. She then returned to Utah to start anew.

Our daughter had a bit of a wild streak, which I attributed to the Huntsman genes. But Karen and I were especially troubled by the realization that she may have lacked the self-confidence we had always attributed to her and that her sense of inferiority was manifested in an excessive emphasis on being thin. The pressures of that obsession led her to anorexia and bulimia. Karen, who has consistently encouraged exercise and good nutrition in our family, was acutely aware of the long-term damage that these practices can inflict on a young body. And they did take their toll through the last eighteen years of her life.

Kathleen attended BYU and the University of Utah where she met Jim Huffman. They fell in love, became engaged, and he quit school. As a stake president in the LDS Church, I had the honor of pronouncing them man and wife, after which Jim went back to finish his degree at the University of Utah and then earned an MBA at Wharton, graduating in the top 10 percent of his class. Kathleen and Jim had seven beautiful children.

But she continued to live on the edge. Due in large part to Kathleen's poor health after years of starving herself, her pregnancies were difficult and each delivery was life threatening. From what I could discern about anorexia and bulimia, they are forms of mental illness involving addictive behavior that most often requires years of therapy to overcome. Kathleen was referred to as my "clone"—we were so much alike in many ways. Her outreach and kindness were contagious. She was such fun and her personality was one of dignity and humor. She was an all-American in every way. When the wheels came off, I was overcome with grief and guilt, as any parent would do in this sort of nightmare.

One afternoon in the spring of 2008, I received a phone call from Jim and Kathleen that left me reeling, as if I had received a swift punch to the gut. They informed me that the long-term effects of her eating disorders and her use of drugs had become serious and that Kathleen needed medical help. I could hardly breathe. I shared the news with Karen and headed for my bedroom. Karen called David and Jon Jr., who was at the time the sitting governor of Utah, telling them that their father needed them immediately. David was the first to arrive and found his mother crying in the kitchen. She told him, and soon Jon Jr., that I was upstairs. They found me sitting on the floor of our large walk-in closet, distraught and weeping as I cradled a portrait of the children. Jon Jr. and David gave me a priesthood blessing, a laying on of hands to someone in need of special counsel, comfort, or healing.

The next day we reached out for professional assistance for Kathleen. She and Jim divorced shortly thereafter, and she went into rehabilitation in California. Within twenty-four hours, we had their seven wonderful, innocent children, ranging in age from eight to seventeen, living in our home. (Most of them remained with us until 2012 when they returned to be with their father. Some are still with us. We love them dearly.)

There are no words to express the depth of our sorrow and the sense of helplessness as we watched our daughter wage her private battle to break the cycle of physical and emotional disorders and their insidious effect on her mind and body. And she tried hard, for more than a year, and confided to Christena on several occasions how she did not want to disappoint her father.

Kathleen seemed to respond to treatment and began looking forward to the next phase of her life. She remarried in Las Vegas to a man who, it tragically turned out, faced severe challenges of his own. Only a month later, we were devastated to learn she had suffered cardiac arrest and slipped into a coma.

We immediately took our daughter to the closest hospital, after which she was transferred to the Huntsman Cancer Hospital in Salt Lake City. Pronounced brain dead by the doctors there, she was placed on life support in the hospital room that we had built for Karen's and my final days on earth. It had been beautifully designed and decorated by Kathleen only a few years earlier. That one of our children would be the first one to use it was unthinkable. Kathleen remained there, unconscious, for a week as we stood by helplessly, scanning for any spark of activity, any sign of hope, any clue she might miraculously recover. It was not to be. In the afternoon of April 20, 2010, her mother and I and her brothers, sisters, and children gathered to say a final good-bye.

Upon her folded hands, I placed a note card on which I had penned, "We have been blessed with so much. We love the Lord. We thank Thee for sweet Kathleen." At 4:00 p.m., her devastated father shut off the resuscitator and Kathleen slipped away serenely in the presence of those most dear to her. My children say I have not been the same since her passing.

The grief over her loss continues to paralyze me when I dwell on it. Whether telling this story publicly can, with the Lord's help, produce closure, I cannot say. What is certain is that I can write no further about this.

21. The Wild Card

IN MY HIGH SCHOOL GOVERNMENT CLASSES, I WAS TAUGHT THAT ANYBODY born in America could grow up to become president of the United States. At that point in our nation's history, I suspect that youngsters who were female, minorities, of non-Christian belief, or of modest means didn't buy that egalitarian premise. It may be that in terms of material success, the American Dream is a brass ring available for any and all to grab. But the likelihood of becoming president today, given the way the process is manipulated by moneyed, special-interest, one-issue neurotics and influenced by uncompromising talk show hosts, is a concept beyond the grasp of most of us. Even when I became wealthy, and my children possessed the material means and societal opportunities to attempt great things, the idea of being elected the most powerful leader on the globe remained theoretical at best.

One of my children heard the drumbeat a bit differently, however, and at 10:00 a.m. on June 21, 2011, the seventy-fourth anniversary of my birth, I became a believer.

Karen and I, along with several of our children and grandchildren, had flown to Newark, New Jersey the day before and spent the night at the Ritz-Carlton in New York City. That morning we boarded a bus back to New Jersey, and the Statue of Liberty National Monument on the Hudson River. The sky was overcast, but the mood was sunny and bright. The atmosphere seemed electric when, standing a few feet to his right on the speaker's platform and with Lady Liberty as a backdrop, I watched my firstborn, Jon M. Huntsman Jr., announce his candidacy for the Republican nomination for president of the United States. "Huntsman Makes It Official: 'I'm a Candidate for the Office of President,'" streamed the electronic reader board minutes later in Times Square across the bay in Midtown Manhattan.

Listening to his relatively short announcement speech, I wondered if the American people would ever get to know what a gifted young leader he is, how he respects people of every socioeconomic strata and can converse comfortably with everyone, how truly honest and decent he is. I was as proud that day as I have ever been in my life. The event took place on the very spot where, twenty-two years earlier, President Ronald Reagan launched his general election campaign for the White House.

Of the nine serious candidates for the Republican nomination, Jon was the only one with combined experience in business, government, philanthropy, and international diplomacy. More importantly, perhaps, was that the political advisers to President Obama dreaded the idea of a general election campaign against Jon Huntsman. He was a magnet for moderates, the constituency that sent Barack Obama to the White House in 2008 and again, as it turned out, in 2012. Obama's campaign manager, Jim Messina, acknowledged after the election that Jon would have been "a very tough candidate" in the general election.

We all knew Jon's primary campaign would not be easy. But we genuinely felt if America got to know him he could pull it off. He was the wild card in the contentious 2012 presidential race. Jon was also the only one of the nine nomination seekers who pledged to conduct his campaign in an arena of civility. He vowed he would not dish up vindictive red meat to the party hardliners and talk-show agitators who, at least in terms of volume and media attention, appear to have hijacked modern GOP primaries. He employed no teleprompter, no formal text.

Jon's pledge was simple and elegant: "Civility, humanity, and respect are sometimes lost in our interactions as Americans. You don't need to run down anyone's reputation to run for president. I respect my fellow Republican candidates. And I respect the president. He and I have a difference of opinion on how to help the country we both love. But the question each of us wants the voters to answer is, who will be the better president, not who is the better American."

Jon kept his word. The other candidates did not follow his lead, and corrosive rhetoric dominated the conversation throughout his seven-month candidacy. Sadly, his consistent display of decency, of balance, of fairness—as well as his late start with little time for preparation—may have contributed to his campaign's downfall.

Jon's pledge of civility was hardly his sole mantra. In his fifteen-minute announcement speech, he noted that our current government does not have to choose between fiscal responsibility and economic growth. What the nation does have to do, he stressed, is make tough decisions to avert being overwhelmed by disastrous entitlement and debt spending. Calling for broad changes in the tax code, he embraced (albeit with kinder rhetoric) the rigorous fiscal plan that was offered by Representative Paul Ryan of Wisconsin. He proposed the nation shift its foreign policy away from overseas conflicts, noting that the most effective global strategy to strengthen our national security would be to rebuild the economic core at home.

My son did not shy from confronting the administration of his former boss, who had been well served by Jon's diplomatic strengths as the ambassador to China, arguably the most important nation, next to ours, on the planet. The nation needs "more than hope," and leaders who can "make hard decisions that are necessary to avert disaster," he said. "For the first time in our history, we are passing down to the next generation a country that is less powerful, less compassionate, less competitive, and less confident than the one we got."

While he took a number of moderate stands, especially on social and environmental issues, he is a solid fiscal conservative, a center-right candidate in the tradition of Presidents Reagan and Bush the First. Indeed, three months after the announcement, an editorial in *The Wall Street Journal*, a bastion of conservative philosophy for the nation's business community, rated Jon's economic blueprint the GOP's best of show among primary candidates. Jon has always embraced careful thought over knee-jerk reaction, a quality lacking in many politicians and commentators today.

Jon M. Huntsman Jr. was an unlikely candidate in the era of the Tea Party, Rush Limbaugh, Fox News, and can-you-top-this political meanness. It was a campaign designed to beat President Obama at his own game. I was—and remain—so proud of him.

Jon had been on the White House's political radar for some time. Some hold that because of Governor Huntsman's popularity with Republicans, Democrats, and Independents alike, the Obama administration had asked him to serve as ambassador to China to get him out of the picture. The thought of facing Jon in the general election did make some Democratic strategists uneasy, but that explanation is too cynical. President Obama had promised to be bipartisan on his key appointments and Jon had the credentials. He had served three presidents before Obama and had held two ambassadorships. As a plus, he spoke fluent Chinese. And, by all accounts, it proved to be a good choice.

I had watched Jon develop over the years. His core values have never varied. The news media made much of his dropping out of high school in favor of his rock-and-roll band, motorcycle riding, and the typical teenage pursuits. Not long after leaving high school, he realized the importance of pursuing his education and went directly into college after passing a rigorous entrance exam. He served a two-year LDS mission to Taiwan, received a degree in international studies from the University of Pennsylvania, and established himself as a Huntsman business executive and foundation president. Before long, he was appointed United States Trade Ambassador, after serving as US Ambassador to Singapore (the youngest ambassador in US history). Later, he would successfully run for governor of Utah—twice.

Even in the midst of such a distinguished career, he's not afraid to let his hair down occasionally. He still plays the keyboard. In fact, while he was governor, Jon and four others—including the mayor of Salt Lake City; the president of Questar; one of Jon's GOP primary opponents; and Jon's son, Jon III—played a mean rock-and-roll repertoire in warm-up acts at a couple of concerts, including one headlined by the Beach Boys.

Jon is also rock-solid faithful to spouse and family. He and Mary Kaye, a remarkable wife and mother, have seven children including two who were adopted from Asian nations. Two of their sons attended the US Naval Academy, one daughter is a concert pianist, one specializes in design, and another is now a program host for MSNBC after stints at ABC News. (Three of the daughters—Abby, Liddy, and Mary Anne—became Twitter stars during the campaign.)

Conservative in most fiscal and social issues and progressive in others, Jon was—and remains—a model of what the Republican Party needs to become if it wants to survive in the future. Jon refused to cater to the right or to the left. He was not beholden to the state's Republican Party or to the powerful LDS Church, of which two out of every three Utahns are members in fact or in name. Jon made people feel important, showing sensitivity to people of all faiths, economic levels, and ethnic backgrounds. He followed his conscience, shunned lobbyists' gifts, and wrapped his office in dignity.

Nobody knew that when Jon Jr. resigned his trade ambassador's post he would return to Utah in late 2003 to declare his candidacy for governor. But if I was born to be in business, Jon was wired for public service. He simply loves public policy.

Utah is the only state in the union that requires state and federal candidates to be selected for the primary election by delegates at a state convention, a biennial gathering intimidated of late by the party's superconservatives. The eight candidates seeking the GOP state convention endorsement in the spring of 2004 included a sitting governor, a just-retired congressman, and the current and former speakers of the Utah House—the crème of the party, all well known to the delegates. When he started his campaign, Jon had three convention delegates backing him. With organization, diplomacy and indefatigable determination, he steadily added delegates to his committed column. He did so by focusing on those areas where he was most conservative. Jon's core message was simple and unwavering: Without economic development, all other issues were irrelevant because the state would not otherwise have the financial wherewithal to improve education, transportation or the environment.

Among the other hurdles he had to overcome were establishing himself in his own right—in other words, differentiating himself from the old man—and dispelling a perception that he was born with a silver spoon. Jon's opponents implied he was buying the election with the family fortune. He shrugged it off, pointing to jobs he has held since he was ten and jokingly handing out tiny silver spoons prior to speaking engagements. In the end, Jon Huntsman Jr. was the top choice of the convention delegates. He and the runner-up—veteran political street fighter Nolan Karras, a former speaker of the Utah House—faced off in a June primary. Jon won, collecting three of every four votes cast and winning every county but his opponent's home county.

In the general election, the Democrat facing him was the bright, honest, articulate dean of the University of Utah Law School and former US

Attorney Scott M. Matheson Jr. His late father, Scott Sr., had been one of the state's most popular governors in the 1970s and early 1980s. Their race was a contest between two outstanding candidates who differed in a few substantive areas. It was a no-lose situation for Utah. If Jon had not been running, I would have voted for Matheson, who abhorred gutter politics as much as Jon did. They were class acts and role models for politicians at every level.

When the election smoke cleared, Jon had received 57 percent of the popular vote, winning 25 of Utah's 29 counties. In an act of stellar statesmanship, Scott Matheson Jr. walked from his election-night hotel headquarters to Jon's hotel headquarters to personally congratulate him on the victory. They embraced and Jon asked Scott to play an advisory role in his new administration. Beholden to no one, he broke with tradition almost immediately. He delivered his State of the State Address in the old territorial capital at Fillmore, our ancestral town. (I am sure his great-uncles Lon and Hal were smiling.)

Most of our state legislators are thoughtful, stand-up folks. Many serve for a brief period of time, then move back to their full-time vocations. Occasionally, a few will throw ethics to the wind and succumb to lobbyist enticements or use their positions to advance their own interests. It's hard to understand, for example, how any legislator who has his or her constituents in mind would let out-of-state nuclear waste be dumped in Utah. But many voted to allow it, and were rewarded handsomely by EnergySolutions, the company seeking approval to store the lucrative waste at its dump site west of Salt Lake City. One past Senate leader, an active member of the LDS Church, ended up representing the tobacco and liquor industries and lobbied legislators to represent those causes. At the same time, he would talk against drinking and smoking at church on Sunday.

Into the mix on Capitol Hill came Jon Huntsman Jr. He managed to accomplish many things as governor: a reformed tax code that employed a flat tax, stronger pro-life legislation, and fortified environmental safeguards. It is hard to pigeonhole him other than to say he chose to support issues he believed were best for the state and its people, who appreciated his practical approach, as did many Democrats, as well. Jon Jr.'s soft-spoken leadership caught the attention of the National Republican Party and the national news media. (While he was governor, Jon loved to haul visiting reporters to his favorite taco cart in downtown Salt Lake City for lunch.)

Governing is never an easy task in Utah, where a fascinating, complex mix of secular and sectarian pressures simmers in a broth of frontier individualism. Jon managed it nicely. He supported a free-market health care plan without an individual mandate. He enacted the most expansive school voucher program in the nation and created jobs without resorting to out-of-control spending and debt. The conservative bible, *National Review*, credited the Huntsman administration with the best overall job-growth rate in the nation.

What many did not know was that the LDS Church was grateful for Jon's leadership in two areas: recognizing civil unions and liquor law reform. Behind the scenes, church leadership was cheering his positive impact on the image of Utah, for taking stands the LDS Church could not embrace for obvious reasons. Jon led reforms that had to happen, but the legislature's biases kept some of them from being enacted.

For example, Governor Huntsman pushed for legislation that would have legalized civil unions and extended pertinent rights to gay citizens, even though the legislature made sure they were never passed. And the LDS Church, unfortunately, took one of its rare public stands when it gave formal financial support to defeating California's Proposition 8, which would have allowed gay marriages in that state. The Church got bloodied in the close fight and earned unwanted national attention even though it was hardly the only religious organization to oppose the measure. Interestingly, its leadership's stance on recognizing civil unions was quite realistic: most had no problem with cohabitating couples receiving joint benefits, or allowing visiting partners in the hospital with the same privileges as immediate family members, or enjoying joint property rights. But for the Church to publicly endorse such privileges would have been somewhat confusing to rank-and-file members.

The same could be said of Jon's efforts to introduce some common sense into some of Utah's goofier liquor regulations. Practicing Mormons don't consume alcohol, and for decades Utah's liquor laws have reflected their abhorrence to it. But at least half the state's inhabitants are not of the Mormon culture or are inactive Mormons who appreciate reasonable access. Moreover, Utah relies heavily on tourism, and many of its cities and resort areas work hard to attract convention business only to have visitors complain or snicker at the state's archaic liquor laws. Jon's steps toward simpler liquor regulations were good for Utah, but the LDS Church could never have initiated or endorsed them.

Governor Huntsman led Utah into the twenty-first century. I can't tell you how many church leaders, including members of the First Presidency (the highest governing office in the LDS Church), told me my son was a brave, honorable leader who understood Utah's image and how to position it for the future. Since then, the LDS Church has taken more progressive stands on certain issues, and it was Jon who did the spadework.

That Jon Jr. was considered for an ambassadorship to China seemed a natural progression, given his interest and experience with the country and the region. He had been appointed ambassador to Singapore by President George H. W. Bush and later named US trade ambassador by President George W. Bush. In my opinion, he was ideally equipped for Asia. I had assigned him to handle relations for our company in China and elsewhere in the Far East when Huntsman Chemical was building facilities in that area of the world many years before.

President Obama was confident in the appropriateness of nominating a GOP governor like Huntsman as ambassador to the second most powerful nation in the world and therefore the second most crucial post in the Department of State. The president and the White House staff followed up with respect to a request for his diplomatic service and their desire to have him accept this critical assignment.

Jon knew it would entail simultaneously getting along with the Chinese government and being assertive in advancing America's interests in the world's most populous nation, which holds trillions of dollars of US debt. He would have to put aside partisan differences because the president and his ambassadors must be of one mind. The US team can have only one coach if it is to be effective. To have a divided front is to court disaster. Jon understood all of this when he accepted the call, even if the partisan pit bulls did not like it. It might have appeared to some at the time that if Jon accepted he would forfeit any political aspirations in 2012. He readily accepted the position with eyes wide open in the spirit of responding to a call to serve his country. And the US Senate confirmed him without dissent—a rarity these days.

Jon Huntsman Jr. and Barack Obama are not polar opposites. They have many things in common, as do all decent, intelligent people, and they enjoyed each other's company. Nearly the same age, each is handsome with a certain amount of star power, as far as that term can be applied to distinguished leaders in their early fifties. Both are caring husbands and fathers. Their spouses (Mary Kaye and Michelle) and their children are self-assured, personable, and smart. Each man possesses a solid moral compass. Each loves his country; each wants to keep Americans free, strong, and healthy; each is respectful of those with whom they politically differ, and each understands what being a public servant is about.

The two also vary in key ways, primarily as to how to go about attaining these common goals and how to insure our future. Jon believes foreign conflicts are not the answer, nor are many of the economic philosophies touted by the Obama administration. For example, Jon differs with the president on the sanctity of entitlement programs and on the subject of taxes as well. Jon has a far better understanding of business needs and burdens than does the president and he has a more promising strategy for creating jobs, as was noted in a *Wall Street Journal* editorial:

> "Mr. Huntsman's (new economic) proposal is as impressive as any today in the GOP presidential field, and certainly better than what we have seen from the frontrunners. Perhaps Mr. Huntsman should be asked to give the Republican response to the president's jobs speech next week. The two views of what makes an economy grow could not be more different."

There are many differences between the two men and plenty of evidence that Jon Huntsman Jr. is a card-carrying conservative, albeit one of conscience and thoughtful vision. But because he does not see political opponents to be evil or un-American simply because they are left of center, because he accepted an ambassadorship when called by a president of all Americans who happened to be a Democrat, because he refused to engage in boorish political behavior or treat divisiveness as a virtue, his presidential bid lasted a short seven months. But what a ride it was!

Some media reports stated that Jon Jr. is an inactive LDS member, but there was no basis for questioning Jon's faith in God, his values, or whether he is fiercely proud of his Mormon legacy. Jon is a person of great integrity who simply stated honestly that, when he was governor, he attended many churches. He was the governor of all the people. We've certainly seen throughout history that presidents attend different church services as a symbolic acknowledgment of the broad religious sweep of America's citizenry. Had Jon won the nomination for the presidency, his personal religion would not have been emblazoned on his sleeve nor would he have used his faith to his advantage, as past presidents have taken pains to avoid doing.

Jon's singular run was in the State of New Hampshire, where he finished in a respectable third place position. The only two candidates ahead of him in this nine-person race were Romney and Paul, who had both run in New Hampshire in 2008 and were well known by the voters. I was very proud of Jon's showing. Probably because of the haste in which the campaign was launched, it really had not been the strategy Jon might have designed if he'd had more time. On January 16, with Mary Kaye at his side, he withdrew his candidacy. I was present at the Myrtle Beach Convention Center when he called it quits. As he had done throughout the national debates, where he was described as the lone adult in the room, Jon took the high ground: "Today our campaign for the presidency ends, but our campaign for a better, and more trustworthy, America continues." He pleaded with the remaining candidates to stop attacking each other, warning that the toxic form of political discourse did not help their cause. A few days after Jon withdrew from the race, syndicated columnist Froma Harrop wrote in more than one hundred newspapers nationwide, "Above all, Huntsman was a class act in a low class campaign . . . He departs with his dignity intact. These days, that's saying something."

As of this writing, Jon is a fellow at the Brookings Institution, serves as a director on several corporate boards, and is a popular global speaker.

He was recently elected chairman of the prestigious foreign policy forum the Atlantic Council, an impressive assembly of authorities in the field of public policy—Dr. Henry Kissinger prominent among them. Perhaps his most significant move since the election was to assume the role of cochair of a new movement called No Labels.

No Labels was founded by veteran Democratic fundraiser Nancy Jacobson, Republican political adviser Mark McKinnon, and former US Comptroller David Walker, among others. With the goal of making America's government work, it also has more than one hundred members of Congress—Republicans, Democrats, and Independents who have grown tired of the political bickering and hard-line partisanship and signed up to become problem solvers. "It's not about centrism," Jon says. "It's about a new attitude toward the realities we face. It's about finding Democrats and Republicans who will check their egos at the door." The organization was officially launched in January 2013. Jon Jr. and Joe Manchin, the Democratic senator from West Virginia, were named to head it and coordinate a weekly national radio show on Sirius satellite. Both are former governors and know how to get things done by building common ground. This nation is not solely red or blue. Much of it is shades of purple. My son and Senator Manchin are doing what they can to recognize, rebuild, and embolden this nation's purple core in order to make America work again.

Where this all goes, I do not know. You will excuse parental exuberance, though, if I declare that Jon Jr. would be a great president or secretary of state.

Meanwhile, something has to be done about the partisan acrimony and divisiveness that continues to bring Washington to a near standstill, leaving the major problems facing this nation to languish. Fox News and a few mean-spirited bloggers foster enormous negativity in the guise of "fair and balanced" reporting. And those on the left, such as most MSNBC commentators, fight back with the same brand of ammunition. Those of us in the middle, who want to see Congress coalesce, seem voiceless. The extremists hold the loudest bullhorns. No respect is shown for different viewpoints; no one seems willing to compromise. It is a tremendously unhealthy situation. I sincerely hope No Labels succeeds. It is important to the health of our beloved America.

22. Riding Into the Sunrise

IT HAS TAKEN ME 77 YEARS TO REACH THIS POINT. ONLY WITHIN THE LAST thirty of them have I become engaged in writing this epistle. I could have included many more experiences, but I figure this is about the maximum a reader can endure. "Good writing," notes L. M. Montgomery, himself a fine writer, "is knowing when to stop." Besides, you get the picture by now.

The ongoing outpouring of family and personal blessings continues to astound me. Karen and our children will continue, as they always have, to be the light of my existence. At age seventy-six, Karen teaches Pilates and aerobics in our home workout center every day but Sunday. She has never spent a night in the hospital (except during childbirth), and her DNA mimics that of her parents, who both lived to be nearly one hundred. Markie, who remains with us, continues to shower us with his trademark joy, innocence, and love. I view each of our children as exceptional and hope each knows how proud their father is of each one of them—as individuals and as representatives of our family name.

And what a joy to watch our grandchildren move into their respective areas of interest. They provide the youthful perspectives and humor that their grandfather so badly needs.

Twelve great-grandchildren have joined our family as of this writing. Karen chastises me because, having found it somewhat challenging to remember every name and birth date, I have begun to call all our great-grandsons Jon and all the great-granddaughters Jane, much to the lighthearted frustration of their parents. Looking down the road, there could be another one hundred names to remember if I live long enough. I see no reason to start memorizing now.

We continue to work through Kathleen's passing. I visit her burial site frequently and sadly, but she is with me wherever I go. Her seven beautiful children in various stages of development are progressing well.

Together, we will continue to work through the children's individual issues as they mature into the productive adults of whom Kathleen would have been so proud.

As to our business, in the second quarter of 2014, our common stock (HUN) reached its highest sustained price as annual revenues exceeded $12 billion. Our corporate researchers are cranking out marvelous new, lightweight, environmentally responsible products each month. The business continues to expand in China, India, Brazil, and a number of emerging countries, as well as the United States and Europe. It currently produces more than 12,000 different materials that, in turn, provide the ingredients for over 120,000 consumer uses. Employee surveys conducted by the online news outlet *Business Insider* resulted in Huntsman Corporation's ranking third among the 50 Best Employers in America for 2013. Huntsman received high praise in particular for employee job satisfaction and workplace flexibility.

The question I'm often asked is whether we are looking to sell Huntsman Corporation or, in the alternative, seeking additional acquisitions. Are we actively shopping the company? No. But a solid business such as ours always generates interest in the marketplace. We are a public company and the decision is not mine, in any case. Should the right buyer offer the right price, at what seems to be the right time, our corporate board of directors would give it serious consideration. Having said this, I must admit that we are in the process of closing a $1.3 billion acquisition in Europe, which will be a solid addition to one of our existing divisions.

Acquisitions are harder to come by these days. The marketplace has changed drastically in the last dozen years. There is no longer easy credit, or the ability to complete heavily leveraged transactions, especially to the extent I did when building the business. Private equity groups and hedge funds have altered the economic landscape. Acquisitions and divestitures are undertaken at breakneck speed with about the same level of care and preparation I might show in picking out a tie. The fun has been taken out of the chase.

That's why I withdrew from Huntsman Gay Global Capital Fund II. Founded in 2007, it was the only equity investment firm to my knowledge with a mission statement having a philanthropic management focus.

Huntsman Gay enjoyed a healthy return on Fund I, collecting more than $1 billion in investment capital.

We are currently embarking on a "family office" financial concept led by Paul. With money from several foundations and family trusts, we are investing over $1 billion in a multitude of areas that we hope will return substantial profits in the future.

I remain grateful for the fundamental belief in myself that enabled my survival. I tried to avoid following the bottom-line advice of the consultants, the let's-make-a-deal lawyers, and the unending supply of habitual naysayers who seem to surround risk-takers. If I had followed the counsel of others, I would not be writing this book. Four times in our corporate history Huntsman should have gone out of business, and we would have, had we listened to the conventional wisdom. Instead, the company figured out how to survive through entrepreneurial ingenuity, a commitment to making it work, and an unshakable belief that it would succeed. The company lived to fight another day—and thrived. No risk, no reward.

People often ask how we got to the top and how we managed to remain there. Part of it is having a vision, of seeing the seventh, eighth, ninth, and tenth steps as opposed to getting hung up on the first and second. I don't spend a lot of time on the initial steps. I am already thinking about the deal after the next one. Success also takes a contrarian mindset. While you have to comply with society to a reasonable extent, you can't do what everybody else is doing.

How does one build great wealth? Through focus, flexibility, hard work; by following one's intuition with self-confidence. And then there's the matter of being willing to bet the farm. A lot of people have those first attributes, but few dare to risk what they have earned to that point. Most would-be executives are reasonably good at conceptualizing, but poor at implementing new ideas and concepts. It is the individual who possesses both of these qualities, particularly the latter, who succeeds most of the time. It is important to be mentally and emotionally tough. Surviving difficult times requires the ability to sustain terrible shocks to the system and still operate with a clear goal in mind. Karen recently asked me how I manage to keep climbing out of bomb craters with only flesh wounds. An excellent question. I am not sure there is a concise, black-and-white, one-size-fits-all answer. Son-in-law Rick Durham believes that once in every four or five generations someone comes along who has it all glued together, who can continue to get up, however wounded, and keep fighting. I believe each one of us has the innate toughness to survive, if pushed. Most of us simply do not realize our abilities when facing a challenging journey.

Our earthly footprint is based on determination, diligence, education, and sacrifice. Don't stand down when the going gets rocky. You are laying the foundation of a great work: your life. Don't cut corners or demean people. Life has little regard for those who waste time. Decide early who you are, your goals, and what reaching those goals entails. Keep in mind that it's not the sermons you give but the sermons you live that will define you.

It would be a fascinating experience to hear in advance what will be said at our eulogies. Would it match what we see in ourselves? What is certain is that we won't be in any physical shape to rebut what is said. Truth be known, few farewell lines at funerals are devoted to one's academic achievements, professional careers, or wealth. Mostly, a eulogy is about what one did for others—as a parent, a volunteer, a teacher, a civic activist, a philanthropist, or one who set good examples. Since we don't get to see the advance text of our eulogies, we might think about living each day as if our actions on that day will establish the record on which we'll be judged. (I received the Giant In Our City Award several years ago by the Salt Lake Chamber of Commerce. I consented to this folderol primarily because I wanted to hear what the bevy of speakers, including the children, had to say about me—a preview, if you will, of what would be said at my funeral.)

These lessons I have learned: Accumulation of wealth is a means to an end, never the endgame. There is more than money to a life well led. If wealth is accumulated in the process, fine, but gain it as a straight shooter. Make your handshake your bond. Trustworthiness is a key ingredient in relationships. No exceptions.

The world is more interconnected today than in any period of history. Personal relationships ought to mean more than ever. Sadly, that is not the case. Instead of developing personal skills, friendships, and love of others, we are letting electronic messages speak for us. My grandchildren are forever urging me to learn to use social media. Are you kidding? I don't know how to operate a computer and they want me to use Twitter? When I am around my grandchildren, I want to talk with them. I make them check their smartphones at the door—no looking down and texting when we are talking. Give me handwritten notes anytime.

But the greatest challenges in the years ahead will be the instillation and acceptance of time-honored values; finding time to serve our nation and churches, synagogues, mosques; and strengthening our ability to respect other people's opinions and beliefs on issues on which we may disagree without resorting to incivility.

Public or private service, of one form or another, adds structure to our lives. Every person ought to be taught in their late teens or early twenties how to serve fellow human beings. I was fortunate to have gained full-time experience in all five areas of service: business, charitable, religious, military, and government. These became the cornerstones of my relationships with people of disparate backgrounds, religions, and ethnicities. All able people should submit two years of their lives to some form of volunteer work in one of the latter four areas. That would instill in us the proper priorities in regard to others.

All in all, it has been a grand time to be alive. Certainly, this is not the only time that history has provided such opportunities for fulfillment. Nor will it be the last great time. But I am glad it was my time.

My most fortunate blessing, outside of family, is to be an American. I hold great respect and love for the people who matured with me, who shared ideas, faith, and loyalty, those who were at my side when empires were built and who loyally accompanied me on this splendorous journey. America is truly a land of freedom and opportunity. Where else could a Blackfoot-born "blue baby," raised in hardscrabble circumstances, have reached such staggering heights? It is a great tribute to those around me— my spouse and family; my late dear brother, Blaine; my sweet mother, to whom this book is dedicated; my father and my fascinating relatives (especially Uncle Hal and Uncle Lon); church officials and others who humbly serve; those who aided me along the way; my unique and gifted corporate teams; the pioneers in cancer research; and so many who have been part of the Jon Huntsman mosaic.

My glass is always half full. The challenge has been to find a creative way to fill it to the brim.

I love writing, as I have throughout my life. The executive chairman of what is one of the world's largest chemical companies may have quit his chemistry class his senior year in high school, but he always loved English. It remains my favorite discipline.

I suppose there is no such thing as a complete autobiography. To have accomplished that feat, one must write from beyond the grave. Memoirs must retrace life to a current point. So now I come to that point. For me, it is but the sunrise of a second beginning. An anonymous writer once offered that a conclusion is the place where you got tired of thinking. Not so. It is a place to catch your breath and take stock. I may stop writing for a while, but I will never stop thinking. I ponder about things more today than at any time in my life. I still dream of new products, of improving the company, of expanding the Huntsman Cancer Institute, of writing other books, of the careers of my children and grandchildren, of community challenges, always of Karen, and maybe a sequel to this memoir.

When people ask Karen if I will ever retire, she says, "No. What would he do?"

I have stuffed several lifetimes into the seven and a half decades throughout which I have traversed the earth. My journey has been fascinating, lucky, risky, satisfying and adventurous. While running that good race and fighting the fights, I have tried hard to forgive transgressions; to provide leadership when needed; to make graciousness, integrity, and decency the fuel that drove my turbines; to be kind even when it was difficult; and to always give back.

I give everlasting credit to God for life's multitude of blessings. No mortal soul could or should take full credit for his or her ride in life. I never expected nor deserved such an outcome. Now, notwithstanding the three decades spent writing elements of this book, it is time to pause. I hope there will be a Volume II. I plan to entitle it *Lucky, Lucky Me.*

Acknowledgments

As poet John Donne phrased it so well, no man is an island. Even writing one's own life story requires assistance from others, and it is important to me to acknowledge those who supported me in such a sizable project. I want to thank my primary editor, James E. Shelledy, former editor of *The Salt Lake Tribune* and now a Louisiana State University journalism professor. Without Jay's help, the story it has taken me three decades to write may never have been completed. I gratefully acknowledge the thoughtful work of the late Lucille Tate, the late James N. Kimball, and Guy Boulton, whose interviews with many of the characters in my personal and professional saga expanded the focus beyond my own recollection. Since I have zero experience with a keyboard, I express my gratitude and appreciation to my assistants, Jannie Spader and Pam Bailey. I sincerely thank Paige Peterson for her expertise in the publishing business and for leading me to my world-class literary agent, Ed Victor, and my publisher, Peter Mayer.

First, last, and always, I acknowledge the love and support of Karen, my sweetheart and best friend, and I thank my children for slogging their way through numerous drafts and providing invaluable feedback.

Index